Stories from the
MINNESOTA BOYS'
STATE HOCKEY
TOURNAMENT
Revised and Updated

David La Vaque and L. R. Nelson

Foreword by Aaron, Neal, and Paul Broten

MINNESOTA
HISTORICAL
SOCIETY PRESS

mnhspress.org

The Minnesota Historical Society Press is a member

of the Association of University Presses.

Manufactured in the United States of America

10 9 8 7 6 5 4 3 2 1

♾ The paper used in this publication meets the minimum

requirements of the American National Standard for

Information Sciences—Permanence for Printed Library

Materials, ANSI Z39.48–1984.

International Standard Book Number

ISBN: 978-1-68134-288-7 [paper]

Library of Congress Control Number: 2023950043

ON THE COVER: Andover's Gavyn Thoreson beats Moorhead goalie Kai Weigel for the game-winning goal in double overtime of the teams' 2022 Class 2A state tournament quarterfinal game. Photo by Tim Kolehmainen/Breakdown Sports Media

FRONTISPIECE: Rochester John Marshall's Todd Lecy expresses his jubilation, and South St. Paul players show their frustration, after Lecy scored the only goal in the Rockets' 1–0 victory over the Packers in a 1977 semifinal. Photo by Pete Hohn/*Minneapolis Tribune*

ON THE TITLE PAGE: *'91 Final—Hill-Murray versus Duluth East,* a study for the painting *Champions,* by Terrence Fogarty. Image courtesy of Karen and Terrence Fogarty

CONTENTS

FOREWORD

Legendary Roseau brothers Neal, Aaron, and Paul Broten dazzled crowds in a combined six state high school hockey tournaments from 1975 to 1984.

The trio representing one of Minnesota's most renowned hockey families left a lasting impression: Neal's four assists in a single period remain a tournament record; Aaron's twelve points in the 1978 tourney were the most since John Mayasich had scored eighteen in 1951; and Paul scored twice in the highest-scoring game in tournament history.

On the following page, the Brotens, playing off each other as deftly as they did during their rink rat childhood, share their memories of and love for the tournament.

Aaron Broten (right) keeps a framed autographed photo of himself and brothers Paul (left) and Neal (center) in Team USA jerseys in his Edina office as a memento of one of the rare times the Roseau-born trio played together. Photo courtesy of Aaron Broten

WE LOVE the stories and all the cool photos of the Minnesota Boys' State Hockey Tournament, from the early years all the way to now, and reading about the excitement the tournament has brought to so many players. We've always been intrigued about whether other players felt the same way we did playing in one of the best sports events in the nation.

If you can make it to the state tournament, that's a big deal. The entire town shuts down if Roseau makes it there. Growing up as Pee Wees and Bantams, watching the high school team that pretty much always made it to state, it was just the thing we wanted to achieve when we got up to tenth, eleventh, or twelfth grade.

You'd be there with all your buddies that you'd played with since you were five or six years old. Everything was kind of like "Wow" to us. Playing in a big rink. Playing in front of all those people. To make it to the state tournament, that was the pinnacle.

After high school we all played for the Gophers and enjoyed NHL careers. Hockey was our focus. But when you're done, you look back at the state tournament experience and realize how fortunate you were just to be able to play in it. You think to yourself, Hey, those were pretty special times.

We still follow the state tournament every year, but it is the years before our time that interest us the most, like the first twenty-five years. What the attendance was like, or where it was held. Players' stats and game summaries have always piqued our interest, too. *Tourney Time* offers this and so much more. Readers will enjoy the many colorful stories—many we hadn't heard before—and interesting facts that bring each year of the state tournament to life.

Aaron Broten
Neal Broten
Paul Broten

From left, Roseau brothers Aaron, Neal, and Paul Broten left their mark on the state tournament in myriad ways despite never winning a championship. Photo by L. R. Nelson/Legacy.Hockey

When I went to the Met Center in Bloomington as a freshman in 1975, I thought, "OK, don't get in anybody's way. If the coach taps you on the back to go out there, don't do anything stupid."
—*Neal Broten*

My first trip in 1977 was with Neal, and by that time the tournament had moved to the St. Paul Civic Center. The clear glass boards stick in my memory. They were unique and added a different element. You really were playing on a stage, because you could see so much more as a fan and as a player.
—*Aaron Broten*

In 1983, we got to practice at the Civic Center the day before our first game. Coach Gary Hokanson put the team all around center ice and had everyone lie down. He said, "Just look at this building. Tomorrow night it is going to be plumb full, and everyone is going to be watching on TV. But it is no different than it is right now." We had people who had never been to the Twin Cities before. They grew up on farms, and this was the first time they got to go to the big cities and see an arena with seventeen thousand people and clear boards and ride up and down in the elevator. I don't know if [Hokanson] was trying to get the jitters out of us. It didn't really help.
—*Paul Broten*

INTRODUCTION

"It is the Stanley Cup, the World Series, and the Super Bowl, all rolled into one. You young men will go on from here and play in many other sports events, but you'll always remember the Minnesota High School Hockey Tournament as the best."

—Herb Brooks

THE MINNESOTA BOYS' high school hockey state tournament, a prep sports pursuit surpassing Indiana basketball and Texas football, was still going strong as it turned eighty in 2024. Collected here, for the first time, are stories that convey the spectacle and drama of this longstanding annual tradition.

The stories—told through rich, firsthand recollections gathered from fresh interviews with more than four hundred former players, coaches, referees, and others—represent hockey's spirit and are sure to elicit smiles and tears. You'll learn about tournament founder Gene Aldrich. Why Herb Brooks, famed coach of the 1980 US Olympic team, valued a state title even more than a gold medal. There's John Mayasich of Eveleth, the Wayne Gretzky of Minnesota high school hockey, who never lost a game in his four-year career. Duluth East forward Dave Spehar, electrifying crowds with three hat tricks in as many games, his Greyhounds falling in an epic five-overtime game the very next season. Centennial goalie Gregg Stutz blanking three consecutive opponents, a feat unlikely to be repeated.

Played in front of tens of thousands of fans at the state's grandest arenas, with a statewide television audience mesmerized from the opening puck drop, the state tournament secured legendary status for successful teams, players, and coaches from Eveleth to Rochester, Edina to Warroad; St. Paul Johnson, first star of the Twin Cities; northern powers International Falls and Roseau; suburban schools; the private schools everyone loves to hate; and the teams that shined only briefly.

Whether you watched the state tournament through the haze of smoke in the St. Paul Auditorium or through the clear boards at the Civic Center, at the old Met Center or in the plush Xcel Energy Center, this book will take you inside the locker rooms, behind the benches, and onto the ice for stories from the nation's greatest high school state tournament.

Drop the puck.

THE EARLY YEARS: 1945–1968

The high school hockey state tournament took root at the St. Paul Auditorium, where the specter of the dominant northern schools loomed like the cigarette smoke that hung thick in the arena's rafters. For twenty-four years, the likes of Eveleth, International Falls, and Roseau ensured that greater Minnesota held sway. The Twin Cities metro area's only answer: St. Paul Johnson, which won four championships in the era. Out-of-towners often arrived in St. Paul by train. Some locals came by streetcar. Increased spectator support and the sport's rising popularity overall helped high school hockey outgrow its capital-city incubator.

Action during the 1957 boys' high school hockey tournament final at the St. Paul Auditorium. Photo by the *Minneapolis Tribune*

FIGHTING FOR EVERY STEP

SURVIVAL FOR TOURNAMENT, AND FOUNDER GENE ALDRICH, AT TIMES TENUOUS

DATES	LOCATION	ATTENDANCE	CHAMPIONSHIP
FEBRUARY 15–17	ST. PAUL AUDITORIUM	8,956	EVELETH 4, THIEF RIVER FALLS 3

Did you know? Two Minnesota Gophers hockey captains, Bob Carley and Bob Graiziger, worked as goal judges during the afternoon quarterfinals.

A FIERCE WIND and drifting snow made each step a chore as Gene Aldrich, St. Paul Public Schools athletic director, trudged the half dozen miles from his downtown office to his home near Cretin High School.

Aldrich faced the Armistice Day Blizzard on November 11, 1940, wearing a light raincoat with no hat or gloves. The historic storm would dump 16.8 inches of heavy, wet snow and claim forty-nine lives, but Aldrich kept walking.

The persistence he showed as he passed abandoned automobiles and stranded streetcars would help him five years later, when he launched the state high school hockey tournament that endured where three previous attempts had failed.

He embodied all the wonderful, clashing elements that provided the tournament's greatness through its first eighty years. Born on April 20, 1898, in St. Paul and raised in Duluth, Aldrich represented north and south. He was private and

In April 1944, Gene Aldrich (left) wrote to the Minnesota State High School League requesting a "State Hockey Meet in 1945." The board agreed, provided that "no expense to the League would be involved." So Aldrich invited eight teams to the St. Paul Auditorium. One year later, the MSHSL officially sponsored the event. The two other men in this picture are unidentified. Photo courtesy of the Minnesota Historical Society

public school, too—a Duluth Cathedral High School graduate who later became a public school administrator.

In between, Aldrich taught social studies at Cretin and coached football, baseball, and golf. Coaching basketball lit the quiet man's competitive fire. He "would destroy at least three towels" during every basketball game, son John Aldrich said. "He would wring them to death."

Whenever Gene Aldrich used his hands to emphasize a point, the middle and index fingers on his right hand flailed. A sickle accident had severed tendons in both digits and left the promising first baseman unable to throw effectively.

Though he dabbled in gardening and played cribbage and bridge, Aldrich shined brightest in the company of student-athletes. Football and basketball players came to his house on Saturday mornings, where Professor Aldrich, as they called him, drew plays in black crayon on the icebox door.

Aldrich left Cretin in 1936 for the St. Paul Public Schools job through which he became an advocate for all sports.

"There really are no minor sports," Aldrich once said. "Gymnastics, golf, tennis, track, and the rest are all valuable. And they are attractive showpieces, too, if they're put on with a little pageantry."

John Aldrich cannot recall ever seeing his father on skates, let alone playing hockey. Yet Gene Aldrich sought to raise the sport's profile through a state tournament.

Others had tried and failed. In February 1940, an invitational state tournament at Gustavus Adolphus College in St. Peter attracted Baudette and Eveleth from the north, Mankato from the south, White Bear Lake, and Minneapolis schools Roosevelt, South, and West. Unseasonably warm temperatures ruined the outdoor ice and forced cancelation.

Nine months later, snowplows pushed back against the Armistice Day Blizzard and Aldrich hitched a ride on one for about a dozen blocks. When the truck became stuck, Aldrich soldiered on by foot.

He arrived home about 7:30 PM, some four and a half hours after he had left the office, "practically frozen," said John, who recalled his father getting into the bathtub and not leaving for over an hour.

Asked why in the world he walked, the elder Aldrich told his wife and son, "I never considered that I couldn't make it."

He held the same conviction about a high school hockey tournament.

In April 1941, Aldrich received Minnesota State High School League sanctioning for "a hockey tournament to be held in St. Paul in 1942." It never happened, possibly due to a lack of funding.

But Aldrich wasn't done trying, even when, in October 1941, permission was given to Roseau High School to host a state tournament in that city the week of February 23, 1942.

Tire and gas rations brought on by World War II prohibited Twin Cities teams from traveling to the event, which was made up of seven northern schools. Thief River Falls, sponsored

Thief River Falls' star defenseman Bob Baker (left) and Jim Shearen of White Bear Lake battle for the puck during the first game in state tournament history. Photo by the *St. Paul Pioneer Press*

by the local 40&8 Voiture Club and playing under the name Hornets, beat Eveleth and future NHL goalie Sam LoPresti 1–0 in the semifinals. The Hornets then defeated Baudette 4–1 to win the tournament.

Roseau never held another event.

Then, in April 1944, Aldrich wrote the MSHSL a letter requesting a "State Hockey Meet in 1945." The board agreed, provided that "no expense to the League would be involved."

Aldrich solidified the host site with St. Paul Auditorium manager Ed Furni. Local businessmen agreed to underwrite any losses, most notably Elmer E. Engelbert, president of St. Paul Book and Stationery Company. The role fit the benevolent Engelbert, who threw annual employee Christmas parties and even dressed as Santa Claus one year.

With expenses covered and an arena secured, Aldrich invited Eveleth, Granite Falls, St. Cloud, St. Paul Washington, Staples, Rochester, Thief River Falls, and White Bear Lake from a pool of twenty-six teams playing prep hockey in 1944–45.

Eveleth and White Bear Lake each had indoor community rinks, both known as the Hippodrome. But indoor hockey was a foreign concept to most players in the tournament, who were

Granite Falls goaltender Gorman Velde (9) occupied the wrong side of history in a 16–0 loss to Eveleth. The final score still ranks as the most lopsided margin in a state tournament game. Velde hung tough, making sixteen saves for the hopelessly outclassed Kilowatts. Photo by the *St. Paul Pioneer Press*

accustomed to outdoor rinks encircled by spectators standing in the snow. The St. Paul Auditorium, later renamed for civil rights activist Roy Wilkins, sticks in players' memories for a dark ice sheet below and cigarette smoke above.

The tournament's humble beginnings were evident in the way players were outfitted. Hockey novices Granite Falls and Staples borrowed jerseys and gear from St. Paul schools Monroe and Mechanic Arts, respectively. Even powerful Eveleth, already a solid hockey community for two decades, donned hand-me-downs. The Golden Bears wore the black and orange jerseys of Eveleth Junior College along with tattered breezers from the Chicago Blackhawks—the latter courtesy of former Eveleth player John Mariucci, who by then had spent two seasons with the NHL club.

To complete the function-over-fashion ensemble, Ron Martinson, an Eveleth forward/defenseman, held his skates together with tape.

On Wednesday, February 14, 1945, players enjoyed a luncheon at the St. Paul Athletic Club. At 2 PM the following day, White Bear Lake and Thief River Falls played the tournament's first quarterfinal game.

White Bear Lake's John Resler, then a fifteen-year-old sophomore wing, recalled teammate George Kieffer, a defenseman, tallying the game's first goal.

"He took the puck down and shot it," Resler said. "The puck went in the net and then he did, too."

Kieffer beat Prowlers goalie Ralph Engelstad, future benefactor of the University of North Dakota. But Thief River Falls won 3–2, disappointing the large White Bear Lake fan contin-

gent that had arrived by train. The Bears' twelve players, wearing black football jerseys with orange numbers, had arrived in two automobiles.

Staples played St. Cloud next, each team led by athletes better known for feats off the ice than on it. St. Cloud's Blake Jaskowiak had hit four home runs out of St. Paul's Lexington Park in the American Legion baseball tournament the previous summer. A forward on the ice, Jaskowiak sported a moustache for good luck.

Teammate Harry Ervin brought his skis to St. Paul because, he said, "I heard they had some pretty big hills around here."

Staples, for its part, featured four Golden Gloves boxers: goalie Emory Dupre (heavyweight); defensemen Dick Bacon (flyweight) and Al Johnson (lightweight); and wing Tony Langer (light heavyweight).

Jaskowiak scored first in a 2–0 St. Cloud victory.

A first-period hat trick by Julius Struntz of St. Paul Washington paced a 5–0 victory against Rochester.

Tournament favorite Eveleth faced Granite Falls, the latter as green as its jerseys, borrowed from St. Paul Monroe.

"Half the guys had never been to Minneapolis or St. Paul in their life, so it was a big deal," said Gorman Velde, the goaltender for the underdog Kilowatts, who recalled the bus ride from the west-central plains.

Breezers? Socks? Kilowatts players never wore them.

"We had no idea how to put everything on," said Velde, who wore jersey number 9 and a leather football helmet without a faceguard. "We had to have the St. Paul [coach] show us."

Players were also ill prepared for the auditorium ice sheet, which dwarfed the small outdoor pond in Granite Falls.

"When we skated out on the rink, we couldn't believe the size of it," Velde said.

Confusion reigned once the action began.

"We played about three or four minutes before the officials stopped the game and had a conference at our bench. 'Do you guys know what a blue line is?' We'd never heard of it," Velde said.

In those days, the goal judge stood on the back of the net. Whenever a puck went in, the goal judge's arm went up. He must have resembled a second-grader eager to be called on as Eveleth, already an established cradle of American hockey that had produced several NHL players, buried Granite Falls 16–0, still the tournament record for most lopsided score.

Eveleth goalie Ron Drobnick's one save remains another tournament record.

"We could have beaten them 50–0," defenseman Clem Cossalter said.

Each member of the Golden Bears' vaunted top line—Neil Celley, Wally Grant, and the red-headed Patrick Finnegan—tallied a hat trick. So did defenseman Milan Begich, who embodied the game's lopsided nature.

"We were just monkeying around and kept feeding him the puck," said Cossalter.

Two teams. Same ice. Different hockey universes.

One of the most dominant forward lines in state tournament history, Eveleth's Wally Grant, Patrick Finnegan, and Neil Celley (left to right), scored a combined twenty-three goals en route to the 1945 championship. Each tallied a hat trick in a 16–0 quarterfinal rout of Granite Falls. The two men at right are unidentified. Photo by the *St. Paul Pioneer Press*

"Eveleth could skate backwards better than we could forward, and that's no crap," Velde said. "Jesus, they could go."

Velde called Eveleth's players "good guys" who "didn't make fun of us" even as the outclassed Kilowatts "were just pushing the puck around."

"We looked at their rear ends a lot," Velde joked.

Granite Falls recovered to win its next game 2–1 before falling in the consolation championship game. Jim Field, a center, played every minute of each game.

"We had a great time," said Velde, who later that summer sailed on a US Navy ship to supply marines who had fought at Iwo Jima. "We were big shots around town as far as we were concerned."

Tournament royalty Eveleth advanced to the semifinals against St. Paul Washington, whose players "were trying to intimidate us in the hotel and on the elevators," Martinson said. "'Oh, you won the first game, but [now] you play us.'"

It was no contest. Celley scored just twenty-eight seconds into the game and tallied a hat trick in the first period. Finnegan and Grant both added hat tricks in a 10–0 victory.

Future Eveleth star John Matchefts hailed Celley, Finnegan,

and Grant as the best line in Minnesota high school hockey history.

"They were doing things with the puck in the early '40s that the Russians were given credit for innovating fifteen years later," Matchefts said. "I've heard Lou Nanne and other guys commenting during the state tournament, talking about the greatest high school lines ever in Minnesota. They never mention Finnegan, Grant, and Celley. They don't know what they're talking about."

Washington's intimidation tactics didn't work on the ice, either. Rougher play resulted in several penalties and did little to slow Eveleth's attack. The Presidents were called once each for boarding, hacking, and interference, and twice for slashing. Though his St. Paul Johnson team wasn't invited, coach Rube Gustafson worked in the penalty box shared by both teams.

"They truly weren't any competition," Cossalter said.

A 26–0 scoring advantage through two games diminished Eveleth's focus for the title game against Thief River Falls.

"We had an attitude," forward Bice Ventrucci said. "We thought it'd be a walk in the park. Guys were clowning around,

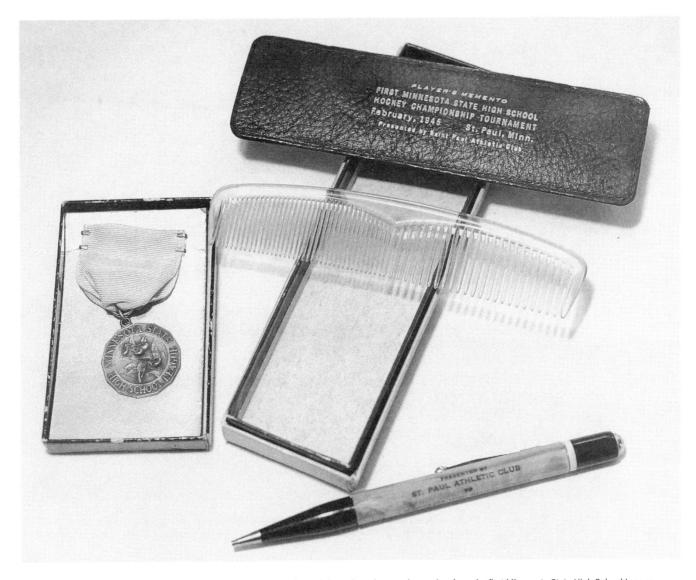

John Resler, of 1945 consolation champion White Bear Lake, received a medal, comb, and pen as keepsakes from the first Minnesota State High School League hockey tournament, sponsored in part by the St. Paul Athletic Club. He also played in the 1946 tournament. Photo by L. R. Nelson/Legacy.Hockey

staying up late. You know how young bucks are. We got a rude awakening the next day and almost lost the game."

Making matters worse, players spent much of Saturday on a state capitol building tour, walking in the underground tunnels for hours.

"By the time we got back, our legs were pretty worn out, and we had to play a few hours later," Cossalter said.

Overconfidence affected even coach Cliff Thompson, who prerecorded a victory interview for a regional NBC radio affiliate about five hours before opening faceoff to be aired Monday night.

Arrogance and tired legs didn't seem to bother Eveleth in the first period. Two Finnegan goals, the first of which deflected off a Prowlers defenseman, produced a 2–0 lead.

But the bad bounce didn't deter Thief River Falls, which responded with three consecutive goals, including a pair from Les Vigness, to take a 3–2 lead at second intermission.

An unfamiliar feeling of desperation crept into Eveleth players' minds. This was "the only game all season in which we were behind," Finnegan said.

"We said, 'We can't lose this,'" Martinson said.

Grant tied the game 3–3 on a power-play goal just 1:37 into the third period. He scored again just fifty-nine seconds later, this one on an assist from Martinson. Normally a second-line center, Martinson was one of the two defensemen on that shift.

"I got the puck and was bringing it down," Martinson said. "I saw Wally come down the other side and passed it to him. And he popped it in."

Grant remembered, "My father was behind the net at the other end. He was cheering us on. He yelled, 'Make sure you keep after them. Keep the puck at the other end.' My father used to come to all the games. He was very aloof, but you knew he was proud after we won."

More drama awaited, courtesy of the auditorium clock,

which slowed down and possibly stopped before recommencing countdown.

"It got to two and a half minutes left, and we thought it should've run out," Cossalter said. "At 4–3, we wanted to get the heck off the ice. Then, all of a sudden, the buzzer went off."

Following Eveleth's 4–3 victory, Grant accepted the trophy, a bronze hockey player atop a plastic base. He also recalled receiving kisses from two drum majorettes.

Grant (nine goals and four assists) and Finnegan (eight goals and five assists) shared the tournament lead with thirteen points.

The players' experiences? Priceless. But the adults underwriting the tournament sweated costs. Not to worry: ticket revenue covered all the three-day event's expenses.

At $1,848.34, rooms and meals at the St. Paul Hotel represented 44 percent of the tournament expenses. Those charges, along with auditorium rental, liability insurance, ticket printing and sales, team transportation, tournament staff (officials, trainers, and scorers), plus miscellaneous items such as towels, pucks, and signs, cost $4,156.80.

Tickets sales brought in $4,291.86 in revenue, leaving a profit of $135.06.

Trophies and medals had cost $232.66, including the champions' trophy affectionately dubbed Bozo by Eveleth players. Grant and Cossalter kept polishing Bozo as a Great Northern train carried the victorious team from St. Paul to Duluth. Automobiles took the players the rest of the way home.

In St. Paul, "we had a little reception in our hotel room, and there were about ten people from Eveleth there," Martinson said. "It was no big deal."

Coming home was a different story.

"I will never forget the parade through town and all the players riding on the car fenders and all the young hockey players standing on the main drag," said Willard Ikola, then a seventh-grader. "We clamored to see them, probably hoping to be in their shoes in a few years as Eveleth Golden Bears and state champions. It made a big impression on us, no doubt."

MSHSL officials felt likewise.

H. R. Peterson, Minnesota State High School League executive secretary, told the *Minneapolis Star* after Saturday's championship game, "While no formal decision has been made yet regarding a second annual state hockey tournament, I'm certain there will be one next year. The first tournament was a success in every way. Crowds, interest, and financial returns were all three very good."

On Monday, two days after the tournament, the *Minneapolis Tribune* reported that "a good share of the board of control members saw their first hockey but all of them are firmly convinced the rugged winter sport has a place in the high school program. It is agreed that inability to obtain equipment may slow the development of the sport until after the war, but then the state tournament may rival basketball as the top winter sport."

The 1945 state tournament legacy lives on through pivotal tournament figures and players:

- Engelbert received a handwritten note dated March 2, 1954, signed by the Thief River Falls team, that read, "For all your trouble and work involved in putting on this 10th annual hockey tournament we, the entire squad and [head coach] Mr. Rolle, would like to thank you from the bottom of our hearts. We had a grand time."

- In 2012, Engelbert's great-grandson Ryan Collins won a state championship with Benilde–St. Margaret's.

- One of Cossalter's five sons, Calvin, played for the Gophers' 1974 national championship team, and another son, Dennis, was the team's student manager. Cossalter's grandson, Nicholas, played on the Eveleth-Gilbert team that won the 1999 Class 1A state championship.

- Grant became a three-time All-American at Michigan and remains the only player from Eveleth's first championship team to be inducted into the US Hockey Hall of Fame, located in Eveleth.

- Velde, born in Granite Falls, farmed his land for more than fifty years and retired in his hometown. He was the last surviving Kilowatts player from the 1945 team. Their alma mater became Yellow Medicine East High School.

- Martinson won two NCAA championships at Michigan (1952, 1953). His grandson Mitch won the 2007 Class 2A state title with Roseau. Another grandson, Erik, officiated tournament games in 2000 and 2001.

Beginning in 1946, the MSHSL officially sponsored the state hockey tournament. Aldrich remained involved, and the sport he never played or coached became his love, which he admitted on February 16, 1959, during Minneapolis Patrick Henry's 5–4 defeat of St. Paul Washington in the Region 1 final.

The game stood as the last one Aldrich attended. He missed his first tournament the following week due to illness. He died on February 26 at age sixty from cancer. In 1994, he was inducted into the Minnesota High School Hockey Coaches Association Hall of Fame.

Two years before his death, Aldrich began another hockey project: he sought to build eight indoor rinks throughout St. Paul. That vision became a collection of Ramsey County arenas, the first of which opened in 1962. Its name? Aldrich Arena, located on White Bear Avenue.

"Dad was a pioneer, *the* influential person in starting up the hockey tournament," John Aldrich said. "I'm sure the numbers are much larger than he would have thought. But I think he sees it all, and I'm sure he's smiling."

~ *DL* ~

THE MASKED MARVEL

ROSEAU'S PINT-SIZED, GOGGLE-WEARING RUBE BJORKMAN AN UNLIKELY SUPERHERO

DATES	LOCATION	ATTENDANCE	CHAMPIONSHIP
FEBRUARY 14–16	ST. PAUL AUDITORIUM	11,035	ROSEAU 6, ROCHESTER 0

 Tournament periods were twelve minutes long, with ten-minute intermissions. Minor penalties were one and a half minutes; majors were three minutes. Rosters were limited to twelve players.

Roseau's Rube Bjorkman (second from right) was nicknamed the Masked Marvel for the combination of his distinctive eyewear and his brilliant play. He was the top goal scorer in the 1946 tournament with four. Photo courtesy of Kyle Oen/Vintage Minnesota Hockey

IT WOULDN'T HAVE taken much imagination to envision a future for the bespectacled Rube Bjorkman—undersized at 5 foot 9 and 155 pounds, and hopelessly nearsighted—that involved crunching numbers as an accountant or hustling vacuum cleaners door to door. As it was, Bjorkman spent his summers in the far reaches of northern Minnesota helping repair old roads and build new ones.

In his job with the Roseau County Highway Department, which he began as a freshman and held through the end of high school, Bjorkman helped prepare construction sites by peering through the telescope-like lens of a transit, then mapping the terrain with his precision measurements.

Come winter, Bjorkman's focus shifted solely to hockey, and he transformed into the real-life superhero known as the Masked Marvel. Precision on the ice came in the form of passes he delivered squarely onto teammates' sticks and the pinpoint shots he unloaded with laser accuracy.

Bjorkman-led Roseau descended on St. Paul for the 1946 state tournament with a 13–3–1 record, two of those losses and the tie coming at the hands of 1945 state tournament runner-up Thief River Falls. Roseau stunned host Thief River Falls 6–4 in the Region 8 championship game to qualify for the school's first state tournament in any sport.

Defending champion Eveleth, unbeaten in more than three seasons, was the overwhelming favorite. Twin Cities newspapers gave Roseau and White Bear Lake the best chance of dethroning the mighty Golden Bears.

The previous year, Bjorkman and teammates Bob Harris and Lowell Ulvin joined coach Oscar Almquist in the 360-mile drive from Roseau to St. Paul to watch the first state tournament. Almquist, a star goaltender for Eveleth in the mid-1920s, knew the auditorium well. He had played pro hockey there for the St. Paul Saints in the American Hockey Association, earning a spot on the league's all-star teams in 1934 and 1936.

"As a coach, he wanted to go down there to watch and support the tournament," Harris said. "For us, that was the epitome of hockey at that time."

Bjorkman, Harris, and Ulvin, inspired by the event's spectacle, issued marching orders to their teammates upon returning home. Reaching the 1946 state tournament was to be their singular focus. Harris, one of just two seniors on the 1946 team, and Bjorkman, the squad's unquestioned leader, pounded home that message.

"We trained and we trained," Harris said. "That was one of our fortes. It was to bed early and no horsing around. We said, 'We're not the basketball team; we are going to be training. And that's all.'

"The basketball team had a couple of guys who were loose about training. Let's just say they were prone to outside activity."

There were no such shenanigans on the hockey team, and the players' physical fitness and mental fortitude were put to an immediate test. Roseau's quarterfinal matchup with White

Bear Lake extended into overtime, during which Harris's goal secured a 2–1 victory.

"Everyone was scrambling around, and I just hoisted one up at the net as I was about to get checked," Harris said. "It wasn't anything fancy."

The *St. Paul Pioneer Press* gave a much more vivid description of the goal in which the hero was described as "chunky little Bill Harris." Harris was, understandably, miffed when he eagerly grabbed the next morning's paper only to see the unflattering adjectives and incorrect first name. Meanwhile, Bjorkman, who didn't crack the scoresheet against the Bears, was making headlines as Roseau's "Masked Marvel."

Bjorkman said his eyesight was so poor he couldn't see the puck unless he was right on top of it. Contact lenses weren't yet in widespread use, so Almquist, keen on having his scoring whiz perform at peak powers, secured a pair of black rubber goggles fitted with prescription lenses.

"I'm not sure where they came from," Bjorkman said. "Lowe and Campbell was a sporting-goods company at the time, and that might be where he got them.

"It kind of looked like an underwater swimming mask. They weren't something I wore over my glasses. They had thick, unbreakable corrective lenses built into them."

Bjorkman's legend was forged in the semifinals, when he scored on a shorthanded solo rush with less than four minutes left in the third period to secure a 2–1 victory over St. Paul Johnson. One newspaper account describes Bjorkman intercepting a Johnson pass at his own blue line, outracing a trio of Johnson pursuers as he flashed down the middle of the ice, moving in on defenseman Orv Anderson and cutting to his right to "ride in on top of goalie Jack McGahn before slapping his crucial shot."

"He looked spooky," Anderson said. "And he skated so fast. The first time he came down, why, it was unbelievable how fast he went."

Sportswriters from four daily newspapers (two each in Minneapolis and St. Paul) were equally impressed. Bjorkman's brilliant play, combined with his unusual eyewear, made him the tournament's first bona fide superstar. He was alternately described as a "bespectacled sensation" and "the wonder man of the tournament," as having a "bandit-like appearance" and wearing "glasses similar to what a welder uses," and as truly otherworldly as "the man from Mars."

Much was also made of Bjorkman's family ties to Harris. Bjorkman's half-sister was Harris's mom, thus making the younger Rube an uncle to Bob and his sister Nancy, Roseau's head cheerleader.

Bjorkman and Harris lived on the opposite sides of town, their upbringings a study in contrasts. Bjorkman's father was an employee of the city, tasked with grading the gravel streets

Led by Rube "the Masked Marvel" Bjorkman (front row, far left), Roseau claimed the title in the second annual boys' high school hockey tournament.
Photo courtesy of Kyle Oen/Vintage Minnesota Hockey

in the summer and maintaining the town's hockey rinks in the winter. He drove a team of horses to accomplish the roadwork, and the Bjorkmans housed the animals in their backyard barn. Bjorkman's mom passed away while giving birth to his younger brother Lavern, and as they grew older the boys were responsible for household chores such as cooking and cleaning.

The son of a dentist, Harris had a more conventional, and admittedly easier, childhood. "I had a soft life at that time," he said.

Harris estimates he stood 5 foot 10 and weighed 185 pounds as a senior. He wasn't lean and chiseled like Bjorkman, but Harris "had grown up playing the game and was a good athlete," Bjorkman said. "He was a key ingredient for us."

As superhero Bjorkman and sidekick Harris were leading Roseau into the championship game, another tournament darling had emerged in Rochester goaltender Clark Wilder. Rochester opened play with a 1–0 victory against Minneapolis West

as Wilder made twenty-five saves and Alan Gilkinson scored the winner in overtime.

With the semifinals up next, Eveleth figured Rochester would be nothing more than a speed bump in the run to the title game. The Rockets, the lone automatic entry into the tournament because of the lack of teams in southern Minnesota, entered with a 5–0 record and the experience of having played in the previous year's tourney (losing both games). Yet they remained a fledgling, unsophisticated operation, as evidenced by Wilder's bare-bones equipment.

Wilder's goalie pads consisted of a baseball catcher's chest protector, elbow pads he turned sideways to protect the outsides of his arms, and a catching glove that most closely resembled a poorly constructed first baseman's mitt. His leg pads were so thin and small he used two of the ancient sets—one strapped atop the other—and still barely managed to cover his knees.

Roseau's Bob Harris (back row, second from right) and Rube Bjorkman (back row, far right) got the better of Rochester's Clark Wilder (front row, far right) in the 1946 title game. All three were named to the all-tournament team. Photo courtesy of Kyle Oen/Vintage Minnesota Hockey

Wilder also used an unusually modified goalie stick. He cut the shaft down to a nub extending just inches above the stick's wider paddle section.

"I did that because it kept getting caught up behind me in the netting," Wilder explained. "If you saw how big I was when I started, you'd understand why."

Wilder's equipment underwent a major upgrade before the tournament thanks to the generosity of St. Paul Washington. The Presidents played in the 1945 tournament but didn't qualify in 1946.

"Since they weren't in the state tournament, they offered to loan us their goal pads," Wilder said. "It was the first time I had goal pads that actually fit me."

Rochester had fielded teams off and on over the years. The program was revived when Wilder and buddies Gilkinson and Dave Alexander, who had grown up playing shinny and skating for miles up and down Rochester's winding Bear Creek, were among a group that successfully begged shop teacher Cliff Monsrud to coach them. Monsrud had been a goalie at North Dakota in the early 1930s, when the program was an independent team in the NCAA.

Monsrud brought Merlin Davey on as an assistant in 1946. It was Davey, an Eveleth native, who dreamed up the game plan he was certain could beat the Golden Bears.

"It was Merl's idea for us to play a defensive game against Eveleth," Wilder said. "Because if we just skated with them, we wouldn't have a chance."

Per Davey's instructions, when Eveleth had the puck, Rochester's forwards and defensemen packed themselves as tightly as sardines in front of the Rockets' goal. The strategy worked. While the game was played predominantly in Rochester's end, the Rockets successfully forced Eveleth to take the bulk of its shots from the outside and blocked several of them before they could reach the goal. The unflappable, "flaxen haired" Wilder was there to stop the shots that did get through—and he did, twenty-four straight, until Eveleth scored late in the third period. By then, Rochester's Ray Purvis had scored two fast-break goals, both courtesy of feeds from Gilkinson, en route to a stunning 2–1 victory.

The next night, in one of the auditorium's dingy locker rooms before the championship game against Roseau, Wilder waited for Monsrud and Davey to instruct the Rockets to deploy the same "defensive hockey" plan that had worked so effectively against Eveleth. Those orders never came. Instead, much to Wilder's dismay, "the coaches said, 'Just go out and play and have fun,'" he said. "I'll never forget that."

After a scoreless first period, Roseau scored in the second when a Harris pass intended for Bjorkman instead ping-ponged off Purvis and Wilder and into the net. Bjorkman was credited with the goal. Less than three minutes later, Harris wove his way through three Rochester players, then deked an onrushing Wilder out of position before firing into an open net for a 2–0 Roseau lead.

"I used to skate with my head down, looking at the puck," Harris said. "Luckily, I looked up, and all of a sudden there was this goalie coming at me. I guess he thought he was going to be able to knock the puck away."

The second-period onslaught continued with a goal by Tom Buran, who played left wing with Bjorkman and Harris. Harris assisted on that goal, then scored on a rebound late in the period to put Roseau up 4–0.

As usual, Bjorkman and Harris played all but a few minutes. The pair would start at forward, then shift back to defense to give starters Ulvin and Vern Johnson a breather. Then it was back to forward. Only occasionally would Almquist signal the pair off the ice.

"I never wanted to come off," Bjorkman said. "I got into the habit of playing a lot."

Bjorkman scored twice in the third period to secure his hat trick and complete the 6–0 triumph over the Rockets.

"Sometimes things just open up and go right in hockey," Bjorkman said. "We were on that night, and it all worked out."

Roseau's celebration consisted of "wandering around town all night and hollering and hooting," Harris said.

The championship caught Roseau's residents off guard. Having navigated the northern wilderness roads that Bjorkman helped build and repair, the three cars carrying the team's coaches and players rolled into town the next evening without a hint of fanfare.

The Masked Marvel and his sidekick, the "chunky little" Harris, returned to being mere mortals.

"We got home at eight or nine o'clock at night," Harris said, "and went to bed."

~ *LRN* ~

PRIDE OF THE EAST SIDE

POCKET OF ST. PAUL IMMIGRANTS NURTURED ST. PAUL JOHNSON INTO POWERHOUSE

DATES	LOCATION	ATTENDANCE	CHAMPIONSHIP
FEBRUARY 13–15	ST. PAUL AUDITORIUM	17,566	ST. PAUL JOHNSON 2, ROSEAU 1

 South St. Paul defenseman Charles "Lefty" Smith helped the Packers win the consolation title and later coached the program to eight tournament appearances.

AT THE TURN OF the twentieth century, immigrants from Sweden, Italy, and Poland populated the neighborhoods surrounding the Payne Avenue and Arcade Street businesses districts of St. Paul, the city's East Side.

When winter came, their children flocked to outdoor ice destinations such as Hastings Pond before migrating a few blocks east to Phalen Park when the rinks were flooded.

The best of them later joined the Johnson High School hockey program, founded in 1913. When the state tournament began more than three decades later, the Governors brought

St. Paul Johnson forward Jim Sedin (left), who skipped fourth grade, was a younger member of the 1947 graduating class but a leader just the same. When Lou Cotroneo joined the team, his peers instructed him, "Jim Sedin calls all the shots"—not coach Rube Gustafson. Photo by the *St. Paul Pioneer Press*

12

pride to their working-class neighbor-hoods by becoming the premier Twin Cities hockey program.

Brothers Orv, Wendell, and Rod Anderson, who lived within a block of Phalen Park, skated for the Phalen Youth Club. Its original home, the epicenter of the Johnson hockey dynasty, was located about where the Phalen Golf Course maintenance facility sits today. The old wooden warming house was just big enough to house a concession stand, skate sharpener, and potbellied stove.

"We would take the poker out of the stove and burn our initials into the wall," Rod Anderson said. "It's amazing the place didn't burn down."

The boys' father, Theodore Anderson, and Herb Brooks Sr., a semipro hockey player who coached many Phalen Youth Club teams, led evening flood brigades.

"Then dad and Herb would come back to the house for a bump," Orv Anderson said.

In the years that followed, folks such as Hjalmar Carlson provided support. George "Skip" Peltier said Carlson, a custodian for St. Paul's Parks and Playgrounds Department for seventeen years, "was like everyone's grandpa."

"He opened the door, got the stove running," Peltier said. "He'd flood and shovel the rink. Even if you didn't have the thirty-five cents, he'd sharpen your skates anyway. If we stayed late, he'd say, 'Just lock it up and put the key over there.'

"Why was Johnson the most successful high school team in the city? Community. You had people supporting the program whether they had kids or not."

In the 1960s and 1970s, Skip Peltier and younger brothers Doug, Ron, and Bob carried on what families such as the Andersons had started.

Oldest Anderson brother Orv, an all-state defenseman, helped Johnson to its 1947 state title. Youngest brother Rod was one of two players who were on the Governors' title teams in both 1953 and 1955.

Middle brother Wendell, who later skated to an Olympic silver medal with the United States and became governor of Minnesota, always lamented never reaching a state tournament.

"I think 'pissed' would be the word," Orv said.

The word to best describe Johnson's 1947 team? Stacked.

The Governors returned ten seniors, including the top line

of all-state selections: Jim "Buzz Bomb" Renstrom and Dave Reipke, plus team leader and future Olympian Jim Sedin.

Anderson and Howie Eckstrom were the top defensive pairing. Goaltender Jack McGahn brought experience, having played on Johnson's fourth-place 1946 tournament team. His backup was Lou Cotroneo, a former basketball player and future Governors coach.

Tournament coaches considered defending champion Roseau and Johnson the favorites for a title-game showdown.

Governors head coach Rube Gustafson, however, worried about quarterfinal opponent Rochester and its goalie, Clark Wilder. The previous year, Wilder had stopped fifty of fifty-one shots in the first two games and propelled Rochester to the championship game.

In the 1947 quarterfinal, Reipke tallied a second period hat trick in a 4–0 Johnson victory.

He scored again in a 3–1 semifinal victory against Minneapolis West.

That sealed an anticipated championship meeting with Roseau. Game-day nerves failed to rattle Orv Anderson.

"On Saturday, my parents left, and I said I'd take the streetcar," he said. "But I fell asleep. So I had to run like hell, with my gear, and I just caught the streetcar. I got downtown and my dad said, 'Where the hell have you been?' I guess I was too nonchalant."

Johnson graduate Ken Haag attended the 1947 tournament and wrote of the atmosphere at the St. Paul Auditorium: "When the skaters first came on the ice, ushered on by the JHS band, it was a spectacle to forever retain. We sat about six rows up in the lower balcony just off center. When the skaters buzzed around the rink to the strains of the 'Johnson Rouser,' Roseau's green raiders in green and white and Johnson in its bumblebee stripes of maroon and white in the pregame loosening up, it appeared if one squinted, to be as colorful insects swarming over a pond."

The Maroon, Johnson High School's yearbook, described the Governors' new uniforms that season as maroon jerseys with white stripes on the arms and white numerals. Silver "pants" were accented with maroon stripes, and socks were maroon-and-white striped.

Roseau, which had beat Johnson 2–1 in the 1946 semifinals, featured the Masked Marvel, Rube Bjorkman.

"He was really the only one we were worried about," said Sedin, who was tasked with covering his future college and Olympic teammate. "He was a smooth stickhandler, and he had a hard shot."

Bjorkman and company drew about seven hundred supporters to St. Paul. Roseau spent $1,600 to charter buses. The inaugural tournament radio broadcast cost $550 and beamed the action through Thief River Falls to whoever remained in Roseau.

They cheered as the Masked Marvel's sixth tournament goal tied the game twenty-four seconds into the third period.

"He went around me like I was nailed to the ice," Anderson said.

Reipke's fifth tournament goal, this one scored with 1:18 remaining, was the game-winner.

McGahn stopped thirty-eight of forty shots he faced in the tournament.

Sedin, who skipped fourth grade and was a young senior class member, said he drank his first beer after the game.

"I don't believe that was his first drink," Eckstrom joked.

About eight weeks later, the victorious Governors returned to the St. Paul Auditorium for an appreciation banquet. Players heard from state tournament founder Gene Aldrich and six-time Stanley Cup champion Lester Patrick.

Donations from more than 140 local residents and businesses on Payne Avenue and Arcade Street made the event possible.

"We had a goal, a mission from day one," Cotroneo said. "It was about your school, but it was always about the East Side."

~DL~

THE IRON THRONE

IRON RANGE'S EVELETH EMERGED AS FORCE FROM THE NORTH

DATES	LOCATION	ATTENDANCE	CHAMPIONSHIP
FEBRUARY 19–21	ST. PAUL AUDITORIUM	19,354	EVELETH 8, WARROAD 2

Did you know? Dave Peterson, goaltender for the St. Paul Harding Maroons (their name before they became the Knights), later coached Minneapolis Southwest to the 1970 state title.

YOUNG EVELETH HOCKEY PLAYERS left their homes on Summit Street, Jackson Street, and nearby blocks, each carrying hand-me-down skates and the one stick they owned, hoping like hell it wouldn't break.

They walked downhill to the Hippodrome, an indoor rink built in 1922 on the town's western edge with a view of the

iron ore mines that put food on their tables and provided raw materials for much of America's steel.

Hockey became Eveleth's other chief export. Standout high school goalies Frank Brimsek, Mike Karakas, and Sam LoPresti all reached the National Hockey League. So did defenseman John Mariucci and forward Aldo Palazzari. Young

Eveleth, winner of the inaugural state tournament in 1945, launched the sport's first dynasty three years later. In 1948, coach Cliff Thompson (front) and the Golden Bears completed the first of four consecutive undefeated seasons. Photo courtesy of the Minnesota Historical Society

Eveleth coach Cliff Thompson, credited with developing the Iron Range town's youth system, helped many skilled Eveleth players flourish. The results became evident every year in February as the Golden Bears won five titles in the first seven years of the state tournament. Photo courtesy of the Minnesota Historical Society

players who idolized them grew to dominate the state tournament's formative years.

Cliff Thompson, Eveleth's coach from 1926 to 1959, presided over it all. In 1945, his Golden Bears won the first state tournament. Three years later, they launched a dynasty. Eveleth's quartet of undefeated championship seasons from 1948 to 1951 remains Thompson's masterpiece.

Granted, the talent was there. Willard Ikola (Jackson Street) and John Matchefts and John Mayasich (Summit Street) became three of the best players not just in their hometown or state but at the collegiate and Olympic levels.

To flourish, however, young talent needs basic equipment and the right balance of organization and freedom—all things Thompson provided.

Before games, the former Minneapolis Central and Gophers forward liked to say, "Let's play businessman hockey."

"I guess he just meant, 'Let's just get down to business and take care of things on the ice, and the winning will take care of itself,'" Ikola said.

Creating a hockey culture within Eveleth wasn't necessary.

Mayasich, a star throughout the 1948–51 championship years, said, "We all had the skills before we got to high school, from playing tennis-ball road hockey or fifteen-to-a-side at the outdoor rink. You learned stickhandling and keeping your head up."

Thompson was credited with developing a youth system in which those skilled players flourished.

"The important thing is getting a certain style of play established so that the youngsters coming up pattern their actions after the first-team boys, and we have a sort of consistency in our style from [younger players] up to high school seniors," Thompson said.

Ikola later coached eight state championship teams at Edina. He said he worked to "stay close to our youth program because that's your bread and butter," one of Thompson's principles.

"Cliff came in every Saturday morning and sat up in the corner," Ikola said, referring to youth games and practices in the Hippodrome. "When he came in, everything picked up."

Thompson invested more than his time. In junior high, he gave Ikola a new leather football. The pigskin had to be well worn before it could be returned for replacement. Same went for hockey equipment.

As a sophomore, Bob "Bobo" Kochevar received a pair of skates from Thompson.

"The stipulation was, 'Don't sharpen them too much,' and, 'When you graduate, you have to pass them down,'" Kochevar said.

With just twelve players on a varsity roster, Thompson made choosing players personal.

"There were no tryouts; he picked his team," said Dave Hendrickson, a member of Eveleth's 1950 and 1951 title teams. "He knew who would play four years down the road. He'd stop you in the hallway at school and say, 'I packed your hockey bag.' That's when you knew you made it."

Thompson valued fundamentals. "A player has to know how to move the puck, how to pass and receive a pass," he said. But like most varsity hockey coaches of the day, he favored scrimmages over repetitive drills.

"I never saw Cliff on the ice," said Ron "Sonny" Castellano, a three-time state champion from 1949 to 1951. "He'd be wearing his fur coat, throw pucks out and say, 'We're going to scrimmage.' We learned to improvise and react. He didn't give us a chalkboard discussion."

"You wouldn't get very far with that today," Hendrickson said.

When Ikola started coaching at Edina in 1958, he allocated the last ten minutes of practice for scrimmage time—as a bonus for productive drills.

Since 1977, the Minnesota Hockey Coaches Association has bestowed the Cliff Thompson Award upon a coach who embodies "long-term outstanding contributions to the sport of hockey in Minnesota." Eight of Thompson's former players have won, including Castellano, Hendrickson, and Ikola.

Thompson's greatest asset, Mayasich said, was "an ability to set lines. He knew who to put with who to get the best out of them."

When Mayasich joined the varsity in 1947–48, Eveleth was positioned for repeated deep playoff runs, and Thompson knew it. After the Golden Bears finished fourth in the previous year's tournament, he said, "We're going to be a whale of a team for the next couple of seasons."

Eveleth went 12–0 in the regular season and blanked both Region 7 opponents to reach the 1948 state tournament.

The postseason shutout streak ended a little more than one minute into the quarterfinals as Rochester scored first. Eveleth wasn't fazed, winning 7–2, thanks to forty-eight shots on goal.

An 8–1 semifinal rout of St. Cloud came next, highlighted by Matchefts's performance. The junior forward scored four goals and assisted on three others.

Eveleth advanced to face Warroad in the title game, a rematch of a regular-season game won 12–5 by the Golden Bears. The Warriors featured Max Oshie—great uncle of T. J. Oshie—who scored an incredible twelve goals against Thief River Falls that season.

Oshie and his brother, Buster, each scored a goal, but Eveleth prevailed 8–2. Tony Tassoni and Matchefts each tallied a hat trick. Matchefts finished as the tournament's leading scorer with fourteen points (nine goals, five assists).

In the dressing room afterward, Thompson once again predicted success at the next tournament.

"We lose hardly anyone, and for every boy who leaves we have a half dozen waiting to take his place," Thompson said.

Lee Cary put that quote and this scene in the *Minneapolis Tribune*: "Cliff was lounging with a hand stuffed in an overcoat pocket and an Eveleth supporter interposed, 'Yeah, all he has to do is pull out that hand and he'll have a hockey player in it.'"

~DL~

MEAN STREAK

EVELETH'S JOHN MATCHEFTS AS NASTY AS NEEDED

DATES	LOCATION	ATTENDANCE	CHAMPIONSHIP
FEBRUARY 24–26	ST. PAUL AUDITORIUM	15,471	EVELETH 4, WILLIAMS 1

 Warroad senior forward Sammy Gibbons scored three power-play goals in the third-place game, a record he held alone for twenty-seven years.

AS EVELETH'S Ron Castellano remembers it, International Falls coaches and players weren't shy about their game plan during a 1949 clash.

The Broncos would render ace forward John Matchefts ineffective by any means necessary.

"Their coach kept yelling, 'Hit him and slow him down,'" Castellano said. "They knew he was our leader. He was the man."

And Castellano, a sophomore at the time, followed senior captain Matchefts anywhere—even as the teams began brawling.

John Matchefts, Eveleth's fierce forward, was the first player selected to three consecutive all-tournament teams. He later won three NCAA titles at Michigan. In 1956, he won an Olympic silver medal playing with former Golden Bears teammates John Mayasich and Willard Ikola under coach and Eveleth native John Mariucci. Photo by the *Minneapolis Tribune*

"I jumped in and ended up on my back and almost broke my jaw," Castellano said.

Better that than defy Matchefts, a rugged rink rat who stood just 5 foot 6 but embodied toughness and tenacity. Invited in 1948 to Boston for an Olympic team tryout, Matchefts couldn't play for the squad due to Minnesota State High School League rules.

He settled for an undefeated season. Matchefts drove Eveleth to the 1948 state championship with a tournament-best fourteen points (nine goals, five assists).

"He had a mean streak to him," former teammate Willard Ikola said. "He was a tiger. He was the most competitive player that I ever played with."

Matchefts tallied only two goals and four assists in the 1949 tournament as John Mayasich came of age. But what Matchefts did off the scoresheet reinforced his value: he set an example for Mayasich, Castellano, and their sophomore peers, LaVerne Hammer, Ed Mrkonich, and Dan Voce. They learned well, winning two additional championships to cement Eveleth's dynasty.

Yielding the spotlight to the sophomore pack never bothered Matchefts.

"I think he was happy to see us," Castellano said. "But we rallied around him. During a game, he might say, 'Suck it up. Let's get going.' But mostly he led by example."

"He was the guy you wanted to be," Mayasich said.

Matchefts's hockey journey began with older sister JoAnn's figure skates.

"They were high blades, but hell, that's all we had, so I used hers," Matchefts said. "Of course, they were too long for me. It probably was good that I learned on them. Because when I got a decent pair of skates, it was like I was skating barefoot."

Jim Matchefts remembers his older brother admiring Neil Celley, Wally Grant, and Pat Finnegan, the untouchable forward line on Eveleth's 1945 state championship team.

As a sophomore in 1947, Matchefts tied for first in tournament scoring with three goals and three assists. His dominance in the 1948 tournament left opponents, fans, and even teammates in awe.

"You dumped the puck to the middle, and John was away,"

In the early days of the tournament at the St. Paul Auditorium, and years before the advent of Plexiglas, chicken wire was used to protect fans, including these two youngsters in 1949, from flying pucks. Photo courtesy of the Minnesota Historical Society

said Tony Tassoni, a senior in 1948. "When he came in on a goalie, the goalie was helpless."

Eveleth players sought to defend their title in 1949 and send Matchefts out a winner.

"After going undefeated the previous year, we were hell-bent on doing it again my junior year," Ikola said. "With Matchefts leading us as a senior and Mayasich starting to dominate as a sophomore, we would be more than a match for anybody. We could score goals in bunches."

The Golden Bears went 13–0, smashing opponents by a combined score of 106–17. They looked as good as they played, ditching the hand-me-down orange-and-black jerseys borrowed from Eveleth Junior College in the 1948 tournament for school colors: maroon with gold trim.

Eveleth exerted its will on foes. Teams take on the identity of their leaders, and the Golden Bears always got a full effort from Matchefts.

"Most of the games were blowouts, and what's most impressive is how consistently hard we played, considering the scoring discrepancies," Ikola said. "The intensity level was always high. We were a strong favorite to defend the state title, and with that team, we knew we were going to win. There was no question about whether or not we would do it—we would win, and that was the focus."

The stocky Matchefts did a little bit of everything on the ice and was strong in other sports as well.

"I think the first touchdown pass I threw was to him in the end zone," Mayasich said.

Eveleth made its first trip to the baseball state tournament in the spring of 1949 with Matchefts at shortstop.

"I labeled him as the Phil Rizzuto of the Range," said Mayasich, referring to the New York Yankees' diminutive Hall of Fame shortstop. "He was small and quick and could run like hell."

Defending champion Eveleth opened state hockey tournament play with a 6–0 quarterfinal victory against White Bear Lake. Voce scored just 1:39 into the game. Tom Ventrucci, school homecoming king as a senior, scored his lone tournament goal. Mayasich tallied a hat trick, and Ikola recorded an eleven-save shutout. Matchefts did not have a point.

He rebounded with one goal and three assists, however, in an 8–0 semifinal rout of Warroad. The remaining script read the same: Voce scored early, Mayasich got a hat trick, and Ikola earned a fifteen-save shutout.

A record third consecutive shutout was Ikola's championship game goal against Williams, but a disputed second-period penalty shot ruined his plans. On the play, John McKinnon shot between Ikola's legs, but the goalie got a piece of the puck. Then McKinnon plowed into Ikola, sending both players—and the puck—into the net. The referee signaled a goal, much to Ikola's dismay.

"I was looking for a damn shutout in that game, and I didn't get it," he said.

Matchefts scored first and added an assist in the 4–1 victory against Williams, coached by Eveleth native Al Braga. Matchefts's record mark of twelve career tournament assists stood nearly five decades. Red Wing's Johnny Pohl, a 1998 graduate, finished with seventeen helpers.

Matchefts became the first player selected to three consecutive all-tournament teams. He later won three NCAA titles at Michigan, two with Ikola. In 1956, he won an Olympic silver medal playing with Mayasich and Ikola under Eveleth native and coach John Mariucci.

"He was a competitor with a mean streak—Italian," Mayasich joked. "He was a winner. We all were."

~*DL*~

"THE BEST GOALIE WE'VE EVER HAD"

EVELETH'S WILLARD IKOLA HAD DRAMATIC FLAIR FOR MAKING THE BIG SAVE

DATES	LOCATION	ATTENDANCE	CHAMPIONSHIP
FEBRUARY 23–25	ST. PAUL AUDITORIUM	14,272	EVELETH 4, WILLIAMS 3

Did you know? St. Paul Murray set a period record for penalties with nine in the final period of the consolation title game. South St. Paul's seven penalties helped set the record for penalties by two teams in a period (sixteen).

Willard Ikola (right) grew up idolizing Eveleth's three NHL goaltenders and made a name for himself as well. His ten victories and five shutouts remain state tournament career records. Ikola won the 1949 tournament opener against White Bear Lake despite forty-two saves by Bears goalie Dick Doyle (left). Photo courtesy of the Minnesota Historical Society

FOR YOUNG GOALTENDER Willard Ikola, a Saturday-night special meant tuning into a *Hockey Night in Canada* broadcast and catching a game featuring one of Eveleth's three National Hockey League netminders: Mike Karakas, Frank Brimsek, and Sam LoPresti.

The play-by-play was beamed from a Fort Frances, Ontario, radio station straight into Ikola's impressionable mind. The broadcasts gave life to the trio, who six other nights each week existed only as pictures on Ikola's bedroom walls.

Lying on the floor in the front room, warmed by the coal

Mighty Eveleth edged Williams 4–3 in the 1950 championship game, the closest the Golden Bears came to losing a state tournament game from 1948 to 1951. Despite losing John Matchefts to graduation, Eveleth maintained its place atop high school hockey thanks to junior John Mayasich (third from right). Photo by the *Minneapolis Tribune*

stove, Ikola, the next great Eveleth goalie, listened to Foster Hewitt call the action. "He shoots! He scores!" became Hewitt's trademark.

Scoring happened less often on the Eveleth trio, and Ikola later met their standards. His ten victories and five shutouts remain state tournament records. He backstopped the Golden Bears to twenty-eight consecutive victories in 1948 and 1949. And Eveleth players desired another flawless season in 1950.

"Coach [Cliff] Thompson was a really low-key guy and never really mentioned anything about our winning streak," Ikola said. "But we were aware of it and certainly wanted to keep it going."

Ikola, the Golden Bears' senior goalie, anchored the defense

for his fourth full varsity season. He also excelled as a halfback on the football team and a catcher in baseball.

"He's one of the best athletes to come out of Eveleth," forward John Mayasich said.

Ikola owed his hockey success to his family's influence. Older sister Doris pulled her six-year-old brother in a sled to the rink. Skating wasn't easy on dull blades attached to hand-me-down boots stuffed with two pairs of wool socks so they'd fit, but Ikola craved more.

He became a goalie in third grade. By sixth grade, he wore an inflatable rubber device for chest protection. A slow leak forced him to reinflate the makeshift pad after each period.

Playing goalie meant following the lead of older brother Roy, Eveleth's netminder. He turned eighteen a few weeks before the inaugural state tournament in 1945 and joined the navy. He later played for Team USA at the 1948 Winter Olympics and won an NCAA title at Colorado College.

Willard Ikola's illustrious career began in 1946 when Thompson asked the eighth-grader to be a practice goalie. Just thirteen years old, Ikola was, as the line in the movie *Rudy* goes, about 5 foot nothing and a hundred and nothing.

Unfazed, he studied starter Ronnie Drobnick, then took the job when jaundice sidelined the senior for a four-game stretch. Ikola helped Eveleth go 3–0–1.

Drobnick returned, Eveleth qualified for the state tournament, and Ikola didn't make the trip. As a freshman in 1947, he and the Golden Bears lost the third-place game. They wouldn't lose for the remainder of the decade.

Before the 1948 season, Ikola received what likely were Brimsek's spare goalie skates from his Boston Bruins days. Brother Tony Brimsek was the local American Legion baseball manager and hooked up Ikola.

"I took them home and I was in seventh heaven," said Ikola, who initially wore three pairs of socks to get a snug fit. He wore one less layer each year as his feet grew.

He filled those skates and his role as Eveleth's next great goalie. Fast on his feet, Ikola played angles well and used poke checks to thwart opposing puck carriers.

"You'd see it time and time again, he'd get his stick out there quick as a flash," said Tony Tassoni, a 1948 graduate.

Practices, even pregame warmups, were competitive sessions pitting Ikola against Eveleth's great forwards. The showdowns made everyone better.

"Anytime you came down on him, he knew he could stop you," Mayasich said. "He knew you better than you knew him."

The Golden Bears rolled through Ikola's senior season. Losing to Grand Rapids in football that fall relegated Ikola and Eveleth to second in the Iron Range Conference, but payback came on the ice. Eveleth crushed Grand Rapids 9–3 and 7–2 in the regular season and 18–0 in the playoffs.

Lopsided results continued at the state tournament. Eveleth blanked Minneapolis Central in a 6–0 quarterfinal victory. Dan Voce tallied a hat trick, and Ikola stopped all fourteen shots.

"He always said, 'Let 'em shoot a little bit. It gets cold,'" Voce said.

Ikola remained perfect in a 7–0 semifinal victory against St. Cloud with fifteen saves. But a six-goal Mayasich outburst grabbed the headlines.

A title game rematch with Williams awaited. The St. Paul Auditorium lights were turned out for team introductions. When a glitch prolonged the darkness, hundreds of fans held lit matches aloft.

Three Eveleth goals in the first period gave no indication of the furious ending to come.

Williams scored in the second period, and Ikola, his dream of three consecutive state tournament shutouts dashed, went to his knees, bowed his head, and remained still for almost a minute.

Bigger concerns loomed as Williams tied the game 3–3 with two goals just fifteen seconds apart in the third period. Then a penalty sent Mayasich to the box late.

"Somebody told me later that my mother was listening to the game and said, 'They're going to lose it, and it's going to be his fault,'" Mayasich said. "How the hell did she know that?"

Sorry, mom. Mayasich returned to backhand the game-winner on a feed from forward Ron Castellano with 1:20 remaining.

If not for a key Ikola stop, Mayasich's goal might have mattered less. Ray Beauchamp, who tied Mayasich for the tournament lead with twelve points, got a breakaway, but Ikola made the save.

"Thank god we had Ike in the net," Castellano said.

"We were as relieved as we were joyous," said Ikola, who stood tall in Eveleth's fiftieth consecutive victory.

He returned to the state tournament a decade later with upstart program Edina-Morningside, having added two NCAA championships with Michigan and the 1958 Olympic silver medal to his résumé. More state tournament success would follow.

A tribute next to Ikola's senior picture in Eveleth's yearbook, *The Carbide,* read, "Not only popular this little lad, but the best goalie we've ever had."

~*DL*~

IRON RANGE IDOL

JOHN MAYASICH DOMINATED PEERS LIKE NO PLAYER BEFORE OR SINCE

DATES	LOCATION	ATTENDANCE	CHAMPIONSHIP
FEBRUARY 22–24	ST. PAUL AUDITORIUM	18,582	EVELETH 4, ST. PAUL JOHNSON 1

Did you know? St. Paul Johnson goaltender Warren Strelow later served as goalie coach for Herb Brooks and the 1980 Olympic team.

JOHN MAYASICH'S GREATNESS in hockey found its way into conversation among St. Paul Johnson teammates at a 2016 celebration-of-life luncheon for departed standout Governors goaltender Tom Wahman.

Roger Bertelsen and Stu Anderson, key forwards on Johnson's 1953 and 1955 state championship teams, respectively, shared their fondness for Mayasich, a fellow Minnesota Gopher who dominated the high school ranks with Eveleth before his college career.

"I said, 'Stewie, my memories are of Mayasich being a hockey player without peer, the finest I ever saw,'" Bertelsen said. "'Was he as good as I remember?'

"And Stewie said, 'He was better than you remember.'"

He's hard to forget. Mayasich still holds ten state tournament records, including most goals in a period (four), game (seven), tournament (fifteen), and career (thirty-six).

As a junior in 1950, Mayasich guided Eveleth to a third consecutive undefeated season. He led all state tournament scorers with eleven goals—six of them in the semifinals alone—and tallied a hat trick in the championship game. Colorado College coach Cheddy Thompson, recruiting at the 1950 tournament, said, "That Mayasich is good enough to make a number of college teams right now; I know he could play on mine."

Eveleth coach Cliff Thompson (no relation) played it coy when he said Mayasich wasn't the best Golden Bears player, "but he may be next year." Was he crazy? Hardly. Thompson knew exactly how his quiet-yet-intense star would respond.

To this day, Mayasich lives by the belief "You should always try to be better than you are."

Despite losing forward John Matchefts in 1949 and goalie Willard Ikola in 1950 to graduation, Eveleth dressed "probably the deepest team we had" in 1951, Ron Castellano said.

Eveleth defenseman Ed Mrkonich (left) and wing Dan Voce (right) made the 1951 state title their third in a row. John Mayasich (middle) enjoyed his fourth consecutive championship to close out a record-setting tournament career. Photo by the *Minneapolis Tribune*

Castellano and Dan Voce were first-line wings. Veterans LaVerne Hammer and Ed Mrkonich solidified the defense. Forwards Mike Castellano and Dave Hendrickson returned, while Bruce Shutte brought fresh talent.

But Mayasich ruled. He supplanted Matchefts as Eveleth's premier forward with his eleven tournament goals in 1950 and fifteen the following season. Not until 2021, when Dodge County's Brody Lamb scored ten tournament goals, did another player reach double digits.

"Voce and I could've sat in the stands sometimes and just watched," Castellano said.

The Iron Range was rich in athletic talent, yet Mayasich stood apart. He was a 6-foot wonder who excelled as a quarterback in football and as a baseball pitcher. His "part-time" spring endeavors weren't too shabby, either: he qualified for state in tennis using a borrowed racket as a sophomore and took fourth in the high jump at the state track and field meet as a senior.

Eveleth linemates John Mayasich (left) and Dan Voce (right), along with Ron "Sonny" Castellano, were united as sophomores and anchored three consecutive state championships (1949–51). Mayasich and Voce are holding the 1951 championship trophy. Photo courtesy of the Minnesota Historical Society

"He was an idol to me and a lot of folks up there," said Vincent Bugliosi, a former Hibbing tennis star who won the state title in 1951 and later gained fame for prosecuting Charles Manson.

The tenth of eleven children, Mayasich learned on the family's lone pair of skates.

Deft hands came from games on crowded rinks and on the street, where a missed shot could mean a lost puck or tennis ball. Stickhandling around defenders and faking goalies became critical.

Later credited with introducing the slapshot to college hockey—Ikola taught him what he'd seen from the Detroit Red Wings—Mayasich had a wicked backhand. Kids dug their hockey goals into snowbanks on the sides of the street. With narrow streets, the goals were not always directly across from each another, so Mayasich honed his backhand rather than always turning to shoot from his forehand.

Undefeated Eveleth reached the 1951 state tournament and opened against Williams in a rematch of the previous year's title game. There was no tension this time as the Golden Bears went ahead 7–0 after one period. Mayasich scored four goals in a 12–1 rout.

Williams goalie Johnny Umhauer, who faced Eveleth in 1950 and 1951, raved, "He was good last year, an all-stater, but he's better this year."

Cliff Thompson was right to prod his prodigy. Before the semifinal against Minneapolis Southwest, star forward Dick Meredith offered another challenge.

"Sure, they'll be tough," said Meredith, sucking an orange after his team's 2–1 quarterfinal victory. "But I think we'll give Eveleth a game. We won tonight, and we were off, way off."

Mayasich, meanwhile, couldn't have been more on against Southwest. He scored a record seven goals in an 11–5 victory.

"Dick Meredith was supposed to be covering me," Mayasich said. "What did I get, seven goals? I always kid him that he's got an assist record."

"They say I was covering him, but I wasn't," Meredith said. "I was all over the ice trying to catch him. In my era, there was no finer hockey player."

Down 5–1 after the first period, Southwest came alive in the second. The Merediths, Dick and younger brother Bob, scored three of the Indians' four goals, cutting their deficit to 6–5.

"We were thinking that we were coming on, but we were tired," Dick Meredith said.

Three Mayasich goals in the third period sank a listing Southwest ship.

"That game was just 'Pass the puck to Mace,'" Voce said.

If only Mayasich's linemates had felt that way more often.

"I was a Croatian playing with two Italian wingmen," Mayasich joked. "They never passed the puck. How did I get it? I'd skate them offside and get a faceoff."

St. Paul Johnson was powerless to stop him in the finale. Neither team scored until Mayasich did so twice in the second period on assists from Castellano.

Mayasich completed the hat trick early in the third period "as the rafters shook to a now familiar refrain—a cheer for Johnny," Halsey Hall wrote in the *Minneapolis Tribune*.

Eveleth won 4–1 and moved its winning streak to sixty-nine games. Mayasich finished with fifteen goals, more than any other team scored in the tournament. Moreover, he fulfilled his goal of being better than he had been the year before.

"We went out to win," Mayasich said. "They say, 'Go out and have fun.' Well, winning was fun. I don't know who the hell ever lost a game and felt good about it."

~DL~

FOUNDING FAMILIES

Merediths, Lundeens, Westbys, and Alms stocked Minneapolis teams with talent

Before outdoor ice became available at Linden Hills Park, one block from his southwest Minneapolis home, Dick Meredith brought his skates and stick to Minnehaha Creek.

Any cattails sticking up through the ice were stomped down in the name of readying his temporary rink for game action.

Meredith graduated from Southwest in 1951, the oldest of five puck-chasing brothers in what became one of four quintessential Minneapolis hockey families.

Minneapolis Southwest coach Dave Peterson talks with forwards Paul Lundeen and John Meredith on the eve of the 1975 state tournament quarterfinals. Southwest appeared in fifteen state tournaments from 1951 to 1980, but only twice without a Meredith or Lundeen on the roster. Photo by Pete Hohn/*Minneapolis Tribune*

The Southwest Indians appeared in fifteen state tournaments from 1951 to 1980 but only two without a Meredith or Lundeen on the roster. The nearby South Tigers reached five state tournaments from 1950 to 1993 and never without an Alm or Westby on or behind the bench.

Charter members of the Minneapolis Hockey Hall of Fame, these four families learned the game on outdoor rinks and later achieved greatness at the high school, college, and international levels.

"These are the builders," said Chris Middlebrook, a 1975 Washburn graduate and Minneapolis Hockey Hall of Fame organizer. "They are an extraordinary story."

Dick Meredith played in the 1950 and 1951 state tournaments before joining the Gophers. In 1960, he and the US Olympic team won the gold medal. All five Meredith brothers reached the state tournament, with Merv tallying a hat trick in the 1955 quarterfinals. Bob and Wayne went on to letter for the Gophers. So did John, the baby of the family, who won an NCAA championship in 1979.

Likewise, the five Lundeen boys boast considerable résumés. Each Pershing Park product played in a state tournament. Oldest brother Bob played on the 1970 state champion Southwest team and assisted on the game-winning overtime goal that clinched the first and still only Minneapolis public-school state title.

Bob, David, Thom, and Paul all played for Wisconsin. Bob won an NCAA title in 1973, and David did the same in 1977. Charlie, the youngest, played at Northern Michigan.

Lloyd Lundeen, the family patriarch, skated for the

TEN NOTABLE TOURNAMENT FAMILIES

1. THE HENDRICKSONS. Three generations reached the state tournament: Larry with Minneapolis Washburn in 1959 and 1960, his sons Dan and Darby for Richfield in 1991, and Darby's son, Mason, who won the 2018 title with Minnetonka. Larry also coached Apple Valley to the 1996 title.

2. THE CARROLLS. Six brothers—Mike, Steve, Tom, Pat, Dan, and Jim—played at Edina from 1973 to 1986. Three reached the state tournament. Steve took second in 1977; Tom (1978 and 1979) and Dan (1982) later won state championships. Pat and Jim officiated tournament championship games in 2000 and 2009, and since 2009, Jim has served as the event's public address announcer. Sister Ann Carroll worked as the 2006 state tournament rinkside reporter for Channel 45 for Class 1A and 2A games.

3. THE POEHLINGS. Lakeville North twin wingers Jack and Nick Poehling helped the Panthers to state in 2013. The next year, younger brother Ryan centered their line, and together they placed second. In 2015, North went 31–0.

4. THE LEMPES. The Grand Rapids championship teams of 1975, 1976, and 1980 all featured Lempes. Dan (1975 and 1976) and Eric and Todd (1980) ensured the family name was prominent among the program's rash of brother combinations.

5. THE BROTENS. Minnesota hockey royalty, the three Broten brothers made the state tournament a springboard to future successes. As a Roseau freshman, Neal joined the 1975 team at state. He and brother Aaron rode undefeated seasons to St. Paul in 1977 and 1978. Younger brother Paul helped the Rams to the 1983 and 1984 tournaments.

now-defunct Minneapolis West Cowboys in the 1946 and 1947 state tournaments. He died in 1980 and didn't see Charlie make the state tournament.

The two families shared the state tournament stage when John Meredith and Paul Lundeen played for the 1975 and 1976 Indian teams.

The Alms and Westbys were much more closely aligned.

The families were neighbors on East Twenty-Fourth Street and played all manner of games on a nearby vacant lot they dubbed Westby's Weedpatch. They called Riverside Park home in the winter and endured the 150 steps down to (and back up from) the rink, a spot since lost to pilings that support the Interstate 94 bridge.

In 1954, Gary and Larry Alm, along with Jerry and Jim Westby, helped South reach the state tournament. A year later, Rick Alm replaced the graduated Gary as the Tigers won an eleven-overtime quarterfinal game against Thief River Falls. Proving the endurance built from those countless trips up and down the stairs, Jerry Westby sent the game to overtime, and Jim tallied the game-winning goal.

"And Larry played the whole game," Gary said.

Gary, Larry, Mike, and Rick Alm all lettered for the Gophers. So did Jerry and Jim Westby. In 1993, Rick coached South to the Tier II state tournament. Larry was his assistant.

"It was a big thing for all of us to go in the Minneapolis Hockey Hall of Fame," Gary Alm said. "People maybe don't remember any of the individual brothers. But they remember the last names."

~DL~

Jim Westby (left) and brother Jerry (right), shown here with sister Judy, played key roles in the 1955 quarterfinal game won by Minneapolis South. Jerry sent the game to overtime, and in the eleventh extra period, Jim tallied the game-winner. Photo courtesy of Kyle Oen/Vintage Minnesota Hockey

The Alm brothers: from left, Tony, Mike, Tim, Rick, Larry, and Gary. From 1950 to 1993, the South Tigers reached five state tournaments, never without one of the Alms or the Westbys, another prominent Minneapolis South family, on or behind the bench. Photo courtesy of Kyle Oen/Vintage Minnesota Hockey

6. THE BJUGSTADS. Brothers Mike and Scott helped put Irondale on the hockey map, leading the New Brighton-based school to its first state appearance in 1979. Mike went the next two years. His son Nick, a Mr. Hockey recipient, also made three consecutive trips with Blaine (2008–10). Scott's son Jesse played on Stillwater's 2016 state team.

7. THE PELTIERS. From 1963 to 1968, St. Paul Johnson made the tournament with at least one Peltier brother on the ice. Skip won the 1963 title as a sophomore and reached the next two tournaments. Ron joined him in 1965. A year later, Doug came aboard. Bob played in the 1970 and 1971 tournaments.

8. THE CHECCOS. When Lakeville South upset number-two seed St. Thomas Academy in the 2017 state quarterfinals, Cory Checco scored a goal, and brother Austin served as backup goaltender. Their cousin, Steve, went

to state with Irondale in 1980 and 1981. Cousin Nick starred for Bloomington Jefferson, winning state titles in 1992 and 1993 and the Mr. Hockey Award.

9. THE SAGISSORS. Tom keyed Hastings's run to the 1985 state tournament, and success followed the next generation north up the St. Croix River. In 2014, sons Sam and Simon (and their cousin Charlie) helped Stillwater make its state tournament debut. In 2016, Sam and Simon's younger brother T. J. added to the family's legacy. Patriarch Don Sagissor was an assistant coach who helped guide Hastings to its first state tournament in 1971, when Don Saatzer was the head coach.

10. THE SAATZERS. St. Cloud Tech brothers Ronald and Don reached the 1950 state tournament and were joined by younger sibling Dick in 1951 and 1952. The Tigers have not returned to state since.

FROM FEARS TO CHEERS

EVEN HIBBING'S CHEERLEADERS HAD DOUBTS ABOUT ENDING EVELETH DYNASTY

DATES	LOCATION	ATTENDANCE	CHAMPIONSHIP
FEBRUARY 21–23	ST. PAUL AUDITORIUM	15,523	HIBBING 4, EVELETH 3

 St. Cloud Tech senior Don Saatzer tallied a hat trick in the consolation semi-finals and later coached Hastings to its first state tournament (1971).

AS LONG AS the great John Mayasich donned an Eveleth jersey, beating the Golden Bears was a concept as foreign in its day as using facemasks and curved sticks.

Players for Hibbing, an Iron Range Conference and Region 7 foe, didn't just expect defeat; they accepted it. Joked about it, even.

"We used to have a pool as to how much we'd lose by when we played Eveleth," defenseman Jerry Calengor said.

Mayasich graduated in 1951 with four consecutive state championships, each one punctuating an undefeated season.

"I was about the happiest person there was when Mayasich moved on," right wing George Jetty said.

As a senior, Jetty dared to dream his hockey team would be the one to end Eveleth's dynasty. That's because the year before, Jetty believed his team was second only to Eveleth. Maybe so. But the Golden Bears mauled Hibbing three times with a combined 27–7 score.

Among Hibbing sports, hockey trailed basketball in popularity by a similar margin. The Bluejackets reached the state

Joanne Tomaino, Jeanne Teske, and Bertha Canelake (left to right) formed Hibbing's inaugural hockey cheer squad just in time for the 1951–52 season. Dressed in white wool sweaters and navy-blue pants, the trio used their skating ability to perform on-ice routines. Photo by the *St. Paul Dispatch*

ABOVE: Linemates George Jetty, Jim Lipovetz, and center Jack Petroske (pictured against Minneapolis Southwest in the semifinal game) were Hibbing's tremendous top unit. Petroske tallied a tournament-best eleven points on three goals and eight assists in 1952. Photo by Bill Seamann/ *Minneapolis Tribune*

LEFT: On three consecutive Saturdays in 1952, Hibbing owned four-time defending state champion Eveleth. A victory at home snapped the Golden Bears' seventy-nine-game winning streak. The Bluejackets won again for the Region 7 title and capped the season with a 4–3 victory for the state title. Captain Jack Petroske is pictured holding the trophy. Photo by the *St. Paul Pioneer Press*

basketball tournament in 1948 and 1949. As the Bluejackets played their 1951–52 season, local basketball star Dick Garmaker was rising to national prominence at Hibbing Junior College.

Heck, Jetty focused on hockey only after not making the basketball team as a ninth-grader.

Cheerleader Joanne Tomaino favored hockey over basketball in large part because she was dating Jim Lipovetz, a talented left wing. She convinced two additional girls to trade the gym for the rink, and Hibbing's inaugural hockey cheer squad was formed in time for the 1951–52 season.

Nothing changed right away. Eveleth beat Hibbing 5–3 in the teams' first meeting.

But as the Bluejackets won eight of their next nine games, citizens of the Ore Capital began attending hockey games in larger numbers.

The regular season ended with a home game against undefeated Eveleth. While her boyfriend, Lipovetz, possessed a quiet confidence, Tomaino said the cheerleaders, typically purveyors of ceaseless pep, "were scared to death."

Not to worry. Jetty scored all five goals in a 5–4 victory, and the Bluejackets snapped the Golden Bears' seventy-nine-game winning streak.

Afterward, many of the estimated six hundred people at Hibbing Memorial Building celebrated the upset on the ice with victorious players.

"Eveleth was dynamic, but our team was really put together," Tomaino said.

Linemates Jetty, Lipovetz, and center Jack Petroske gave the Bluejackets a tremendous top unit. Jetty considered Petroske "our catalyst. He was a cut above; I fed off him."

The second line of Bill Webb, Howie Wallene, and Don Holcomb added key goals.

Calengor and defensive partner Martin "Zooner" Sundvall were undersized but tough. Martin Sundvall Sr. unintentionally coined his son's nickname: "Zooner" was how "Junior" sounded through a thick Finnish accent.

"Zooner couldn't hold a tune, but he would always be humming when he came by and hip-checked somebody," Calengor said.

Third defenseman Herb Sellars lived in Eveleth until age eleven, with one house between his and the Mayasichs' on Summit Street. A job at Stevenson Mine led to the Sellars family moving about twenty-five miles west.

Goalie Don Vaia switched from forward as a freshman and played with poise beyond his experience level.

One week after derailing Eveleth's winning streak, Hibbing traveled to the Golden Bears' den for a Region 7 finals rematch. An estimated 3,500 fans packed the Hippodrome and roared as their boys went ahead 1–0 just fifty-two seconds into the game.

Hibbing returned fire with six consecutive goals, ending in a 6–2 victory that clinched the team's first state tournament appearance. Eveleth also made the field, since the Region 7 runner-up was automatically entered as the "backdoor" Region 3 representative.

Despite being state tournament newcomers, Hibbing's players didn't lack confidence.

"I didn't anticipate any problems with winning the tournament," Jetty said.

They certainly didn't have any in the quarterfinal. Jetty and Lipovetz each tallied a hat trick in a 10–0 rout of St. Cloud. Earlier Thursday, Mayasich, now a freshman with the Minnesota Golden Gophers next door in Minneapolis, had watched Eveleth's victory against Thief River Falls, then greeted former teammates in the locker room.

Hibbing's semifinal against Minneapolis Southwest proved challenging. Both teams entered the third period scoreless. Then a flurry ensued as all four goals came in a span of 1:34. Jetty scored his team's first and last goals, and Lipovetz ended up with the game-winner in a 3–1 victory.

The victory set up a third consecutive Saturday meeting with Eveleth.

Before the title game, Hibbing coach Mauritz Uhrbom received a telegram from the Charleson Iron Mining Company congratulating him on the semifinal victory.

"I'm going to keep this," Uhrbom joked. "Might need a job this summer."

By the end of the Eveleth game, he needed to lie down. The Bluejackets skated to a 4–1 lead a little more than one minute into the third period and then relaxed.

"I warned the kids, 'Now stay on the offensive. Don't go into a shell,'" Uhrbom said. "They sort of forgot it for a while."

Fatigue, not forgetfulness, was really to blame. Jetty and Petroske never left the ice that night. When the second line came on, Petroske and Jetty replaced defensemen Calengor and Sundvall.

Play became "extremely one-sided in our end," Sellars said. Eveleth fired fifteen shots on goal, but only two beat Vaia, and Hibbing survived with a 4–3 victory.

Vaia, first to reach the team room, hugged each teammate as they entered. An official gave him the game puck.

"That was the big thrill," Vaia said. "With a gang like that out in front, it isn't hard to look good."

That was more than could be said for Petroske's skates. He had tallied a tournament-best eleven points (three goals, eight assists) on skates that looked like they had been tied to a car's rear fender in Hibbing and dragged to St. Paul.

"Don't worry, Coach," he told Uhrbom. "Only thing important are the blades."

Unproven at season's start, Hibbing had left no doubt. On three consecutive Saturdays, from Hibbing to Eveleth to St. Paul, the Bluejackets bested Eveleth.

Tomaino, who later married Lipovetz, recalled the cheerleaders celebrated by "splitting a Hershey bar in the St. Paul Hotel lobby. We toasted our great team and the experience we had."

~DL~

A PLACE AMONG NORTHERN STARS

ST. PAUL JOHNSON PROVED CHAMPIONSHIP METTLE BY BEATING EVELETH AND WARROAD

DATES	LOCATION	ATTENDANCE	CHAMPIONSHIP	
FEBRUARY 19–21	ST. PAUL AUDITORIUM	19,924	ST. PAUL JOHNSON 4, WARROAD 1	31

 Pete Passolt, uncle of accomplished hockey player and longtime local television broadcaster Jeff Passolt, scored two goals for Minneapolis Southwest in the consolation semifinals.

ONE POSTPRACTICE conditioning drill sticks in the memories of 1953 St. Paul Johnson Governors players.

"There was a pretty good snowstorm during practice, and Rube's car couldn't get up a hill," said Gene Picha, a senior goalie that year. Rube, as in Gustafson, was the Governors' coach. His mid-1930s dark-blue Chevrolet required youthful horsepower.

"So we pushed it," Picha said.

Success for Twin Cities schools in the tournament's early years was much the same thing—an uphill battle. Northern hockey teams won a combined seven of the first eight championships: five for Eveleth and one each for Hibbing and Roseau.

But Johnson, 1947 state champion, reaffirmed its elite status by beating two northern teams en route to the 1953 championship.

Coach Rube Gustafson (back row, second from left) helped Johnson become one of the state's early hockey powers by winning it all in 1953. The Governors joined Eveleth as the only program to win two or more titles in the first nine years of tournament play. Photo courtesy of the Minnesota Historical Society

St. Paul Johnson sophomore wing Rod Anderson could not beat Warroad junior goalie Bob Lewis on this play, but the Governors' ultimate 4–1 victory meant Anderson joined older brother Orv as a state champion. Photo by Russ Bull/*Minneapolis Tribune*

Picha witnessed the rise. He was a backup in 1951 when John Mayasich scored all four Eveleth goals against Johnson and capped an unparalleled prep career with a fourth consecutive state title. In 1952, the Governors lost in the first round and again in the consolation championship game.

"I must say, I didn't play well," said Picha, who allowed eleven tournament goals. "I felt that nobody should score on me and that any goal was my fault."

Picha met his high standards as a senior. The Governors' only all-city selection in football and hockey, he helped his gridiron teammates go undefeated and win the St. Paul City Conference championship. Johnson later defeated Minneapolis North for its first Twin Cities championship.

The success proved contagious for a hockey team that returned nine players from the 1952 tournament.

"We had confidence that we weren't going to lose," Picha said. "It wasn't a verbal thing. It was a within thing."

But that overconfidence hurt the team late in the season.

Johnson lost 3–2 to Minneapolis Southwest in the Twin Cities championship game after crushing the Indians 8–0 earlier in the season.

"We thought that game was going to be a walk in the park," senior forward Roger Bertelsen said. "We got our comeuppance."

The Governors also got a tough draw in the state tournament quarterfinals: St. Louis Park lost its season opener, then reeled off fourteen consecutive victories.

Players took the ice for the 9 PM game. Johnson forward Gary Shea, called Red for his hair, almost saw his night end early when he took a stick to the face.

"It knocked me out," said Shea, who later needed two stitches in his chin. "I went to the bench, and Rube handed me something and said, 'Smell this, Red.' I never missed a shift."

Tied 1–1 after regulation, the teams ground their way to a fourth overtime. Then Bertelsen made his move.

"I came down on their two defensemen hoping they would make a mistake so I could do something," Bertelsen said. "But they didn't, so I shot between them hoping to get a rebound."

Instead, his team received a gift.

"The puck hopped over the goalie's stick; it didn't even get to the back of the net," Shea said.

Bertelsen joked, "I could tell you that it was a laser shot, but I won't."

After the game, an ecstatic Bertelsen said, "I was sure lucky on that one. I'll never forget that shot if I live to be a hundred."

Even if Bertelsen wanted to forget, his teammates won't let him.

"He still catches a lot of grief for that," Shea said. "We'll say, 'Good thing he couldn't raise the puck. We wouldn't have won.'"

Johnson survived the tournament's longest game to date and earned a semifinal against Eveleth, royalty among northern schools. Not since 1947 had the Golden Bears missed the title game.

With Johnson seemingly sapped by its marathon game, the *Pioneer Press* opined, "Johnson will be at a disadvantage in the tussle with Eveleth."

Bertelsen didn't see those words before the game. Fearing their son's discouragement, his parents hid the paper.

Extra! Extra! The Governors were magnificent, blitzing Eveleth for three goals before the game was four minutes old and leading 4–0 after the first period.

"We just took it to them," Bertelsen said "They were standing still, and we were moving."

Jack Holstrom, Johnson's precocious sophomore defenseman, was dumbstruck.

"They no more than dropped the puck and it was 3–0," he said. "Everything we shot went into the net."

Forward Bob Wahman tallied a hat trick in a 7–1 rout, which he called "the crowning achievement in my athletic career."

Johnson's strength came from two strong forward lines. Bertelsen played on the first unit with Wahman and Glenn Peterson.

"Bob and I were closer than the one and the two," Bertelsen said. "I knew exactly what he was doing, and he knew where I was going to be whether I had the puck or not.

"And Glenn was Ichabod Crane. He was all knees and elbows but always going like hell."

Holstrom played across from Ray Karnuth on the blue line.

"Rube paired Jack with Ray, and it was a perfect match," Bertelsen said. "Jack was a pure stay-at-home defenseman, whereas Ray liked to wander a little bit."

Shea said of Holstrom, "I can't remember him making a mistake." Holstrom shrugged.

"He's being kind," he said. As for Picha, Holstrom raved, "There's a guy who was steady."

Bertelsen considered Picha and Karnuth "arguably two of the best hockey players in the state."

After defeating Eveleth, Bertelsen said, "It dawned on me that we can play with these northern schools."

A timely realization considering Warroad, located six miles south of the Canadian border, was the Governors' title game opponent.

Brothers and future Olympic gold medalists Bill and Roger Christian were two of Warroad's 250 students.

Two Bertelsen goals made the score 2–0 after one period. Rod Anderson and Karnuth doubled the lead in the second period, and Picha, one year after disappointing himself in tournament play, held a shutout into the third period before yielding his lone goal of the final. He was selected to the all-tournament team.

"Johnson is the first team to outskate us this year," Warroad coach Bernie Broderick said afterward. "No, I don't feel too bad about losing. We lost to a great team."

~*DL*~

RENAISSANCE MEN

MUSIC, MOTORS AMONG PROWLERS' MANY NONHOCKEY INTERESTS

34

DATES	LOCATION	ATTENDANCE	CHAMPIONSHIP
FEBRUARY 25–27	ST. PAUL AUDITORIUM	24,508	THIEF RIVER FALLS 4, EVELETH 1

 Central, with a 13–4 record, became the first Duluth team to reach the tournament. The Trojans, coached by John Vucinovich, went 0–2.

LOREN "SID" VRAA played the coronet, Lyle Guttu the trombone. Marv Jorde was a disc jockey at a local radio station.

Dennis Rolle, coach of Thief River Falls' hockey team, provided the vocals. And not just in his stirring pregame speeches and behind-the-bench chatter.

"I remember one time we were going to Warroad," forward Joe Poole said. "[Rolle] said, 'If you beat them, I'll sing all the way home.'"

The Prowlers won. Rolle was true to his word.

"He sang like Al Jolson," Poole said. Rolle evidently did a dead-on impression of the wildly popular and influential early-1900s singer, comedian, and actor. "He was really good.

With dashing coach Dennis Rolle (right) leading the way, Thief River Falls completed an undefeated season in 1954 by outscoring its three state tournament opponents by a combined 18–3. Photo by the *Minneapolis Tribune*, courtesy of Kyle Oen/Vintage Minnesota Hockey

Loren "Sid" Vraa of Thief River Falls breaks in alone on South St. Paul goaltender Henry Metcalf during a 1954 state semifinal. Vraa scored Thief River Falls' second goal in an 8–1 rout. Photo by the *Minneapolis Tribune*

We couldn't believe it. Everyone just sat with their mouths open."

Multitalented doesn't begin to describe the Prowlers' 1954 squad. Most every player was a standout in several sports, including Poole, who also starred in cross-country and as a baseball shortstop. Vraa was an ace pitcher and the football team's all-state quarterback.

When he wasn't spinning records or serving in the National Guard, Jorde, another multisport star, transformed old cars into hot rods. Robert Helgeland, a discus thrower, sprinter, and left fielder, dabbled in electronics with an eye on a TV repair career. And Guttu, a top hurdler who played baseball and captained the football team, also served as the narrator for the town's annual Christmas program.

"Lyle is the idol of the town's younger hockey players," Rolle said about Guttu, a varsity regular beginning in the eighth grade.

Thief River Falls entered the 1954 state tournament with a 17–0 record. The Prowlers, making their fourth tourney appearance, were tabbed as the favorite ahead of defending champion St. Paul Johnson and perennial powerhouse Eveleth.

Jorde, the team's leading scorer, centered a forward line that included fellow senior Guttu and junior Vraa. All three stood at least 6 feet.

Poole, a junior who was second on the team in scoring, centered two more towering seniors in Helgeland and Darryl Durgin.

There was no distinguishing between a first and second line. Jorde's unit entered the tournament with a combined thirty-five goals, while Poole's had thirty-four. Just as effective was the defense, led by twin hammers Mike McMahon and Les Sabo, burly seniors known for their physical play and efficient puck movement. They played in front of goalie Jack Hoppe, a senior co-captain. The Prowlers allowed a mere eighteen goals in their seventeen victories.

Thief River Falls dispatched Minneapolis South 6–1 in the quarterfinals, the only unexpected plot twist coming in the form of a Helgeland hat trick.

"Can't understand it," Helgeland, known mostly for his defense, told reporters. "I've scored only eight goals altogether this season."

The 5-foot-9, 145-pound Poole notched only an assist in

WHITEY AND BEAVER
Jersey switch backfired on colorful South St. Paul characters

First, there's that name and nickname.

Dick Lick became known around South St. Paul hockey circles as Beaver. The youngster with prominent front teeth always skated at the "Mudhole," the outdoor rink in town where so many future Packers honed their trade.

Lick palled around with Don "Whitey" Willer, whom Lick recalled as being prone to episodes in which he would be disoriented and unresponsive, though conscious. Like the time Beaver was getting a ride on the handlebars of Whitey's bicycle.

"He was quiet, so I turned my head the best I could, and I could see he wasn't with it," said Beaver, a middle schooler at the time.

Thankfully, Whitey recovered after a half block, and the ride down Marie Avenue continued without incident.

Beaver and Whitey co-authored one of the great comic-relief moments in state tournament history by switching jerseys before the 1954 third-place game for strategic reasons.

Eventual champion Thief River Falls shellacked the Packers 8-1 in the semifinals, so the idea was to give Beaver, the more prominent scorer, better opportunities against a sure-to-be-fooled St. Paul Johnson defense.

To the ice they went, Beaver donning Whitey's number 7 and Whitey wearing Beaver's number 8.

You know how this ends, right? Whitey scored twice, but Beaver's name went in the box score for eternity.

Later, both became referees, calling scores of hockey games from youth to college. In 1968, they worked George Kern's first game at Notre Dame. Never mind that Kern had been their varsity coach at South St. Paul.

Beaver and Whitey's real claim to fame was teaching football coach Ara Parseghian to skate at South Bend.

"He was hanging around at the morning skate, and, by god, we got him going pretty darn good," Lick said.

Beaver and Whitey worked three games together at the 1979 state tournament and were especially busy during the semifinal between Edina East and Roseau—the teams combined for a state record seven power-play goals.

As for his given name, Beaver gave his parents a break.

"They were pretty religious, so I didn't want to bring it up," he said. "Besides, if I wasn't Richard, I'd probably have been named Peter."

What's in a name? The vanity plates on his truck say it all: "THE BEAV."

~DL~

Childhood pals from South St. Paul, Don "Whitey" Willer (left) and Dick "Beaver" Lick (middle) co-authored one of the great comic-relief moments in state tournament history by switching jerseys before the 1954 third-place game. Whitey scored twice, but Beaver's name went in the box score for eternity. At right is teammate Bob Sharrow. Photo courtesy of the Minnesota Historical Society

the opener but still emerged as the tournament's darling. Described as "the sweetheart of the crowd with his swift sallies up ice and his clever stickhandling" in one newspaper report, the red-haired Poole also caught the eye of University of Minnesota coach John Mariucci.

"I must be dreaming," Mariucci remembered thinking. "That fellow's too good for this league."

Poole grew up thirty miles north of Thief River Falls (and about the same distance south of the Canadian border) in tiny Strathcona, learning to skate in roadside ditches. The second oldest of ten children (all but two of them boys), Poole was in the fifth grade when his family moved to Thief River Falls.

The town's indoor ice proved too tempting for Poole. He would unlatch a window in the arena's equipment room, then, along with younger brothers Jack and Pat, sneak in early on weekend mornings.

"We loved skating on that perfect ice," Poole said. "Then we would go right back out through the same window."

Poole had a goal and an assist in the Prowlers' 8–1 semifinal win over South St. Paul. This time, Durgin was thrust into the spotlight with his three goals.

"I don't think [Helgeland or Durgin] had ever had a hat trick in their careers before that tournament," Poole said of his linemates.

As Eveleth coach Cliff Thompson had predicted, Eveleth reached the championship game with a 3–2 victory over St. Paul Johnson. Meanwhile, the Prowlers' hopes for their first title dimmed when Poole awoke Saturday morning with a balky right leg. Rolle drove the centerman to the University of Minnesota campus for treatment from trainer Lloyd "Snapper" Stein.

"I don't know how he did it, but I could hardly walk when I got there," Poole said, "and my leg felt great when we left."

As Rolle and Poole were driving back to their hotel, they were surprised to hear a radio announcer report, "Joe Poole will not play tonight because of a broken jaw."

Poole was, indeed, in the lineup for the opening puck drop.

"We're not afraid of Thief River," Thompson said in a pregame salvo that only reinforced the Prowlers' favored status.

Thief River Falls led 3–0 with 2:20 remaining in the second period on Guttu's second goal of the game, and Jorde scored six seconds later on an assist from Poole, setting a tournament record that still stands for the fastest two goals.

"Poole started the whole works," Eveleth's Bob Kochevar, who scored late in the third, said about the Prowlers' quick-strike goals. "He could skate like crazy, and he was very tricky with the stick."

The 4–1 victory earned Thief River Falls its first championship and an undefeated season. Described as "immortals" in the local newspaper, the players were greeted as such at the outskirts of town.

"They said they were going to have a little meeting at the auditorium," Poole said. "But most of the town was out lining the streets when we drove in. It was amazing."

The players rode parade style in separate cars to the city auditorium, entering to an ovation from a raucous crowd of about 1,500.

The school band was there, too, offering a fitting final serenade to the Prowlers' musically inclined group of Renaissance men.

~*LRN*~

GREATER THAN GOLD

OLYMPIC "MIRACLE" COACH HERB BROOKS SAID TITLE WITH JOHNSON WAS THRILL OF LIFETIME

DATES	LOCATION	ATTENDANCE	CHAMPIONSHIP
FEBRUARY 24–26	ST. PAUL AUDITORIUM	27,213	ST. PAUL JOHNSON 3, MINNEAPOLIS SOUTHWEST 1

 NHL president Clarence Campbell attended Thursday's quarterfinal session. He was in town to watch Chicago play Boston at the St. Paul Auditorium on Wednesday and stayed an additional day to watch the preps play.

ONLY SECONDS REMAINED in the 1954 state tournament semifinals when St. Paul Johnson junior Stu Anderson missed a great chance for a tying goal.

But he didn't take the 3–2 loss to Eveleth too hard. He simply smashed his hockey stick on a goalpost after time expired. Then he tried walking home from the St. Paul Auditorium.

He might have hoofed it the whole way, but Orv Anderson, a defenseman on the Governors' 1947 state championship team and no relation, picked up the perturbed pedestrian on the old Third Street Bridge at the eastern edge of downtown St. Paul.

"I didn't think I deserved a ride," said Stu Anderson, who ultimately acquiesced.

Once home, he shot pucks against a basement wall late into the night. Like a coiled spring, Anderson unleashed his energy in the third-place game against South St. Paul. His first-period hat trick set state tournament records that still stand: fastest three goals to start a game (5:27) and least amount of time between three goals (2:07).

The performance wasn't about redemption. It sent a message to his eight teammates returning in 1954–55. They responded with a dominant 26–1–2 season and the program's third state championship.

Herb Brooks became the most famous of Johnson's 1955 state champs. But Anderson, an eccentric talent who sang a song called "Pickles" to himself as he skated, was the catalyst.

"Stewie had a way of making the rest of us more competitive," Roger Wigen said.

Intrasquad scrimmages at Phalen Park fueled the Governors' success, largely because the boys always played for keeps.

After a heated scrimmage, Rod Anderson, Orv's younger brother, "took my stick and threw it on the hill because I scored the game-winning goal," Stu Anderson recalled.

St. Paul City Conference opponents stood no chance. Johnson went 7–0–1 and outscored the opposition 53–1. The Governors avenged their lone blemish, a 0–0 tie against East Side rival Harding, with an 8–0 shellacking in the Region 4 playoffs.

Johnson rolled into the state tournament as a favorite. Both Stu and Rod Anderson were all-state selections along with defenseman Jack Holstrom and goalie Tom Wahman. All-city

honors were bestowed on Brooks and defenseman Chuck Rodgers. Rounding out the top two forward lines were Wigen and state tournament veterans Karl Dahlberg and Ken Fanger.

Coach Rube Gustafson, a two-time state champion, believed, "This gang of mine has a better chance to reach its full potential in this tourney than some of the other teams I've had in the meet."

He would have to wait. Johnson and Roseau were scheduled to start tournament play about 9 PM, but a landmark game postponed the puck drop.

Minneapolis South and Thief River Falls, tied 2–2 after regulation, needed a five-minute overtime. Then a second. Then a third. Then a fifth. Then a seventh. Then a ninth. Johnson and Roseau players passed the time playing cards or cribbage. They knew one another from annual games in the "Kaffee Kup" traveling trophy series, including a 3–3 tie late in the regular season.

Finally, after the ninth overtime, officials started the Johnson/Roseau game and gave the gassed Minneapolis South and Thief River Falls players a longer break. Fanger scored, and Johnson led 1–0 after the first period.

After a tenth scoreless overtime for Minneapolis and Thief River Falls, Johnson and Roseau played the second period.

Minneapolis South won in the eleventh overtime. The elapsed game time of 87:57 was a record that would stand until 1996, when Apple Valley outlasted Duluth East for 93:12.

Then Johnson, despite getting outshot 21–12, completed its 1–0 shutout. Wahman anchored the victory, claimed at 12:43 AM.

"He earned it that day," Wigen said. "They came on like gangbusters."

Johnson's successful nightcap produced a tournament first: an all-metro semifinal.

Johnson's draw appeared favorable. Minneapolis South, which the Governors had defeated twice during the season, was sure to be fatigued. Yet the teams were tied 1–1 after two periods. Stu Anderson and Wigen scored thirty-two seconds apart in the third to seal the 3–1 outcome.

"No alibis, we lost to a better team," Tigers coach Rudy Kogl said afterward.

ABOVE: Herb Brooks (top) huddles with teammates (from left) Stu Anderson, Tom Wahman, and Roger Wigen after winning in the state tournament semifinals. The Governors went on to win the program's third title. "Every one of the guys I played with were competitors," Wigen said. "That made the whole team better." Photo by the *St. Paul Dispatch*

LEFT: NHL president Clarence Campbell (right) attended Thursday's quarterfinal session with tournament founder Gene Aldrich (left). Campbell was in town to watch Chicago play Boston at the St. Paul Auditorium on Wednesday and stayed an additional day to watch the schoolboys play. Photo by the *St. Paul Pioneer Press*

Johnson would play Minneapolis Southwest in the first all-metro title game. With a grinning Gustafson looking on, Kogl told Southwest coach Paul Wohlford, "Beat those guys tomorrow night and give Minneapolis its first championship."

Wohlford, coaching his final high school game, had served as scoutmaster for a young Gustafson.

The student overcame the teacher as Johnson pounced early. Brooks scored before and after a Stu Anderson tally for a 3–0 lead at first intermission.

But penalties plagued the Governors throughout. They were called for two infractions each period.

"They got me for an elbow," Wigen said. "When I came back to the ice, Herb said, 'Let's see if you can stay out here the rest of the game.'"

But Stu Anderson dazzled on the penalty kill. On two occasions when Southwest had a five-on-three advantage, his fluid skating and deft puck handling nullified the power plays. A 3–1 victory capped a championship season that resonated with Brooks.

Almost three decades later, *Sports Illustrated's* E. M. Swift wrote a state tournament profile called "The Thrill of a Lifetime." By then, Brooks had coached Minnesota to three NCAA titles from 1974 to 1979. He had engineered the "Miracle on Ice" and Olympic gold in 1980. But they didn't match 1955, Brooks said.

"It's because you do that with kids you've come up through the ranks with," he said. "You lived for the day you had a chance to try out for the high school team, hoping you'd get the sweater number of some guy you admired. Then you lived for the day you made the tournament, so you could win it and share that with your mates. It sounds like bull, but that win in high school was a bigger thrill than the gold medal."

Wigen said, "Herb signed a poster of the 1980 team and wrote, 'Roger, the names are different but it's the same as 1955.' That comes from the fact that teamwork is what won it."

~DL~

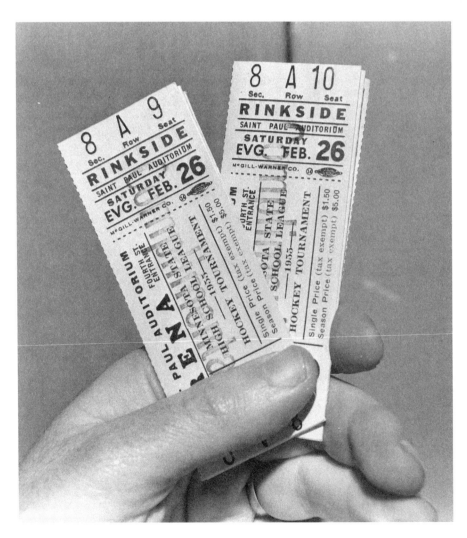

Fans with a ticket to the 1955 final saw St. Paul Johnson battle Minneapolis Southwest in the first all-metro title game. The Governors earned the Capital City bragging rights with a 3-1 victory. Photo courtesy of the Minnesota Historical Society

ENDURANCE TEST

Sleep-deprived Thief River Falls, Minneapolis South played eleven overtimes

One of the tournament's most enduring games, the eleven-overtime quarterfinal between Thief River Falls and Minneapolis South in 1955, almost never happened—and, Prowler players maintain, it sure as hell never should have ended how it did.

Drama had existed well before the overtime sessions. Selected as the home team, defending state champion Thief River Falls was required to wear white jerseys. Since the Prowlers only had dark jerseys, they risked forfeiting.

Desperate, coach Dennis Rolle asked St. Paul Harding coach John Rossi, an old friend, for a favor. Junior wing Glen Carlson said the Knights' white jerseys "were brought into the locker room . . . just before we went out onto the ice."

Carlson's second-period goal gave top-ranked Thief River Falls a 2–1 lead. South's Jerry Westby scored in the third period, and the teams went to overtime unaware of the historic grind ahead.

The Prowlers' Loren "Sid" Vraa scored a regulation goal but also hit pipes several times. The mounting extra sessions were unkind.

Carlson said, "[Vraa] goes in on the goalie and fakes him right out of the crease. He's got twenty-four square feet to shoot at in about the seventh overtime, and he goes to his backhand and he shot toward the net. He hit the crossbar . . . and it went over the net."

After the ninth overtime, officials started the Johnson/Roseau quarterfinal to give the Prowlers and Tigers a breather and to prevent the Governors and Rams from going too long into the night. South's Jim Westby, whose brother forced overtime, said teammates refueled on oranges and Coca-Cola. Senior defenseman Larry Alm played the entire game.

In the eleventh overtime, Jim Westby scored the game-winner.

"Just inside the blue line, I took a slapshot, and it was just plain lucky that it went in," he said. "Maybe their goalie was sleepy."

The game ended at 12:23 AM. With regulation periods lasting twelve minutes and overtime periods five minutes each, the game's elapsed time of 87:50 stood as a record for forty-one years.

Hard feelings among Thief River Falls players linger because Westby's winner came on the power play.

Duane Glass, a junior defenseman, was called for a tripping penalty in the eleventh overtime.

"I asked the referee what I did and told him, 'That's bull. That's a poor call,'" Glass said. "He said, and I'll never forget this as long as I live, 'We have to get this game over with some way.' Those were his exact words. What a call."

What a game.

Though his Prowlers won eight of nine games and the 1954 and 1956 titles, Carlson lamented, "The only one people want to talk about is the one we lost in eleven overtimes. That comes up time and time and time again."

~DL~

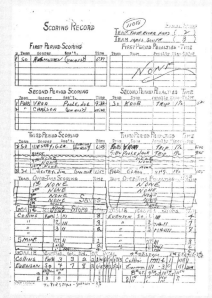

ABOVE: Jim Westby (right) scored to end a record eleven-overtime quarterfinal and bring Minneapolis South a 3–2 victory against Thief River Falls. The defeated Prowlers wore borrowed jerseys from St. Paul Harding. As the home team, they were required to wear white, but they had only brought dark. Photo courtesy of the Minnesota Historical Society

TOP: The scoresheet from the eleven-overtime quarterfinal in which Minneapolis South outlasted defending state champion Thief River Falls. Courtesy of the Minnesota State High School League

WALKING WOUNDED

NO INJURY TOO SERIOUS FOR MANGLED, SHORTHANDED PROWLERS

DATES	LOCATION	ATTENDANCE	CHAMPIONSHIP
FEBRUARY 23–25	ST. PAUL AUDITORIUM	30,949	THIEF RIVER FALLS 3, INTERNATIONAL FALLS 2

Did you know? Eveleth made its twelfth straight appearance, a record that still stands.

A RUNAWAY GARAGE DOOR, a deadly winter snowstorm, and an allegedly vengeful basketball coach all conspired against a Thief River Falls team that entered the 1956 state tournament held together by nothing more than gauze pads and athletic tape.

Outside forces aside, the Prowlers didn't possess the typical building blocks of a championship team. Their best forward was a pack-a-day smoker, their goaltender was prone to lapses in concentration, and their top defenseman was mo-

nopolizing much of that tape and gauze to keep a mangled hand patched together.

Senior defenseman Duane Glass was so skilled he played most every minute of every game. His ironman role continued even after his out-of-control garage door made such a mess of his right hand that his modified glove had to be taped to his hand before every playoff game.

Glass was just one member of the Prowlers' walking wounded in St. Paul, joining the battered Jim Hall (three bruised ribs

Thief River Falls players were a bruised and battered bunch upon their arrival at the St. Paul Auditorium in 1956. The Prowlers, who won the title despite their abundance of injuries, were immortalized in the book *River of Champions*. Front row, left to right: Ken Sauve, Cliff Strand, Fred Dablow, Jim Hall, Glen Carlson, Art Cloutier, and Duane Glass. Back row, left to right: student manager Art Overbye, Rodney Collins, Dale Glass, Wendy Johnson, Darryl Smith, Ron Reese, Jack Poole, and coach Dennis Rolle. Photo by the *Minneapolis Tribune*

Jack Poole of Thief River Falls controls the puck in front of Prowlers goaltender Rodney Collins as defenseman Duane Glass (9) plows into two International Falls players during the 1956 championship game. Thief River Falls beat the Broncos 3–2 for its second state title in three years. Photo by the *Minneapolis Tribune*

and a head injury), Ron "Cookie" Reese (swollen and blackened left eye), Fred Dablow (gashed forehead), Glen Carlson (battered nose), and Jackie Poole (sprained wrist).

The diminutive Poole was hardly bothered by his bandaged wrist. As the third oldest in a family of ten children, bumps and bruises were a daily fact of life.

"We didn't have to go out and look for hockey players because we had all we needed right there in the house," said Poole, who spent countless hours with his brothers on the Northrop Park rinks across the street from their home.

Older brother Joe had helped lead the Prowlers to the 1954 state championship and an undefeated season. Built like his brother, Jackie was 5 foot 7, 145 pounds, and tough as boot leather. Also like Joe, Jackie had a silky skating stride and soft hands. And that's where the similarities stopped.

While Joe walked the straight and narrow as an A student, the incorrigible Jackie was prone to taking the occasional detour. The Pooles' father ran a bar and dancehall in town, and Jackie's path to and from school would often lead him there.

"It was easy enough to walk by the tavern on the way to school and have a couple of smokes," Poole said.

Smoking was a recurring topic in *River of Champions*, a book by Mary Halvorson Schofield that chronicled the Prowlers' 1954 championship season. As detailed in the book, second-line forward Jimmy Reese was kicked off the team on the eve of the regional playoffs after it was reported he had been seen smoking outside the City Service gas station.

According to the book, however, the wrong man was fingered. It was Reese's older brother, Bernard, home on leave from the navy, smoking outside the station.

Schofield wrote, without naming him, that the school's basketball coach reported the high school league rules infraction. Al Adams was the Prowlers' basketball coach at the time.

"Some pretty reliable sources told me it was Adams who turned him in," Carlson said.

With the suspended Reese out for the rest of the season, Thief River Falls won the Region 8 championship and entered the state tournament with a 17–1 record. It was the Prowlers' fifth state tournament appearance in Dennis Rolle's seven years as coach. He had built the Prowlers into an elite program, a notch below the level of five-time champion Eveleth, his alma mater, and St. Paul Johnson, winner of three titles.

The 1955 champion Governors dealt the Prowlers their lone loss, a potentially fatal brush with a brutal northwestern Minnesota blizzard factoring into the outcome.

The night before the Johnson game, Glass and forwards Cliff "Chipper" Strand and Carlson, Poole's wings on the Prowlers' high-scoring "Pony Line," headed west toward Grand Forks to watch the University of North Dakota hockey team. Driving into the teeth of a howling northern prairie snowstorm, they aborted their fifty-mile trip and turned back but became hopelessly stuck in a snowdrift. With temperatures plummeting and their car dangerously low on gas, frostbite or worse was a real concern.

"I thought we were dead, I really did," Carlson said.

The boys were saved by a Greyhound bus hauling passengers to Thief River Falls. With the bus plowing a trail through the deep snow, they followed in its tracks, reaching town in the early hours of the morning. (The boys' parents all thought they were sleeping over at goaltender Rod Collins's house.) All

three were noticeably sluggish and ineffective that night in the 3–1 loss to Johnson.

The Prowlers survived another close call in St. Paul. Strand scored in triple overtime to lift the Prowlers past Edina 3–2 in the quarterfinals despite the brilliant play of Hornets goaltender Murray MacPherson, who made fifty-four saves. Thief River Falls dispatched rival Eveleth 3–0 in the semifinals behind a goal and an assist from Strand and seventeen saves from Collins.

Collins stunned Rolle and his teammates in the championship game against International Falls when, with the score tied 2–2 in the second period and the play in the Broncos' end, he calmly glided up to the Thief River Falls bench and asked for a drink of water.

"I thought Rolle was going to have a heart attack," Poole said. "Hell, I thought *I* was going to have a heart attack."

Collins returned to his net just in time to thwart a scoring attempt by Oscar Mahle, the superstar forward who scored both Broncos' goals. Poole scored his fourth of the tournament moments later, the winning goal in the Prowlers' 3–2 triumph.

More drama came after the tournament. Rolle abruptly announced his retirement from coaching to focus on his counseling work at the school.

"That sure surprised me," Hall said. "The word I heard was that the guy was mighty smart. He had the good years, and he knew when to get out."

The Prowlers made just three more tourney appearances in the next fifty-plus years, finishing no better than fifth.

~LRN~

Thief River Falls players proudly wore patches signifying their 1956 state championship on their lettermen's jackets. Photo courtesy of Kyle Oen/Vintage Minnesota Hockey

LARGER THAN LIFE

INTERNATIONAL FALLS ACE OSCAR MAHLE'S FEATS THE STUFF OF LEGEND

DATES	LOCATION	ATTENDANCE	CHAMPIONSHIP
FEBRUARY 21–23	ST. PAUL AUDITORIUM	33,041	INTERNATIONAL FALLS 3, ROSEAU 1

Did you know? The losing teams combined scored just eight goals, matching the tournament low set in 1945 and duplicated in '46.

INTERNATIONAL FALLS made a second consecutive trip to the state tournament in 1957, and by then Oscar Mahle's legend had grown to Paul Bunyan–esque proportions.

Fact almost always trumped fiction when it came to Mahle. The senior forward entered the state tournament having scored a stunning fifty-seven goals—including twelve hat tricks or better—for the 20–2 Broncos.

"Mahle was the kind of player who, if the coach said, 'We need three from you,' he would go out and score four," said Les Etienne, a junior defenseman in 1956–57.

A year earlier, Thief River Falls' Glen Carlson had skated onto the glassy black St. Paul Auditorium ice and straight into the purple-and-gold-clad crucible that was Mahle.

The occasion was the 1956 state championship game. The assignment was to prevent Mahle from scoring. Stop Mahle, the thinking went, and you beat International Falls.

"That was pretty much it," Carlson said about Thief River Falls' game plan. "Cover him at all times."

Mahle was a smooth, fast skater who, together with linemate David Frank, did the bulk of the Broncos' scoring.

International Falls' Oscar Mahle, pictured here walking to the St. Paul Auditorium ice, ranks among the greatest state tournament performers. The winger renowned for his wicked backhand shot scored a tournament-best seven goals to lead the Broncos to the 1957 title. Photo by the *Minneapolis Tribune*

"He was their right wing, and I was our left wing," Carlson said about Mahle. "I played right opposite him, eyeball to eyeball."

Carlson believed he was doing a bang-up job holding Mahle in check until a stunning development midway through the first period. Mahle crossed the blue line into the Prowlers' end of the rink with Carlson attached to his hip.

"He was coming down along the boards on his wrong wing, and he was going to take a backhand shot from way out," Carlson said. "And I thought, 'Let him shoot, that's going to be harmless.' Bing, it went right into the upper corner of the net.

"I thought, 'Wow, I am going to have to watch him a lot closer.'"

Mahle scored again in the second period, but Carlson and the Prowlers held on for a 3–2 victory.

A year later, Broncos coach Larry Ross, a Duluth native and former standout goaltender at the University of Minnesota, proclaimed Mahle the state's best player before the 1957 tournament, placing him on a pedestal with Eveleth's incomparable John Mayasich.

The Broncos, making their third state tournament appearance and second under Ross, had top-level talent at every position. Ross had a knack for maximizing his players' talents by plugging them into ideal positions, and he had done a masterful job assigning roles for an International Falls team primed to win the school's first championship in any sport.

Frank, the Broncos' fastest player and a superb passer, grew up playing outdoor hockey with Mahle at the Carson Lupie Rink in South International Falls. The chemistry between the two neighbors, forged beginning when they were five years old, was unmistakable. Each knew how to get the puck to the other, often without bothering to look.

Bob Miggins, undersized but determined and fearless in the corners, was the third member of the top line. His job was to pass the puck to Mahle and Frank—preferably Mahle.

"He couldn't break a slab of butter with his shot," Jim Wherley, the Broncos' goalie, said about Miggins. "But he knew how to get the puck to Mahle."

Added Etienne: "Miggins was out there for one reason and one reason only. I don't know if he ever took a shot."

Miggins played his role to perfection in the 1957 tournament quarterfinals when he notched a tournament record for most assists in a game with five in a 10–0 rout of Hallock.

"No kidding. Did I really?" the unassuming Miggins, a junior not used to being in the spotlight, asked reporters after being told about the record. "You're not kidding me."

Frank and Mahle, both seniors, each had four goals in the victory. Wherley, a junior, made just seven saves—including one each in the second and third periods.

Wherley was a rough-and-tumble character who was constantly getting in scraps with his younger brother Jerry, also a goaltender.

"He never forgets to remind me about the time I threw a brick at him," Jim said. "I hit him in the head.

"We were both tough. We didn't back down from anybody, including each other."

Wherley had been all but flawless in the Region 7 playoffs, when International Falls dispatched Duluth Central, Duluth Denfeld, and Eveleth by a combined score of 19–1. The 3–1 victory over Eveleth in the regional championship kept the Golden Bears, five-time state champions, from reaching the tournament for the first time in the event's thirteen-year history.

"Jim was a kid who, even if he didn't have a mask on, he would stop a shot with his mouth if he had to," Etienne said.

Another International Falls tough guy, forward Gene Steele, played a key role in the monumental victory against Eveleth and its star forward, Gustave "Gus" Hendrickson.

"Hendrickson was a big guy, husky," said Tom Neveau, the Broncos' top defenseman in 1957. "Ross took Steele aside and said, 'Every time Hendrickson is on the ice, I want you on the ice.' Then he made sure everybody heard him say, 'Every time Hendrickson touches the puck, I want you to knock him on his ass.' I still remember seeing Hendrickson being knocked down by Steele what seemed like a dozen times in that game.

"After the game I skated by Hendrickson and said, 'How do you like that, Gus?'"

Neveau rarely left the ice for the Broncos, coming off only when summoned by Ross. His value was such that he played the entire 1956 championship game with one eye swollen shut after being hit in the face with a puck. Although known more for his impeccable defense than his scoring prowess, Neveau scored a goal in a 4–0 semifinal rout of Minneapolis South.

Just as he had done a year earlier, Mahle scored twice in the championship game, a 3–1 triumph over Roseau. Both goals came courtesy of his fabled backhand.

"As good as we were, the bottom line is it was Oscar Mahle's team," Etienne said.

~LRN~

BORDER CROSSING

BULAUCA BROTHERS ROSEAU'S HANDSOME, CONTROVERSIAL CANADIAN CONNECTION

DATES	LOCATION	ATTENDANCE	CHAMPIONSHIP
FEBRUARY 20–22	ST. PAUL AUDITORIUM	35,243	ROSEAU 1, ST. PAUL HARDING 0

 *Did you know?* In 1958, a northern team skated off with the title for the eleventh time in the tournament's fourteen editions.

AS TEENAGERS, Ed and Bill Bulauca made daily trips across the border dividing middle-of-nowhere Manitoba from equally remote northwestern Minnesota, barely slowing as they cruised past the uniformed customs agents stationed on both sides of the invisible line separating Canada from the United States.

"In those days, you would drive by the customs house and they would just wave to you," Ed said. "And after eight at night, everything was closed. You just drove right through."

The Bulauca brothers grew up in South Junction, Manitoba, a one-church, one-store, zero-stoplight community three miles due north of the US border on Highway 310. As high school sophomores, the Bulaucas began attending school fourteen miles to the south in Roseau. The new kids were instant celebrities.

"He was the best-looking guy in the school," Jim Stordahl, who starred at center for Roseau, said about the dark-haired, square-jawed Ed Bulauca. "The girls liked him. Heck, he drove a car. None of us had cars. We were lucky if we rode bicycles."

The Bulaucas' athletic prowess further boosted their popularity. Both were starters on Roseau's football team (Ed as a running back and Bill as a receiver), and they excelled in hockey, too. As juniors, Ed was a high-geared forward and Bill a rock-steady defenseman for the 1957 Roseau team that lost 3–1 to International Falls in the state championship game.

"They were accepted [in Roseau] just like they had been there forever," said Dick Roth, Roseau's starting goalie for three seasons beginning in 1957–58. "They were nice guys, even though they said 'eh' a lot."

Roseau brothers Ed and Bill Bulauca (second and third from left) were congratulated by St. Paul Johnson players Gary Schmalzbauer, Dave Brooks, and Harold Vinnes after the Rams beat International Falls 4–0 in the quarterfinals of the 1958 state tournament. Led by the Bulaucas, Roseau went on to win the tournament, defeating St. Paul Harding in the title game. Photo by the *St. Paul Pioneer Press*

St. Paul Pioneer Press and *Dispatch* editorial cartoonist Jerry Fearing previewed the 1958 state tournament with this *Dispatch* illustration showing the eight qualifying teams descending on the "Hockey Capitol of the Nation." Courtesy of the Minnesota Historical Society

While they were embraced in Roseau, the Canadians' presence in St. Paul drew criticism from some corners. Newspaper readers expressed concerns in letters published in the *Minneapolis Star* sports section after the 1957 tournament.

"As a taxpayer, I object to paying for the education of Canadians" and "Somehow it doesn't seem quite right that Canadians should be represented on a Minnesota high school hockey team" were some of the printed criticisms.

Roseau's school superintendent responded with his own letter, initially published in the *Roseau Times-Region*: "Their father requested that they be permitted to attend high school here . . . rather than go to Winnipeg. . . . They [were] accepted on a strictly non-resident basis, at no cost to the local district or any other Minnesota taxpayers. We did not ask whether they could play hockey, basketball or a bass drum."

Bill Bulauca was a year younger than Ed but had skipped a grade in elementary school so he could join his brother in the same classes. As freshmen, the Bulaucas had attended a boarding school in Winnipeg, one hundred miles to the north.

"I was really pleased," Ed Bulauca said about attending Roseau High. "Because this way I got a car."

Ed, who did all the driving, piloted a four-door 1950 Pontiac Chieftain the first year the boys commuted to Roseau, then upgraded to a sporty blue-and-white 1956 Pontiac Laurentian two-door hardtop for their junior and senior years.

The Bulauca brothers bolstered a lineup that featured several other multisport stars, including Roth, the Stordahl brothers (Jim and Larry), bullet-shooting forward Don Ross, and superb defensemen Dale Olson and Keith Brandt.

Roseau reached the state title game again in 1958, entering the finale against St. Paul Harding with a twelve-game unbeaten streak, including a 4–0 victory over defending champion International Falls in the quarterfinals and a 6–3 rout of South St. Paul in the semifinals. The return of Larry Stordahl from an early-season knee injury and the shifting of Larry Anderson from defense to a high-scoring all-senior forward line with Ed Bulauca and Dave Wensloff ignited the Rams' late-season surge.

Unheralded Harding's role as a surprise finalist was reminiscent of Rochester's stunning run to the 1946 title game. Harding secured its spot in the tournament with a 5–2 victory over Minneapolis Patrick Henry in the Region 1 championship.

Earlier in the playoffs, Harding had shocked St. Paul Johnson 4–3, a result so unlikely it initiated discussions about changing the regional playoff format. Governors players roamed the halls of Harding High School insisting they hadn't been "robbed" of a chance to play in the state tournament (as some Johnson backers were claiming) and pledging their support for the Knights.

Gary Schmalzbauer, Dave Brooks, and Glen Marien were the Johnson players who showed up unannounced at Harding coach John Rossi's biology class.

"That's part of tournament play," they told Rossi. "We have no complaints."

"Cinderella" Harding continued to make headlines and amass nicknames (Giant-Killers, Miracle Men of 1958, the Wonder Boys from Dayton's Bluff) with a 3–2 quarterfinal victory against St. Paul Murray and a 3–1 semifinal triumph against St. Louis Park. The Knights, outshot in both games, relied heavily on the spectacular play of senior goaltender Arnie Johnson.

"He was always a pretty good goalie," Harding's Joe Schwartzbauer, then a sophomore forward, said about Johnson, "but I don't know—all of a sudden he was hotter than a pistol."

Johnson was sizzling again in the championship game, making thirty-eight saves while continually frustrating the Rams' legion of sharpshooters. Larry Anderson's goal early in the first period proved the winner in the Rams' 1–0 victory. Harding managed just eleven shots.

"In most of our games, we would get an early lead and then just go out and play and have fun as we won handily," Larry Stordahl said. "We kind of expected that to happen in the championship game. But we just couldn't get a second goal."

As usual, the Bulaucas played key roles. Bill scored the winner against International Falls. Ed was named to the all-tournament team for the second straight year. The victory celebration in South Junction, home to about thirty-five families, was as raucous as it was in Roseau.

"Oh yeah, it was a big deal," Bulauca said. "In those days, everybody shopped in Roseau, everybody went to the movie theater in Roseau. We were there all the time.

"The border didn't really mean anything."

~LRN~

SLEEPING GIANT

ROSEAU POWER FORWARD LARRY STORDAHL ALMOST DOZED THROUGH SEMIFINAL GAME

DATES	LOCATION	ATTENDANCE	CHAMPIONSHIP
FEBRUARY 19–21	ST. PAUL AUDITORIUM	36,023	ROSEAU 4, MINNEAPOLIS WASHBURN 2

Did you know? Thief River Falls' entry was coached by John Matchefts, the 1940s Eveleth scoring superstar who also led the University of Michigan to three national championships.

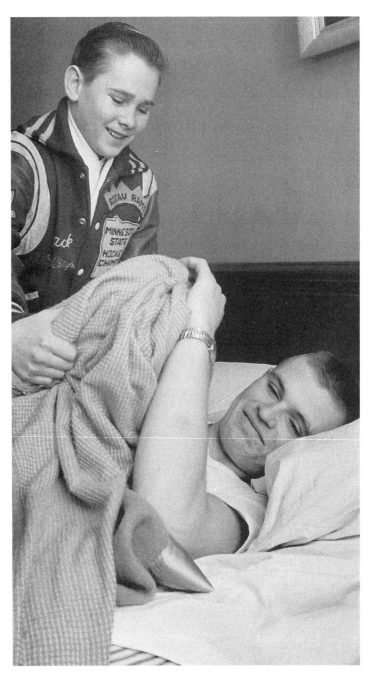

LARRY STORDAHL preferred to do his sleeping at night.

As a veteran of multiple state tournament trips, the standout Roseau forward had a trusted, proven pregame routine. Afternoon naps weren't part of it.

But a good night's rest had been hard to come by during the first few days of the 1959 tourney. An unfamiliar bed and loud big-city surroundings contributed to his fitfulness. By Friday afternoon, the worn-out Stordahl decided a quick snooze would leave him refreshed and ready for that night's semifinal showdown with International Falls.

So Stordahl shut off the lights and closed the curtains in his room at the St. Paul Hotel, stretched out in his bed, and settled into a deep sleep.

As Roseau's student manager, Jackie McDonald tended to many of the team's behind-the-scenes tasks. He filled water bottles, he taped sticks, he washed uniforms, he folded towels.

McDonald's responsibilities ramped up during the state tournament. Before every game, it was his job to roust players from their hotel rooms, then help herd the stragglers across the street and through Rice Park to the St. Paul Auditorium.

McDonald was good at his work. He made his rounds with efficiency. He pounded on doors with authority. He checked and double-checked each player's room diligently. On this evening, however, Roseau was minutes away from hitting the ice for warmups, and Larry Stordahl was nowhere to be found. The first tremors of panic began to reverberate in the Rams' locker room.

International Falls had become an annual state tournament opponent for Roseau, the winner of the all-northern-team showdown capturing the state title each of the previous two years (International Falls in 1957, Roseau in 1958). Beating the Broncos was a difficult task under the best of conditions. Beating them without a player with the skills and stature of Stordahl shoved the degree of difficulty to the edge of impossible.

Roseau manager Jackie McDonald rousts star forward Don Ross from bed during the 1959 state tournament. One of McDonald's tasks was to ensure all players were out of their rooms and at the rink at least an hour before every game. Photo courtesy of the Minnesota Historical Society

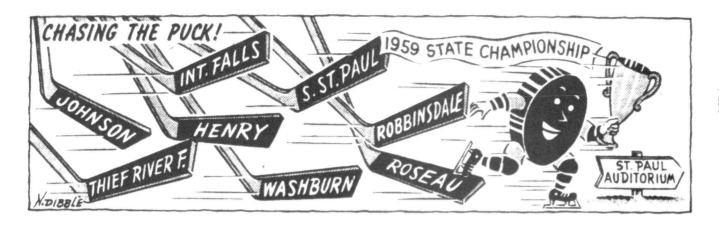

Stordahl, a junior, was an irreplaceable component on Roseau's top line. On one of the most prolific scoring units in state history, he was the left wing; brother Jim Stordahl, a senior, was the center; and junior Don Ross was the right wing.

Jim Stordahl was the playmaker. Also the star quarterback on the Rams' undefeated football team, he excelled at reading defenses. He took pride in the fact that he was given the freedom to call his own plays, and he always solicited feedback from his teammates.

"We had a playbook from our coach, and we would go over the plays before a game," Stordahl said, "but after that we talked it over in the huddle and called our own plays."

Stordahl played center the same way he played quarterback. He preferred to have the puck as the Rams crossed the opposing team's blue line. Then he would simply study his reads and dish the puck to the open man. Easy.

"He was a very unselfish playmaker, and very smart," Ross said about Stordahl.

Ross was the shooter. The slapshot was a new technique, and Ross was one of the first Rams players to experiment

ABOVE: The *Minneapolis Tribune* ran this cartoon of a spry puck racing ahead of eight sticks representing the 1959 state tournament qualifiers. Courtesy of the Minnesota Historical Society

LEFT: Roseau's Jim Stordahl, coach Oscar Almquist, and Larry Stordahl (from left) admire the 1959 state championship trophy. Both Stordahl brothers were named to the all-tournament team. Photo by John Croft/ *Minneapolis Tribune*

with it, taking his stick back high above his head in a windmill windup. A stocky 5 foot 11 and 195 pounds, Ross had the strength and coordination to parlay the shot into a fearsome, dangerous, and at times destructive weapon.

Ross was goofing around with teammates one morning at Roseau's arena when he uncorked slapshots that shattered two windows of the warming area that looked down on the ice sheet.

"I let a couple of them go a little high over the chicken wire," Ross said. "My dad got the bill for it. Luckily windows weren't too expensive back then."

Larry Stordahl was the puck hound. No one was better at working the corners than big Larry, who at 6 foot 1 was the tallest of the trio. His wiry frame and tenacity made life miserable for opposing defensemen.

"Larry was a strong kid, and he had that long reach and could poke the puck away," brother Jim said.

Jackie McDonald and Larry Stordahl were roommates, and earlier in the evening, as part of McDonald's appointed rounds, the sophomore manager had stuck his head in their darkened room and called out. There was no response and no movement. Stordahl must have already left for the rink, McDonald figured.

He figured wrong.

After being alerted to Stordahl's absence, Roseau coach Oscar Almquist dispatched McDonald back to the hotel. Sure enough, Stordahl was buried under his blankets, still in a deep slumber. McDonald woke him up and the two raced back through Rice Park to the auditorium. Stordahl was a whirlwind as he threw on his equipment.

"They went out and warmed up without me," said Stordahl, who stepped on the ice just in time for the opening faceoff. "You couldn't hold up everything for one guy."

Stordahl was still rubbing the sleep from his eyes during a scoreless first period, but he fully awoke in the second to score Roseau's first goal. It was all the Rams would need in a 2–0 triumph.

"I guess he was well rested," Ross said with a laugh.

Almquist, who demanded discipline and effort from his players, never did punish Stordahl for his tardiness.

"I think he was just happy that I scored," Stordahl said.

Roseau completed its 31–0 season the next night with a 4–2 triumph over Minneapolis Washburn, giving the Rams their second championship in as many years.

Ross scored a hat trick in the title game, one of the goals coming shorthanded on a blistering slapshot from the blue line that sailed into the upper right corner.

Among the celebration photos is one showing the apple-cheeked Ross grinning from ear to ear and wearing Almquist's wide-brimmed hat. Standing next to him are Almquist and the Stordahl brothers, all three also flashing expressions of pure joy. And why not? Roseau's top line had scored eleven of the team's thirteen tournament goals, and Almquist had amassed three state titles.

Sleepy little Roseau (population: 2,231) had become the state's newest dynasty.

~LRN~

'HOUNDS AT THE DOOR

DULUTH EAST MADE HISTORY BY BARGING THROUGH "BACKDOOR" TO TITLE

DATES	LOCATION	ATTENDANCE	CHAMPIONSHIP
FEBRUARY 25–27	ST. PAUL AUDITORIUM	39,488	DULUTH EAST 3, ST. PAUL WASHINGTON 1

 Edina-Morningside, coached by Willard Ikola, defeated Eveleth, coached by Ikola's former Eveleth teammate John Matchefts, in the consolation semifinals.

TWO HOCKEY UNDERDOG stories played out simultaneously in late February 1960 as the United States pushed for its first Olympic gold medal and Duluth East aimed to become the first "backdoor" state tournament qualifier to win it all.

On the afternoon of February 27, the Yanks upset the Soviet Union 3–2 in the semifinals—ample motivation for the Duluth team making its championship debut that evening.

"[Goaltender Don] Hilsen came in the locker room saying, 'Beat Russia,'" defenseman Dick Fisher said. "It became our rallying cry."

The deep, talented, and motivated Greyhounds would beat St. Paul Washington 3–1 for their first state title. But Duluth had lost the Region 7 finals, so what were the Greyhounds doing at the St. Paul Auditorium in the first place? In those days, the runner-up from Section 7 or 8 alternated each year as the automatic Region 3 representative.

Granted, four previous backdoor qualifiers had reached the state championship game, but no one even made a dark horse of Duluth East, which had lost both games in its lone previous tournament appearance in 1958.

Not to mention these Greyhounds were young and inexperienced at several spots. Senior Hilsen was a converted defenseman playing his first season between the pipes. But he skated well and playing centerfield in baseball gave him a superior glove hand.

"[Coach Glenn] Rolle told us, 'He's going to be our goalie next year, so shoot pucks at him all summer,'" defenseman John Bonte said. "He filled in quite admirably. His style wasn't great, but he got to pucks."

Bonte and Fisher were both converted forwards. They were joined by Bob Hill and Mark Williams, whose cousin, Tommy, would play on the 1960 US Olympic team.

Though a bit unconventional on the back end, Duluth East boasted a strong forward line of Bill McGiffert, Jim Ross, and Bill Sivertson. Two transfers from Duluth Cathedral, Bob and Mike Hoene, improved the Greyhounds' depth.

And these guys were winners. Much of the roster came from Glen Avon, the park team that in 1958 had gone to Lake Placid, New York, and won the national Pee Wee championship.

Still, Rolle had written off any state tournament plans.

"I admit, at the season's start, I was building for next year," he said. "But the way we jelled in midseason, I changed my mind pretty fast."

Duluth East lost the Region 7 title game to Eveleth and opened state tournament play against favored Minneapolis Washburn, runner-up the previous year. The physical Millers featured defenseman Larry Hendrickson, a 200-pound guard in football. He was called for six penalties during the 1959 hockey tournament.

But the Greyhounds would not be intimidated.

"One of their captains said before the game, 'This is our year,'" Ross said. "I told him, 'Keep your head up.'"

Washburn, clad in orange jerseys with matching socks, led 1–0 after one period, 2–1 after two, and 3–1 in the third. The Greyhounds persisted, and "when Sivertson stole the puck and tied the score against Washburn, it set us afire for the tournament," Rolle said.

The Greyhounds went ahead to stay as Ross completed the hat trick. A final tally from Bill Savolainen gave Duluth East four unanswered goals in a span of 4:52, three of those on the power play. Ross and Sivertson each scored during a five-on-three advantage.

"I warned the kids before the tournament to keep away from foolish penalties," Washburn coach Carl Carlson said.

Duluth East won 5–3, but neither team was done playing. Hendrickson and Hilsen tangled at the final buzzer, prompting a brawl.

"Hendy took a shot at Don, who also had a short fuse," Ross said.

Hendrickson claimed, "Their goalie said something pretty rude, and it triggered me at seventeen, I guess."

Jim Byrne of the *Minneapolis Star* wrote that Hendrickson "poked [Hilsen] with the handle of his stick. As the game ended, Hilsen charged back and right away all hands on deck joined in."

Byrne's choice of phrase proved prophetic, as Hilsen later worked as a watchman on the *Edmund Fitzgerald*. (He was not on duty for its fateful voyage in November 1975.)

Duluth East's quartet of (from left) Jim Ross, Bill Sivertson, Mike Hoene, and Dick Fisher earned all-tournament honors as the Greyhounds made tournament history. No previous "backdoor" state tournament qualifier had won it all. Photo courtesy of the Minnesota Historical Society

Hendrickson was booted from the remainder of the tournament.

Duluth East played on. The Greyhounds rallied for three goals in the second period and netted the first three goals of the third period in a 6–2 semifinal victory against South St. Paul. Sivertson recorded a hat trick.

"We really hit our stride in that game and were flying," Rolle said afterward. "We did everything perfectly against them; our passing was accurate, and we skated like the dickens."

Saturday's championship against St. Paul Washington began with a 2–0 Duluth East lead on first-period goals from Sivertson and McGiffert just fifty-one seconds apart. Washington cut its deficit to 2–1 after two periods. And though the Presidents peppered the Greyhounds for thirteen shots in the third period, Hilsen denied them all.

Mike Hoene, who centered the second and third lines, scored the final goal. He had taken a stick to the nose in the regional final at Eveleth and wore a softball catcher's mask at the state tournament.

Winning a high school championship, which Duluth East wouldn't do again for thirty-five years, "was a feather in the cap for the city of Duluth," McGiffert said. "It was a big deal. It put us on the map."

And the team's victories came against future legendary coaches: Hendrickson would win the 1996 Class 2A state title with Apple Valley. South St. Paul's Doug Woog would bring the Gophers to six Frozen Fours. And St. Paul Washington's Jeff Sauer would win two NCAA titles with Wisconsin. Even so, Sauer said the state tournament was "still my biggest thrill in hockey."

On Sunday morning, February 28, 1960, the United States men's hockey team won its first Olympic gold medal by defeating Czechoslovakia—a precursor to the 1980 Miracle on Ice. The American roster included Duluth's own Tommy Williams and state tournament veterans John Mayasich (Eveleth), Dick Meredith (Minneapolis Southwest), brothers Bill and Roger Christian (Warroad), and Bob Owen (St. Louis Park).

~DL~

FORGOTTEN RAMS

LACK OF FANFARE SUITED STARLESS ROSEAU JUST FINE

DATES	LOCATION	ATTENDANCE	CHAMPIONSHIP
FEBRUARY 23–25	ST. PAUL AUDITORIUM	40,607	ROSEAU 1, SOUTH ST. PAUL 0

 Tiny Hallock, from the far northwestern region of the state, made its second appearance in 1961—and its last, as the school is now known as Kittson County Central. Hallock coach Ken Wellen played in the state tournament in 1946 and 1947 for Roseau.

HUNDREDS OF WELL-LUBRICATED FANS spilled onto the ice, many of them throwing wild haymakers in a melee that had all the logic and precision of a shotgun blast. For the twelve law enforcement officials working the 1961 Region 7 championship game, halting the mayhem was a Sisyphean task.

"Fifty of them couldn't have broken up that scuffle," tournament director Jack Malevich said about the violent aftermath of Duluth East's 3–2 victory over International Falls in front of a record Eveleth Hippodrome crowd of 3,800.

Duluth East was the defending state champion and, with

eleven returning regulars, the obvious tournament favorite in 1961. But the Greyhounds were a bruised and battered bunch. As they limped into St. Paul, star forward Mike Hoene's gashed and swollen scalp was the most troubling of the injuries (he had been knocked to the ice as the clock expired in the regional final, precipitating the brawl).

Two other tournament entrants faced serious injury concerns, while a family rivalry and a semifinal "jinx" also made headlines.

Ron Naslund, who had scored thirty-seven of Minneapolis

Roseau's Gary Johnson (in goal) and Gordon Hipsher (10) battle for the puck against South St. Paul's Ray Funes (13) and Tony Palodichuk (6) during the 1961 state championship game. Johnson stopped all fourteen shots he faced as Roseau won 1–0 for its third title in four years. Photo by the *St. Paul Pioneer Press,* courtesy of the Minnesota Historical Society

Roseau's Gordon Hipsher (left) and David Backlund accept the 1961 championship trophy. Photo by the *St. Paul Pioneer Press,* courtesy of the Minnesota Historical Society

Roosevelt's seventy-four goals entering the tournament, was struck in the head by the butt end of a stick during the Twin Cities championship game. He was hospitalized and, with both eyes bandaged shut, ruled out of the tournament. North St. Paul co-captain Gene Hoff underwent stomach surgery just days after the Polars' Region 2 title game triumph. He, too, would spend the tournament in the hospital.

Meanwhile, drama swirled around St. Paul Johnson, what with legendary coach Rube Gustafson facing the prospect of coaching against his son. Steve Gustafson was a four-year starter and co-captain for North St. Paul, and the teams were

in opposite sides of the bracket, spurring speculation of a potential father-son championship showdown.

South St. Paul had its own distraction. The Packers had been knocked out in the semifinals each of the previous three years, forcing coach Charles "Lefty" Smith to answer questions about the dubious streak and how it, in his words, "had reached the stage where it was a complex with our players."

First-time entrant Bloomington wasn't expected to have the experience or horsepower to compete for the championship. Neither was Hallock, which emerged from the far northwest region of the state with seven losses, the most of any team.

That left Roseau.

The Rams had won back-to-back titles in 1958 and '59 before suffering one of the biggest upsets in region playoff history, the ultratalented 1960 team losing 1–0 to Warroad. The 1961 team included only a handful of returnees, none of the superstar variety. At best, Roseau was considered a dark horse to win the title.

Unlike previous Roseau teams that had featured future college and Olympic standouts such as Rube Bjorkman, Bob Harris, Don Ross, and brothers Jim and Larry Stordahl, this collection of Rams was lacking severely in star power.

"Individual talent–wise, the 1960 team was definitely better," said Rick Ulvin, who, like many of the Rams, had been a junior varsity player the previous season. "But team-wise, we were pretty darn good in 1961."

There was precious little fanfare as Roseau rolled into St. Paul in its yellow school bus.

"I don't think anybody paid any attention to us when we got down there," Ulvin said.

Though Roseau's players were dapper in their matching set of blue blazers—Rams logo and crossed hockey sticks stitched on the breast pockets—in most eyes, they didn't have the look of champions.

"We were just ordinary kids," said Dave Backlund, who scored two game-winning goals for the Rams in the tournament. "We weren't expecting anything great. We just went out and played."

Backlund had played on a forward line with Larry Stordahl and Don Ross in 1960. In 1961, he was paired with fellow seniors Jeff Vacura and David Peterson. In terms of speed, maneuverability, and elusiveness, Roseau's top line had been downgraded from a sports car to a pickup truck.

"We weren't up at their caliber," Backlund said in comparing himself, Vacura, and Peterson to Stordahl and Ross.

Once they got rolling, though, the plucky Rams proved difficult to stop. Backlund scored in overtime as Roseau slipped past Minneapolis Roosevelt in the quarterfinals. The Rams rotated two forward lines, and the other unit, consisting of Ulvin, junior Paul Rygh, and sophomore Bob Lillo, did the heavy lifting in the semifinals. Ulvin scored his third goal of the game in triple overtime, and Roseau outlasted North St. Paul 4–3.

"The young guys on the team saved us in that one," Backlund said.

Meanwhile, South St. Paul broke its semifinal hex by stunning Duluth East 2–1. In an iconic tournament photo, Smith, overcome by the moment, is shown with head bowed, weeping with joy after the victory.

Roseau coach Oscar Almquist wondered aloud whether his Rams would be physically drained for the championship game, but it was South St. Paul that appeared emotionally spent. Neither team mustered much for prime scoring chances; Roseau won 1–0 on a first-period Backlund goal.

"We had actually shot the puck down the ice, and it would have been an icing," Backlund said. "But Paul [Rygh] took off and beat the South St. Paul defenseman to the puck and just fired it out in front. It landed on my stick out in front of the net.

"It was just kind of a magical time."

Roseau sophomore goaltender Gary Johnson needed just fourteen saves to earn the shutout. Doug Woog, the precocious South St. Paul junior forward playing in his third state tournament, was rendered ineffective by Roseau's defense.

"He didn't have a shot on goal," Todd Oseid, a 6-foot-2, 200-pound brick wall of a senior defenseman, said about Woog.

Sunday morning, as Roseau climbed aboard its bus for the 358-mile trip home, a Twin Cities newspaper was there to document the departure.

"They had a picture of us, and the caption read, 'The Rams left St. Paul as quietly as they arrived,'" said Paul Dorwart, a junior defenseman. "I thought that was a cool line."

~LRN~

TOURNAMENT DARLING
South St. Paul's diminutive Doug Woog beloved by fans, teammates

Doug Woog became synonymous with the Minnesota Gophers hockey program as a standout player (1963–66), successful coach for fourteen seasons (1985–99), and television analyst for a decade.

Not bad for a kid who grew up in 1950s South St. Paul learning his craft at the "Mudhole" in his older sister's figure skates—which he painted black to avoid schoolboy taunts.

Woog became the varsity program's first and most unlikely star. Basketball was his preferred winter sport, but he failed a basketball physical in fifth grade due to an irregular heartbeat. Doctors' tests revealed nothing, but Woog wasn't allowed on the court.

So he headed for the Mudhole. Puck chasers throughout town met at the frozen marsh, located off Southview Boulevard between Twelfth and Thirteenth Avenues.

"Basketball was the sport," said Woog, who only grew to about 5 foot 7. "You were crazy to go out there and play hockey in the cold weather. Hockey wasn't the elite. It was the working class."

The hearty bunch welcomed Woog, who shifted his extracurricular loyalties to the ice. He even ventured to Southview Country Club, skating on the first-hole water hazard, where he could see Titleist golf balls under the ice.

"Was that safe?" Woog said. "Depends on how deep the water was."

Folks stood two and three deep around South St. Paul High School's outdoor ice rink as the Packers rose to prominence. The hockey program made six consecutive state tournament trips from 1957 to 1962 and gave the town an identity beyond stockyards and meatpacking.

Woog, a forward, finished all four of his varsity seasons at the tournament (1959–62). He scored in his first tournament game, a 1–0 quarterfinal victory against Minneapolis Patrick Henry.

The next morning, *Minneapolis Tribune* readers were greeted by one of the tournament's iconic images: a large front-page photograph of Packers goalie Gary McAlpine kissing a smiling Woog's right cheek.

Woog finished his prep career with twelve goals and seven assists in twelve state tournament games. He was named to the all-tournament team three times.

"To get recognized as a good athlete in hockey, you had to get to the state tournament," Woog said. "The

South St. Paul goaltender Gary McAlpine kissed teammate Doug Woog after the freshman scored the lone goal in a 1–0 quarterfinal victory against Minneapolis Patrick Henry. Photo by Paul Siegel/*Minneapolis Tribune*

exposure did a lot for you in terms of self-confidence and a chance for a college scholarship."

All four of Woog's teams reached the semifinals, but only one earned a title shot. South St. Paul's 1961 team fell 1–0 to Roseau in the championship game.

"We just ran out of time," Woog said. "There were about four thousand South St. Paul fans there, and they gave us a standing ovation."

Woog returned to the tournament in 1978 as South St. Paul's coach. His 1980 and 1981 teams also got there but fell short of a title.

In 2015, the city renamed Wakota Arena after Doug Woog. He feels honored to be part of South St. Paul's proud, if incomplete, tradition. The Packers were winners but never champions.

"The pressure was there," Woog said. "You weren't a success until you made it to the tournament. Whatever marbles you picked up after that, fine."

~*DL*~

ESCAPE ARTIST

IMPORTED FROM CANADA, TINY HUFFER CHRISTIANSEN HAD HOUDINI-LIKE ABILITIES

DATES	LOCATION	ATTENDANCE	CHAMPIONSHIP
FEBRUARY 22–24	ST. PAUL AUDITORIUM	41,571	INTERNATIONAL FALLS 4, ROSEAU 0

Did you know? Before playing professionally for the St. Paul Saints, Roseau coach Oscar Almquist, an Eveleth native, was a standout goaltender for Saint Mary's University in Winona, where he attained all-American status in 1933.

DRESSED IN STREET CLOTHES, Keith Christiansen looked as fearsome as a lilac bush.

The rosy-cheeked forward with a constant twinkle in his eyes stood 5 foot 5 and weighed 145 pounds.

A killer hockey player? This cherub? No way.

Once strapped into his skates with a hockey stick in his hands, however, Christiansen cut an altogether different figure.

As a high school junior, the kid known to all only as "Huffer" was Minnesota's top talent, a stickhandling magician who terrorized flailing, overmatched opponents.

With Huffer orchestrating, International Falls games during the 1961–62 season weren't as much athletic endeavors as they were big-top circus entertainment. The Broncos played in front of sold-out crowds not only at their "home" arena across

Keith "Huffer" Christiansen of International Falls dances in alone on Richfield goalie Lee Stokes during a 1962 quarterfinal. Christiansen's first-period goal proved to be the winner as the Broncos beat the Spartans 4–0 en route to the title. Photo by the *St. Paul Pioneer Press,* courtesy of the Minnesota Historical Society

Coaching icons Oscar Almquist of Roseau (left) and Larry Ross of International Falls (right) make a toast before the 1962 tournament. Photo by the *St. Paul Pioneer Press,* courtesy of the Minnesota Historical Society

the Rainy River in Fort Frances, Ontario, but up and down northern Minnesota's hockey-crazed Iron Range.

Everyone came to see the dazzling play of Huffer, the little wunderkind who was so quick on his skates and deft with his stick that he routinely worked his way out of near-certain calamities.

"He was lined up for train wrecks all his life," said Mike "Lefty" Curran, International Falls' senior goalie that season. "But checking him was like trying to pick up a greased pig."

Huffer grew up in Fort Frances, the middle of Walter and Nathalie Christiansen's three sons. Walter was a standout hockey player himself, starring for the Fort Frances Canadians in 1952 as they won the prestigious Allan Cup, awarded to Canada's best senior team. Walter and International Falls coach Larry Ross were close friends, and in summer 1960 they hatched a plan to send Huffer and older brother Ken, a standout defenseman, over the river to attend high school and play for the Broncos.

Ross had seen firsthand the impact Canadian imports could have on the state tournament in 1958 when brothers Ed and Bill Bulauca crossed the border from Manitoba to star on Roseau's championship team. The Rams beat International Falls 4–0 in the quarterfinals that year, and Ross quipped, "We could make a shambles out of the state tournament every year if we used the kids from Fort Frances."

As part of the "rink rat" crew that helped scrape and flood the ice between periods at Fort Frances's Memorial Arena, the Christiansen brothers had long been infatuated with the Broncos. They watched in awe as their heroes packed the arena with close to three thousand fans for all their home games.

(International Falls didn't have indoor ice at the time.)

"I was a Bronco long before I ever even played for them," Huffer said.

The Christiansens earned a dollar a night and free entry into games. But the biggest payoff was being allowed to play hockey into the early hours of the morning inside the arena after Friday- and Saturday-night games.

"Huffer was a natural," Ken said. "We played a lot of road hockey, too, and ever since he was a wee guy, he could just do things."

If Huffer's prodigious talents were blessed upon him at birth, so too, it seems, was his nickname. No one, not his brothers, friends, or teammates, nor his high school sweetheart and eventual wife Evie—not even Huffer himself—knew how, why, or from whom his moniker came.

"That's just what we called him, for as far back as I can remember," Ken said.

It was discovered early in the 1961–62 season that Ken, as a senior, was ineligible for the team because he had repeated the ninth grade while attending school in Fort Frances. Two of the Broncos' early victories were declared forfeit losses as a result. Huffer also had repeated the ninth grade and, though just a junior, was ruled to be in his final season of eligibility.

Determined to make the most of his one full campaign with the Broncos (he had been forced to sit out half of his sophomore season), Huffer teamed with best buddy Bobby "Slopjohn" O'Leary and co-captain Jim Thompson to form one of the state's most fearsome forward lines. Incredibly, the Broncos' other forward trio of Jim Amidon, Glen Blumer, and Matt Donahue was just as productive.

Which line was better?

"That will be something that will be contested forever, until they are all on the wrong side of the ice," Curran said.

The Broncos, ranked number one for most of the season and unbeaten in twenty-five games entering the tournament (except for switching those two victories to forfeit losses), defeated highly regarded Greenway twice in the regular season and again in the Region 7 final. They beat the Raiders—who, along with Roseau, were considered International Falls' biggest challengers—a fourth time in the state tournament semifinals, with Amidon scoring twice and adding an assist in the 3–2 victory.

Huffer scored an unassisted goal 3:49 into the title game against longtime nemesis Roseau, the defending champion, with what one newspaper account described as an "audacious maneuver" in which he was "holding the puck for a full ten seconds." He added a dazzling assist on an O'Leary goal in the 4–0 victory. Curran made twenty-nine saves, including two on Roseau breakaways, for his second shutout of the tournament.

Despite Amidon's heroics, the spectacular play of Curran in goal, and the brilliance of workhorse defenseman Don Milette, it was Huffer who garnered most of the headlines and accolades. Like the undersized state tournament darlings who had come before him, such as Roseau's Rube "the Masked Marvel" Bjorkman and Thief River Falls' Joey and Jackie Poole, Huffer launched the St. Paul Auditorium's fans (numbering close to eight thousand for the title game) onto their feet every time

he touched the puck. He was compared alternately to Eveleth great John Mayasich and to International Falls' Oscar Mahle, the goal-scoring machine who in 1957 had led the Broncos to their only previous state title.

After losing 4–0 to International Falls in the quarterfinals, Richfield coach Gene Olive summed up the trouble with stopping Huffer (who had a goal and an assist in that game) to reporters in beautifully succinct fashion: "We tried to check him, but we couldn't."

~LRN~

Captains Don Milette (4) and Jim Thompson (12) hoist the championship trophy as International Falls players and cheerleaders gather for a group photo after the Broncos won the 1962 tournament. Photo by the *St. Paul Pioneer Press,* courtesy of the Minnesota Historical Society

SLOPJOHN'S REVENGE

Stick-swinging incident between International Falls and Greenway might have been premeditated

Greenway's Bob Zuehlke reared back and uncorked a howitzer of a slapshot. The rising puck rocketed straight at the International Falls goal. Players from both teams were only too happy to jump out of the path of the chin-high widow-maker.

The seas parted too slowly for Broncos goalie Mike "Lefty" Curran.

"I can kind of remember it coming at me," Curran said.

Goalies didn't wear masks at the time, and the puck struck Curran square on the jaw. He dropped to the ice like a sack of coal. Knocked out. Cold.

Curran was hauled off the ice on a stretcher with 1:40 left in the Broncos' eventual 3–2 victory over the Raiders in the 1962 Region 7 championship game in Virginia. The standout goaltender was taken to the hospital, although Curran said, "When they got me off the ice, I was already standing up."

Curran, who received five stitches, said there was never any doubt he would be ready to play in the following week's state tournament in St. Paul.

"They didn't talk about concussions back then like they do now," he said.

The incident left an impression on Bobby "Slopjohn" O'Leary. An International Falls forward with a short fuse and a long memory, O'Leary wouldn't hesitate to use his stick on teammates in practice but saved his worst punishment for opponents.

Despite losing the region title game, Greenway reached the state tournament by virtue of the old "backdoor" rule that gave a northern region runner-up entry by representing the vacant Region 3. The Raiders entered the tournament with just three losses, all to the Broncos.

Players from Greenway and International Falls were mingling in the lobby of their downtown St. Paul hotel when Zuehlke strolled up to Curran and leaned in close to inspect his handiwork.

Bob "Slopjohn" O'Leary of International Falls (front) was accused of intentionally whacking Greenway's Bob Zuehlke (back) on the head with his stick before both players tumbled to the ice during a 1962 quarterfinal. The incident was ruled to have been an accident, and O'Leary was cleared to play in the championship game, during which he scored a goal in the Broncos' 4–0 victory over Roseau. Photo by the *St. Paul Pioneer Press*, courtesy of the Minnesota Historical Society

"Doesn't look so bad," Zuehlke said of Curran's bandaged chin.

"He was kind of cocky about it," Curran said.

O'Leary witnessed the exchange and told Curran, "Don't worry about a thing, I'll take care of him."

International Falls was a penalty-prone team that season—the Broncos were called for eighteen infractions in three state tournament games, twice as many as the next most penalized team—and O'Leary most often led the procession to the box. Even in practice, he was known to cross the line from fair to foul play, such as the time he repeatedly whacked the back of teammate Jim Amidon's legs with his stick.

The 6-foot, 190-pound Amidon complained to International Falls coach Larry Ross about the transgression. Ross replied, "Well then go get him, Ammy!"

The confrontation ended with O'Leary's nose bloody and broken.

"Amidon turned and just put that stick right in [O'Leary's face]," Curran said. "And Ross didn't mind, as long as O'Leary could still play."

The Broncos and Raiders met for a fourth time that season in the state semifinals. In the closing seconds of International Falls' 3–2 victory, O'Leary hit Zuehlke over the head with his stick. Zuehlke was carted from the ice on a stretcher and treated for a gash above his eye.

Greenway coach Rube Bjorkman, a former Roseau star, was incensed and submitted a formal protest with the Minnesota State High School League Board of Control, seeking to have O'Leary kicked out of the next day's championship game. Earlier, in the quarterfinals, Roseau's Paul Dorwart and St. Paul Monroe's Ken Nelson had been disqualified for the rest of the tournament for throwing punches at each other.

O'Leary professed his innocence by saying he had been hit, lost his balance, and was falling backward when his stick accidently hit Zuehlke on the head.

"I'd bet my life O'Leary didn't hit him on purpose," said Ross, who vowed, "If they put O'Leary out of the championship game, I hope to never bring a team to the state tournament again."

Officials ruled the incident a "routine hockey accident," and O'Leary was cleared to play in the championship against Roseau. After International Falls' 4–0 rout of the Rams, a headline in the Sunday *Minneapolis Tribune* read, "Falls 'Thanks' Bjorkman for 'Firing Us Up.'"

"We can be very thankful for Rube Bjorkman," Ross said about his former University of Minnesota teammate and roommate. "His statements about Bob O'Leary after the semifinal game Friday night just fired up our players."

~LRN~

FOND FAREWELL

ST. PAUL JOHNSON SENT BELOVED COACH RUBE GUSTAFSON OUT IN STYLE

DATES	LOCATION	ATTENDANCE	CHAMPIONSHIP
FEBRUARY 21–23	ST. PAUL AUDITORIUM	43,061	ST. PAUL JOHNSON 4, INTERNATIONAL FALLS 3 (OT)

 *Did you know?* The waterway that inspired Johnson's "Grand Army of Phalen Creek" nickname once snaked through the East Side from Lake Phalen's south shore to the Mississippi River. Engineers enclosed Phalen Creek in underground tunnels in the 1930s.

HASTINGS POND in wintertime provided a place for young Bill Metzger to play out his hockey fantasies.

Stick in hand, his skates cutting the ice, Metzger visualized winning the state tournament with Johnson High School. He'd be the hero, scoring goals just like older cousin Herb Brooks had done for the Governors' 1955 championship team.

By 1963, changes had come to St. Paul's East Side. Dirt transported from the construction of Interstate 94 buried Hastings Pond, the neighborhood gathering place until outdoor rinks

St. Paul Johnson's dynamic forward line of (from left) Mike Crupi, Greg Hughes, and Rob Shattuck reached consecutive championship games against International Falls. They won in 1963 but fell short a year later. All three later played at the University of Minnesota. Photo by the *St. Paul Pioneer Press*

were flooded. The marshland became part of the new Johnson High School campus, which opened in the fall. Metzger's senior class was the last to graduate from the building located about a mile south on Arcade Street.

These weren't the only ways an era ended in 1963. Before the hockey season, coach Rube Gustafson announced he was stepping down after seventeen seasons to become athletic director.

Both he and Metzger went out as champions, with a playoff run and championship game finish sweeter than any Metzger had dared to dream of.

Two equally talented forward lines fueled the Governors, who went 15–0–1 in the St. Paul City Conference and averaged six goals per game.

First-line center Jon Kulstad led the conference with twenty goals. Co-captain Metzger skated at left wing, and Dick Nordlund played right wing.

The senior trio was pushed by second-line juniors Mike Crupi, Greg Hughes, and Rob Shattuck. All three later played at the University of Minnesota.

"No one changed lines to match our second line, so opponents' second lines were never a match for them," said George "Skip" Peltier, a third-line sophomore.

Hughes centered the line with quick feet and a quicker shot.

"Yeah, he was a shooter," Shattuck said. "Notice I said shooter, not scorer. He missed the net a lot. I was a passer. I couldn't shoot for anything."

Hughes disagreed, crediting his left wing for being good in the tight spots where goals are scored.

Crupi, the right wing, brought toughness.

"There was no give-up in that kid," Hughes said.

Co-captain Ron Evenson, who like Metzger led without ego, and Phil Kellor anchored the defense.

Then there was Hank Remackel, who started his varsity career on defense before switching to goalie.

"He was probably the biggest question mark," Metzger said. "They said his fundamentals were terrible. If you were a goalie coach watching him, you'd say, 'How the hell is he doing that?' But he was a competitor who liked to win."

Remackel played for Lockwood Playground, not the Phalen

Players from St. Paul Johnson (foreground) and International Falls stand quiet and still for the national anthem at the St. Paul Auditorium before going all-out in the 1963 title game in what would be the first tournament championship decided in overtime. Photo courtesy of the Minnesota Historical Society

Youth Club run by Herb Brooks Sr. that served as finishing school for Johnson varsity hopefuls.

"And they were all Swedes or Italians and Protestants or Lutherans," said Remackel, a German Polish Catholic. "I was the only fish-eater on the team."

Of Johnson's four state championship teams, the 1962–63 team faced the greatest odds. The Governors survived the backdoor of the region tournament just to qualify for state but ultimately made Gustafson the third coach to win four titles.

Not bad for a guy who never skated.

Born in 1911, Rueben O. Gustafson, known as Rube or Gus, graduated from Johnson in 1929. He asked about playing hockey but was denied because the team was full. So he played basketball.

Gustafson graduated from Concordia College in Moorhead and pursued teaching and coaching. He led the girls' basketball team at tiny Ayr High School in North Dakota to the 1938 state championship.

After stints in Dilworth and Farmington, Gustafson returned to Johnson in 1944 as a mathematics teacher and wound up coaching hockey.

Lou Cotroneo joined Johnson's hockey team for the 1946–47 season as a rare backup goalie and learned Gustafson wasn't the man in charge.

"They told me, 'Don't pay attention to Rube. Jim Sedin calls all the shots,'" Cotroneo said.

The Governors held a captain's practice the morning of a 1947 state tournament game—without Gustafson.

"He was a nice guy, supportive," Sedin said. "But we didn't think he knew anything about hockey at that time."

Orv Anderson, a defenseman on the 1947 team, said, "He blew his whistle and said, 'You can't kick the puck.' We said, 'Rube, this isn't basketball.'"

Players grew to appreciate the big Swede's other talents.

"Rube wasn't an overly technical coach," said Roger Wigen,

a forward on the 1955 championship team. "He was a builder of men. He was a disciplinarian, a father figure."

"One time we were playing Cretin outside at Phalen in front of about three thousand people," Wigen recalled. "I came back to the bench and said, 'Goddammit, I missed the net.' And Rube tells me, 'You never want to swear when priests are around.'"

Remembered for his practice ensemble of buckle overshoes, a heavy brown coat, and a sheepskin hat with ear flaps, Gustafson also carried a hockey stick—but not for passing.

"You'd get it across the butt while doing laps for conditioning," Peltier said.

Years of success changed players' perceptions of Gustafson.

"He was god," Shattuck said. "He called me Short Stuff. I remember our first team meeting. I worshipped every word he said. Gus never skated in his life, but he was a great coach."

Said Hughes: "If you made a mistake he'd say, 'I want to talk to you,' and then take you out of the locker room. But there were never put-downs; he was always positive. You wanted to play hard for him. I listened to him like I listened to my dad."

Players primarily scrimmaged during practice. None recalled Gustafson designing plays, though he did emphasize puck movement.

"He knew what he needed to know about game management," Peltier said. "He knew more than most about how to deal with kids. He endeared himself. You wanted to play hard for him. Herbie [Brooks] had a lot of those qualities—getting you to play with your heart and not just your physical and mental abilities."

A torrid stretch of five playoff games in six days challenged players' bodies, hearts, and minds. They won the Region 4 semifinal but were upset by St. Paul Murray the next day in overtime of the championship game. That meant going through the backdoor Region 1.

"This is where 'Win for Gus' came into play," Peltier said.

After a one-day break, Johnson beat White Bear Lake and Edina on consecutive nights and qualified for state. About twenty-four hours later, the Governors lost the Twin Cities championship game to Minneapolis Roosevelt, their upcoming opponent in the state tournament quarterfinal.

"Maybe psychologically it was good to have lost to them because at the state tournament they thought they'd won the game before they stepped on the ice," Metzger said.

In the rematch, Roosevelt led 2–1 after two periods before Metzger took control. Metzger's father, also named Bill, was a defenseman on Johnson's 1945 team. The elder Metzger encouraged his son to play more aggressive.

Living out his Hastings Pond dreams, Metzger scored twice in the third period for a 3–2 victory.

"He had a heart as big as the St. Paul Auditorium," Peltier said.

Roosevelt disputed Metzger's second goal, knocked in with thirty-eight seconds remaining after goalie John Bjeldanes thought he had frozen the puck and gotten a whistle.

"I didn't think it was frozen, so I went after it," Metzger said. "It was an aggressive play."

The semifinals brought a familiar foe in Roseau. The teams had played a home-and-home "Kaffee Kup" series for years, mixing good hockey with off-ice shenanigans. Cotroneo, a Johnson assistant coach from 1954 to 1963 and Gustafson's successor as head coach, recalled a Roseau trip during which a player's snowmobile slid out of an alley and into a highway patrol car.

Johnson and Roseau collided twice during the regular season, with the Rams prevailing each time. The Governors won the all-important third showdown 2–1 on a pair of Shattuck goals in the second period. Remackel made twenty-eight saves.

That left defending champion International Falls (23–0–2), a matchup Metzger felt was fate. Had Johnson (23–2–1) won the Region 4 title, the teams would have met in the state semifinals.

International Falls star forward Jim Amidon believed the finals provided more appropriate turf.

"All year long, one of the papers has been rating Johnson first in the state and us second," Amidon said. "Now we'll have a chance to find out who really is the best."

The Broncos went ahead 1–0. Johnson responded with two goals seventeen seconds apart from Crupi and Hughes. Toward the period's end, Crupi scuffled in front of Johnson's net. He collapsed on the bench and was carried into the dressing room on a stretcher. A bruised windpipe left him struggling to breathe.

The player who later became the namesake of the Minnesota Gophers' "Most Determined Player" award returned for the second period. Gustafson, who attended Johnson with Mike Crupi Sr., called Mike Jr. "the toughest player I've ever seen when he has nothing left to go on but instinct."

Speaking of tough, International Falls senior defenseman Dick Haugland played despite acute appendicitis, which would require surgery the next day. He evened the score 2–2 with a second-period goal.

Metzger gave Johnson a 3–2 lead after two periods. But his primary assignment was shadowing Amidon, who had tallied a hat trick in the quarterfinals.

"Gus told Metzger, 'Wherever Amidon goes, you go. If he goes to the bathroom, you go,'" Hughes said.

Metzger wasn't on the ice when Amidon, who assisted the first two International Falls goals, broke free on a tremendous end-to-end rush and scored with forty-two seconds remaining in regulation. For the first time in nineteen years of the state tournament, the title game went to overtime.

"We could've gotten down, but we didn't," Metzger said.

Metzger was coming back to the bench as Crupi got the puck behind Remackel and started down the left side. Crupi picked up speed as he left the Governors' end and blew by a Broncos skater. Deep in the offensive zone, he curved around the bottom of the circle toward the net and sent a backhand pass into the slot.

Shattuck, trailing the play, proved himself a shooter after all. He wasted no time, redirecting Crupi's pass and beating the goalie. He said after the game, "Falls' goalie was still on the other side looking for Crupi when the puck hit my stick. All I had to do was tip it in."

Kathy Peltier (Brullo), Skip's older sister and a former Johnson cheerleader, said, "That whole play is burned in my memory. We were on the floor in front of the student section. The goal was scored in the net closest to us; we were right there to see it."

Jubilant players piled up on the ice. Shattuck said, "People to this day remind me of that goal."

The unorthodox Remackel had helped Johnson overcome the Broncos' 34–26 shots-on-goal advantage.

"They called this boy the weak link in our ball club," Gustafson said. "How wrong can they be?"

For Metzger, the tournament exposure led to recruiting interest. He played at Colorado College, where he met his wife, Sue.

"We just celebrated our fiftieth anniversary [in December 2017]," said Metzger, who considers Johnson's championship run "a life-changing event."

Gustafson won 375 games, made twelve state tournament appearances, and won four state championships. He called the 1963 title "a wonderful way to bow out. I'm proud of those kids as I could possibly be."

He retired from Johnson in 1976 but remained involved with the school's booster club. He died from cancer in January 1991 at age seventy-nine. His memorial service was held at Gustavus Adolphus Lutheran Church, where he had sung with the Swedish Male Chorus.

About a month later, the Governors hockey team reached the 1991 state tournament wearing jerseys bearing a silver star patch with "Gus" written in maroon.

The arena next to Johnson High School was later renamed "Gustafson-Phalen" in his honor.

"He was a master," Cotroneo said. "Rube never played the game. He never put on a pair of skates. But he knew how to deal with people. When you win four state championships and you never played the game, you're doing something right."

~DL~

"A REAL SCRAPPER"

MERE FLESH WOUNDS COULDN'T KEEP BRONCOS' PETE FICHUK OUT OF CHAMPIONSHIP

DATES	LOCATION	ATTENDANCE	CHAMPIONSHIP
FEBRUARY 20–22	ST. PAUL AUDITORIUM	44,362	INTERNATIONAL FALLS 7, ST. PAUL JOHNSON 3

 Harry Brown, who was instrumental in the growth of Minnesota hockey outside the traditional winter season, made his lone state tournament appearance as a coach, leading Minneapolis Patrick Henry to a third-place finish.

THE BUSINESS END of a wayward stick caught Pete Fichuk squarely above the left eye. The gash was long and deep. Blood flowed like water from a spigot.

International Falls was playing Richfield in the semifinals of the 1964 state tournament, and it appeared Fichuk's night was over midway through the first period.

Fichuk, the triggerman on the Broncos' top line, headed to the bench for emergency repairs. Generous use of gauze bandages and athletic tape stopped the bleeding. The junior center was back on the ice in no time flat, never mind that his eye was all but swollen shut.

Mere flesh wounds weren't enough to keep Fichuk off the ice. Perseverance and grit were programmed into his DNA; his father drove a tank in World War II and was wounded in service before returning home to a paper mill job.

"His tank got blown up, and when he was getting out, he got wounded in the arm," Fichuk said. "He was a pretty tough guy."

Fichuk took his share of lumps, too. As a kid, he would skate for hours on end at International Falls' Eleventh Street outdoor rink against players twice his age, high schoolers who weren't shy about putting pint-sized rink rats in their place.

By the time he reached high school himself, Fichuk's stickhandling and skating prowess were renowned around town. As a sophomore he squared off daily in practice against the likes of Jim Amidon, the big, strong senior center who was the brightest of Broncos stars in the 1963 state tournament.

"His line beat us up pretty good that season," Fichuk said.

St. Paul Johnson had stunned previously unbeaten International Falls 4–3 in overtime in the 1963 championship game, a loss that stoked Fichuk's already white-hot competitive fire.

"We felt like we blew that 1963 game," he said. "We had our eyes on [winning the 1964 championship] from day one."

The pretournament festivities in 1964 included a banquet for all the participating teams. Johnson's Rob Shattuck, who scored the winning goal the previous season, was introduced to Larry Roche, the International Falls goalie who surrendered it.

Roche yearned to play Johnson again, and he wasn't shy about saying so.

"I wouldn't be human if I didn't," he said.

Johnson entered the 1964 tournament at the peak of its powers. The Governors, state champs in 1947, '53, '55, and '63, were 22–0–1 and held a twenty-eight-game unbeaten streak. They had thirteen shutouts, allowing only sixteen goals and no more than two in any game.

Johnson's all-senior top line of Shattuck, Mike Crupi, and Greg Hughes ranked among the best in state history, and all three were being recruited to play at the University of Minnesota.

The Governors' status as overwhelming 1964 tournament favorites grew to titanic proportions after they shut out Alexander Ramsey 4–0 and Patrick Henry 9–0 to reach the championship. International Falls (19–4–1) entered the tournament through the backdoor of vacant Region 3 after losing to Duluth East in the Region 7 championship. The Broncos played Duluth East again in the state tournament quarterfinals, slipping past the Greyhounds 2–1 to set up their semifinal showdown with rugged Richfield.

Richfield's lineup included nine players from its number-one-ranked football team of the previous fall. The Spartans' plan was to pummel the Broncos at every opportunity. Football on ice.

"We wanted to hit them hard, to use our size," Richfield coach Gene Olive said.

The 5-foot-9, 160-pound Fichuk absorbed the brunt of the beatdown. Not long after suffering the cut above his eye, he took another stick to the face. This time he was hit square in the mouth, losing two teeth. He slammed his stick to the ice in disgust after suffering the injury, then collapsed near the scorer's table.

Fichuk was helped off the ice and didn't return. His first-period departure caused chaos on the bench and ice as lines were shuffled to account for his absence.

"When Pete went out, that was a big blow to us," said Tony Curran, Fichuk's longtime winger. "We had played together for all those years. We were lost without Peter."

The Broncos eked out a 3–2 victory on the strength of two third-period goals from sophomore sensation Tim Sheehy.

The fabled International Falls "Cotton Rockets" forward line of (from left) Tony Curran, Pete Fichuk, and Keith Bolin team up to autograph a stick at the 1964 tournament. Photo by the *Minneapolis Tribune,* courtesy of the Minnesota Historical Society

International Falls had earned its title game rematch with Johnson, but there was talk Fichuk might have to undergo oral surgery and miss the rematch. The Broncos' outlook was bleak at best.

After beating Richfield, Broncos coach Larry Ross was confident Fichuk would play the next day. "If I know him, he'll be back," Ross commented. "That one's a real scrapper."

Sure enough, Fichuk—his head heavily bandaged, his left eye and mouth bruised and swollen—strolled into the locker room before the championship game carrying his gear.

"That was inspirational," said Ron Beck, the Broncos' back-up goaltender.

Weeks later, X-rays revealed that one of Fichuk's missing teeth had been shoved straight up into his gums.

"Yeah, it hurt," Fichuk said. "But I put that aside. I wanted to play against Johnson."

"That would have knocked other guys out of the championship game, but not him," said Jim Carter, a bruising South St. Paul defenseman who played against Fichuk in high school and with him for two seasons at the University of Minnesota. "He was a tough little son of a bitch."

Hughes opened the scoring for Johnson early in the first period of the championship game, but Fichuk responded with an unassisted goal a little more than a minute later. The pair exchanged goals again later in the first, this time Fichuk answering eleven seconds after Hughes.

The Broncos scored the next four goals (the first two assisted by Fichuk), and Roche made eighteen saves en route to a stunning 7–3 thrashing of the Governors.

Against all odds, the battered Fichuk had willed himself into a one-man wrecking ball.

"[The championship game] was like a car accident," St. Paul Johnson coach Lou Cotroneo said. "We got totaled."

~LRN~

INTERNAL COMBUSTION

PRACTICE FLAREUPS PREPARED DOMINANT INTERNATIONAL FALLS FOR "EASY" GAMES

DATES	LOCATION	ATTENDANCE	CHAMPIONSHIP
FEBRUARY 25–27	ST. PAUL AUDITORIUM	43,728	INTERNATIONAL FALLS 7, BLOOMINGTON 0

 South St. Paul's Terry Abram, a towering senior who drew the attention of the New York Rangers, was described by Packers coach Lefty Smith in a *Minneapolis Tribune* article as "the finest defenseman I've seen in high school."

WHEN THE BELL RANG at precisely 3:33 PM to signal the end of the school day, International Falls hockey players made a mad dash to the gymnasium locker room, where they put on their gear in preparation for practice, held a short bus ride across the Rainy River at Memorial Arena in Fort Frances, Ontario.

Members of the daily stampede during the 1964–65 season included Marshall Sether, a 200-pound defenseman built like a whiskey barrel, and Dan Mahle, a rugged 6-foot-3 forward who used his elbows and knees in corner battles as effectively as a chef wields a carving knife.

Ahead of a spring when the state would be ravaged by floods and tornadoes, the Broncos, too, were a force of nature, as unstoppable as the rising waters and devastating winds.

The 1964–65 International Falls team, one of the most dominant in state history, completed a 24–0 season by routing Bloomington 7–0 in the 1965 state championship game. Photo courtesy of the Minnesota Historical Society

One of the greatest teams in state history featured a who's who of International Falls legends. They became household names not only around town but throughout Minnesota, all of them eager to rush to the rink and prove their mettle. Their training sessions weren't so much practices as they were tests of will, toughness, and endurance.

Think of it as hockey's version of *Survivor*.

"If you could get through practice, the games were easy," said Peter Fichuk, a senior center during the 1964–65 season.

Fichuk and longtime linemates and fellow seniors Tony Curran and Keith Bolin scrimmaged daily against the equally dominant line of juniors Tim Sheehy, Peter Hegg, and Dan Mahle. Sheehy, a center, stood 6 foot 1, weighed 185 pounds, and was coveted by every college in the country.

"We were older and thought it was our turn to dish out some lumps to the younger guys, but Sheehy and Mahle were big boys," said Fichuk, who stood 5 foot 9.

Fichuk's line was derisively nicknamed the Cotton Rockets by Broncos goaltender Larry Roche, a senior in 1964 who deemed the group's shots as soft as "a puffball of cotton coming at me." Not that the trio needed rocket shots. They were known for their tic-tac-toe passing, the dizzying puck movement often resulting in tap-in goals at the side of the net.

"Those guys weren't happy unless they had five passes inside the blue line," Roche said.

Sheehy's line relied less on finesse and more on brute force. The group had a shoot-first mentality.

"We were told that for every ten shots, you should get a goal," said Mahle, younger brother of Oscar Mahle, star of the Broncos' 1957 state championship team. "We figured if that was the average, why not shoot every chance you got?"

The defensemen were just as skilled. Sether and fellow seniors Gary Wood and Brian Glennie were all above average in size, as was junior Steve Ross, the son of coach Larry Ross. The wide-bodied Sether was unusually nimble for a player of his build.

"He wasn't flashy, but when he got the puck, boy could that guy find me," Fichuk said.

Glennie, also a superb passer, stood out for his exceptional skating skills honed during summer lessons in Rockton, Illinois, with figure-skating instructor Art Nichols. Fichuk, Sheehy, and Steve Ross also spent a summer in Rockton working at the rink and perfecting their strides.

Wood possessed the rawest talent of any player in the group. The first Minnesota-born player ever selected in the NHL Amateur Draft, he was taken in the second round (number twelve overall) by the Oakland Seals in 1967.

Wood's signature skill was the slapshot, and he uncorked it at every opportunity.

"Boy he could shoot the puck," goaltender Ron Beck said. "But he had no idea where it was going."

Beck played a handful of games as a sophomore backing up Roche and would become the Broncos' full-time starter as a junior and senior. Beck is the only Minnesota high school goaltender to play two or more seasons and never lose a game in his career, racking up fifty-five victories.

Larry Ross didn't stumble into this abundance of talent (twelve of the fifteen players on the 1965 tournament roster received Division I scholarships). Four bustling outdoor rinks—Eighth Street, Eleventh Street, Carson Lupie, and the Bandshell—all were strategically located within about a half mile of each other, providing walking-distance hockey opportunities to most every kid in town. The Broncos' 1957 state championship team, coupled with the Olympic gold medal won by the US hockey team in 1960, launched local interest in the sport to the moon.

"Every kid in town wanted to play hockey," Sheehy said.

The stacked Broncos entered the 1964–65 season as defending state champions who had graduated just three seniors. They reached the state tournament with a 24–0 record, having outscored their opponents 198–37.

"It is the deepest team I have had in ten years at the Falls," Ross said leading up to the tourney. "It is very sound in every way."

University of Minnesota coach John Mariucci was equally impressed: "I don't think there has ever been a better high school hockey team than International Falls. They not only have a number of great individuals, but the big thing is they have fifteen men who can play and not hurt them at any time."

The Broncos trailed Roseau by a goal early in the third period of the quarterfinals, then rallied for a 5–3 victory thanks to unanswered goals by Bolin, Mahle, and Fichuk. The rest of the tournament was decidedly anticlimactic.

A Sheehy hat trick highlighted a 5–1 semifinal rout of South St. Paul. International Falls capped its unbeaten season by overwhelming Bloomington 7–0 on the strength of a Mahle hat trick and two goals each from Fichuk and Curran. The margin of victory remains tied for the largest ever in a state championship game.

Turns out the best competition for the Broncos all season had been . . . the Broncos.

"They were heated scrimmages," Beck said. "They went at it pretty good."

Added Sheehy: "You had a lot to think about during the day before that bell rang."

~LRN~

NO STRANGER TO DANGER

ULTIMATE SURVIVOR TIM SHEEHY SET GOLD STANDARD AS DO-IT-ALL SUPERSTAR

DATES	LOCATION	ATTENDANCE	CHAMPIONSHIP
FEBRUARY 24–26	ST. PAUL AUDITORIUM	46,016	INTERNATIONAL FALLS 5, ROSEAU 0

Did you know? Roseau senior Bryan Grand, playing in his fourth tournament, scored all four Rams goals in a 4–2 quarterfinal victory over Greenway. Grand later coached Bemidji to the state tournament in 1985 and '86.

TIMOTHY KANE SHEEHY never set out to tempt fate. Crazy, weird, deadly stuff just seemed to happen to him.

Like the time he rolled off the top of his bunk bed. A corner post jutting from the single bed below broke the grade-schooler's fall.

"I cracked my ribs," said Sheehy, widely considered the greatest of all the legendary players churned out by Canadian border town International Falls during its two-decade reign as a state superpower. "I was out of commission for weeks. To this day I still hate bunk beds."

Danger lurked everywhere for Sheehy, the fourth oldest of nine children who grew up wedged between two of International Falls' most famous landmarks. The town's massive, soot-belching paper mill was a mere slapshot to the east of the Sheehy home. Directly to the north were the Rainy River and, on the other side, Canada.

It was a ninety-foot drop from the top of the riverbank to the water below. Perfect for high-speed sledding come winter. Well, except for that water below.

"That was a real steep hill—straight down," Sheehy said. "You ended up in the river if you couldn't put the brakes on in time."

Two houses down from the Sheehys were the Amidons. Jim Amidon, another International Falls hockey icon and Sheehy's idol and mentor, tells the story of how his mother witnessed one of Sheehy's daring sledding runs gone wrong. She rushed down the hill and plucked the youngster out of the ice-cold water.

"He would have drowned, probably," Amidon said.

By the time he was a senior, Sheehy had played in three straight state championship games, winning titles as a sophomore and junior. He stood 6 foot 1, weighed 185 pounds, and oozed athleticism. The nephew of dominant 1930s-era Chicago Bears fullback and International Falls–raised Bronko Nagurski, Sheehy was courted by every collegiate hockey coach in the country as he entered the 1966 state tournament with fifty-three goals and forty assists in twenty-five games.

Sheehy's legion of admirers included University of Minnesota coach John Mariucci, who was among the four thousand in attendance at Hibbing's Memorial Arena watching in awe as

International Falls star Tim Sheehy won three straight state championships, including the 1966 title to close out his stellar career. Photo by the *Minneapolis Tribune*, courtesy of the Minnesota Historical Society

Peter Hegg (center) donned a chef's hat before serving pancakes to his International Falls linemates, Tim Sheehy (left) and Dan Mahle (right), during a break from the 1966 state tournament. The trio formed one of the state's all-time great forward lines. Photo by the *Minneapolis Tribune,* courtesy of the Minnesota Historical Society

She happened to be the twin sister of the 6-foot-4, 210-pound Carter. Unwittingly, Sheehy once again was courting disaster.

"He gave me a two-hander, and I thought he'd broken my arm," Sheehy said about Carter. "I had to leave the game. I know he had seen me talking to his sister. Maybe he was sending a message."

Carter, recruited to play football by most every major college in the nation, never left the ice during South St. Paul's 3–1 quarterfinal victory over White Bear Lake. The Packers, like all teams, relished the opportunity to end International Falls' win streak.

"We were a bunch of tough Polish kids from the rough side of town," said Carter, who played linebacker for the Green Bay Packers for eight seasons. "Our dads worked at the stockyards. We would play teams like Edina and call them 'cake eaters.'

"Then we would play the Falls, and I looked at those guys and thought, 'Man, they must really be from the sticks because they don't seem very cultured.' They weren't easy to play against. They didn't just cruise by you. They were hitters."

Sheehy drew comfort from playing alongside longtime winger Dan Mahle, whose bruising style left opposing players quivering in their skates.

"Other teams were intimidated by him, very much so," Sheehy said. "That's why I liked him on my line. He was a horse.

"We always put him on Carter's side of the ice."

South St. Paul scored first in the semifinal, going up 1–0 midway through the first period on a goal by Joe Bonk. International Falls tied it later in the first on a goal by first-line wing Peter Hegg. Ten seconds later, Sheehy scored the winner in the Broncos' eventual 2–1 triumph.

Hegg and Mahle were talented goal scorers, but they knew the best option in most any situation was to get the puck to Sheehy.

"We played together for so long, I always knew where Timmy was going to be," Mahle said. "I knew he would have a better chance of scoring than me."

Ron Beck, the Broncos' starting goaltender at the 1965 and '66 state tournaments, appreciated a different aspect of Sheehy's game.

"He played both ends of the rink," Beck said. "The play would be coming at me, and I would look back and he would have his head down, digging to catch up."

For the third straight year, International Falls won the championship in a rout, overwhelming Roseau 5–0 for a fifty-eighth straight victory. Sheehy managed just an assist in the triumph. No matter. His deep impact on the Broncos' dynasty—and Minnesota hockey in general—would resonate forever.

Carter said, "He was the player that we all aspired to be."

~LRN~

the silky powerhouse scored all of International Falls' goals in a 5–3 triumph over Greenway in the Region 7 final.

The victory was the Broncos' fifty-fifth straight.

"They have the best high school senior hockey player I have ever seen in Tim Sheehy," Mariucci said. "There isn't anything that Sheehy can't do. He is big, strong, fast, has great desire and a lot of nerve. He can backcheck, stickhandle, and do everything a good hockey player should be able to do."

Sheehy scored twice in the state tournament quarterfinals as the Broncos eased past Bloomington Kennedy and star goaltender Bob Vroman 3–1. South St. Paul and hulking defenseman Jim Carter came next. International Falls had played the Packers twice in the regular season, winning 5–1 and 5–0.

Before the regular-season game in South St. Paul, Sheehy, described as "darkly handsome" by one Twin Cities newspaper, chatted innocently with one of the Packers' cheerleaders.

TEAMMATE TURMOIL

FEUDING GREENWAY PLAYERS PUT WINNING ABOVE LOYALTY TO "FIEFDOMS"

DATES	LOCATION	ATTENDANCE	CHAMPIONSHIP
FEBRUARY 23–25	ST. PAUL AUDITORIUM	45,140	GREENWAY 4, ST. PAUL JOHNSON 2

Did you know? There were no shutouts in the 1967 tournament, one of just seven times that's happened in the event's history.

TINY TOWNS on the southwestern tip of Minnesota's Iron Range are strung along Highway 169 like lights on a Christmas tree. Pengilly into Calumet into Marble into Taconite into Bovey into Coleraine.

Back in the 1960s, each of those outposts amounted to, give or take, a few hundred people, a general store, a post office, an elementary school, a bar, a church, and an outdoor hockey rink.

Kids spent hours on those rinks with their buddies, emulating the stars of the Taconite Hornets, the local senior semipro

Greenway's Mike Antonovich darts past St. Paul Johnson's Jim Prouxl (2) and Glen Goski (10) during the 1967 championship game. Antonovich, a sophomore, completed the scoring with ten seconds left in Greenway's 4–2 triumph over the Governors. Photo courtesy of the Minnesota Historical Society

men's team, and preparing for battle against the other youth teams proudly representing the surrounding mining towns.

Youngsters on the maroon-and-gold Marble Mallards, blue-and-white Calumet Coots, iron-ore-red Bovey Bombers, red-white-and-blue Taconite Hornets, and other colorful teams were fiercely loyal to their fiefdoms.

"We all hated to lose," said Mike "Gordy" Holland.

Holland was from Coleraine. The Coleraine kids didn't particularly care for the kids from Taconite. Same went for the Calumet kids and their Marble neighbors.

"Marble was only a mile away," said Calumet's Mike Antonovich, "and they didn't like us much over there. Most of the guys didn't like each other.

"It was always a competition between the cities as to who had the best hockey and the best players."

Add outliers Cloverdale and Lawrence Lake to the mix, and there was an amalgamation of towns and townships that supplied hockey players to Greenway High School in Coleraine. When all those kids who had spent years trying to sledgehammer each other into submission (not just in hockey but in base-

ball and other sports, too) became high schoolers, they were expected to tug on the same color jerseys and play nice.

So, how did they all get along?

"Not very well," said Bob Gernander, Greenway's hockey coach starting in the 1966–67 season.

The Raiders overflowed with both talent and bad blood. Just before the Region 7 playoffs, tempers reached their boiling point during practice. Punches were thrown, sticks were swung, and voices were raised as payback for dozens of long-standing grievances. Coleraine and Taconite supplied the most players of any of the towns, and battle lines were drawn between those two constantly feuding groups. Think Hatfields and McCoys on ice.

"It was kind of spread out all over the ice," Holland said about the melee. "The coaches finally threw us all in the locker room. There was a lot of screaming and yelling in there, guys complaining about favoritism this and favoritism that."

Gernander was never overly concerned by the constant bickering or even the occasional brawl.

"When we were playing another team, and the puck

Greenway players gather with the championship trophy after beating St. Paul Johnson 4–2 for the 1967 championship, the first state title for the Raiders. Photo courtesy of the Minnesota Historical Society

74

dropped, all that went away," he said. "Our guys were such competitors. All they wanted to do was win."

As for favoritism, the biggest criticism Gernander heard was that *too many* players were getting a regular shift.

Gernander had planned on rotating two forward lines in 1966–67, as most teams did in an era when periods lasted just twelve minutes. But with time winding down in a 5–2 season-opening win over Eveleth, Gernander sent out the third line of sophomore Mike Antonovich, junior Jim Stephens, and senior Jim MacNeil for the first time.

"We got out there for two or three shifts, and I don't think the puck ever got out of Eveleth's end," said Stephens, who grew up playing alongside Antonovich in Calumet. "After that, all three lines got equal ice time."

Gernander, who even rotated the starting lines, said some fans weren't shy about voicing their concerns over his equal-play deployment.

"People would say, 'Gee, if you are going to win you have to cut that down to two lines and play your best six forwards,'" Gernander said. "I would say, 'OK, you tell me which guys are the six best, because I sure can't tell.'"

Depth and balanced scoring proved critical in the Raiders' most important games. After a 1–1 tie in the teams' first meeting, Greenway beat high-powered Hibbing by a single goal in four subsequent matchups, three of them in the playoffs (district, region, and state). The final meeting in the pentalogy came in the semifinals of the state tournament. While Hibbing was getting all its scoring from its fabulous "Mafia Line" of seniors Bill Baldrica, Bob Collyard, and Mark Barbato, the Raiders had four goal scorers representing all three lines and the defensive corps.

Baldrica's second goal of the game tied the score 3–3 with one minute remaining in the third period. But Gary Lawson's goal sixteen seconds later gave the Raiders a 4–3 triumph and their inaugural state title game appearance.

St. Paul Johnson, led by the dazzling forward combination of brothers Doug and Ron Peltier, entered the tournament unbeaten in twenty-two games. The Governors were considered heavy favorites to win the title, along with their quarterfinal opponent, 21–0–1 Edina. Johnson beat the Hornets 3–1, then slipped past North St. Paul 5–4 in overtime on a Ron Peltier goal.

Entering the championship game, the Peltiers had scored six of Johnson's eight goals. Greenway, in contrast, had different scorers on all nine of its goals in the quarterfinals (5–1 win over Minneapolis Roosevelt) and semifinals.

Balance again trumped individual stars in the title game, as each Greenway line contributed at least one goal in a 4–2 triumph over the Governors and their wildly aggressive—and effective—goaltender, Terry Del Monte. Johnson was outshot 40–26, and most of the Governors' best chances came courtesy of the Peltiers and linemate Russ Zahradka.

Despite (or maybe because of) all those grudges, the hatred for being called "Coleraine" by Twin Cities media outlets, and the multitudes of fierce practices, Greenway had risen to the top of Minnesota schoolboy hockey.

"Once the game started, we all probably disliked the other team more than we did each other," Holland said. "If you were supposed to get the puck, you got the puck, no matter what town you were from."

~LRN~

DANGER ZONE

Goalies once allowed to skate to opposite end – at their own risk

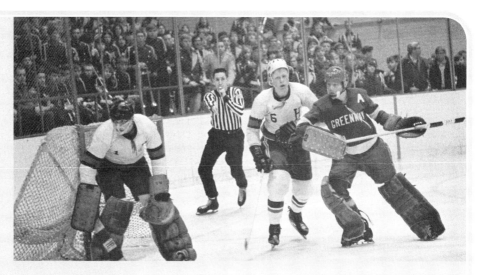

Goaltenders were allowed to cross center ice in the late 1960s, and Greenway's Bill "Pie" Joy delighted in creating havoc in front of the opposing team's net during delayed penalty calls, as he did here in front of goaltender Andy Micheletti and defenseman Ron Olson in a 1967 semifinal against Hibbing. Photo courtesy of the Minnesota Historical Society

The referee raised his arm to signal a penalty. This was Ron Beck's starting bell.

Like a thoroughbred bursting from the starting gates, the International Falls goaltender raced full speed to the other end of the rink.

Because the penalty was being called on the opposing team, in this case South St. Paul, Beck knew there was no threat of being scored upon. By rule, the whistle would blow as soon as the Packers controlled the puck. Until then, it was Beck's job to position himself in front of the crease and block the vision of the opposing goaltender.

Beck was a senior during the 1965–66 season when International Falls coach Larry Ross implemented the highly unusual goalie-screening-goalie tactic.

"I don't know where the idea came from," Beck said. "I suppose they figured, 'Beck is a pretty good skater; let's send him down there.'"

"Down there" could be a dangerous place. Opposing players salivated at the chance to bump and jostle Beck. Against South St. Paul and defenseman Jim Carter, a future NFL linebacker who stood 6 foot 4 and weighed 210 pounds, the bumping and jostling was taken to the extreme.

Carter slammed into Beck, knocking him into the air.

"I'll tell you, my feet were higher than my head," Beck said. "I didn't know exactly where I was when I got up."

The Broncos didn't have a proven backup goaltender. Losing Beck to injury would have been a disaster for a team in the midst of a fifty-nine-game winning streak and run of three straight state championships.

"I came to the bench, and Larry Ross said, 'That's the end of that,'" Beck said.

At about the same time Ross was decommissioning Beck as a front-of-net presence, Greenway coach Grant Standbrook stumbled upon the same idea. The Raiders were struggling with delayed penalties, failing to control the puck long enough for the goalie to come to the bench for an extra skater. Standbrook was practicing the goalie-skater exchange one day when he raised his arm to signal goaltender Rick Metzer to come to the bench.

Bob Tok was the player designated to go on the ice for Metzer. Problem was, Tok happened to be tightening his skates when Metzer arrived at the bench.

"He was frustrated by the fact that Bobby wasn't ready," Standbrook said about Metzer. "So he kept on going to the other end."

The innovative Standbrook liked the look of Metzer screening the opposing goalie and assigned Metzer to that duty on occasion, just as Ross had briefly deployed Beck. When Bill "Pie" Joy took over as the Raiders' goaltender in the 1965–66 season, Standbrook sent him to the other end on delayed penalties, too.

"He just said it makes sense, rather than me coming over to the box," Joy said. "He said, 'We could get down to the other end quicker if I just did it myself.'"

Bob Gernander took over as Greenway's coach entering the 1966–67 season. He continued to send Joy, then a senior, to the other end on delayed penalties.

"It was a big part of his game, and he loved it," Gernander said about Joy. "And anything that would make the goaltender happy, I would let it go."

Joy was racing end to end regularly during the 1967 state tournament. He tripped on his straps while joining the attack on a delayed penalty in the quarterfinals against Minneapolis Roosevelt. In the semifinals, against Hibbing, he was involved in a jousting match in front of the Bluejackets' goal and was called for high-sticking.

He rushed the length of the ice to join the attack in Greenway's 4–2 championship victory over St. Paul Johnson.

"I almost scored in the state tournament after the puck went off the opposing goalie," Joy said. "It might have been against Hibbing. I whiffed on it. The puck was sitting right there."

The way Gernander remembers it, the practice was outlawed the following season. Goaltenders no longer were allowed to participate in the play in any manner past the red line. The NHL implemented rule no. 27.7, aka the Gary Smith Rule, after the 1966–67 season when Smith, then a Toronto Maple Leafs goalie, was knocked out cold after carrying the puck beyond the red line.

"It was novel," Joy said. "It was different. People still remember me as the goalie who would skate to the other end. I guess I was famous because of it."

~LRN~

SLUGGO, STAR, AND STINKY

NICKNAMES A RITE OF PASSAGE FOR GREENWAY'S CHAMPIONS

DATES	LOCATION	ATTENDANCE	CHAMPIONSHIP
FEBRUARY 22–24	ST. PAUL AUDITORIUM	45,369	GREENWAY 6, SOUTH ST. PAUL 1

 Greenway's championship was the twentieth for a northern school in the first twenty-four years of the tournament.

THERE WAS A Sluggo, a Bucko, a Jughead, and a Tonto.

And on it went with a Farmer and a Cotton and an obligatory Moose.

Tom Peluso had the best nickname: Star.

Mike Antonovich had the worst: Stinky.

Nicknames were so woven into the fabric of the 1967–68 Greenway team that Raiders coach Bob Gernander didn't know the birth names of at least half his players.

"I just called them by their nicknames," he said. "That's all I knew. I would have had to have looked them up in the school records to know their real names."

One newspaper reporter attempted to list all the Raiders' nicknames, omitting defenseman Mike "Gordy" Holland because, according to Holland, "everyone just thought Gordy was my real name."

Greenway's cast of characters was a half-and-half mixture of returning players from the previous season's state championship team and varsity newcomers such as sophomores Peluso, Jim Hoey, and Bob Lawson. Seniors Sandy Markovich and Dave Stangl also were new to the team, as were juniors Bill Guyer and Dave Prestige.

"We didn't have quite the depth we had the previous year," Gernander said. "We went back to playing mostly two lines."

The Raiders had less scoring balance but more star power. The 5-foot-5, 150-pound Antonovich, an all-state tournament pick in 1967 as a sophomore center, emerged as the team's scoring behemoth. Senior defenseman Ken Lawson (Bob's cousin), 5 foot 10 and 200 pounds of chiseled granite, also was a returning all-state tournament pick.

"Kenny Lawson was the leader probably on both of those teams," Gernander said. "There wasn't anything he couldn't do."

Added Hoey: "[Lawson] could play both offense and defense. He was a good skater. He was smart. He used his body well. My sophomore year, he ran the team."

Unlike Lawson, the bespectacled Antonovich didn't cut an intimidating figure. His oversized hockey gloves reached all the way to his elbows, and he refused to wear shoulder pads.

The nickname only added to Antonovich's aura. He typically bolted from practice without showering, hitchhiking the ten

Greenway's Mike Antonovich (left) and Kenny Lawson haul hockey sticks into their hotel as they prepare for the 1968 tournament. Photo courtesy of the Minnesota Historical Society

miles from the arena in Coleraine to his home in Calumet. And if the Raiders were on a win streak, superstition dictated that his favorite T-shirt go unwashed until they lost.

Stinky, indeed.

"I didn't have many clothes at home anyway," Antonovich said. "I didn't have anything."

Antonovich grew up idolizing Jim "Slim" Troumbly, a standout center for the Taconite Hornets, the area's semipro senior men's team. Troumbly had starred for the US national team in 1950.

"He could pass, he could score, he could skate," Antonovich said. "I wanted to be just like him."

With Lawson and Antonovich forming the backbone of the team, Greenway went 19–1 in the regular season, losing only to Hibbing. The Bluejackets beat the Raiders again in the final of the district playoffs, but both teams advanced to the Region 7 tournament, where Greenway lost 1–0 in overtime to International Falls in the championship game. Despite yet another playoff loss, the Raiders reached the state tournament via the

backdoor, beating Region 8 runner-up Thief River Falls 4–1 for the vacant Region 3 title.

The oddity of qualifying for the state tournament with two playoff losses failed to dent Gernander's confidence in his team's chances for a repeat.

"I was good friends with [International Falls coach] Larry Ross," he said. "And we talked all the time about how it was harder to get out of our regional, with so many great teams, than it was to win the state tournament."

The state tournament was in its final season at the old St. Paul Auditorium. The plan was to move the event to the new, more spacious Metropolitan Sports Center in Bloomington (home of the NHL's fledgling Minnesota North Stars) until a new arena was built in downtown St. Paul.

It was time for a change. The auditorium had been a fine home for the event in its infancy, but by the twenty-fourth tournament its seating capacity of just more than eight thousand was unable to accommodate what had become rabid fan interest.

Greenway goaltender Terry Casey carries the championship trophy to coach Bob Gernander after the Raiders won their second-straight state title by beating South St. Paul 6–1 in the 1968 championship. Photo courtesy of the Minnesota Historical Society

The smoke billowing from the stands (smoking was allowed inside the arena) and outdated accommodations also generated little fondness with the players.

"The place was a dump," said Edina's Bobby Krieger, a sophomore in 1968.

Greenway's Hoey also was less than impressed.

"There were no locker rooms for us—all they had was a screen up," he said. "We dressed in our hotel, then we would walk over with the fans to the games. What a scene that was."

Mounds View, Greenway's quarterfinal opponent, was a state tournament newcomer. The Raiders, however, were intimately familiar with the Mustangs' formidable lineup, which featured the Buetow brothers: Bart, a 6-foot-5 wing, and Brad, a 6-foot-2 defenseman. A few years earlier, Mounds View and Greenway had met in the state Bantam tournament, and the Mustangs had won.

A goal by Bart with fifteen seconds left in the third period pushed the quarterfinal game into overtime.

"The tying goal they got was 100 percent on me," said Holland, a standout defenseman for two seasons. "I had had the puck in open ice and tried to beat a guy. The kid stripped me.

"When Davey Stangl scored that goal to win it, that was a big burden off me."

Stangl's overtime goal launched the Raiders into the semifinals, where they beat St. Paul Johnson 4–3 in a rematch of the previous year's championship game. Then the Raiders routed South St. Paul 6–1 in the title game, getting two goals each from linemates Antonovich and Peluso.

As a freshman, Peluso had watched intently the previous year while Antonovich was mobbed by fans and interviewed by reporters after the championship game.

"Tommy is watching, and he is telling me, 'That's what I want. I want people to know me like they know Anton,'" Gernander said. "In other words, he wanted to be the star."

And a nickname was born.

~LRN~

THE GOLDEN ERA: 1969–1991

The best the state tournament had to offer began in 1969, when affluent suburban Edina defeated tiny Warroad in the competition's first year at the Met Center in Bloomington, which offered twice the seating capacity of the St. Paul Auditorium. The success of "villain" Edina brought a new intensity to the north vs. south intrastate rivalry, and in 1975, private schools came on board. The tournament returned home to St. Paul in 1976, this time to the Civic Center. The elite schoolboy hockey began to receive national buzz, and stars of television and movies couldn't resist the tournament excitement. In 1979, the eight-team affair broke the hundred-thousand-attendance barrier, and hockey had overthrown basketball as Minnesota's top prep tournament pursuit.

After moving to the Metropolitan Sports Center in Bloomington in 1969, the state tournament attracted 83,625 fans in 1970, marking the first time attendance topped 80,000. By the end of the decade, after it had moved to the St. Paul Civic Center, total attendance would break the 100,000 mark in a single tournament. Photo by the *Minneapolis Tribune,* courtesy of the Minnesota Historical Society

COLLISION COURSE

WARROAD'S BELOVED HENRY BOUCHA AND EDINA'S ROLE AS VILLAIN BOOSTED DRAMA TO NEW HEIGHTS

DATES	LOCATION	ATTENDANCE	CHAMPIONSHIP
FEBRUARY 20–22	METROPOLITAN SPORTS CENTER, BLOOMINGTON	79,868	EDINA 5, WARROAD 4 (OT)

Did you know? Warroad's four goals tie a record for the most by a losing team in a championship game. It's happened five other times, three of those by Hermantown (2011, '13, and '15).

"STOP OR I'LL SHOOT!"

In front of the startled state patrol officer, Henry Boucha burst out the rear driver's-side door of the sedan and took off sprinting over the bridge spanning the Roseau River.

Boucha was in trouble of the worst kind: a Warroad kid deep in the heart of Roseau, enemy territory, ignoring commands from an agitated lawman with a firearm strapped to his waist and the authority to use it.

The standout running back for Warroad High School's football team and ace pitcher and star slugger on the Warriors' baseball team, Boucha was one of the finest athletes ever born in the far northern reaches of Minnesota—or anywhere in the state, for that matter.

Now he was putting his athletic prowess to the ultimate test. Could he outrun a speeding bullet?

"Stop or I'll shoot!"

The command was bellowed again as Boucha fled, his arms and legs pumping like pistons on a locomotive. The order only fueled Boucha to run faster.

It was late summer. Football season. Boucha was a senior, and as skilled as he was at football and baseball (colleges offered him scholarships in both sports), hockey not only was Boucha's greatest passion but also offered the most likely path to professional stardom. He had made Warroad's varsity team as an eighth-grader, and the legend of Henry Charles Boucha, state hockey champion as a Bantam-aged (seventh-grade) star who could turn on a dime, rush the puck with the flash and flair of a young Bobby Orr, and play an entire game without leaving the ice, only grew with each succeeding season.

Opposing players and fans spoke about Boucha in hushed tones of reverence. Born to George and Alice Boucha, great-grandson of medicine woman Maymushagubiek, a healer known as Laughing Mary, Boucha was the Ojibwe kid with superhuman abilities. His shot was so powerful it bent goalposts and shattered pucks. Why, did you hear the story about how he once shot a puck through the side of an arena and into the frigid night air?

But right now, Boucha, slender and sneaky strong, required speed, not power. He needed his legs to carry him to safety. Earlier that day, he, Lee Moyer, and two friends from

Warroad's Henry Boucha, shown here being interviewed at the Met Sports Center during the 1969 state tournament, was as much a celebrity as he was a hockey player. Photo by the *Minneapolis Tribune,* courtesy of the Minnesota Historical Society

the football team had decided to head west to Roseau to attend a dance. Now they were wanted by the law.

"Please, god, let me get out of this," Boucha thought to himself as he reached the far end of the bridge.

Roseau sits twenty-two miles due west of Warroad, the towns inextricably linked by their geography, history, industry, and, perhaps above all else, their hockey. The rivalry between the town's hockey teams dates to 1908.

On this night, Boucha and his buddies had gone to a dance at Roseau's municipal building. The dance was deemed a dud, and the Warroad foursome were convinced by a group of Roseau boys to leave together for a different, better party.

Eight of them piled into the car driven by one of the Roseau boys. It was speeding and swerving all over the road. Boucha, starting to sweat, asked whether they could turn around and head back. Too late. Lights flashed and sirens wailed. They were being pulled over.

The state patrol officer started asking questions. "Have you been drinking?" He circled to the passenger side and noticed a beer bottle on the floor. More questions. Boucha had heard enough. If he was going to make it to state, he figured he had to get as far away from this car, this situation, as fast as possible.

Out the back door and across the bridge he went. Boucha raced down Roseau's back streets and alleys. He was heading east, toward Warroad, sprinting. He must have run at full speed for two miles.

Boucha hitchhiked home and spent a fitful night in his bed, tossing, turning, and "praying for a miracle," as he put it. The next morning, he ventured tentatively into town. All of Warroad was abuzz about the previous night's incident. Oddly, he

thought, he never was questioned by the authorities, or anyone else for that matter.

No shots had been fired. But Boucha had, figuratively, dodged a bullet.

"I couldn't believe how lucky I was," he said.

Some six months earlier and nearly four hundred miles to the south, Willard Ikola sat in his room at the St. Paul Hotel, fuming. He had just watched the 1968 state tournament championship game on television, and he hadn't enjoyed a second of Greenway's 6–1 blowout victory over South St. Paul.

Ikola, the young Edina coach who had won three state titles as a goaltender for Eveleth (racking up fifty straight wins in the process), had just guided his Hornets to another disappointing state tournament finish. Seven times Edina had reached the state tournament, and seven times the Hornets had lost their opening-round game, the last four of those losses coming under Ikola's watch.

Times were changing in Edina, which now had its own indoor arena, a rare amenity for Twin Cities schools at the time. The city's youth teams were enjoying top-level success at state and national tournaments, and there was pressure for the high school team to do the same.

Watching Greenway win its second straight state title in 1968 ticked off Ikola. It was late, approaching midnight, and he already was thinking about next season, specifically the state tournament. He couldn't take losing on the big stage anymore. It had to stop.

"Ed, we've got to go tell the underclassmen we are done with this consolation crap," Ikola said to longtime assistant coach Ed Zins. "We have to tell them right now!"

"Yeah!" Zins said enthusiastically. "That's a good idea. Let's go do it!"

Out they went, down the hall, banging on hotel room doors.

"Get out here!" Ikola ordered the still half-asleep boys dressed only in their underwear and T-shirts.

Ikola and Zins were military men. Ikola had served under Zins in the US Air Force Reserve and brought more than a little of that if-you-are-not-early-you-are-late mentality to coaching.

"The rule was, when I stepped on the bus, we started moving," Ikola said. "We weren't going to wait for anyone who was late."

Ikola was in California finishing out his commitment to the air force when Edina's coaching job opened late in the fall of 1958. Ikola already had turned down multiple offers from Cal Marvin, his coach on the 1958 US national team, to coach Warroad's high school team. Then Edina came calling, and the twenty-six-year-old Ikola took the job without so much as an interview.

The Hornets went 4–9–5 in Ikola's first season. It would be the only losing season in his thirty-three-year head coaching career.

Ikola had the Hornets in the state tournament by year two, but they were hardly ready for prime time. Despite the repeated disappointments at state, however, Ikola saw championship potential. A group of skilled sophomores—led by forwards

Bobby Krieger and Bruce Carlson and defensemen Bill Nyrop and Steve Curry—ranked among the best players Edina had produced. Throw in juniors such as forward Rick Fretland, defensemen Jim Knutson and Skip Thomas, and goaltender Doug Hastings, and Ikola believed the Hornets boasted championship-level talent.

Now those players were sticking their heads into the hallway, listening to their coach tell them, in no uncertain terms, they were done with "this consolation crap."

"I remember the words 'pissed off' being said a lot," Carlson said. "We had never seen Ikola like that before. We were a little bit scared."

The first twenty-four state high school hockey tournaments were held at the St. Paul Auditorium, an obvious choice for the fledgling event given the size of the arena (it held more than eight thousand spectators for hockey games) and its location in the heart of hockey-crazed St. Paul's downtown.

But the growing popularity of the tournament and the increasingly noticeable dinginess and lack of amenities in the arena had made it clear it was time to move on to a newer, larger venue.

The Metropolitan Sports Center in Bloomington, home of the Minnesota North Stars NHL franchise, became host of the event starting in 1969.

The Met was completed in 1967 at a cost of $6 million. It held 14,400 for hockey games, offered abundant parking, and was dubbed in promotional materials as "hockey's best arena." With the biggest and best arena Minnesota had ever seen set to host the state tournament, all that was needed were players and teams worthy of the grand stage.

Edina, laser focused since Ikola's late-night tirade, assembled a season stunning in its dominance. Thirteen shutouts in twenty regular-season games. Twelve wins by five or more goals. The only setback was a 3–1 loss to Minneapolis Southwest late in the regular season.

Edina, 19–1, won its three regional playoff games by scores of 7–2, 7–1, and 7–0. The Hornets were looking square in the eye of their first-round state tournament hex. Another quarterfinal loss, they were sure, would ignite the wrath of their normally good-natured coach.

Warroad lost 2–1 to Roseau in the 1969 Region 8 championship game, but Boucha still had one last opportunity to shed the tag of "Greatest Player Never to Have Appeared in the State Tournament."

Eveleth, which had lost to Greenway 3–2 in the Region 7 championship game, was the Warriors' opponent in the "backdoor" game played at the Hibbing Memorial Building for the vacant Region 3 title.

The overflow crowd arrived early, and the back-and-forth game didn't disappoint. With the scored tied at two early in the third, Boucha was making one of his trademark spin moves when the stick of a flailing Eveleth defender clipped him above

Speedy junior forward Bobby Krieger was one of Edina's top scorers in 1969, although he was held without a point during his team's overtime victory in the 1969 championship game against Warroad. Photo courtesy of the Minnesota Historical Society

his right eye. Blood from the gash spilled down Boucha's face, stained his jersey, and pooled onto the ice.

The bleeding had to be stopped or Boucha was done for the night. In a stroke of good fortune, Ben Owens, longtime physician for all of Hibbing's high school teams and known around town simply as Dr. Ben, was there to assist. He deftly butterflied Boucha's cut, then covered his handiwork with wide strips of tape.

While Boucha was being taped back together, Warroad coach Dick Roberts emptied his bag of tricks. He called forward Mike Marvin, who had scored earlier in the game, over for a conversation at the bench.

"What is the matter, Coach?" Marvin asked.

"Nothing is the matter. Just stall for time," Roberts said. "I want to get Henry out here."

Officials restarted the game just as Boucha emerged up the ramp to Warroad's bench.

The game extended into an eight-minute overtime period. Then another. A third overtime seemed imminent when, with the clock winding down, Warroad winger Frank Krahn whipped a pass from behind the net to an open Boucha at the point. Krahn yelled, "Shoot!" Boucha obliged.

From twenty-five feet out, the thigh-high shot eluded Eveleth goaltender Ralph Koiber. An instant after the puck hit the back of the net, the clock hit zero.

LEFT: Warroad's Henry Boucha (right) goes low as he wheels around Roseau defenseman Tim Lillo during a 1969 semifinal at the Met Sports Center in Bloomington. Warroad beat Roseau 3–2, with Boucha scoring the winning goal. Photo by the *Minneapolis Tribune,* courtesy of the Minnesota Historical Society

BELOW: Edina defenseman Jim Knutson (left) battles for the puck with Warroad's Henry Boucha during the 1969 state championship game. A hard hit by Knutson in the second period ruptured Boucha's eardrum, forcing him to leave the game. Photo by the *Minneapolis Tribune,* courtesy of the Minnesota Historical Society

"We were all standing there in suspense," Boucha said. "We didn't know if the goal counted."

The goal light had turned red an instant before the clock struck zero. It counted. The partisan Warroad crowd went bonkers with joy, spilling onto the ice and mobbing Warriors players.

Boucha, having further cemented his legend with his gladiator-like return and most dramatic of goals, described the feeling as having "just jumped out of an airplane and sky-dived down to earth."

After five long years on the varsity, and numerous close calls—on and off the ice—Boucha and the Warriors were finally headed to state.

The atmosphere was electric in the shiny new Met Center. The largest crowd ever to see a state championship hockey game, more than fifteen thousand, buzzed in anticipation of tiny Warroad's showdown with metro behemoth Edina.

The Hornets weren't yet a hockey powerhouse, but they had won state basketball championships in 1966, '67, and '68. In addition, Edina had been named the mythical state football champion in 1965 and '66, and the school had won a state baseball championship in 1968. The Hornets, seemingly, were championship caliber in everything.

"We were the big school everybody loved to play and beat," Knutson said.

Edina crushed Mounds View 5–0 and South St. Paul 7–1 to reach the title game. Warroad, meanwhile, slipped past Minneapolis Southwest 4–3 and Roseau 3–2. The Warriors, even with the great Boucha rarely leaving the ice, were the underdog. Yet another reason for the overwhelming crowd support.

Among the sliver of fans cheering for Edina was Knutson's older brother, Dave, who was in the service and headed to Vietnam by way of Fort Sam Houston in San Antonio. Dave was more than a brother to Jim. He was a friend, mentor, and, when it came to hockey, Jim's biggest fan.

During warmups, Knutson was called over to the penalty box. Unsure of what was happening, he was stunned when game officials pointed to the stands. There was Dave, smiling and waving.

"Nyrop's father ran Northwest airlines, and somehow they were able to get him to the game," Knutson said.

Another surprise came during the announcement of the starting lineups. Boucha, who wore number 16 and was the second-to-last player listed on the Warriors' roster, was announced *after* his younger brother Ed, who was dressed as the backup goaltender and wore number 17. Henry, who launched fans onto their feet every time he touched the puck, got a deafening ovation.

"I thought they had forgotten me, I really did," Boucha said. "I was shaking because I was so surprised at the reaction of the crowd."

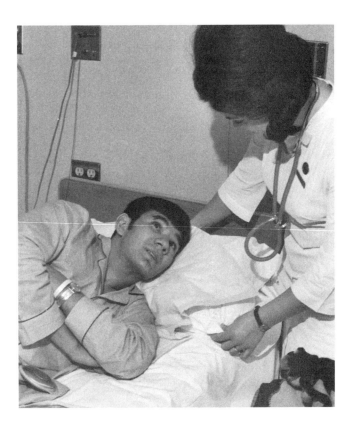

Warroad star Henry Boucha at Ramsey County Hospital after suffering a ruptured eardrum during the 1969 championship game. Photo by the *St. Paul Pioneer Press,* courtesy of the Minnesota Historical Society

Edina scoring twenty-two seconds into the first period on a Rick Fretland breakaway, Warroad rallying for a 2–1 lead by the end of the first, Edina storming ahead 3–2 with two early goals in the second—all of the game's early highlights and wild momentum shifts were reduced to mere afterthoughts when Knutson and Boucha collided against the boards in the most infamous body check in state hockey history.

Boucha, on a rush late in the second period, fired a shot on goal that Hastings steered toward the right corner. Boucha chased after the rebound, arriving at the puck a split second before Knutson.

Knutson delivered a high, hard hit. The side of Boucha's head slammed off the Plexiglas, and the Warroad star slumped to the ice.

Boucha was still lying on the ice when Knutson, called for elbowing, headed to the penalty box. Boucha was helped up from the ice but was unable to regain his equilibrium—the ice was permanently tilted.

"I'm done," he told Roberts before he was taken to the Met Center's training room for examination. The Warroad coach slammed his fist on top of the boards in disgust and was crying between the second and third periods when interviewed by reporters.

Was the hit dirty? A photo taken by an amateur photographer in the stands at the opposite end of the rink shows Knutson's elbow at the level of Boucha's ear, but the Warroad star was already sagging toward the ice. By all accounts, there was no calculated attempt to injure.

Rick Fretland (9) was among the first to mob goaltender Doug Hastings (1) after Edina beat Warroad 5–4 in overtime to win the 1969 state championship. Photo by the *St. Paul Pioneer Press,* courtesy of the Minnesota Historical Society

"His elbow was high, you can see it in the photo," Boucha said. "But I don't think he was trying to knock me out of the game."

"You are always going to try your hardest against the other team's number-one player," Knutson said.

Boucha was taken to Ramsey County Hospital with a ruptured eardrum. Roseau radio announcer Bernie Burggraf broadcasted that Boucha had *died,* sending the few families left listening back home in Warroad into hysterics. Burggraf quickly amended that call with information that Boucha was, indeed, still alive and at the hospital.

Meanwhile, the Met Center crowd, whipped into even more of a frenzy, aimed its vitriol at Knutson. The boos thundered every time he touched the puck.

Edina took a 4–2 lead late in the second on a Tim McGlynn goal, eliciting more jeers. All signs indicated Warroad, like Boucha, was done.

But then, junior wing Frank Krahn brought Warroad back to life, scoring twenty-one seconds after McGlynn and then again with 1:19 left in the second to tie it at four.

Warroad outshot Edina 11–9 in a scoreless third, but the Hornets prevailed 5–4 in overtime on a shot through traffic from the point from senior defenseman Skip Thomas. The Hornets celebrated wildly, ignoring the crowd's deafening dissatisfaction with the outcome. An exhausted Krieger handed the championship trophy to Ikola like a weary retriever dropping a pheasant at a hunter's feet.

The crowd's viciousness drained some of the joy from Knutson.

"I didn't mind the fans booing at me during the game," Knutson said. "I kind of understood that. But when they announced my name for the all-tournament team and they still booed me, I remember that really upset me."

Boucha learned of the game's outcome from his mother late that night after being examined and escorted to his hospital room. "She said, 'The boys lost in overtime,'" Boucha said.

He spent the next four days in the hospital, where he underwent surgery on his ear and received flowers, stacks of get-well cards, boxes of chocolates, and various other gifts from fans wishing their best.

Among the hordes of visitors were Knutson and his father. There were no hard feelings.

In contrast to that summer night when he had raced out of Roseau and slipped quietly into Warroad, praying to avoid attention, Boucha was flown home in a private plane and met with a hero's reception. The loss to Edina, the injury—all the disappointment washed away as the high school band played and what seemed like the entire town offered smiles and support, handshakes and hugs.

"It was a glorious time for Warroad hockey," Boucha wrote in his autobiography.

~*LRN*~

BAG OF RAGS

Henry Boucha's jersey cut to shreds by souvenir seekers during hospital stay

The black-and-gold number 16 Warroad jersey, what remained of it, sat on a table next to Henry Boucha's hospital bed. Reduced to a heap of ribbons, it was collateral damage from the infamous and devastating hit that felled the Warriors' superstar defenseman in the 1969 state championship game.

Boucha suffered a ruptured left eardrum as a result of Edina defenseman Jim Knutson's high and hard second-period check along the boards and was rushed to Ramsey County Hospital. Boucha's bloodstained jersey and equipment were sliced off his torso and tossed aside as emergency room staff attended to him.

The jersey was brought to Boucha's room, where it attracted souvenir hunters—doctors and nurses among them—like bees to nectar.

"They were cutting off little pieces of it to take home as mementos, I guess," said Boucha, who, as the darling of the tournament, launched fans onto their feet and touched off sonic-boom roars every time he touched the puck.

The swatch-cutting escalated to something more when someone cut away and pocketed the jersey's crest.

"I never found out who took that," Boucha said.

A steady stream of people had come to visit him, including newspaper reporters and opposing players and their parents. Knutson and his father were among the well-wishers. After spending four days in the hospital, the last three recovering from surgery to repair his eardrum, Boucha and his

Henry Boucha stands next to the Warroad jersey he wore in the 1969 tournament. The jersey, reduced to rags during Boucha's hospital stay, was reconstructed decades later using matching materials. Photo by L. R. Nelson/Legacy.Hockey

mother left the hospital with the jersey, such as it was, in tow.

"They put what was left of it in a bag and handed it to us," Boucha said. "Basically, it was just a sack of rags."

For the next four decades, Boucha never gave his old jersey much thought. He stashed it in a storage shed in Warroad after he retired from hockey, leaving it there as he bounced from town to town and job to job.

A chance mid-2000s meeting between Boucha and memorabilia collector John Lindberg at the state tournament was step one in bringing the jersey back to life. Boucha was at the Xcel Energy Center selling copies of his autobiography when Lindberg stopped to chat. The two had never met.

"I said, 'You wouldn't happen to know where your high school jersey

is?'" Lindberg said. "My jaw must have hit the floor when he told me he had it."

Lindberg is a native of Kennedy, Minnesota, a town of fewer than two hundred people that sits eighty-three miles due west of Warroad. Lindberg and Boucha made plans to meet in Warroad and inspect the jersey.

"It turns out it was in one of those little sheds you put out in your yard to put a lawnmower in," Lindberg said. "It was in one of those green Rubbermaid totes."

The jersey was in the same condition as it had been when Boucha left the hospital all those years ago.

"I thought it was a rug," Lindberg said.

About a month after their meeting, "[Lindberg] called me and said he couldn't sleep because he wanted that jersey so bad," Boucha said. "So I ended up selling it to him."

Lindberg spent years scouring the internet for a replacement crest and matching black and gold materials. He enlisted seamstress Peggy Jackson to reconstruct the jersey, a process that took months.

"She did every stitch by hand," said Lindberg, who agreed to loan the jersey to a museum in Warroad. Boucha also has access to the jersey for appearances and other special events.

The reconstructed jersey, with all its unique and bizarre history, is one of the state tournament's great enduring artifacts. A piece of history Lindberg isn't interested in parting with.

Besides, he said with a laugh, "I don't know that there is anyone that wants to pay me a king's ransom to own it."

~LRN~

BATTLE OF 50TH AND FRANCE

MINNEAPOLIS SOUTHWEST PREVAILED IN SHOWDOWN WITH BORDER RIVAL EDINA

DATES	LOCATION	ATTENDANCE	CHAMPIONSHIP
MARCH 5–7	METROPOLITAN SPORTS CENTER, BLOOMINGTON	83,625	MINNEAPOLIS SOUTHWEST 1, EDINA 0 (OT)

Did you know? Eight teams have been shut out in the tournament, including White Bear Lake in 1970. The Bears also are the only team to have been shut out in multiple tournaments, having also gone scoreless in 1951.

TELEVISION CAMERAS were rolling when a microphone was shoved in a giddy Bill Shaw's face.

The Minneapolis Southwest junior had just extracted himself from the bottom of a mound of jubilant teammates, and now inquiring minds wanted to know.

How did you score the winning goal?

Shaw was speechless. He had nothing to say to the reporter and a regional audience numbering in the hundreds of thousands. Not a single word.

Ask Shaw the same question today, about how, exactly, he ended one of the most dramatic games and historic state tournaments in the event's eight-plus decades, and he offers only a slightly more effusive response.

"I don't know," he says.

The 1970 state tournament set records for most overtime games (six) and overtime periods (twelve). St. Paul Johnson goaltender Doug Long made sixty-one saves, a single-game record that stood for twenty-six years, in a five-overtime quarterfinal victory over Greenway. Long was brilliant again the following night in the semifinals, making fifty-two stops as the Governors fell 2–1 in three overtimes to undefeated Edina and superstar forwards Bobby Krieger and Bruce Carlson.

While Long, Krieger (who scored in double overtime in the quarterfinals against Warroad), Carlson (author of the OT winner against Johnson), and the drama-soaked run of overtime games were fixtures in the headlines and highlight reels, Shaw and fellow third-liners Tom Mitchell and Julian "Jay" Idzorek were dangerously close to being glued to Southwest's bench. The undefeated Indians were set on playing just two lines in the tournament, a strategy that had served them well throughout the regional playoffs.

But crisis has a way of trashing even the most meticulous plans. Southwest trailed North St. Paul by three goals entering the third period of the teams' quarterfinal matchup, and Indians assistant coach Larry Larson convinced head coach Dave Peterson to start deploying the third line. The change awakened the offense, which erupted for four unanswered goals (the final three from senior Paul Miller) in the 4–3 overtime victory.

"We decided if we were going down, we'd play everyone in uniform," Peterson said. "I'm thankful we did."

With standout senior goaltender Brad Shelstad back in top form after an admittedly shaky performance against North St. Paul, and Peterson now set on rotating all three forward lines, Southwest cruised past Hibbing 3–1 in the semifinals.

Southwest's title game matchup against Edina only heightened the tournament's drama. Southwest was 23–0–1, Edina 24–0–1, and undefeated teams had met for the championship just once previously (and never since), when Eveleth (10–0) beat Thief River Falls (12–0–1) for the 1945 title. It was also just the second time a northern school was excluded from the championship.

The showdown was billed in one banner newspaper headline as "50th & France—State Title Crossroad," a nod to the intersection that served as the boundary between the neighboring school districts. Battle lines were crossed. Southwest students hung out daily at the Red Barn restaurant on the Edina side; Indians fans successfully lobbied a gas station in enemy territory to remove its pro-Hornets banner.

Junior Bill Shaw, a member of Minneapolis Southwest's third line, was an unlikely hero, leading his team to its first and, to date, only state title in 1970. Photo by the *Minneapolis Tribune*, courtesy of the Minnesota Historical Society

The biggest point of contention, however, came from Edina coach Willard Ikola dropping Southwest from his schedule. The Indians had defeated the Hornets in their lone meeting each of the previous two seasons, but Southwest had graduated its best two forward lines and top two defensemen from its 1969 state tournament squad. In search of stiffer competition, Ikola swapped Southwest out for Minneapolis Roosevelt.

"Peterson made sure we knew that, too," John Taft, a Southwest sophomore defenseman in 1970, said about the perceived slight, which was used as a rallying point.

Video footage from the 1970 championship never has been available for widespread public consumption (Shelstad calls them the Lost Tapes). Yet Shelstad's showdown with Krieger in the closing seconds of the third period of a 0–0 tie has been described in meticulous detail over the years.

"One of our defensemen, who shall remain nameless at this point, I think fell over or something at the left point," Shelstad said in a Fox Sports North documentary on the tournament.

Taft, who would go on to play for the 1976 US Olympic team and in the NHL for the Detroit Red Wings, fesses up as being *that* defenseman.

"I remember it because I was like a cone at the blue line," Taft said. "Krieger just blew by me."

As Krieger raced in and cut through the crease, Shelstad uncharacteristically flopped to the ice and stacked his pads. Krieger, knowing the buzzer signaling the end of the period was about to sound, couldn't lift the puck high enough to get it over the outstretched goaltender.

"I rushed it a little bit and didn't create enough space to lift it over his pads," Krieger said.

Carlson swooped in for the rebound.

"The puck came off Shelstad fluttering like a gyroscope," Carlson said. "The corner was pretty wide open, and I just kind of slapped at it just before the period ended."

Carlson's shot sailed wide right. The game remained scoreless.

Shaw, in just his third year of organized hockey and wearing skates Peterson had purchased for him, might have been the most unlikely player on either roster to score the winning goal. But there he was, stationed in front of the net, when workhorse Southwest defenseman Bob Lundeen took a pass from Idzorek and uncorked a shot from the point.

"The puck came rolling out toward me, and all I wanted to do was put it back into the zone," said Lundeen, who would also play in the 1976 Olympics. "I shot the puck and kind of lost track of it."

What happened next remains one of the tournament's great mysteries.

Written accounts describe Lundeen's shot going off Shaw's stick, chest, or upper torso and into the net for a 1–0 victory, the only championship won by a Minneapolis public school.

How did you score the winning goal?

Shaw wanted answers, too.

"Bobby had one hell of a shot, so the next day I looked for bruises on my chest," Shaw said. "I couldn't find any."

~LRN~

Minneapolis Southwest's Bill Shaw (9) deflects the winning goal past Edina goaltender Larry Thayer in overtime as the Indians win the 1970 state championship and complete a 24-0-1 record on the season. Photo by the *Minneapolis Tribune,* courtesy of the Minnesota Historical Society

LONG ON TALENT

Pint-sized goaltender Doug Long had tournament for the ages in 1970

Lou Cotroneo, St. Paul Johnson coach from 1963 to 1974, had laid down four rules for his varsity hockey players: I want to see you in school. I want to see you in church. I want to see you in a barbershop. I want to see you in my office with your report card — Cs or better.

No one was exempt. Not even promising sophomore goalie Doug Long. On the Friday before Monday tryouts, Cotroneo sought Long and found him, shoulder-length hair and all, in the school library.

"He was reading a damn comic book," Cotroneo said. "I gave him the rules early and told him, 'I'd appreciate it if you got a haircut before Monday.'"

Early Monday morning, Cotroneo heard a knock on his office door, looked over, and initially failed to recognize the freshly shorn Long.

"I said, 'Dougie, I think this is gonna be a good relationship,'" Cotroneo said. "After that, I called him Yul Brynner."

The Governors' leading man in goal for three seasons stood about 5 foot 5 but loomed much larger throughout his tournament for the ages as a junior in 1970.

In the quarterfinals, his sixty-one saves sparked a five-overtime upset of Greenway. The record stood twenty-six years.

"He was on, you could tell," said Jim Hoey, a senior wing for Greenway. "You couldn't just throw the puck on net. A lot of our shots started missing the net because we were trying to be too fine. It gets in the back of your head when someone has your number."

"Tom Peluso had a great snapshot," Hoey said. "Doug stopped him two or three times on breakaways. For him to play just as well if not better the next night was incredible."

Long shined in the semifinals against undefeated Edina, stopping fifty-two shots in a three-overtime loss.

"Later, I got mail from some Edina girls who told me I shouldn't feel bad," Long said.

Long, who played Ping-Pong to sharpen his hand-eye coordination, said, "I was really sharp that tournament. If you can square up to 'em, you can stop 'em."

A standing ovation greeted Long when Cotroneo pulled him in the second period of the third-place game against Hibbing. The Governors trailed 3–1 at the time, and Cotroneo said he wanted to give his busy goaltender "a well-deserved rest." Long left with 124 saves, a tournament record that stood forty-nine years.

"You talk about a kid who paid the price every day he was on the ice," Cotroneo said.

About two decades later, Hoey bumped into Peluso as they waited in line to enter the St. Paul Civic Center for a Thursday state tournament quarterfinal game. They shared tournament memories with a fellow hockey fan, and the conversation turned to 1970.

The tournament was a testament to great goaltending. But only one name came up.

"This guy says, 'Remember Doug Long?'" Hoey said. "It's one of the most memorable performances in state tournament history."

~DL~

When not making spectacular save after spectacular save, St. Paul Johnson goaltender Doug Long, an all-tournament pick in 1970 and 1971, roamed well outside his crease to play the puck. He made a record 124 saves in the 1970 tournament despite playing only half of the Governors' third game. Photo by the *Minneapolis Tribune,* courtesy of the Minnesota Historical Society

PROMISES, PROMISES

EDINA'S UNASSUMING TIM CARLSON BROKE CHARACTER WITH OUTLANDISH ASSURANCE

DATES	LOCATION	ATTENDANCE	CHAMPIONSHIP
MARCH 11–13	METROPOLITAN SPORTS CENTER, BLOOMINGTON	79,362	EDINA 1, ROSEAU 0

 Hastings, making its first tourney appearance, was led by 6-foot-4 Dean Talafous, who would play eight NHL seasons with the Atlanta Flames, Minnesota North Stars, and New York Islanders. Talafous had two goals and three assists to lead the Raiders to the consolation title.

TIM CARLSON planted the seeds of his Joe Namath moment in the devastating aftermath of the 1970 state championship game.

Previously unbeaten Edina had just suffered a crushing 1–0 overtime loss to Minneapolis Southwest, and Carlson was about to leave the bench area when he caught a glimpse of dejected coach Willard Ikola. The junior forward agonized for the man who had offered so much support, understanding, and encouragement a month earlier when Carlson's mother died suddenly from a brain aneurysm.

"He was just standing there by himself, and I went up to him and said, 'Don't worry, Coach. We'll win it next year,'" Carlson recalled. "What else can you say?"

Carlson spent his first two seasons as a varsity player toiling in the shadow of his older brother Bruce, a star forward who played alongside Bobby Krieger, the legendary speedster and scoring phenom who was the poster boy of Edina's emergence as a state superpower.

Bruce Carlson and Krieger had been among the twelve seniors on Edina's 1970 state tournament team, a group that led the Hornets to the 1969 state championship (the first in school history) and was unquestionably the best single class of players the program had produced. Included was Bill Nyrop, a defenseman who would win three consecutive Stanley Cup titles with the Montreal Canadiens.

It stood to reason that if the Hornets couldn't win a title with that star-filled, senior-laden team in 1970, there was no chance they would do so the following season with just five returning players. Ikola shrugged off Tim Carlson's postgame promise as nothing more than a heartfelt pick-me-up from the typically quiet and unassuming kid.

A few days later, the Hornets held their postseason banquet. Per tradition, the player who had been voted the next season's captain, in this instance Carlson, was required to stand up and say a few words. Reminiscent of Joe Namath, the cocky New York Jets quarterback who in 1969 had made a bold banquet boast that his afterthought of a team would upend the heavily favored Baltimore Colts in Super Bowl III, Carlson told the crowd, "We didn't win it this year, but we're going to next year."

Carlson's words created a buzz in the room, most of it generated by the snickering of players and parents.

"He went back to his seat, and he is all red," Ikola said. "He puts his chin down, acting like, 'What did I say?' So I go up to him and say, 'Now Timmy, you said it, let's go do it.'"

On a wall just outside the sauna in Ikola's basement was a board he used as an oversized depth chart. Players' names were written on pieces of paper and tacked in groups by their projected positions. Ikola removed names and added new ones immediately after the completion of a season, fussing and tinkering with the forward and defense combinations like a mad scientist. In later years, Ikola would sometimes have his team set long before tryouts.

In spring 1970, he stared at a mostly blank piece of plywood.

"At least we had all summer to figure it out," he said.

Edina's Braemar Arena was built in 1965, at a time when there were about fifty kids in the youth program. The Hornets were decent, but not great. They had negligible state tournament success (seven quarterfinal losses in as many appearances) before their 1969 breakthrough.

"We had a tough time competing with the northern teams," Ikola said. "But once we got that inside ice, then our youth teams got inside ice. Then we became a three-line team."

Numbers in Edina's youth program skyrocketed into the hundreds by the early 1970s, and teams at every level regularly competed for state and even national championships. Ikola mined players for his 1970–71 squad from this stream of talent.

Senior first-line forward Bill Broback came from a program called Juveniles, a precursor to today's Junior Gold programs. Senior Rick Cabalka, another first-line wing, was one of several players who the previous season had played Midgets, a now-defunct level that was for high schoolers who had aged out of Bantams. The junior varsity supplied another handful of promising but unproven players.

"It was pretty slim pickings," said Todd Nieland, a junior defenseman who had played on the varsity the previous season. "Or so it seemed, right?"

Added Broback: "We were a bunch of guys who weren't supposed to win anything."

Edina players celebrate a 4–3 overtime victory in a 1971 quarterfinal as the puck sits in the net behind Minneapolis Southwest goaltender Mike Dibble.
Photo by the *Minneapolis Tribune,* courtesy of the Minnesota Historical Society

Edina lost its opener 5–3 to Duluth East. Six straight wins later, the Hornets fell to International Falls 5–4. Ikola was pleasantly surprised his group of no-namers had given the perennial powerhouse Broncos all they could handle. Even in defeat, he thought to himself, "Maybe I have something here after all."

The Hornets didn't lose again in the regular season and won four sectional playoff games by a combined score of 26–3. They earned a state tournament rematch with Minneapolis Southwest, winning the quarterfinal 4–3 in overtime. Dave Ottness, one of four sophomores who played key roles, scored in the third period. Junior Steve Eichorn notched the winner in overtime.

All three lines scored in a 4–2 semifinal victory over St. Paul Johnson and goaltender Doug Long, the darling of the previous year's tournament.

Junior Rick Wineberg, a spare forward Ikola sent out as part of a makeshift fourth line, scored the lone goal late in the third period, and junior goaltender Dave Bremer made nineteen saves in Edina's 1–0 championship triumph over Roseau.

"We had depth, and I think more than anything, that's what won it for us," Broback said.

Carlson came dangerously close to sabotaging the victory, and his prophetic "We'll win it next year" promise, when he took an elbowing penalty with 1:26 remaining.

"I remember after the game a radio reporter came up to me on the ice as we were celebrating," Carlson said. "He said, 'Carlson, what the hell were you thinking about while you were sitting in the box?' I said, 'All I can tell you is prayers can be answered.'"

And predictions, no matter how outlandish they might seem, can come true.

~LRN~

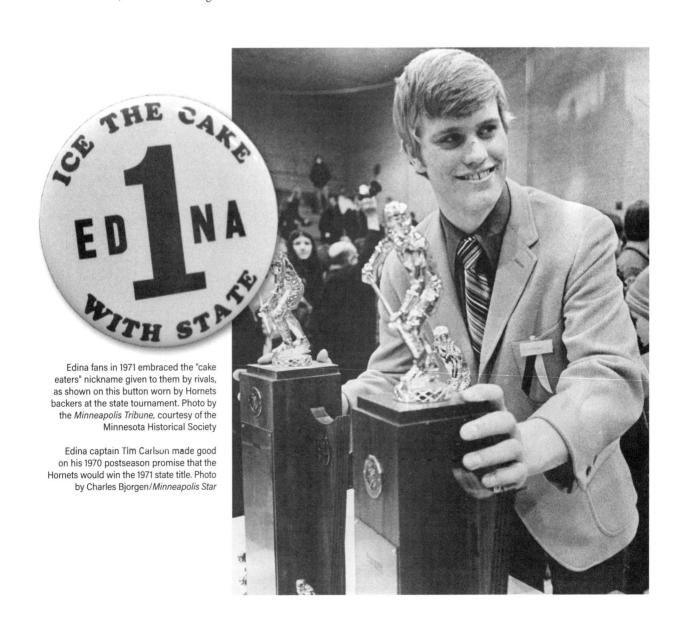

Edina fans in 1971 embraced the "cake eaters" nickname given to them by rivals, as shown on this button worn by Hornets backers at the state tournament. Photo by the *Minneapolis Tribune,* courtesy of the Minnesota Historical Society

Edina captain Tim Carlson made good on his 1970 postseason promise that the Hornets would win the 1971 state title. Photo by Charles Bjorgen/*Minneapolis Star*

LIVING THE DREAM

TROPHY PRESENTATION MATCHED JIM KNAPP'S PREMONITION DOWN TO LAST DETAIL

DATES	LOCATION	ATTENDANCE	CHAMPIONSHIP
MARCH 9–11	METROPOLITAN SPORTS CENTER	82,300	INTERNATIONAL FALLS 3, GRAND RAPIDS 2

Did you know? Northern hockey havens Bemidji and Grand Rapids each made their first tournament appearance in 1972.

OUT CAME THE cloth-covered table—and with it, two trophies.

Two men wearing blazers, one of them holding a microphone, strolled onto the ice. The runner-up team was announced, and its captains led the slow, somber procession to the table and the smaller of the two trophies. The handoff was made, and the players, moving as if their skates were stuck in cement, trudged away with hardware in hand, just as dejected as when they had arrived.

The master of ceremonies appeared in no hurry to complete his job. As the anticipation amped up, so did the electricity. The still-packed arena might as well have been a powder keg.

"And now, the captains from the championship team from International Falls, please come forward and accept your trophy!"

The crowd roared. Jim Knapp was skating on air as he reached center ice, fellow senior captain Craig Dahl at his side. Their teammates, bursting with excitement, trailed behind. The trophy, heavy with its large, box-like wooden base and shiny, solid metal hockey player perched atop, was raised off the table, and . . .

"Jimmy, wake up! Time to get ready for school!"

Knapp's eyelids, as heavy as manhole covers, cracked open. He eased his head off the pillow and swung his feet toward the floor. His recurring dream, in all its wonderful Technicolor detail, was put on hold for another day.

As a kid growing up in International Falls, Knapp had watched in awe as the Broncos won four state championships in the 1960s. He'd seen the processions of police cars and fire trucks escort the winning teams back to the border town, fans lining the streets as if it were the Fourth of July, not still-frigid late February.

Knapp had also gotten a taste of the state tournament in 1971, when the Broncos finished third. Now he wanted the full experience, right down to the moment that championship trophy was plopped into his hands. He was so sure the Broncos would turn that nightly dream into reality he brokered a decidedly brash deal with Dahl.

"I wanted to work it out before the season," Knapp said. "I told Craig, 'When they hand out the region championship tro-phy, you are going to accept it. Then, when we get the state championship trophy, I am going to take it.'"

Dahl accepted. Confidence was not a problem for the two Broncos who wore armbands emblazoned with the letter C.

"We felt like, with the talent we had, we should win every game," Dahl said.

Knapp led a group of four 6-foot-plus, hard-hitting heavyweight defensemen, all of whom were fleet skaters able to rush the puck on a whim. All four went on to play at the Division I level in college, with Knapp (Minnesota Duluth) and Paul Green (St. Louis University) as the senior veterans joined by junior Jim Lundquist (Brown) and burly sophomore Cal Sandbeck (Denver).

With the lightning-quick junior Peter Waselovich, a future North Dakota star, in goal, the Broncos were as loaded defensively as any team in the state.

The sharpshooting Dahl and smooth-skating junior David Brown led the offense. Forechecking demon Al Karsnia joined them on the top line. Sophomore Paul Brown, David's younger brother, teamed with senior Jim Jorgenson and junior Buzzy LaFond on a unit that had a knack for scoring at opportune moments.

All that talent was required to compete at the level of Grand Rapids, which beat International Falls for state Pee Wee and Bantam championships and then, as high schoolers, fired another shot across the Broncos' bow with a 5–4 triumph in the 1971–72 season opener.

International Falls returned the favor by pounding the Indians 5–1 in the Region 7 title game. As he and Knapp had agreed upon, Dahl accepted the regional championship trophy on behalf of the team.

Energized by having vanquished their old rival so decisively, the Broncos eased past Bemidji 8–3 in the state quarterfinals on the strength of a Dahl hat trick.

Jorgenson couldn't believe it when, in overtime in the semifinals against Minneapolis Southwest, he saw two defenders charging at him behind the Southwest net. That left Paul Brown all alone in front. Jorgenson's quick pass and Brown's laser shot gave the Broncos a 2–1 victory.

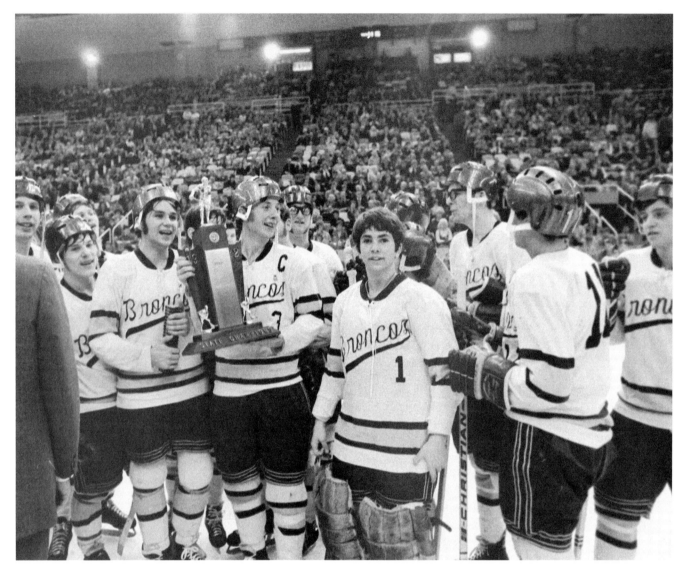

The 1972 championship ceremony played out just as International Falls' Jim Knapp had dreamed so many times: with Knapp (center) holding the championship trophy and fellow Broncos captain Craig Dahl (to his right) at his side. Photo by the *Minneapolis Tribune,* courtesy of the Minnesota Historical Society

"Upper corner," Jorgenson said about Brown's goal. "He could always score."

Grand Rapids awaited in the title game. The Indians had reached their first state tournament by the backdoor, beating Region 8 runner-up East Grand Forks for the vacant Region 3 title.

The Indians appeared poised to beat the Broncos for yet another championship, as they led 1–0 heading into the third. Exactly what was said in the Broncos' locker room, and by whom, before the final period is up for debate, although one newspaper account credited Waselovich for a dose of inspiration: "If anybody here doesn't want to go out on the ice in the third period and give out 100 percent, I'd suggest they take their skates off and quit for the night."

Added Dahl: "All I can remember is that, as that was being said, Al Karsnia happened to be reaching down to tighten his skates. We all thought for a second he was taking them off."

The Broncos hit the ice for the third period looking like a loose, rejuvenated team and immediately went on the attack. A rising backhander by David Brown at 2:40 of the period tied the score at one. Just more than two minutes later, Paul Brown put the Broncos ahead 2–1. Dahl wheeled and fired a low shot into the net with 4:15 remaining to give International Falls a 3–1 cushion.

A Grand Rapids goal in the final minute made for a frantic finish.

The postgame ceremonies played out just as Knapp had dreamed, right down to the part where he was handed the trophy and raised it high in the air. Except this time there was no wake-up call.

"Oh, boy," Knapp said. "I had done it so many times in my dreams, it was déjà vu."

~LRN~

"POPS" KNOWS BEST

International Falls coach Larry Ross was father figure to talent-laden Broncos

Larry Ross was a high school social studies teacher, with emphasis on the word *social*.

Ross, who also served as International Falls' hockey coach, delighted in beckoning his players from their classes for one-on-one chats about the importance of heart and desire or the mindset needed to beat an upcoming foe.

"He would pull me right out of the classroom in the morning and tell me what I had to do in the game that night," said Dean Blais, who starred for the Broncos in the late 1960s. "You would spend all day thinking about what he had said. By game time, I was so ready to play I could have run through the locker-room door to get out on the ice."

A Duluth native and the son of a stonemason who built his family's brick home, Ross played goalie at Morgan Park High School. After graduating in 1940, he joined the navy, serving in World War II as a salvage diver and playing for the navy's hockey team. Ross was twenty-seven by the time he enrolled at the University of Minnesota, already a husband and the father of an infant son, Steve.

Prone to ulcer attacks, Ross was playing for the Gophers one night when a public address brought on heightened anxiety.

Would the parents of Steve Ross please claim their son? He has been turned in at the scorer's table.

Little Stevie, still in diapers and barely old enough to walk, had waddled from the bleachers to the concession stand area, becoming lost.

"Imagine what Larry thought!" a mortified Dorothy Ross, Larry's wife, said

in a *Minneapolis Tribune* article. "I was supposed to be watching after Stevie."

Larry, Dorothy, Stevie, and daughter Patty moved to International Falls in the summer of 1954, and soon after a high school hockey dynasty was born.

With Ross at the helm, the Broncos reached their first state championship game in 1956, won their first title in 1957, and appeared in five straight championship games starting in 1962 (winning three in a row from 1964 to 1966). Ross won his sixth and final state championship in 1972. Only former Edina and Edina East coach Willard Ikola has more, with eight.

"He was a people person," said Steve Waselovich, who played goal for three of Ross's state tournament teams, including the 1972 squad. "Everybody called him Pops. But you wouldn't call him that to his face. We had too much respect."

An avid golfer who carried a handicap of two, Ross was also the head coach for the Broncos' boys' golf team for thirty-three years. He started the men's ice hockey program at Rainy River Community College in 1968 and coached both the college and high school teams at the same time.

Ross, who presided over a remarkable run of fifty-nine straight victories from 1964 to 1966, was a master motivator with a knack for striking the right tone with his players. Take the time the Broncos were playing in Roseau and Ross made note of the rink's subpar lighting.

"He said, 'Boys, it's a pretty dark rink out there,'" said 1971–72 senior co-captain Craig Dahl. "And then he unscrewed every other light bulb in the ceiling and said, 'Are you ready?'"

"We just flew out the door. I think we beat them 5–1."

Ross finished with a 566–169–21 record in his thirty-one seasons leading the Broncos, helping produce dozens upon dozens of future college, Olympic, and professional standouts. Little Stevie grew up to be strapping defenseman Steve Ross, one of the Broncos' best players in their 1960s heyday.

Larry Ross was most proud of the relationships he forged with his players, sometimes at the expense of less meaningful endeavors, like schoolwork.

"He would just take me downtown to Riley's [Sporting Goods] and he'd pick out a couple of sticks for me and bring me back to school," said Dan Mahle, a senior forward in 1965–66. "It wasn't like we had any big conversation. He used to get me in trouble all the time with the other teachers."

Ross turned down head coaching job offers from Colorado College and the University of Wisconsin, adopted teenager Ron Beck into his family after both of the goaltender's parents died, and gave endless thanks to Doc Romnes, the Minnesota hockey coach who had convinced Ross to enroll at the school.

"Wisest move I ever made," Ross said.

The architect of a sprawling youth hockey system that was the envy of the state, he wrote a book, *Hockey for Everyone*, as a guide for young coaches.

Lawrence A. Ross died May 1, 1995, at his home in International Falls. Nobody loved the game of hockey more. And nobody, his players insist, coached it better.

~LRN~

THE GRADUATE

HIBBING'S DAVE HERBST PUT DIPLOMA IN JEOPARDY WITH HOCKEY HOOKY

DATES	LOCATION	ATTENDANCE	CHAMPIONSHIP
MARCH 8–10	METROPOLITAN SPORTS CENTER, BLOOMINGTON	84,039	HIBBING 6, ALEXANDER RAMSEY 3

 Alexander Ramsey goaltender Dave Tegenfeldt, whose father was a missionary, was born in Burma. He played soccer from age eight and first put on hockey skates in eighth grade.

HIBBING SENIOR Dave Herbst's school day ended at 2 PM, an hour before his peers, so he could participate in a work-study program as the manager of an A&W Root Beer stand.

Though the program ended when the A&W closed for the season in mid-September, Herbst kept exiting school early. Only instead of the root beer stand he headed for the Hib-

bing Memorial Building rink, where he shot pucks and worked toward his real desired job: pro hockey player.

Then one January afternoon, high school guidance director Elmer Salvog came to the rink and warned Herbst that this recently discovered abuse of privilege and the resulting school hours missed could prevent the young man from graduating.

Hibbing forward Dave Herbst (3) made good on a brash preseason boast to a teacher that the Bluejackets would win the state title. Herbst played a big role in a semifinal victory, scoring twice to get Hibbing out of a 2–0 hole against International Falls. Photo courtesy of the Minnesota Historical Society

Hibbing linemates George Perpich (10) and Joe Micheletti (7) took turns lighting up Alexander Ramsey in the 1973 championship game. Each scored twice in the third period as the Bluejackets pulled away for a 6–3 triumph. Micheletti netted a hat trick. Photo by John Croft/*Minneapolis Tribune*

Herbst replied, "I don't think that's going to happen. We're going to win the state championship and put Hibbing on the map."

Salvog "was not happy at all with that answer," Herbst said.

Flustering Herbst wasn't easy. Buried beneath a collapsing snow pile at age six, he needed to be revived by the fire-department rescue squad.

A handful of years later, a wayward puck gashed him above his right eye while he was tying his skates. Varsity hockey coach George Perpich happened to be at the Hibbing Memorial Building and took the bleeding Herbst to the doctor for stitches. His Saturday-morning hockey practice now ruined, Herbst returned to gather his equipment.

That's when Perpich made him forget all about the wound. "He brought me in the locker room and said, 'I've been

watching you play. You remind me of [Hibbing standout] Bob Collyard. Someday, you're going to play for me,'" Herbst said.

To local hockey enthusiasts, who had last seen Hibbing win a state title in 1952, Perpich promised, "We're going to win this thing with my boys someday."

The 1972–73 Bluejackets included two of the coach's sons: George Jr., a senior wing, and younger brother Jim, a sophomore defenseman. Other standouts were Herbst, senior defenseman Gary Samson, and senior goalie Tim Pogorels. Center Joe Micheletti was the star, a three-sport standout who did his best work in skates.

Hibbing started the season 14–0–2 and vaulted to the state's top ranking. Pogorels posted five shutouts in the Bluejackets' first six victories.

"You get to the point where you expect to win every night," Jim Perpich said.

Hibbing traveled to International Falls during the season and beat the defending state champions 5–3. But the Broncos dominated the Region 7 playoff rematch 8–3, the low point of Hibbing's season.

"We were embarrassed," Micheletti said. "But sometimes those things are good for you."

Humbled Hibbing routed Region 8 runner-up Roseau 9–2 to secure the state tournament's backdoor as Region 3 champion.

Hibbing opened with a 4–2 defeat of Bemidji. That meant a third meeting with International Falls. This time, Hibbing players felt ready.

They were loose.

They were confident.

And they were behind 2–0 to start.

Kevin Nagurski, whose father, Bronko, was a Minnesota football legend, scored his team's second goal. The elder Nagurski watched from home due to arthritis in his leg.

Fresh lumber helped Herbst draw the Bluejackets even. When his stick broke, Herbst borrowed one of Micheletti's spares and scored a first-period goal. During the first intermission, Herbst spent $10 on two new sticks from the Metropolitan Sports Center pro shop and used one to tie the game 2–2 in the second period.

Hibbing gained an advantage heading into the third period. Wary of his players wearing their heavy wool away jerseys inside the balmy Met Center, Falls coach Larry Ross requested a pregame coin flip with coach George Perpich Sr. for jersey selection. Perpich agreed—and won.

"In the third period, their jerseys looked like they'd been in a swimming pool," Jim Perpich said.

Hibbing cranked the heat with three consecutive goals in a little more than four minutes, one from Micheletti and two from George Perpich Jr.

International Falls cut Hibbing's lead to 5–4 with two late goals, but the Bluejackets prevailed.

Perpich Jr. told John Gilbert of the *Minneapolis Tribune*, "We wanted to get a shot at International Falls even more than we thought about winning any state championship. We had something to prove."

Hibbing would face Roseville-based Alexander Ramsey for the championship, giving coach George Perpich Sr. his first (and only) title shot. Born in Croatia, he arrived at age nine in Leetonia, then an unincorporated community just west of Hibbing. His first cousin, Rudy Perpich, later served as Minnesota's governor.

"Big George," a 260-pound offensive lineman, played for Georgetown's football team. He also played in the All-America Football Conference for a season each with the Brooklyn Dodgers and Baltimore Colts.

He returned to Hibbing in the fall of 1952 to coach football and then got the hockey job as well. He attended or coached at every state tournament thereafter, missing only 1955 because George Jr. was born on the evening of the February 26 championship game.

Now they had a chance to win a championship together.

Alexander Ramsey went ahead 2–1 early in the second period and then went on a power play, seemingly poised for an upset victory. Then Micheletti changed the game's complexion with an unassisted shorthanded goal.

"I saw that they tried to go up the middle on the breakout all game," Micheletti said. "They did it again, and I read it as well as I've ever read a play. I thought, 'Here it is.'"

In the third period, Hibbing erupted with three goals in a tournament-record twenty-three seconds. Micheletti led all tournament players with seven goals and eleven points.

With the 6–3 outcome almost decided, Herbst told his coach, "Take a look around. I think everyone in Hibbing is here watching us win."

Big George scanned the blue-and-white-clad fans and told Herbst, "I think you're right."

Back home for Sunday's victory celebration at the junior high, Herbst noticed Salvog coming his way.

"He put his arm around me and said, 'This is awesome,'" Herbst said.

"I said, 'Elmer, am I going to graduate?'"

"He said, 'You're graduating.'"

~DL~

1974

THE FINAL COUNTDOWN

CRAIG NORWICH–LED PREGAME RITUAL KEPT HORNETS FOCUSED ON UNDEFEATED SEASON

DATES	LOCATION	ATTENDANCE	CHAMPIONSHIP
MARCH 7–9	METROPOLITAN SPORTS CENTER, BLOOMINGTON	84,210	EDINA EAST 6, BEMIDJI 0

99

Did you know? Frank B. Kellogg High School made its lone state tournament appearance, reaching the consolation championship. Kellogg merged with Alexander Ramsey High School in 1986 to form Roseville Area High School.

HE ATTRACTED STARSTRUCK college recruiters like moths to a streetlamp, watched with delight as his stoic coach momentarily broke character, and survived an awkward elevator ride during which rival fans shredded his team's photo in disgust.

Edina's 1973–74 season was brimming with moments that were alternately glorious, near-catastrophic, and flat-out bizarre. And the Hornets' Craig Norwich, the best player on one of the state's all-time great teams, was at the center of them all.

"Norwich was the straw that stirred the drink," said Bill Thayer, the Hornets' leading scorer that season.

A defenseman who rushed the puck with jaw-dropping flair and finesse, Norwich spent his senior season not only in the glare of the spotlight but also, for a couple of weeks, in command of the team.

The 1973 oil crisis led to a gas shortage in 1974. As a result, the Hornets' annual road trip to northern Minnesota was canceled. "They were having truck pull-offs," Norwich said. "Monster trucks that would race up hills or whatever. But we couldn't go up to northern Minnesota. They didn't have enough gas."

Schools around the state were closed for two full weeks during the holidays. Coaches were forbidden to run practices during that period, but players could still skate during the school shutdown, so Edina coach Willard Ikola handed over the reins to Norwich, the team's captain.

Norwich took the responsibility seriously. He organized practices filled with two-on-ones, three-on-twos, two-on-twos, and so on, just as Ikola ran them.

When Ikola returned, Norwich suggested the Hornets add

Senior defenseman and captain Craig Norwich kept Edina East focused on its goal of an undefeated season in 1973–74. The Hornets beat Bemidji 6–0 in the 1974 state title game to go 24–0. Photo by the *Minneapolis Tribune,* courtesy of the Minnesota Historical Society

a new wrinkle to their power play. Ikola quickly put the state's most heavily recruited player back in his place.

"I said, 'Norwich, that C on your jersey means you are a captain. It doesn't mean you are a coach,'" Ikola recalled.

As a sophomore and junior, Norwich had played on the Edina and Edina East teams, respectively, which had the best records of any team entering the state tournament (Edina split into East and West high schools before the 1972–73 season). Both times, however, the Hornets lost in the quarterfinals.

"I was determined there would be no more screwing up this thing in the end," Norwich said.

Added Thayer, another of the team's twelve seniors: "We had a very bad taste in our mouths. We said we are going to win them all."

Starting with the season opener against Blake, Norwich, whom Ikola described as "the best competitor I ever had," gathered the team around the Hornets' net before the opening puck drop and said, "This is where it starts! We've got twenty-four games to go boys!" The Hornets beat the Bears 5–2.

The pregame routine never changed as the victories kept coming, most of them blowouts. The Hornets' only one-goal win in an undefeated eighteen-game regular season was in the finale, a 5–4 triumph against Robbinsdale.

Six to go, boys!

"That first playoff game, I always was scared of it," Ikola said. "You're playing somebody you should handle or somebody you beat up during the season. There's no band, the rink is half full, no atmosphere at all."

Edina East's Craig Norwich holds the 1974 state championship trophy as he stands next to Hornets coach Willard Ikola during a celebration at the school. Photo by the *Minneapolis Tribune,* courtesy of the Minnesota Historical Society

Edina opened with Bloomington Lincoln, a squad it had blasted 9–2.

The rematch was tied 2–2 after regulation. "Here's the best team we ever had, and now we are in overtime," Ikola said incredulously.

The Hornets' Jerry Johnson scored less than a minute after the opening faceoff in the extra period to avert one of the biggest upsets in state history.

Edina East routed Robbinsdale 7–1 in the section semifinals, then eased past Bloomington Kennedy 2–1 in the final.

Three to go, boys!

Edina's 9–0 bludgeoning of St. Paul Harding in the state tournament quarterfinals was so clinically thorough many observers all but handed the Hornets the championship trophy. The *Minneapolis Star* published an article with the banner headline "Edina East called best in 16 years," referencing Ikola's comment that this was his best team in his sixteen seasons at the helm. Former and current high school, college, and NHL coaches used words such as "exceptional," "almost perfect," and "tremendous" to describe the team's play.

Two to go, boys!

Henry Sibley led Edina East 3–0 early in the third period in the semifinals. The Hornets' dreams of an undefeated season were all but nuked. Then Tim Pavek scored on a breakaway at 5:39 to spark hope. Charlie Petersen pulled the Hornets to within 3–2 less than two minutes later.

The Hornets scored three more goals in a span of sixty-three seconds on their way to a 5–3 triumph that ranks as one of the greatest comebacks in state tournament history.

"I'll never forget watching Willard jump up and down like a little kid," Norwich said. "I'd never seen that side of him before."

Sibley fans didn't suffer the defeat well.

The Hornets were staying at the Curtis Hotel in downtown Minneapolis. On the elevator up to their rooms, they were joined by a group of dejected Sibley supporters.

"I don't know if they were some Sibley cheerleaders or just female fans," Thayer said. "One of them ripped our team photo out of the program, tore it into pieces, and said to Norwich, 'You ruined everything.'"

One to go, boys!

Johnson scored thirty seconds into the championship game against Bemidji, and they might as well have halted it there. The only drama in Edina East's 6–0 victory came in the closing seconds when Ikola, desperate to insert senior backup Steve Sherman, switched his goaltenders during play instead of waiting for a whistle.

Bemidji coach Chuck Grillo, thinking his team was being shown up by Ikola's unconventional move, did the same with his goaltenders about thirty seconds later, much to the delight of the Met Sports Center crowd of 15,069.

The victory completed what would be the only undefeated season in Ikola's thirty-three-year career. The Norwich-led Hornets finished 24–0 and are frequently mentioned in the same breath with undefeated teams from Eveleth, International Falls, and Bloomington Jefferson.

Greatest team ever?

"Well, they won all their games," Ikola said. "And you can't do any better than that."

~LRN~

GONE IN SIX MINUTES

Henry Sibley's three-goal lead disappeared instantly as Edina fashioned amazing comeback

Henry Sibley's game plan for its 1974 state tournament semifinal with Edina East was remarkable in its simplicity. And effectiveness.

The idea was to hit the fleet-skating, slick-passing Hornets at every opportunity. Hit them at the blue line, behind the net, in open ice, and along the boards. Hit them everywhere. Hit, hit, hit.

"Sibley just came out and ran the [expletive] out of us," said Craig Norwich, Edina East's senior captain. "We weren't used to that. That was the first team that came right at us, and we didn't figure it out for a while."

Unbeaten in twenty-two games, Edina East had no answer for the 21–1 Warriors as they elbowed, shouldered, and forearm-shivered their way to a 2–0 first-period lead on two Bob Baumgartner goals.

Sibley's physical play reached its apex when a savage hip check by defenseman John Albers sent Edina East's Charlie Petersen skyward, skates pointing straight at the Met Sports Center ceiling. The impact was such that it jarred the stick out of Petersen's grip and, upon his face-first landing, the glove off his left hand.

"They played rough with us," acknowledged Bill Thayer, a senior who led the Hornets in scoring.

After a scoreless second period, the Hornets figured all they needed was an early goal in the third. Score the next goal and the comeback victory was inevitable, they thought.

Sibley goal-scoring wizard Doug Spoden wasn't in an accommodating mood. He scored 2:13 into the third, and the Warriors led 3–0.

Warriors fans went wild with joy. Hornets fans were overcome with sorrow.

"I had a friend who was so depressed he tore up his championship game tickets, thinking we were done," senior wing Tim Pavek said. "He couldn't get into the game the next night."

Edina East players Larry Johnson (left), Charlie Petersen (middle), Steve Polfuss (15), Bob Frawley (far right, middle), and Andy Overman (far right, top) celebrate their improbable 5–3 comeback victory over Henry Sibley in the 1974 semifinals. Photo by the *Minneapolis Tribune*, courtesy of the Minnesota Historical Society

Pavek ignited one of the most improbable comebacks in state tournament history 5:39 into the third when he took a long pass from Norwich and streaked in alone on scorching-hot Warriors goaltender Paul Rutherford.

"Boom—the goal light came on, the crowd came up, and the band started playing," said Pavek, who hit the upper right corner. "The momentum changed."

Shaken but undeterred, Petersen scored a power-play goal 1:43 later to pull the Hornets to 3–2. After killing a hooking penalty to Larry Johnson, Edina East scored three more goals [from Thayer, Bob Frawley, and Petersen] in a span of sixty-three seconds en route to a stunning 5–3 victory.

Five goals in 6:09.

"It was the most amazing thing in hockey I have ever seen," said Willard Ikola. The normally stoic Edina East coach went wild on the bench, jumping up and down and screaming in delight both during the comeback and after the game.

"We outplayed them for two periods," Sibley's Spoden said. "But they only needed one."

The following summer, Ikola was headed north to his cabin when he made a pit stop in Hinckley. A fan who had tried unsuccessfully to buy a ticket to Edina East's game against Sibley and ended up watching it at a bar recognized Ikola and sparked up a conversation.

"He says to me, 'Geez, in the third period, you guys were behind 3–0 and I had to go to the bathroom,'" Ikola said. "He said he came back from the bathroom, sat in the same chair he was at before, looked up at the score, and saw it was 5–3. He says to me, 'What the hell happened?'

"I said, 'What happened? You took a six-minute crap, that's what happened.'"

~LRN~

1975
CHOCOLATE MAKES EVERYTHING BETTER

GRAND RAPIDS GOALIE WITH SWEET TOOTH OFFERED CLUTCH SAVES, COMIC RELIEF

DATES	LOCATION	ATTENDANCE	CHAMPIONSHIP
MARCH 6–8	METROPOLITAN SPORTS CENTER	83,089	GRAND RAPIDS 6, MINNEAPOLIS SOUTHWEST 1

Did you know? French polio (Guillain-Barré syndrome) in the eighth grade left future Roseau High goalie Tim Erickson unsure of his ability to walk, let alone play hockey. But he worked his way back into form and was a starter for three years.

"PITTER, PATTER, LET'S GET AT 'ER."

Grand Rapids goaltender Dan "Chocolate" Clafton used the phrase before each game as the Indians left their locker room. And while it was no "Win one for the Gipper" or St. Crispin's Day Speech, the homespun rallying cry found its mark.

A style all his own made Clafton the right man between the pipes for a ridiculously talented Grand Rapids team on the cusp of greatness.

Behind the wheel of his 1964 Ford Fairlane, yellow with a hand-painted black roof, Clafton couldn't be missed driving

Grand Rapids center John Rothstein loathed his "Johnny R., Superstar" nickname. Drafted by the Minnesota Fighting Saints of the World Hockey Association after his junior season, the speedy centerman remained focused and led Grand Rapids to a state title. Photo by Jack Gillis/*Minneapolis Star*

along Highway 38 to and from the Itasca Recreation Association Civic Center, where Grand Rapids practiced and played.

On game nights, the student section serenaded the fun-loving goalie with an edited version of an old Nestlé jingle: "N-E-S-T-L-E-S, the Indians have the very best. Choooooc-laaaaaate."

"We just knew Chocolate was Chocolate, but in big games he repeatedly came up big," senior wing John Rothstein said. "He'd make a big save and bounce up, and the crowd loved it."

Playing with joy was the only way for Clafton, who suffered from a bone disease as a child and wondered whether he'd ever play at all. He wore leg braces around age five to correct hip problems. The chubby youngster was put on a diet to help lower his weight and lessen the burden on his hips. But a neighbor kid saw Clafton sneaking candy, and "Chocolate" was born.

He made varsity as a sophomore, the first time Clafton ever played on a top team. A starter his junior year, he helped the team to a third-place state tournament finish.

Third in 1974 after taking second in 1972, Grand Rapids announced itself as the coming prep hockey power from the Iron Range, though logging and the Blandin paper mill, not mining, were the Mississippi River town's primary economic pillars.

In Clafton's mind, 1975 was Grand Rapids' turn to get at 'er.

"Chocolate came up with the big saves and the right thing to say at all times," assistant coach Mike Sertich said.

While Chocolate embraced his nickname, "Johnny R., Superstar" didn't sit well with Rothstein.

Based on his performances, however, the moniker fit like an orange-and-white Grand Rapids jersey. Rothstein could fly. And the right wing could finish, often on slapshots from the circle.

Rothstein made varsity as a freshman in 1971–72, and the Indians won their first Iron Range Conference title.

A few months after the 1974 state tournament, Rothstein's profile rose like the many pucks he blistered. The Minnesota Fighting Saints of the World Hockey Association made him a rarity by drafting the high school junior as their final pick of the seventeenth round. The Saints' first pick? Future Minnesota Wild coach Bruce Boudreau.

Already the team's leading scorer—he tallied thirty-six goals and twenty-four assists as a junior—Rothstein struggled with celebrity status. No one recalls where the Superstar nickname began. But teammates remember Rothstein's embarrassment when fans at other rinks taunted him with it.

"He didn't like that tag at all," said Erin Roth, who played left wing, opposite Rothstein.

Yet Rothstein admits he got caught up in the hype. In turn, he and title-hungry Grand Rapids struggled. The Indians marred a 3–0 start by dropping consecutive games to Region 7 teams International Falls and Greenway.

"I remember feeling that I was entitled to be the best," Rothstein said. "Then Sert came and talked to me."

Sertich and Rothstein shared more than one meaningful conversation that season. In fall 1974, just weeks before the hockey season started, Sertich had lost his wife, Carlene, in an automobile accident.

The Grand Rapids hockey family, players and coaches, cared for one another. But nobody quite knew how to address the tragedy.

"I was afraid to look him in the eye," Rothstein said. "At practice a month later, he got his nose six inches from me."

It's OK to grieve, Sertich assured Rothstein.

"It drew us all closer," Sertich said.

Rothstein's scoring slump paled in comparison. Nevertheless, Sertich said he helped get the young man "recentered" in mid-December.

Around that same time, head coach Gus Hendrickson helped Rothstein by promoting Pete DeCenzo to top-line center.

Older brother Mark DeCenzo had centered Rothstein the previous season to great success, and Rothstein wasn't shy about dictating terms to his new center.

"He said, 'The reason you're here is to get me the puck,'" Pete DeCenzo said.

Not that he minded.

"If you could hit John at full stride in the neutral zone, you're probably getting an assist," DeCenzo said.

Retooled Grand Rapids swept Edina East, the defending state champions, and Edina West on the road and reestablished itself among the state's elite.

Few teams could match Grand Rapids' powerful lineup. After the DeCenzo-Rothstein-Roth line, opposing teams faced lines centered by Dan Lempe and Doug Bymark. On defense, seniors Steve Fleming and Jeff Oakley, along with junior Bill Hoolihan and sophomores Don Lucia and Tom Madson, provided additional grit and personality.

The leader of the defensive corps was Bill Baker, a future NCAA champion with the Gophers and Olympic gold medalist.

"[Baker] was a hard worker and a role model," Lucia said. "He lived life the right way. On the ice, he had a low panic point and great hockey sense. He controlled the game on the back end, and he could do everything well."

In 1975, unflappable senior defenseman Bill Baker helped lead Grand Rapids to its first state championship with impeccable play. "I don't ever remember him having a bad game," teammate Pete DeCenzo said. Photo courtesy of the Minnesota Historical Society

DeCenzo said, "I don't ever remember him having a bad game."

Grand Rapids was good, but Virginia was the Region 7 favorite after winning the Iron Range Conference ahead of Eveleth. Third-place Grand Rapids split with both teams in the regular season.

In the past, whichever team lost the Region 7 title game faced the Region 8 runner-up for the Region 3 backdoor crown. But before the 1974–75 season, the Minnesota State High School League added teams, shuffled regions, and closed the backdoor. The net result: northern Minnesota received one fewer state tournament entrant.

Northern programs had dominated the first thirty years of state tournament play, winning twenty-two titles. A second avenue for their northern neighbors ranked metro-area coaches—especially one with Iron Range roots.

"They think up there that they're the only ones who play hockey," said Edina East coach Willard Ikola, the former Eveleth goalie who helped the Golden Bears win three titles. "They've had an extra representative for too long. We're as good as they are."

Grand Rapids felt the same about its Region 7 semifinal opponent, number-one-ranked Virginia. With a 5–2 victory, they beat coach Gus Hendrickson's older brother Dave (Blue Devils coach) and nephew Keith (Blue Devils standout), as well as Sertich's alma mater.

After the Indians dropped Eveleth 4–2 in the regional final, *Minneapolis Tribune* reporter John Gilbert dubbed them the Halloween Machine. Sertich made good on a pregame wager with players and shaved off his mustache.

"After getting through Region 7, I thought we had a good chance," Baker said. "Several Iron Range Conference teams were able to win it before us, and that's because there were no nights off."

Grand Rapids arrived at the Met Center in Bloomington shorthanded. Fleming had taken an accidental stick to the eye in the first round of the regional playoffs, leaving him unable to finish the season. No Fleming meant the Indians lacked a solid penalty killer and shot blocker.

Wearing an eye patch, Fleming made the trip anyway and visited the locker room before each game.

In the quarterfinal, Grand Rapids trounced Henry Sibley 8–3 behind a DeCenzo hat trick and a two-goal, three-assist Rothstein performance.

Next up: Hill-Murray, a private school that represented an evolving state tournament. On August 1, 1974, thirty-four non-public schools had been accepted as MSHSL members. Half of them sponsored hockey, including Hill-Murray, a two-time Independent Tournament champion (1970 as Hill and 1972).

The Pioneers won Region 3 and gained admission to what coach Terry Skrypek called "the number-one show in town. We were excited to be there. We had the players."

Senior center Rod Romanchuk (fifty-three goals) and senior goalie Steve Janaszak, who later joined Baker as an NCAA champion with the Gophers and an Olympic gold medalist, gave the Pioneers star power.

Hill-Murray proved it belonged with a 3–1 quarterfinal defeat of Duluth East. Gaining acceptance was another matter.

Color commentator Lou Nanne interviewed Brother Francis Carr, Hill-Murray's athletic director, after the Duluth East victory. Nanne's second question pertained to player recruiting accusations, which Carr denied.

Nanne praised the Pioneers' skill and said their presence would "erase forever the doubts of who is the best team in the state."

Best goalie in the tournament? Clafton wanted the title. He made the semifinal matchup with the more heralded Janaszak personal. And he delivered with a 2–0 shutout victory.

"I heard about him, and I admit I went out there to prove something," Clafton said afterward. "I just wanted to beat him."

But not this way. Not stopping just twelve shots. Clafton marveled as St. Paul Johnson's Doug Long made sixty-one saves to beat Greenway in the 1970 quarterfinals and desired something similar.

Plus, Clafton said Gophers coach Herb Brooks had shown some recruiting interest.

"Because our team was pretty stout defensively, I only had a small number of saves," Clafton said. "I still have some regret that I didn't see more shots."

Blame Baker, who DeCenzo said "probably had as many saves as Chocolate against Hill-Murray."

"The other teams knew that if Billy was out there, they weren't going to score," Rothstein said. "I don't think he was on the ice for a goal the whole state tournament."

Roth scored twice in the second period and took his spotlight turn. He considered himself a "garbage guy" who feasted on rebounds. But he brought more to the game.

"He had a refusal to be second to the puck," Sertich said.

"Johnny had more skill, but Roth was the more natural goal scorer," DeCenzo said.

The Hill-Murray victory took a toll. Baker was hobbled after blocking a shot. Rothstein suffered a charley horse in his right leg.

Uncertainty lingered as Grands Rapids prepared to face Minneapolis Southwest for the championship. The teams had scrimmaged in late December, a 7–5 Grand Rapids "victory" that meant little now.

Quiet and tense best described the Grand Rapids team bus ride to the Met Center. And since chocolate makes everything better, Sertich put the loquacious goalie on the spot.

"Mike handed me the bus microphone and said, 'Say something,'" Clafton said.

"He gets up, grabs the microphone, and says, 'Ladies and gentlemen, there's no reason to panic,'" Sertich said. "That was it. We came off the bus roaring."

Southwest took charge with a 1–0 lead at first intermission. A Southwest player alone in the slot was poised to strike again in the second period, but he failed to get a shot off. Roth passed

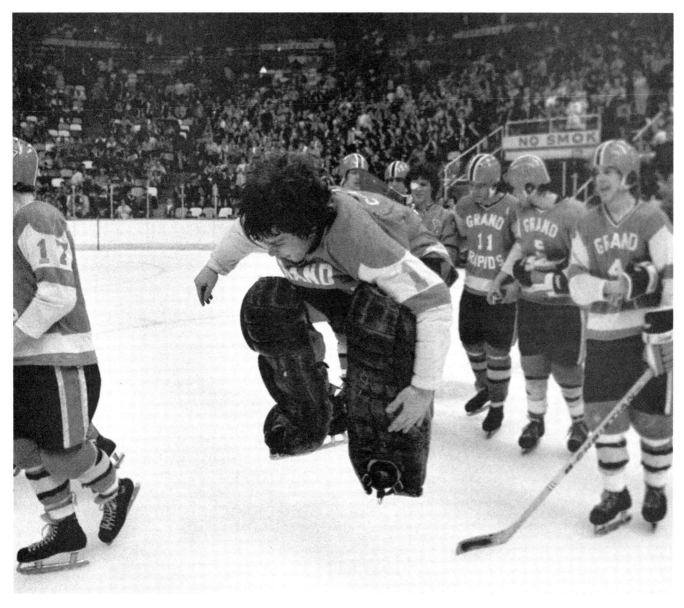

Grand Rapids goaltender Dan "Chocolate" Clafton jumps in elation after winning the 1975 state title. Clafton, both eccentric and effective, played with an infectious swagger. He always used the phrase, "Pitter, patter, let's get at 'er," before games. And he drained the tension on the team bus before the championship game by grabbing the microphone and blurting out, "Ladies and gentlemen, there's no reason to panic." Photo courtesy of the Minnesota Historical Society

the puck to Rothstein, and he raced toward the net. Rothstein pedaled a stationary bike before the game to loosen up, but stiffness slowed him early. Not on this rush.

"Johnny R., Superstar, came alive with a rocket," Roth said. "Right side. Top of the circle. Let 'er rip, top shelf."

"That was the kind of play he'd make to change momentum," Sertich said. "He did it quite often. That goal took away the guys' apprehension. It lit a fire and released the tension."

Grand Rapids awoke. Two Dan Lempe goals 2:30 apart and another from Dennis Doyle just thirty-six seconds later put Grand Rapids ahead 4–1 at second intermission. Roth and De-Cenzo added third-period goals, and the 6–1 victory proved northern Minnesota wasn't done churning out power programs.

Three games against Twin Cities foes. Three victories.

"We always thought we had an edge when we played southern teams," Rothstein said. "I think we played a little tougher."

Graduation claimed Baker, Clafton, and Rothstein. Hendrickson left for the University of Minnesota Duluth job and took Sertich along. But none of the returning players feared for their program's future.

"Somebody said the northern hockey wasn't good anymore," Roth told reporters afterward. "Guess we showed them. We'll show them again next year, too."

~*DL*~

UNBRIDLED SUCCESS

ROOKIE GRAND RAPIDS COACH LET PLAYERS TAKE REINS

DATES	LOCATION	ATTENDANCE	CHAMPIONSHIP
MARCH 4–6	ST. PAUL CIVIC CENTER	92,333	GRAND RAPIDS 4, RICHFIELD 3

 Undefeated Mounds View, led by star forward Rob McClanahan, fell in the quarterfinals to McClanahan's future Gophers and Olympic teammate Steve Christoff.

A CROWDED SCHOOL gymnasium welcomed home the 1975–76 Grand Rapids hockey team, state champions for a second consecutive year.

Mayor Robert Horn exalted the winners and then introduced first-year head coach Jim Nelson.

"If we had an election today," Horn told the audience, "he'd have my job."

Nelson, a baby-faced twenty-six-year-old, grabbed the microphone.

Scanning the happy faces, he remarked, "Yeah, and there was a time in January that if we had an election, any one of you would have had my job."

Pete DeCenzo, a senior center, said that exchange spoke to the challenges Nelson faced and the guile he possessed to help everything turn out fine.

Nelson, a Roseau native who played goalie at North Dakota, got promoted after three seasons as goaltender coach. His staff of fellow twenty-somethings, Rod "Buzzy" Christensen (North Dakota) and Lyn Ellingson (Minnesota Duluth), made all the right moves.

Which is to say this hockey version of the *Friends* cast did little.

"I was so young and naïve," Nelson said. He replaced Gus Hendrickson, older by about a decade. "The smartest thing I did was let the horses run."

In all, sixteen of the eighteen 1975–76 Grand Rapids players would go on to play Division I hockey. Standouts included Dan Lempe (team leader with fifty points on twenty-four goals), Erin Roth (27–22), and DeCenzo (21–17), plus forwards Doug Bymark and Al Cleveland and defensemen Bill Hoolihan, Don Lucia, and sophomore Scot Kleinendorst.

Eight consecutive victories to start the season indicated the defending champions should again be a factor in March. Good thing because three state tournament appearances in four seasons created "intense pressure to get to state each year," goaltender Jim Jetland said.

"You'd hear, 'Hey, we've got our rooms booked,'" Jetland said. "You felt a sense of obligation to all these people counting on you. People's winters revolved around this hockey team."

Concerns arose in late December and early January as

Grand Rapids sophomore goalie Jim Jetland played with veteran moxie after taking over the starting job midseason. He went on to anchor the school's run to a second consecutive state title. Photo courtesy of the Minnesota Historical Society

Grand Rapids' Pete DeCenzo (left) celebrates a goal he tipped home on a shot from teammate Al Cleveland. The goal drew Grand Rapids even with 1976 quarterfinal opponent Bloomington Kennedy. DeCenzo scored again for a 2–1 victory. Photo by the *St. Paul Pioneer Press*

Grand Rapids lost three consecutive games to Richfield, Edina West, and Edina East. Rock bottom followed in a 7–3 thrashing by Eveleth.

A local hockey fan told Nelson, sulking at a bar one evening during the slump, "Your power play sucks."

"I slid him a napkin and said, 'Draw one up and I'll use it,'" Nelson said.

The young coach knew a tougher decision loomed: ending the goalie rotation of sophomore Jetland and junior Jim Leone.

Nape, as friends and even players called Nelson, "took us seniors individually into the locker room and asked, 'Who do you want as your goalie?'" Roth said. "We unanimously picked Jet.

"Jet had that moxie, that 'it' factor between the pipes."

And on the mound. Jetland, with his dazzling curveball, was the pitching ace the previous summer as the Grand Rapids Legion team won the state title.

In his first game as the undisputed starter between the pipes, Jetland earned a 3–0 shutout of Hibbing. But not everyone was convinced.

Larry Ross, architect of the International Falls dynasty, said

publicly that teams couldn't win with a sophomore goalie. Nonsense. Nelson won the starting job as a sophomore and helped Roseau to three consecutive state tournaments.

Jetland's reaction: "Anybody that's competitive takes it as a challenge."

Nelson had all his horses in place. Grand Rapids won nine of its next ten games.

Still, Eveleth was the Region 7 favorite. Led by Mark Pavelich, Ronn Tomassoni, Craig Homola, and Bob Hallstrom, the Golden Bears were poised to reach their first state tournament since 1960 and revitalize the original Iron Range dynasty.

The teams, which split two regular-season meetings, met in the regional final in front of a crowd of 4,450 jammed into the Hibbing Memorial Building.

Jetland finished with twenty-four saves in a 3–0 victory. Roth, battling a 103-degree fever, was too fatigued to celebrate.

DeCenzo, whose family had moved from Eveleth to Grand Rapids when he was a freshman, said breaking the Golden Bears' hearts meant "friends I grew up with wouldn't talk to me. I couldn't go back there for a few years."

Victory also meant a trip to St. Paul, the tournament's original home from 1945 to 1968 and its destination again after seven seasons at the Met Center in Bloomington. A new venue, the Civic Center, offered distinctive clear boards and double the capacity of the old St. Paul Auditorium.

The Civic Center drew mixed reviews. "I would have kept it at the Met," Nelson said. But quarterfinal Thursday was spectacular.

A lone goal separated all four winners and losers. Grand Rapids (19–5) drew Bloomington Kennedy (22–1), and only Jetland's play kept a 1–0 first intermission deficit from being worse.

DeCenzo scored both goals in a 2–1 victory.

The semifinals brought a rematch with Hill-Murray, which bludgeoned Minneapolis Southwest throughout a quarterfinal victory that went to overtime.

"They were physical and a little cheap—nice Catholic boys," DeCenzo said.

Its once-broken power play fixed by Nelson's tinkering, Grand Rapids got four man-advantage goals, including a tournament-record-tying three from Cleveland, in a 7–4 victory.

The title game meant a rematch with Richfield and standout Steve Christoff, who had scored the game-winning goal in the teams' first meeting.

Taking aim before the puck dropped, Lempe said of Christoff, "I know he's very good. But maybe he's a little overrated."

Gulp.

"Gus had been recruiting and gave us a scouting report on Christoff," said Roth, assigned to cover the skilled center. "He said, 'When he comes down, he'll always go to his left. Or right.' There was no reading him. He wasn't overrated at all."

Christoff scored twice, but Grand Rapids redeemed its earlier loss with a 4–3 victory.

The team became the first back-to-back state champion since rival Greenway, located eight miles northeast in Coleraine, had won in 1967 and 1968. That was especially sweet for Roth's father, Gene, who during Greenway's heyday had referred to Coleraine as home to "the -iches, the -viches, and the son-of-a-bitches."

Lempe, after his haughty comments about Christoff, was humbled by the journey.

"A month ago, I never thought we could win it," Lempe told the *Minneapolis Tribune*'s John Gilbert. "In fact, I never believed it until we won our first game down here."

~ *DL* ~

Grand Rapids lost its regular-season meeting with Richfield but won the all-important state championship game rematch. Richfield standout Steve Christoff (foreground) skates away as Grand Rapids players revel in the first back-to-back state championship since Greenway did it in the late 1960s. Photo courtesy of the Minnesota Historical Society

THE CLOWN PRINCE

COLORFUL ROCHESTER JOHN MARSHALL COACH GENE SACK PUSHED ALL THE RIGHT BUTTONS

DATES	LOCATION	ATTENDANCE	CHAMPIONSHIP
MARCH 17–19	ST. PAUL CIVIC CENTER	94,772	ROCHESTER JOHN MARSHALL 4, EDINA EAST 2

Did you know? This was the first time since 1970, and just the third since the tournament's inception, that a northern team failed to reach the championship game.

HE SPOKE OF FROGS and princes and butter and cream, drew from a bottomless pool of one-liners, wore a toupee under his houndstooth cap, and had a puck-sized button on the lapel of his checkered blazer that read, "We're In It! Let's Win It!"

Rochester John Marshall's collection of mostly anonymous, remarkably loose, and blissfully carefree players was a reflection of their flamboyant leader as they barged into the 1977 state tournament with shoulder-length hair flowing from mismatched helmets.

"He was just a fun-loving guy," Rockets scoring leader Scott Lecy said about Gene Sack, who was as much a comedian as he was a coach. "You wanted to win for him."

Sack gave his players nicknames that changed daily, called them all "hamburgers" as a term of endearment, and repeatedly warned in practice, "Keep your dobber up."

He had starred at Cretin High School and played semipro hockey as a rough-and-tumble defenseman in his hometown for the St. Paul Koppys and 7-Ups, and later for the Rochester Mustangs. He wasn't an Xs and Os guy. Never pretended to be.

When Lecy suggested the Rockets mimic the power play deployed by the University of Wisconsin's squad, Sack responded by asking which players Lecy wanted on the unit.

"Then he said, 'OK. Take them down to the other end and work on it,'" Lecy recalled.

Sack empowered his players. He made them laugh. He kept the game simple and fun.

"Whenever Gene was around, the world seemed brighter

Rochester John Marshall coach Gene Sack's infectious smile and penchant for nicknames made him a lovable, larger-than-life character to his players. Photo by the *Minneapolis Tribune,* courtesy of the Minnesota Historical Society

and the load seemed lighter," said Les Neeb, who served as an assistant coach under Sack.

Asked once about his strategy for winning the biggest game of his career, Sack responded, "We had the horses."

And he knew enough not to harness them. When sophomore goaltender Paul Butters asked to wear the number 10—highly unusual for a netminder—Sack acquiesced. (Butters's reasoning? The 1 stands for the traditional goalie number and the 0 for a shutout.)

"Eccentric," Sack said about the precocious goaltender.

Facemasks and half shields were just coming into vogue in the late 1970s and were not yet mandatory during the 1976–77 season. Still, at Sack's request, all the Rockets were wearing them in their season debut. During his opening shift, Lecy, caught looking down for the puck, was sent flying with a thunderous check.

"I came off the ice and said, 'I'm not wearing this damn thing,'" Lecy said about his mask. "Geno said, 'Then take it off.' All of a sudden, screwdrivers were flying all over the bench."

One of the few ideas Sack, a high school history teacher, vetoed came from John Marshall athletic director Kerwin Englehart, who suggested buttons supporting the team's state tournament trip should read, "Sack 'Em." Sack suggested they use the "We're In It! Let's Win It!" slogan instead.

Typical Sack, treating a Rochester team's first appearance in the state tournament since 1948 as casually as if it were a trip to the grocery store.

"He would talk about himself and his playing days," said Paul Brandrup, a junior defenseman in 1977. "He played for the Mustangs back in the [1950s], and he was a fan favorite. The one story he would always tell us was when he got a puck into the face and laid on the ice with medics around him. They said, 'Sack are you OK? Are you OK?' He said, 'Yeah, I am fine. But how is the crowd taking it?'"

Rochester John Marshall's big breakthrough, the Rockets beating emerging metro powers Burnsville and Bloomington Jefferson to reach the state tournament, was met with a hearty dose of skepticism. Southern Minnesota was known for its prowess in basketball, wrestling, and football—most every major sport but hockey.

Pretournament chatter in the metro newspapers centered on the excellence of Twin Cities kingpin Edina, unbeaten and tradition-laden Roseau (the Neal Broten–led darlings from the Canadian border), and two-time defending champion Grand Rapids from the edge of the fabled, hockey-crazed Iron Range.

John Marshall was noted for the novelty of being the first southern team in twenty-nine years to appear in the tourney (Rochester High had made a four-year run of appearances starting with the inaugural event in 1945, finishing second in 1946), having a wise-guy head coach, and boasting a high-scoring offense . . . and that was all.

The Rockets had spent much of the season blowing out southern Minnesota programs new to hockey. Double-digit victories were both commonplace and, as far as the Twin Cities media was concerned, unimpressive. One of their two losses was at home to unranked Sibley, a 7–1 drubbing that planted more seeds of doubt.

"I can't speak for everybody," Brandrup said about the team's confidence level at the state tournament. "But that Sibley game just kept running through my brain, that it is possible to get smoked."

Brandrup's worries proved unfounded. The Rockets blitzed state tournament regular Minneapolis Southwest 4–1 in the quarterfinals as the 5-foot-8½, 160-pound Lecy scored his thirteenth hat trick of the season.

The wise-cracking Sack also was in top form.

"It's amazing, really," he told reporters after the game. "Butters got out there in front of seventeen thousand fans and didn't turn to cream."

Despite the dominating, feel-good triumph, questions about John Marshall's legitimacy lingered.

"Does a Rochester team belong in this tournament?" a reporter asked Lecy.

"We showed today we can play hockey with these guys," Lecy replied.

Gophers coach Herb Brooks was among the thousands of onlookers smitten with Lecy's racehorse speed, deft scoring touch, and refuse-to-lose attitude. "He weighs 155 pounds, and 140 of that is heart," Brooks said about the sandy-haired, freckle-faced Lecy, who was also the Rockets' backup quarterback in football and starting shortstop in baseball.

Todd Lecy, Scott's sophomore brother and linemate along with junior Bruce Aikens, scored the lone goal in the third pe-

Rochester John Marshall's Scott Lecy, one the most prolific goal scorers in state history, was a fan and media darling during the 1977 state tournament in St. Paul. Photo by the *Minneapolis Tribune*, courtesy of the Minnesota Historical Society

riod as John Marshall escaped the semifinals with a 1–0 victory over South St. Paul, another longtime state power. The big, strong Packers used a punishing, bone-jarring style to effectively shackle John Marshall's Smurf-sized top line (the diminutive Scott Lecy was the biggest of the bunch).

"I remember they were just really physical," Scott Lecy said. "They pounded us. And their goalie [Duane Bodie], I think he was like 6 foot 3, 225. A big boy. I just couldn't get anything past him."

Butters, 5 foot 7 and 140 pounds, again measured up to the challenge. He made thirty-seven saves, a tournament record that still stands as the most ever in a shutout.

The Rockets had reached the championship, but their naysayers wouldn't relent. South St. Paul coach Denny Tetu was among the loudest, even after the semifinal loss, calling John Marshall a "mystery team."

"They've got these three seniors [actually four], plus a defenseman who plays the whole game and a sophomore goalie

. . . and they're going to be in the finals of the state hockey tournament," Tetu said incredulously. "I don't know what in the world they've got going for them."

Maybe Tetu couldn't see it, but Sack was right. John Marshall had the horses. Lecy's 61 goals and 112 points as a senior rank sixth and seventh, respectively, among the state's all-time leaders. He's one of the best athletes to ever come out of Rochester. The same could be said for his sidekick Aikens, a 5-foot-8, 155-pound speedster whose 250 career points rank in the state's all-time top twenty. Aikens, like Lecy, also excelled in baseball and football.

Scott Lecy and Aikens were required to carry the offense starting early in the 1976–77 season when Todd Lecy, their center, was suspended for nine weeks after an athletic code violation incurred at a Christmas party. The 5-foot-7, 165-pound Todd, nicknamed Pudly, returned in time for the playoffs and scored twice in the final 2:12 in a 6–4 section semifinal win over Burnsville.

Defenseman Jeff Nelson, a junior, was a shot-blocking maniac who rarely left the ice. Brandrup, a slick puck mover, developed a knack for springing Lecy and Aikens on breakaways with long passes. Nelson, Brandrup, and third defenseman Tom Taylor, an offensive lineman from the football team, all stood taller than 6 feet and weighed in at around 200 pounds.

The Rockets were talented and finely tuned. The fathers of Aikens and the Lecy brothers played for the Mustangs in the United States Hockey League that attracted top talent from the Midwest and Canada. Every Sunday afternoon, the old Mustangs, many of whom served as youth coaches, would mix with the youthful Rockets in pickup games that were loaded with teaching moments.

"I remember [second-line center] Jeff Teal's dad showing us how to block shots," Todd Lecy said. "He was literally taking slapshots at us telling us to step into them. That was as scary as any game I ever played in."

As much as he enjoyed playing the role of court jester,

Rochester John Marshall's Todd Lecy expresses his jubilation, and South St. Paul players show their frustration, after Lecy scored the only goal in the Rockets' 1–0 victory over the Packers in a 1977 semifinal. Photo by Pete Hohn/*Minneapolis Tribune*

Rochester John Marshall players carry coach Gene Sack off the ice after the Rockets' 4–2 victory over Edina East in the 1977 state championship game. Photo by Pete Hohn/*Minneapolis Tribune*

Sack, who joined the marines while still in high school and fought in World War II as a turret gunner, was serious about avoiding a repeat of 1960. That year his Thief River Falls team had entered the tournament with just one loss and the state's number-one ranking. The Prowlers lost both their games.

Because of that dismal performance, Sack likened himself to a frog who could now transform himself into a prince with a Rockets championship.

"It's easy to get overawed by just being in the state tournament," he said. "I've got to make sure everybody is settled down."

Nerves weren't an issue in the title game. Todd Lecy said he got a chuckle as he watched the Edina student section's choreographed indifference—holding newspapers in front of their faces—as the Rockets' lineup was announced.

"That was classic," Lecy said. "And of course Aiks scores thirty seconds into the game and three-quarters of the building goes crazy."

Scott Lecy sprang Aikens with a Hail Mary pass that somehow slipped under an Edina defenseman's stick in the neutral zone. Aikens crossed the left faceoff circle and ripped a shot high over Hornets goaltender Steve Carroll. It took only thirty-six seconds for one of the biggest underdogs in state championship game history to take a 1–0 lead.

"The entire state was pulling for Rochester except for our little wedge of fans in the corner," Carroll said.

The Rockets worked their quick-strike magic again less than seven minutes later when, with John Marshall shorthanded, Lecy snuck behind the Edina defense and caught a long pass

from Brandrup in stride. Lecy deked Carroll to the ice and flipped a backhand shot over the sprawling goaltender. The game was less than eight minutes old, and the Rockets led 2–0.

Edina was unimpressed.

"I still remember one of their big guys saying, 'You little so-and-sos, you don't even belong here,'" Todd Lecy said.

Edina rallied to tie the score at two after two periods, then Scott Lecy struck again 1:01 into the third. The Rockets were clinging to that 3–2 lead (Butters was superb again with thirty-seven saves, including fifteen in the third period) when Todd Lecy scored an empty-net goal with fifty-eight seconds left to clinch a 4–2 victory. His goal celebration one was for the ages, his feet spinning one hundred miles per hour as he ran on the ice like a sprinter, straight into the arms of his big brother.

"And is he happy? Yes sir! He'll run from here to Rochester!" was the call on the TV broadcast.

Sack flung his hat high into the air as the final horn sounded. He was beaming as his players hoisted him on their shoulders and carried him off the ice. The Prince of Rochester.

The 1977 championship remains the only one ever won by a school from the deep southern part of the state, a one-of-a-kind title paired with the Rockets' uniquely brilliant coach. Sack was seventy-five when he died of leukemia in 2002.

"His greatest gift was to just let us play," Brandrup said. "We couldn't have won it without him."

~LRN~

"YOU'RE STARTING, KID"

EDINA GOALTENDERS AT CENTER OF MULTIEPISODE DRAMA

DATES	LOCATION	ATTENDANCE	CHAMPIONSHIP
MARCH 9–11	ST. PAUL CIVIC CENTER	98,870	EDINA EAST 5, GRAND RAPIDS 4 (2 OT)

 This was the first year state high school players were required to wear face-masks, although several teams had donned them the previous season.

MIKE VACANTI dropped to the ice to make a save.

Whummmp!

The puck made a sickening sound as it smacked the Edina East goaltender's exposed knee.

"I took a shot, and it went underneath my pad and broke my kneecap," Vacanti said. "I couldn't stand up."

Play was stopped. Hornets coach Willard Ikola marched onto the ice to check the condition of his junior netminder.

When he reached the crease, Vacanti still was sprawled on the ice.

Ikola: "What's wrong? What's wrong? Is it your hamstring?"

Vacanti: "No, it's my knee. I can't stand up."

Ikola: "You're fine. You started this game, you're going to finish it. Get up."

Ikola glanced at the Hornets' bench. There sat backup goaltender Bruce Bonstrom, barely tall enough to see over the boards. Bonstrom was a junior varsity goaltender. He was dressed for the late-December 1977 game in Grand Rapids only because senior Gary Aulik, who had been rotating starts with Vacanti, was sitting in the bleachers in street clothes with a wrist injury.

"I am leaning over Mike when Ike comes out," said Steve Brown, a senior defenseman. "Mike is grabbing his knee, and Ike turns around and looks at the bench. [Bonstrom] weighed a hundred pounds wringing wet. All you could see was a bob of blond hair."

Said Ikola, a three-time state champion goaltender for Eveleth in 1948–50: "I figured [Vacanti] can play better with the one leg than this kid with two."

Brown helped Vacanti up. With his arms draped over the crossbar for support, Vacanti finished out the frantic final three minutes of the 4–3 victory over the previously undefeated Indians.

Goaltending drama was a recurring theme for the Hornets that season.

Aulik returned home from Grand Rapids, sawed the cast off his injured wrist, and declared himself fit to play.

Less than two months later, Vacanti ditched his crutches and donned his skates weeks ahead of schedule. Ikola resumed rotating the two goaltenders, and the Hornets entered the postseason with a 19–1 record. Aulik and Vacanti continued to alternate starts in the regional playoffs, during which the Hornets allowed one goal in each of their three victories.

Edina East, which had lost to Rochester John Marshall in the 1977 title game, opened the 1978 state tournament with a 3–2 win against Minneapolis Roosevelt led by defenseman Mike Ramsey, a future Olympian and NHL standout. Vacanti was solid in making twenty saves, ten of them in the first period. Steve Ikola, Willard's son, scored with fifty-six seconds left in the third period, batting the puck into the net baseball style off the shaft of his stick, to secure the victory.

Undefeated Roseau, led by the fabled forward line of brothers Neal and Aaron Broten and fellow rink rat Bryan "Butsy" Erickson, awaited in the semifinals. The trio had amassed just fewer than 150 goals entering the state tournament.

Neal Broten and Erickson, both seniors, scored against Edina East. But it was speedy Edina right wing Mike Lauen who emerged as the highlight-reel hero, notching a hat trick to lead the Hornets to a 5–3 victory. Lauen's final two goals came in the third period as Edina East broke a 3–3 tie.

Aulik was steady bordering on spectacular in making twenty-seven saves, several of them point-blank attempts by the slippery Neal Broten.

Coach Ikola hadn't reached his team's locker room and already the decision of which goaltender to start in the championship was weighing on him.

"Gary for us did an outstanding job, as he has done all season," Ikola said in a TV interview. "Vacanti, our other goaltender, plays well, too. I don't know which one we are going to use yet.

"We'll sleep on it and make a decision tomorrow."

The decision was slow in coming. Aulik was walking above the Mississippi River outside the team hotel at about 4:30 in the afternoon when a teammate yelled down from the seventh floor, "Hey, Aulik. Coach wants to see you in his room!"

Aulik sprinted up to Ikola's room, where the coach, assistant Ed Zins, Vacanti, and senior captain Tom Kelly awaited.

"It stood to reason that Vacanti would get the start," Aulik said. "But I hoped against hope I would have the opportunity to go out and win one more."

FABLED FAMILY
Roseau's Broten brothers made mark on tournament despite dreaded Edina hex

Roseau's Neal Broten was a freshman making his first trip to the state tournament when he lost the $20 in spending cash his dad had given him. Twenty bucks was a significant sum back in 1975.

"And I lost it the first day," he said. "I was sick to my stomach."

Younger brother Aaron remembers an unexpected climate change after making the six-hour trip south from the Canadian border.

The St. Paul Civic Center "was warmer and hotter, and the ice wasn't as good as you were used to," he said. "It's not very often when you come off the ice after a period up north and it's still wet."

Paul, the youngest of Newell and Carol Broten's five children, made

a tidy profit as a middle schooler selling Roseau hats in the Civic Center concourse.

"Everyone wanted to buy your hat, because it said 'Roseau' on it," said Paul, six years younger than Neal. "They cost like five bucks. Guys would offer me fifteen bucks or ten bucks, and I would say, 'Sold!' Then I would go put on another one."

The Brotens are one of the most fabled families in high school hockey history. Though they never won a title in a combined six tries, thanks in large part to eternal roadblock Edina, they left their mark on the event in a multitude of ways:

• Neal's four first-period assists in the 1978 third-place game—a 5–3 victory over Mounds View—remains

a tournament record for most assists in a period.

• Aaron's twelve points in the 1978 tournament were the most since John Mayasich had scored eighteen in 1951.

• Paul scored twice in Roseau's 9–8 consolation championship victory over Burnsville in 1984. The combined seventeen goals still stand as the most scored by two teams in a single game. Roseau tied another state record by rallying from a four-goal deficit.

The Brotens' appearances on the state's grandest stage were all but inevitable. Neal was walking at eight months ("He was always good on his feet," Newell says) and playing in a Roseau third- and fourth-grade league as a first-grader. He made headlines in the *Minneapolis Tribune* as an eleven-year-old, seventy-two-pound Pee Wee described as having the qualities of, alternately, Boston Bruins legends Phil Esposito and Bobby Orr.

Ridiculous comparisons? Hardly.

"He was a little Gretzky is what he was," said Gary Hokanson, Roseau's head coach when all three Broten brothers made state tournament appearances in the late 1970s and into the mid-'80s.

Years before he hit middle school, the diminutive Neal was scoring one hundred–plus goals a season.

"Here would be this teeny guy out there, and all these big dudes, they would take runs at him," Hokanson said. "He would just zip right around them and keep on going."

As a freshman, Neal was a third-line center on the Roseau team that reached the 1975 state tournament, losing both games.

The Rams returned in 1977 as an

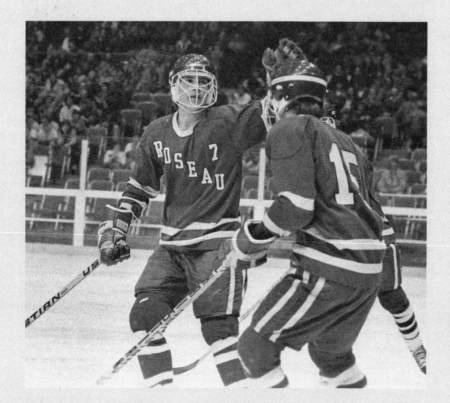

Roseau's Neal Broten (7) celebrates with linemate Bryan "Butsy" Erickson (15) during the 1978 state tournament. Broten registered four assists in one period (the first) against Mounds View in the 1978 consolation championship, a record that still stands. Photo by the *Minneapolis Star Tribune*

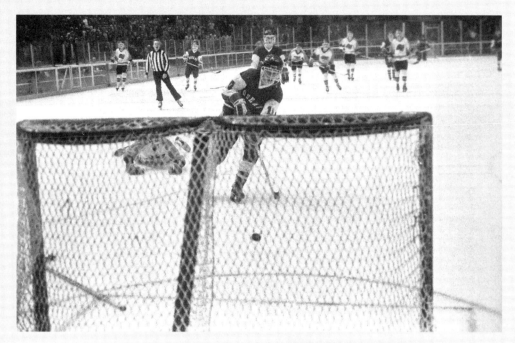

LEFT: With six Grand Rapids skaters on the ice behind him and a thrown stick in front, Roseau's Aaron Broten flipped the puck into an empty net with four seconds left to secure a 6–4 state quarterfinal victory over the previously undefeated Indians. Photo by the *Minneapolis Star Tribune*, courtesy of Kyle Oen/Vintage Minnesota Hockey

BELOW: In a 1983 *Minneapolis Star Tribune* feature story before the state tournament, Paul, the youngest of the three Broten brothers, said, "If you're a Broten, everybody's looking at you." Photo by *Minneapolis Star Tribune*

undefeated juggernaut. This time, Neal, now a junior, had sharpshooting brother Aaron, a sophomore, at his side. Junior forward Bryan "Butsy" Erickson, who joined them in endless games of street hockey, was yet another scoring machine. All three were byproducts of rare natural-born talent, an insatiable love for the game, and Roseau's one-of-a-kind hockey incubator known as the North Rink, a no-frills indoor ice sheet that allowed for pickup games for all ages anytime, day or night.

"They would play in a Saturday-morning league that started at eight," Newell said. "At seven o'clock at night they wouldn't have come home yet. If we happened to bring them home to have a bite to eat, they would be gone. They were back at the rink."

Roseau lost 2–0 to one-loss Edina East in the 1977 quarterfinals. The notoriously humble and soft-spoken Neal was denied on numerous prime scoring chances by Hornets' goaltender Steve Carroll.

"He scores on those 90 percent of the time, and this time it didn't happen," Aaron said. "It's like, that's just the way it goes."

In 1977–78, the Brotens and Erickson had one of the most dominating seasons in state history, racking up point totals reminiscent of the great Roseau "Production Line" of Jim and Larry Stordahl and Don Ross in the late 1950s. Neal had 115 points, Aaron 106, and Erickson 79 for a combined 300. Hokanson said in eight of twenty regular-season games, the trio sat out the third period of blowouts.

Roseau again reached the state tournament undefeated, this time knocking off defending champion Rochester John Marshall 4–2 in the quarterfinals. But the Rams lost 5–3 to Edina East in the semifinals, with one of the Hornets' goals coming short-handed on a center-ice shot from Tom Kelly.

"It was a goal he would save 99.9 percent of the time," Neal said about Rams goaltender Dean Grindahl. "I don't know about sitting on the bench going, 'Frickin' Edina is so damn lucky' or whatever, but I mean, come on, really?"

Aaron returned as a senior in 1979, leading the Rams past previously unbeaten Grand Rapids in the quarterfinals before losing the semifinals in a stunning 12–4 thrashing to, of course, Edina East.

Paul, six years younger than Neal, played in the state tournament in 1983 and 1984. In both, the Rams lost to—you guessed it—Edina.

Things might have turned out differently for the Brotens.

Perhaps not coincidentally, Newell, a longtime Roseau city employee, received job offers from multiple hockey hotbeds when it became obvious his boys were special talents. Among those that came calling was Warroad.

"They would have written a paycheck from [Marvin Windows] and told Newell [to] put on there as many zeroes as he wanted," said Hokanson, a Warroad native.

Newell was working for Solar Gas when he was offered a job at the company's home office. The lifelong Roseau resident declined. "I wasn't made for office work," he says.

The location of that central office? Edina.

~*LRN*~

116

Edina East cheerleaders show their spirit during the 1978 tournament. Photo by the *Minneapolis Tribune,* courtesy of the Minnesota Historical Society

Ikola, as much drill sergeant as he was hockey coach, wasn't long on words.

"He said, 'Aurick'—ever since the seventh grade, he always replaced the *l* with an *r*—'you are getting the start tonight,'" Aulik recalled.

Vacanti was crushed.

"I didn't handle it very well," said Vacanti, who skipped the team meal that night. "I went to my room and pouted."

Both Aulik and Vacanti were ready for the opening puck drop against championship foe Grand Rapids. Vacanti, as instructed by Ikola, played the role of good soldier, offering words of encouragement and slaps on the back for his teammates from his end of the bench.

Aulik, meanwhile, played the game of his life. He made forty saves in regulation and eight more in two overtime periods. Edina mustered twenty-three shots compared to Grand Rapids' fifty-two.

"He was just unconscious," Ikola said. "If it wasn't for him, we wouldn't have won."

The same could be said for fourth-line forward Tom Carroll. When Lauen crashed into the boards in the first period and couldn't return because of a back injury, Ikola plucked Carroll off the bench as a replacement.

Carroll, a junior, scored the winning goal when the rebound of his initial shot squirted free in the slot. With Grand Rapids goaltender Jim Jetland flat on his back thinking he had frozen the puck, Carroll swatted it into the net for the 5–4 victory.

A feeling of relief washed over Aulik.

"I just remember being glad it was over," he said.

Grand Rapids was left in a state of disbelief.

"I feel like a football coach who had a territorial advantage all day," Grand Rapids coach Jim Nelson told reporters, "and then got stung with the bomb."

~LRN~

EVERY DAY I NEED ATTENTION

GLITZY TOURNAMENT BOOSTED HORNETS' CELEBRITY STATUS

DATES	LOCATION	ATTENDANCE	CHAMPIONSHIP	
MARCH 15–17	ST. PAUL CIVIC CENTER	100,902	EDINA EAST 4, ROCHESTER JOHN MARSHALL 3 (OT)	117

 The same year minor penalties increased from one and a half to two minutes, a record 106 goals were scored in the tournament, including twenty by champion Edina East. Eveleth holds the record for most goals scored in a tournament with thirty in 1945.

COLLEGE COACHES on scouting missions from the East Coast were regular attendees at Edina East practices. Celebrities such as Cheryl Tiegs, Richard Dawson, and Howard Cosell came from all corners of the country and watched the Hornets. Starry-eyed girls were caught outside players' hotel room doors after curfew.

Twin Cities newspapers loved Edina East, too, hailing the defending state champions as the state's number-one-ranked team to start a 1978–79 Hornets season that had all the trappings of a Led Zeppelin concert tour.

Edina's players, nine of them back from the previous season's squad, enjoyed the scrutiny.

"It was kind of an unusual thing," senior captain John Donnelly said about the abundant fanfare. "But, you know, Edina is short for Every Day I Need Attention."

Not all the attention was flattering. The Hornets incurred the wrath of head coach Willard Ikola more than once that season, including during the two-game swing at Hibbing and Eveleth. After the team pounded Hibbing 8–1 in the opener, Ikola set a 10 PM curfew ahead of the next day's game.

And when Ikola said 10, he meant 9:45. Or earlier. He had no patience for tardiness, as senior forward Mark Gagnon can attest.

"My girlfriend is at my door, and it is about ten something,"

Supermodel, fashion designer, and Minnesota native Cheryl Tiegs was among the numerous ABC network–affiliated celebrities who made appearances at the 1979 state tournament. Photo by the *Minneapolis Tribune,* courtesy of the Minnesota Historical Society

118

Gagnon said. "Ikola comes down the hall by himself. I thought to myself, 'OK, we have a situation here.' He looks at me, and the girl kind of scampers off. He didn't scold me at that point."

The Hornets started sluggishly the next day. Eveleth was Ikola's hometown, and the former Golden Bears goaltender who had won three state titles wanted a grand showing against his former team.

Ikola stormed into the locker room after the lackluster first period. This time, Gagnon didn't escape the coach's wrath.

"Gagnon, you are running around out there like a dog in heat," Ikola growled. "Let's get some ice for that guy's balls."

What was intended as a stern speech instead became comic relief.

"We were putting our jerseys over our heads because we were laughing so hard and didn't want to get yelled at," said Steve Brown, a senior defenseman.

The Hornets beat Eveleth 5–2 but suffered four losses in their next eleven games. Two of the setbacks came against archrival Edina West by scores of 6–2 and 6–1.

Ikola didn't suffer defeats lightly, and the second of those losses to West all but blew his mind. He held a no-puck practice, ninety minutes of hard skating. He called his players spoiled and arrogant, then pulled aside the seniors for some final words.

"Ikola never swore," senior goalie Mike Vacanti said. "He would say, 'You big ape' or 'You dummy,' but he never swore.

"He said to us, 'I don't understand what is going on, why you are not prepared in what we are doing.' He said, 'I've got to tell you, I am lost. I am a goddamn hockey coach, not a [expletive] psychiatrist.'

"It was a big shocker, to hear him drop an f-bomb," Vacanti said. "We didn't lose again."

Edina East fully expected to meet Edina West in the Region 6 championship. But the Cougars were stunned by Robbinsdale Cooper 2–1 in the semifinals. East beat Cooper 5–1 for its eighth tournament appearance of the decade (counting 1970–72 as Edina).

A heightened element of glitz and glamour accompanied the Hornets in St. Paul. KSTP was the new television broadcast rights holder, and supermodel Tiegs, actor and game-show host Dawson, and sports broadcaster Cosell were brought in to celebrate the station's new ABC affiliation.

Edina East edged Hill-Murray 4–3 in the quarterfinals, setting up a third state tournament meeting with Roseau in as many years.

Mike Lauen, who had scored a hat trick in Edina East's 5–3 semifinal win over Roseau the previous year, scored with twenty-three seconds left in the first period to put the Hornets ahead 3–2. Edina East outscored the Rams 5–1 in the second period and 4–1 in the third en route to a dizzying 12–4 triumph. Lauen finished with another hat trick, as did linemate Gagnon.

"That was really kind of a shock even to us that we were able to score that many," said senior forward Tom Carroll, who

Edina East goaltender Mike Vacanti (left) and forward Mike Lauen, dabbing his bloody chin with the remnants of a toilet-paper streamer, savor their 4–3 overtime victory after Lauen scored the winning goal against Rochester John Marshall in the 1979 title game. Photo by Pete Hohn/*Minneapolis Tribune*

scored twice. "If we played them a hundred times I don't think that would have ever happened again."

Rochester John Marshall scored a combined twelve goals in its first two tournament games on its way to the championship. The Rockets, from the deep southern portion of the state, were the darlings of the tournament, just as they had been in 1977 when they shocked Edina East 4–2 in the championship game.

With Cosell, known best for his work on *Monday Night Football* and boxing broadcasts, commentating, John Marshall led 3–2 late in the third period. Ikola was preparing to pull Vacanti for an extra skater when Carroll scored on a feed from Brad Benson with 1:13 left in regulation.

Lauen burst down the right side early in overtime, beating a John Marshall defenseman to the puck and hammering a shot off superb Rockets goaltender Paul Butters's right arm and into the net.

"He made it look so easy, so nonchalant," Donnelly said about Lauen.

Tripped just after he shot, Lauen went sliding face first into the boards behind the John Marshall net. He was too tired to get up and served as a landing pad for joyous teammates.

"We had a saying on our team," Donnelly said about the Hornets' brash approach to overtime. "'Meet me at the hog pile.'"

Lauen emerged from the pile with a battered chin and blood-spattered jersey, but he stemmed the bleeding by applying a three foot length of toilet paper from the rolls that doubled as streamers thrown onto the ice.

Holding his makeshift bandage to his chin, the leftover portion of the strip flapping in the breeze behind him, Lauen took a victory lap with his teammates. The farewell tour for a team that loved every minute of its season in the spotlight.

~LRN~

GIFT OF GAB

Famed sports broadcaster Howard Cosell waxed poetic about tournament's greatness

Howard Cosell was tight with Muhammad Ali, flew on private jets to the world's biggest sporting events, and brought his blustery intelligence to number-one-rated *Monday Night Football* broadcasts, coining the phrase "He could...go...all...the...way!"

Of all the celebrities—movie stars, supermodels, politicians, and comedians—who have attended the state tournament, it's likely none created a bigger buzz than Cosell.

He was at the peak of his fame when he arrived at the St. Paul Civic Center in 1979, wife Emmy part of his entourage. KSTP-TV was in its first year broadcasting the state tournament, and the station had recently affiliated with ABC. Cosell, supermodel Cheryl Tiegs (a Minnesota native), and *Family Feud* game show host Richard Dawson were also in the cadre of stars brought in to promote the partnership.

"It was no stunt," KSTP owner Stanley Hubbard told the *Star Tribune's* Joe Soucheray. "The tournament was a perfect showcase for Howard."

When Cosell wasn't smoking stogies, signing autographs, and bumping elbows with *Star Tribune* columnist and friend Sid Hartman (playfully introducing Hartman as "the man who wants the Vikings moved out of Minnesota"), he watched some of the hockey.

"This is sport the way it should be," he said, launching into one of his trademark soliloquies during the championship game between Rochester John Marshall and Edina East. "The fun. The joy of participation. The learning experience. The interdependence that grows between and among young people. The synthesis, the cohesion. This is what sport really is all about. I tell you this has been a thrilling experience for me."

Players and coaches were awestruck by having Cosell in their midst. Former tournament great John Mayasich, working for KSTP, brought Cosell down to the arena floor to interview Edina East coach Willard Ikola. Maysich and Ikola had been teammates on state championship Eveleth teams in 1948, '49, and '50, and Maysich gave Cosell some quick background, noting that former goaltender Ikola had starred for Michigan and on several US national teams.

"Howard didn't know me from beans," Ikola said. "When I started talking to him, the first thing he says is, 'I remember when you played at Michigan.' Hell, he never saw me play at Michigan."

Ikola said he tried to muster the courage to ask Cosell who his favorite heavyweight boxer was, knowing the answer would be Ali.

"I was going to try to interview him a little," said Ikola, who has a framed picture of his conversation with Cosell hanging in his rec room. "I didn't have the guts to do it."

Edina East players spilled out of their locker room to witness their coach's exchange with Cosell, which began with Cosell giving Ikola a playful jab to the chin.

"We are all out there watching it because it is kind of a spectacle," goaltender Mike Vacanti said. "Then, when Ikola was done and walking away, he sticks his tongue out at us, like 'Ha, ha.' Something a little kid would do. We saw this other side of him that we had never seen."

Cosell, who professed his admiration for the play of John Marshall's Todd Lecy and Paul Butters and raved about Edina's speed and depth, truly seemed to relish his dalliance with Minnesota high school hockey.

"This is a delight," Cosell said. "I just can't convey to your viewers how much I have enjoyed this high school tournament."

~LRN~

Famed sports broadcaster Howard Cosell lands a playful jab as he interviews Edina East coach Willard Ikola during the 1979 state tournament. Photo by Pete Hohn/*Minneapolis Tribune*

COMEDY CENTRAL

WISE-CRACKING GRAND RAPIDS KNEW WHEN TO SHOW SERIOUS SIDE

DATES	LOCATION	ATTENDANCE	CHAMPIONSHIP
MARCH 13–15	ST. PAUL CIVIC CENTER	102,197	GRAND RAPIDS 2, HILL-MURRAY 1

 Minneapolis Southwest became the city's last public-school state tournament entrant until 1993, when South reached the Tier II event.

AN UNPROVEN HEAD COACH with an unheralded senior class that one player described as uncoachable.

No one could have predicted the 1979–80 Grand Rapids team capturing the program's third state championship in six seasons.

"If you look at the rosters from about 1975–80, you wouldn't pick them," said Rod "Buzz" Christensen, who in 1979 was in his first year as head coach after four seasons as a Grand Rapids assistant.

"The 1978–79 senior group won everything at the youth levels," said forward John DeCenzo. "The 1980 seniors didn't, so it made us looser."

Too loose, much of the time.

"We were kind of uncoachable, as a whole," said defenseman Scott Billeadeau.

The team that would later put its mix of shenanigans and skill on full display at the state tournament started the season 1–3.

Then the eleven seniors, several of them players whose older brothers had helped Grand Rapids win state titles in 1975 and 1976, got serious.

A seniors-only meeting renewed their purpose. The previous season, many of them had played on the undefeated team upset by Roseau in the state tournament quarterfinals.

They had to get back to state. And they had to win. But they would do it their way—as characters playing with character. What followed was a 14–2 run through the remainder of the regular season.

"The attitude of the team was 'We're not going to be perfect but we're going to win,'" said forward Tom Rothstein.

"Buzzy let us be us," DeCenzo said. "There was no way I'd have coached that team."

Buzz, or Buzzy—a nickname bestowed by his mother because of a strange sound he made in the crib—had won two state titles as a forward at International Falls (1965 and 1966) and played at North Dakota.

He also served as an army combat medic in Vietnam for twenty months in 1970–71. He said the experience taught him that "you don't have to be freaking out when things go a little haywire."

Instead, whenever players made practice mistakes, Christensen shot them the evil eye.

Stern looks weren't necessary for goalie Jon Casey. Though surrounded by screwballs, Casey maintained a frightening intensity.

An errant Eric Lempe shot buzzed Casey's head during warmups before one early-season game. Enraged, Casey gave chase and threw his goalie stick at Lempe. Teammates had to go retrieve the paddle from the other end of the ice.

"With the pads on, he was a completely different person," Billeadeau said. "On the ice, no one was more serious."

After lackadaisical play by teammates during a scramble in front of the net resulted in a goal, Casey pulled himself during the regular-season finale, a 10–4 victory at Bemidji.

"He came to the bench and went right into the locker room," Christensen said.

"I was always very competitive, and I wanted to win at all times, at all costs," Casey said.

Casey and younger brother David, a forward, had transferred from nearby Greenway before the 1978–79 season. The move drew ire along the Iron Range.

"It was a family situation. There were reasons beyond hockey," DeCenzo said.

Grand Rapids claimed its seventh consecutive Region 7 title and brought its traveling circus to the St. Paul Civic Center.

Teams practiced Wednesday, and Christensen and players remember the precision of tournament newcomer Bloomington Jefferson. The Jaguars looked sharp and ran crisp drills.

Grand Rapids, meanwhile, resembled hockey hillbillies.

"We had guys wearing different jerseys, and we scrimmaged with a tennis ball," Christensen said. "We weren't trying to prove or accomplish anything."

"We weren't a drill team," DeCenzo said.

In the quarterfinals, Grand Rapids drilled Hopkins Lindbergh 8–3. Rothstein and Todd Lempe each scored twice, and DeCenzo added three assists.

Upstart Jefferson waited in Friday's second semifinal. And Grand Rapids hit the ice loose as ever thanks to a television segment gone hilariously wrong.

Channel 5, the Twin Cities' ABC television affiliate, had risked a live behind-the-scenes interview from the Grand Rapids locker room.

A loosey-goosey Grand Rapids bunch knew better than to cross goalie Jon Casey, an intense competitor who was at his best in big games. Hill-Murray entered the 1980 championship game undefeated, but Casey proved unbeatable. He helped Grand Rapids overcome a 32-16 deficit in shots on goal in a 2-1 victory. Photo courtesy of the Minnesota Historical Society

Viewers watching between periods of the first semifinal game, Hill-Murray versus Minneapolis Southwest, received a stick-taping tutorial from Rothstein. But off camera, a line of teammates ranging from half dressed to completely naked stood chuckling. Rothstein heard but did not see them—until he turned to grab his stick to close the segment. Good thing the cameras didn't show what Rothstein saw.

"I started laughing and couldn't stop," Rothstein said.

Rob Leer, then a young reporter, quickly closed with, "Well, I guess they are loose down here."

Recalling that moment, Leer said, "That team was goofier than anybody advertised. But it made for great TV."

Grand Rapids trailed Jefferson 1–0 at first intermission, then took the lead on goals from Rothstein and Jim Malwitz. Billeadeau assisted on both goals but did his best work hounding Jaguar forward Jay North.

North tallied a quarterfinal hat trick but couldn't find a seam in the Grand Rapids defense. Billeadeau found North.

"Scooter popped him, and that changed North's game," DeCenzo said.

Holding a one-goal lead in the third period only heightened Casey's competitiveness. He dived to knock away a puck and thwart a two-on-none Jefferson chance.

"I was able to be more aggressive because our defense was so strong," Casey said.

A 3–1 victory earned unflappable Grand Rapids a title game showdown with undefeated Hill-Murray (27–0).

DeCenzo, Malwitz, and Rothstein engaged in pregame locker-room gymnastics—tumbles, rolls, and jumps for teammates to judge.

All business on the ice, Grand Rapids struck first on an unassisted, shorthanded DeCenzo goal.

"The hardest hit DeCenzo took in the tournament was when I jumped on him," Billeadeau said. "He goes, 'Scooter, what the hell?'"

Hill-Murray players had to be asking a similar question of Casey. The Pioneers outshot Grand Rapids 32–16 but only beat Casey once. Todd Lempe put Grand Rapids ahead 2–1 late in the second period, and that's how the game ended.

Reflecting on the team's harried journey and the coaching staff's mostly hands-off approach, assistant coach Lyn Ellingson told John Gilbert of the *Minneapolis Tribune*, "We figured that they might be just wacky enough to go all the way if we left them alone."

—DL~

SIGHT TO BEHOLD

South St. Paul's silky skating Phil Housley was NHL-ready as a high schooler

Phil Housley formed roots in South St. Paul hockey by rendezvousing with friends at the Bromley Street rink or catching a late-afternoon ride with his father and brother down to Veterans Field.

He started as so many young puck chasers do: trying to impress the older players. He later surpassed them all. A stellar defenseman, Housley played in the state tournament as a sophomore and junior. Not long after his 1982 graduation, Buffalo Sabres coach Scotty Bowman made him the sixth pick in the NHL draft.

"He's the closest thing I've seen to Bobby Orr," Bowman said.

Remarkably, Housley went straight from high school to the NHL without playing college or minor-league hockey. No Minnesota-born player before or since has been able to make that claim.

"I've never seen anybody from Minnesota that is as talented and as skilled and as beautiful to watch as Phil," said Doug Woog, the former South St. Paul player who coached Housley.

The young man was so good, his number 20 home jersey was retired upon his graduation. There wasn't a ceremony. Just larceny.

"I took it," Housley said with a

laugh. "The white number 20 jersey is still in my basement."

Housley drew raves for his offensive skill set. Fast, fluid, and a finisher, he became an instant force upon touching the puck.

He bagged 108 goals as a ten-year-old Squirt, 113 as a Pee Wee. Woog played him as a freshman. A year later, Housley tallied sixteen goals and twenty-nine assists and led the Packers across the Mississippi River to the St. Paul Civic Center for the state tournament.

"Just standing there and hearing the national anthem, I thought it was the greatest thing," Housley said.

In that first state tournament game, Housley scored the tying goal with less than one minute remaining in regulation. But the Packers fell in overtime.

As a junior, Housley assisted on his team's first goal and older brother Larry scored the game-winner in a 2–1 quarterfinal upset of Edina West. Phil's semifinal performance of a goal and two assists wasn't enough in a 5–3 loss to Irondale.

He never got another chance to race around the Civic Center in those briefly popular Cooperall pants only he could make stylish. Henry Sibley eliminated South St. Paul in the sectional final the following year and ended Housley's prep career. The loss still haunts him.

But rich state tournament memories linger as well, important to him as an incredible NHL career of twenty-two seasons and 1,495 regular season games.

"That is something you wish every hockey player in Minnesota could experience," Housley said. "I would tell anyone that gets there to cherish it and have fun with it because you'll take it with you the rest of your life."

Chosen sixth overall by the Buffalo Sabres in the 1982 NHL draft, Phil Housley never spent a day in college or the minors. Yet some of his fondest memories are from his two state tournament trips with South St. Paul. Photo by Regene Radniecki/*Minneapolis Tribune*

~DL~

SATS AND THE PYLON

UNLIKELY BLOOMINGTON JEFFERSON COACHING DUO FORMED CHAMPIONSHIP COMBINATION

DATES	LOCATION	ATTENDANCE	CHAMPIONSHIP
MARCH 12–14	ST. PAUL CIVIC CENTER	100,914	BLOOMINGTON JEFFERSON 3, IRONDALE 2

 Jefferson goalie Chris Robideau broke his femur and dislocated his knee playing soccer as a sophomore. Doctors said he was done playing hockey. But he back-stopped the Jaguars to glory as a senior.

TOM SATERDALEN arrived in 1973 as Bloomington Jefferson's head coach and soon found a solid coaching résumé did not equal job security.

Seven parents, most of whom had sons who hadn't made the team, petitioned for Saterdalen's ouster during his second season. Administrators backed Saterdalen, who had learned under Minnesota coaching legends and directed Wisconsin high school hockey championships, but he needed another ally.

So, after the season, he called on John Bianchi to be his assistant. Bianchi, a lousy pond-hockey player with one season of Squirt-hockey coaching experience in the Jefferson youth ranks, was incredulous.

"I couldn't demonstrate anything to anyone," Bianchi said. "I felt like a pylon."

Saterdalen felt otherwise.

"Tom said he didn't want me for my skill, he wanted me for my enthusiasm and dedication," Bianchi said. "He said, 'I watched you coach one year, and you're a winner.'"

Saterdalen sharpened players' minds, and Bianchi spoke to their hearts. Together, they formed the foundation of Minnesota's next great high school hockey program.

As a kid, Saterdalen toiled on a Rochester farm and later played football, hockey, and baseball at John Marshall. He played two years of amateur hockey before enrolling in 1962 at Bemidji State. As a senior, he served as hockey team captain.

Bianchi grew up about 275 miles north in Mountain Iron but wasn't involved in the prevalent mining industry. His athletic loves were basketball (despite standing 5 foot 4) and baseball. Hockey was something he played on the pond—poorly.

As a senior at Bemidji State, Bianchi led the baseball team with a .488 batting average and made only one error at shortstop. He graduated with a degree in elementary education in 1962 just months before Saterdalen's arrival.

Then Bianchi moved to the Twin Cities and became an elementary school teacher in the growing Bloomington school district.

Saterdalen arrived at Jefferson after coaching stints at Cloquet, Bemidji State, the University of Minnesota, and Superior (Wisconsin) High School. During his three seasons at Min-

nesota, Saterdalen learned under Herb Brooks, Glen Sonmor, and Ken Yackel. In four seasons at Superior, he won two Wisconsin state championships.

This hockey odd couple used strengths as different as their upbringings to bring Bloomington Jefferson into power.

"They were both psychologists in different ways," said defenseman Jim Becker, senior captain in 1980–81. "Sats would ride you. John loved you. With John, you didn't want to lose for him. With Sats, you were afraid to lose for him."

The Jaguars defeated Rochester Mayo in 1980 to gain their first state tournament appearance. Tom Kurvers, Jay North, and several additional seniors who went on to play college hockey, placed third.

No one predicted a championship in 1980–81 even though nine players returned.

"We always saw ourselves as underdogs," said Steve Bianchi, the oldest of John's three sons and a junior center. "It was like, 'You can kick dirt in our face, that's OK.' We weren't the most skilled team, but we were well coached and worked hard."

These Jaguars never shied from competition. Becker said driveway hockey games after school with Bianchi and Kurvers "didn't stop until there was blood."

Players kept score even in the lighter moments.

"We would clog the drains in the shower room, get four or five inches of water and see who could slide on their ass farthest," Becker said.

Jefferson returned to the state tournament and drew Grand Rapids in the quarterfinals. The defending champions led 3–1 in the third period and looked poised to vanquish the Jaguars for a second consecutive year.

A power-play goal from Jefferson senior wing Dan Beaty, whose father was from Grand Rapids, cut the Jaguars' deficit to 3–2. Then Bianchi scored the goal of his life.

Pushing the puck past a fallen Grand Rapids defenseman and then putting a move on the other, Bianchi freed himself for an unassisted tying goal.

"Every game had a turning point, and we always seemed to rise to it," Steve Bianchi said.

His father concurred.

"That shot has stayed in a lot of people's minds," John Bianchi said. "But really, it was a team goal. Everybody hung in there."

Just forty-nine seconds into overtime, Steve Nornes slid a backhand pass from behind the net past three Grand Rapids players and into the slot for Paul Gess to bury. Jefferson won 4–3.

The semifinal between Jefferson and Apple Valley featured two teams with inflated loss totals. Using ineligible players meant both teams were forced to change victories to losses by forfeit: Apple Valley eleven and Jefferson six.

Two weeks earlier, Apple Valley had crushed Jefferson in a scrimmage.

"We came out flat, but it ended up being a little psychological advantage," Steve Bianchi said.

Jefferson handled Apple Valley 4–1 in the rematch.

Revenge once again served Jefferson well in the championship game against Irondale. The Knights of New Brighton "beat us all the time growing up," said John Bianchi, who challenged players "to be a man and say, 'I'm going to go out there and do it.'"

Saterdalen's game plan complemented Bianchi's speech. Ace defensive forwards Nornes and Tony Mazzu neutralized Irondale scorers Mike Bjugstad and Steve Hoppe. The Knights duo managed a lone assist.

Hardworking wing Tony Mazzu personified a Bloomington Jefferson team short on star power but long on grit and determination. He scored a goal against Irondale in the championship game and provided excellent defense against top Knights scorers Mike Bjugstad and Steve Hoppe. Photo courtesy of the Minnesota Historical Society

"That was the best defensive team I ever played on," Becker said. "Everyone backchecked. It was a defenseman's dream."

His team down 1–0, Becker scored a power-play goal to draw even. John Bianchi praised Becker as someone who would "jump in front of a truck to stop it from hitting a dog. He was not afraid to show you who he was. He held everybody up."

Gess scored again forty-eight seconds later. A physical presence throughout the tournament, Gess had television color commentator Herb Brooks comparing him to former Gophers tough guy Paul Holmgren.

Mazzu, who had missed several games around midseason

for college football recruiting visits, scored the clinching goal in a 3–2 Jaguars victory.

Jefferson became the second Twin Cities suburban program to win a state title.

"This is the biggest thrill ever; nothing I've experienced has come close to approaching this," Saterdalen said. "These are good, hard-digging kids. They've been winners all their lives."

Saterdalen and Bianchi, an odd but undeniable duo, had only just begun their winning ways.

~DL~

Bloomington Jefferson became just the second Twin Cities suburban team to win a state championship. Heading into the 1981 tournament, few observers picked the Jaguars, who had graduated a lot of talented players from the 1980 team, but the no-stars approach worked well. Photo courtesy of Kyle Oen/Vintage Minnesota Hockey

SUPERTEAM

EAST-WEST EDINA MERGER CREATED ABUNDANCE OF TALENT—AND HEADACHES

DATES	LOCATION	ATTENDANCE	CHAMPIONSHIP
MARCH 11–13	ST. PAUL CIVIC CENTER	101,006	EDINA 6, WHITE BEAR MARINER 0

 Cloquet, Rochester Mayo, and White Bear Mariner all made their tourney debuts. Mariner High School, which opened in 1972, never returned, eventually merging with White Bear Lake High School in 1983.

"YOU'RE NOT MY CAPTAIN!"

Edina was a team in disarray early in the 1981–82 season, and those four words drilled straight into the heart of the Hornets' issues.

The freshly minted merger of Edina's high-powered East and West hockey programs had created a superteam, an array of top-caliber veteran talent the likes of which the state had never seen. More than ninety players showed up for tryouts that fall, many of them returning letter winners who had no shot at making the squad.

"That was a waste of five days," said Hornets coach Willard Ikola, whose embarrassment of riches included fourteen future Division I college players (including five who became NHL draft picks). "I already knew who was going to be on the team before they ever stepped on the ice."

In an attempt to spark diplomacy between groups of players who had grown up as heated rivals ("mortal enemies," as better described by John DeVoe), a captain was chosen to represent each faction. The honors went to senior defenseman Bill Brauer from East and senior center Dave Maley from West.

Leadership was required when a sloppy, uninspired early-season practice blew Ikola's top and sent the Hornets to the showers early.

"Ike kicked us off the ice," Brauer said, "and told us, 'You captains go talk to your team and figure this out.'"

Brauer had an oversized personality, big enough to match his hulking 6-foot-3, 200-pound frame. "I was kind of a yeller, a rah-rah guy," he said.

With Maley at his side, Brauer tried to jumpstart the flatlining team.

Come on, guys, Coach is mad at us! We've got to get this thing going! We've got all the talent in the world—we've got to start using it!

DeVoe wasn't buying it. A senior, he was Maley's longtime running mate. They had been terrors growing up, causing mayhem in the Valley View Junior High School hallways. The high school's principal asked West hockey coach Bart Larson to try to rein in the two mischievous freshmen.

"They tended to fool around maybe more than they should

have," Larson said. "I told them, 'You guys have to shape up outside of the classroom.'"

The 6-foot-2, 175-pound DeVoe was a natural goal scorer who, along with Maley, had cracked West's varsity lineup as a freshman. DeVoe and the bruising Brauer had been involved in more than a few run-ins over the years, including the time Brauer broke DeVoe's shoulder with a devastating hit.

DeVoe, who naturally bristled at authority, was now supposed to follow Brauer's orders? Not going to happen.

Having reached his boiling point, DeVoe stood up and had his say:

"You're not my captain! I didn't vote for you! I don't have to listen to you!"

"They literally were standing toe to toe," said Wally Chapman, a senior forward. "We were all kind of going, 'Wow, this is crazy.'"

DeVoe and Brauer almost came to blows leaving the rink that day. Larson, who had become Ikola's assistant coach, intervened.

Slowly, the frosty relationship between the two groups (and, by extension, Brauer and DeVoe) began to thaw.

Ikola, fearing he didn't have enough scoring balance in his forward lines, broke up his all-West unit of Maley, DeVoe, and Chapman. He inserted East-sider Brian Cutshall on the line with DeVoe and Maley.

"I said, 'Cutshall, just go in the corner and feed those two guys,'" Ikola said. "'And then get out of their way. And then you backcheck all the way back to the net. That's all you've got to do. Feed them and come back. Feed them and come back.'

"That line took off."

DeVoe instantly appreciated the work of the relentless Cutshall, despite his East roots.

Chapman, a third-liner the previous season who had been thriving on the top line, was paired with junior varsity call-ups Dan Carroll and Mike DeVoe (John's younger brother). DeVoe was from West, Carroll from East. Both were juniors.

"They were two JV guys," said Chapman, who was given the news of the shakeup in Ikola's hotel room before a game at

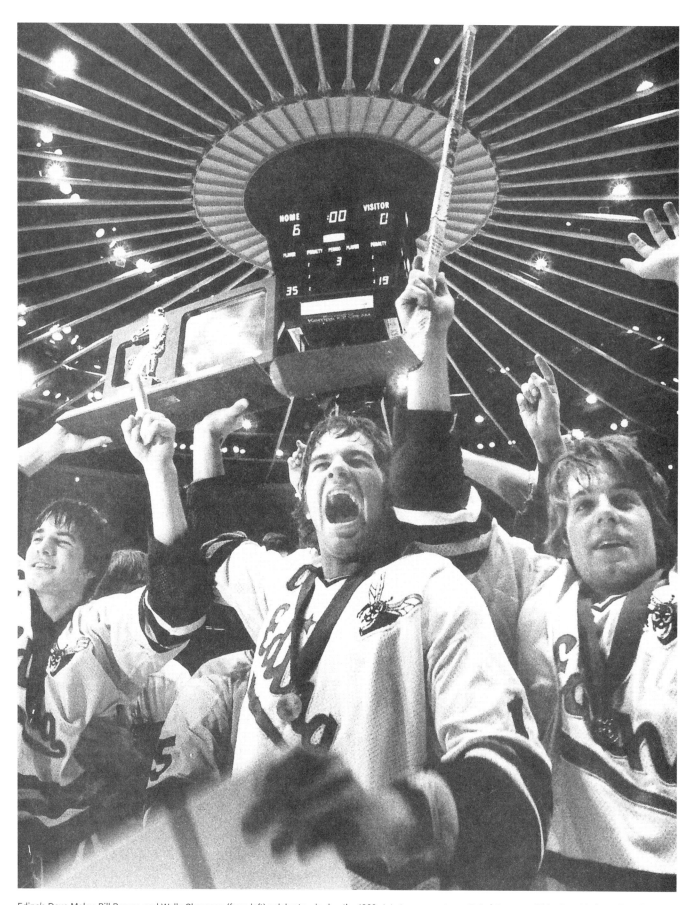

Edina's Dave Maley, Bill Brauer, and Wally Chapman (from left) celebrate winning the 1982 state tournament on a 6–0 victory over White Bear Mariner. Photo by Mike Zerby/*Minneapolis Tribune*

Duluth East. "I thought, 'Oh my gosh, I am going from the penthouse to I don't know what.'"

Ikola explained the move wasn't intended as a demotion. On the contrary, he made Chapman a de facto coach with the authority to manage the trio as he saw fit.

"Wally was a great kid," Ikola said. "I said, 'Wally, I am not even going to coach your line. You are the guy. Tell those two juniors what you want.' So I gave him an assignment, so to speak."

That line took off, too.

"Danny, like all the Carroll brothers, could score from anywhere," Chapman said. "Mike was a grinder and could score. It wasn't like they were crappy players."

Added Carroll: "Mike and I were like, 'Holy [expletive], Wally Chapman? We're playing with Wally Chapman?' We clicked from the get-go. It was phenomenal how we bonded."

A third forward unit consisting of center Mike McCarthy and wings Paul Roff and Jeff Vacanti gave the Hornets yet another potent scoring line.

Nicknames were given to the defensemen and forward units based on the color of their practice jerseys.

"The defensemen wore red and were the Red Guns," Chapman said. "We were the gold line, and our nickname became the Solid Gold Dancers. Don't ask me why—we were just being dumb high school kids. Maley's line was the Whiteheads.

"The nicknames created a bond. You never wanted to be the worst line. There was a lot of pride."

As new, more healthy rivalries were born, the divide between East and West narrowed.

Seven games into the season, Edina beat Hibbing 4–2 in a matchup of the state's first- and second-ranked teams. The Hornets were outshot by a two-to-one margin and relied heavily on the stellar play of senior goaltender Jim Lozinski to eke out the win.

Ikola wasn't pleased with his team's performance, the latest in a growing list of irritants. He didn't like the boom boxes blasting in the locker room. ("Get those damned things out of here!") He didn't like players wearing mismatched socks in practice. ("Go change. You look like clowns!") He especially didn't like the rumors about West players implying he was soft.

"They were saying, 'I've heard a lot of stories about that Ikola, that he's kind of a hard-ass at times. But he doesn't seem that way to me,'" Ikola said.

During the practice following the Hibbing game, Ikola saw Maley and John DeVoe "playing grab-ass, just screwing around," Ikola said. "I never planned no-puck practices, but I had quite a few of them over the years. It is something that just happens."

For the next hour and a half, the Hornets did sprints, starts and stops, and a variety of other conditioning drills. They never touched a puck.

"Ikola kept yelling at us, 'Jimmy [Lozinski] has whiplash from all the shots he saw against Hibbing! Jimmy is in the hospital because he has got goddamn whiplash!'" John DeVoe said.

Added Chapman: "Lozinski wasn't there at practice. None of us knew why. I thought, 'Is Lou really in the hospital?' Turns out he was just sick or something and just happened to not be there that day."

Nurtured by burning lungs and aching legs ("I skated their asses off," Ikola said), team unity continued to blossom. Edina reeled off ten straight victories heading into the final two games of the regular season, when it inexplicably lost 3–2 in overtime to Bloomington Kennedy and 4–3 to Minnetonka.

"We took our foot off the gas," John DeVoe said. "Lost focus. In retrospect, I'm glad we lost those games because it woke us the hell up."

The Hornets righted themselves in time for the playoffs, reeling off lopsided sectional wins over Cooper (8–1), Minnetonka (7–2), and Wayzata (8–1).

Before the season, Ikola, in a tradition borrowed from Vince Dooley's Georgia football program, had T-shirts made for his players that read "BIG TEAM, little me."

"We all came to believe in that saying over the course of the season," Maley said.

Edina opened the state tournament with a 7–4 triumph over Rochester Mayo in which the Hornets scored six of the final seven goals and outshot the Spartans 38–20.

Chapman scored the tournament's signature goal in overtime in a semifinal victory against defending

THIRTY-EIGHTH ANNUAL MINNESOTA STATE HIGH SCHOOL
HOCKEY TOURNAMENT
MARCH 11, 12, 13, 1982
66th YEAR OF SERVICE—1916-1982
OFFICIAL PROGRAM $1.50

champion Bloomington Jefferson. With just more than a minute left in overtime, Carroll, off a faceoff, burst out of the Hornets' zone with the puck. He hit Mike DeVoe in stride as the right winger made center ice. DeVoe crossed the blue line and dropped a pass back to Chapman, who whipped the puck off the right goalpost and into the net. A dazzling play from the Solid Gold Dancers.

"That was as fine a goal as you're gonna see," longtime tournament TV analyst Lou Nanne said on the broadcast.

Nanne was impressed with White Bear Mariner, too. The Dolphins, making their first and only state tournament appearance, upended Hibbing 4–1 in the other semifinal. With twelve players standing 6 feet or taller, Mariner figured to try to impose its will on the speedy Hornets.

"Lou Nanne was on TV," DeVoe said. "He talked about how big White Bear Mariner was and how Edina better watch out. We were at the hotel walking around the hallways on our floor laughing and saying, 'We are going to get killed! They are giants!'"

Edina had ten players 6 feet or taller and none shorter than 5 foot 10. But the championship game was hardly a board-shaking affair. Edina was unrivaled in terms of speed, skill, and depth, and it showed in a freewheeling 6–0 rout.

The score could have been even worse for the Dolphins. Two Hornets goals were disallowed, including one by John DeVoe when he was ruled to have scored using an illegal stick.

"Classic DeVoe," Chapman said.

In was common practice for DeVoe to heat the blades of his sticks over a stove and then slide them under a door, bending the curves to banana-like proportions.

"They were meat hooks," said DeVoe, who after scoring would usually switch sticks briefly with defensemen Tom Rzeszut or Andy Kasid, just in case there was an inquiry.

DeVoe was so excited to have scored late in the first period

he forgot all about his switcheroo trick as he celebrated with teammates in front of the Mariner bench, practically waving his stick in front of Dolphins coach Tom Simpson's nose. Simpson asked the officials to check the curve. Not that DeVoe's stick altering was a guarded secret.

"It was very well known that he had the biggest curve on the planet," Chapman said.

The Hornets led 1–0 after the first period, and by the time DeVoe served his ten-minute misconduct, they were up 4–0.

"Damn, he got me mad," Ikola said about DeVoe, "I was going to sit him down, but we were playing well, and I thought, 'The hell with it.'"

Ikola wasn't much into studying videotape, but weeks later as he watched the championship game, he marveled again at his team's play.

"I knew we played about as good as you can play for a high school team," Ikola said. "But I watched the video, and everything was zip, zip, zip, zip. We didn't make a bad pass the whole game. Everything was tape to tape. The forechecking was unbelievable.

"I never saw a team play a game with no mistakes. Not at any level. I thought to myself, 'We played a perfect game.'"

Imagine that. The team that, in Ikola's eyes, couldn't do anything right ended its season by doing no wrong.

And the guys who just couldn't get along? After a night of celebrating, and after their teammates all had fallen asleep, Brauer and DeVoe quietly slipped out of the downtown Radisson Hotel.

Off they went, just the two of them, to share a late-night meal at Mickey's Diner, mortal enemies having become the best of buddies.

~LRN~

PURSUIT OF PERFECTION

HILL-MURRAY'S UNBEATEN SEASON REQUIRED CONTRIBUTIONS FROM ALL

DATES	LOCATION	ATTENDANCE	CHAMPIONSHIP
MARCH 10–12	ST. PAUL CIVIC CENTER	102,596	HILL-MURRAY 4, BURNSVILLE 3

Did you know? WCCO-TV began televising the state tournament in 1983, spending $450,000 to secure the rights for three years. The production featured ten cameras for game action and memorable music videos shot at all eight qualifying schools.

"LET'S HIT DOUBLE FIGURES in the third period," a Rochester John Marshall hockey player crowed.

"No way they score five goals," another proclaimed.

Stunned Hill-Murray players, down 7–3 after two periods on the road, listened from the adjoining locker room inside Graham Arena.

Coach Terry Skrypek watched as his Pioneers quietly turned the taunts into fuel. Blow their undefeated record? Not here. Not tonight.

"It was like someone inflated us," Skrypek said.

Hill-Murray's four-goal barrage in the final 8:36 of regulation tied the game. Co-captain Mark Horvath's overtime goal capped an astounding 8–7 comeback victory.

"To walk out of that arena with a victory set us up for what was to come," co-captain Mark Krois said.

Beating Rochester John Marshall, coupled with a Twin City game victory four days later, made Hill-Murray 21–0 heading into the playoffs. Two options remained: lose and go home . . . or go undefeated.

Krois knew the stakes. As a ninth-grader, he had made varsity but hadn't cracked the 1980 state tournament roster. Those undefeated Pioneers lost 2–1 to Grand Rapids in the championship game.

"I had to get back," Krois said.

So did Skrypek, who called the 1980 championship "the toughest game I ever lost."

Until their Rochester John Marshall comeback, the 1982–83 Pioneers had rolled through the regular season virtually unchallenged. They averaged 10.6 goals per game in sixteen St. Paul City Conference victories.

Hill-Murray enjoyed a perfect 1983 season, going 28–0 and becoming the first private school to hoist a state championship trophy. Co-captain Mark Krois (left) scored twice in the title game, and Tom Follmer (right) posted two assists. Photo courtesy of the Minnesota Historical Society

Of course, attracting top players from several of those public schools' neighborhoods made Hill-Murray, a Catholic school located in Maplewood just over the border from St. Paul's East Side, a target.

"Everyone took their shots," said Krois, who grew up in St. Paul Johnson's area program. "Everyone said, 'You guys recruit.'"

Tony Curella lived near St. Paul Harding. Pat Heffernan fought his dad about leaving St. Paul Highland Park. Tom Follmer hailed from St. Paul's North End—Como Park territory.

Pooling his players' talents for the greater good started with Skrypek shrinking their heads.

"He told us, 'There's only one superstar on this team, and it's none of you,'" Horvath said.

"He instilled an attitude of unselfishness," Heffernan said. "Pass from the heart, wish the best for your linemates and teammates."

Teams throughout Skrypek's career played arduous scrimmage schedules. The 1982–83 Pioneers took it further, practicing after some of their roughly two dozen scrimmages.

"If we were going to win the tournament, we needed something extra," Skrypek said. "We talked about paying the price. Don't have any regrets."

The third round of the Section 3 playoffs brought Stillwater, coached by Andre Beaulieu. In 1970, Beaulieu had been coaching at Hill (then an all-boys school) and made Skrypek his assistant.

Hill-Murray tied the game 4–4, then braced as Stillwater went on a five-on-three power play.

"Then Krois controlled the puck himself for almost forty seconds to kill off the first penalty," Skrypek said. "It was one of the best efforts I ever saw."

Krois said, "My stick got slashed out of my hand, so I kept working along the boards with my feet. Coach gave me a slap on the helmet."

Hill-Murray won 5–4 and advanced to the sectional championship game against North St. Paul. Season-ending playoff losses to the Polars the past two seasons made Hill-Murray's 9–2 shellacking even sweeter.

Krois returned to the state tournament, this time to play. Getting there also meant a great deal to Horvath; a knee injury suffered during fall soccer season had lingered throughout hockey season.

"They wheelchaired me from the hotel across the street into the Civic Center," Horvath said. "I'd get dressed in the locker room and they'd wheel me to the ice."

"He couldn't even kneel for the team prayer," Krois said. "Everyone picked up on his gritty determination."

Memories of practicing at the Civic Center on the eve of the state tournament still stir Horvath, the team's emotional leader.

Hill-Murray's fans cheered their team to a 4–3 victory against Burnsville to clinch the program's first state title in seven tries. The Pioneers punctuated the feat by posting the first undefeated season since Edina East in 1974. Photo courtesy of Kyle Oen/Vintage Minnesota Hockey

"You step on that ice," said Horvath, pausing as tears welled in his eyes. "It takes your breath away. You've arrived. There's nothing better."

Skrypek attempted to relieve pressure by encouraging players: "We won twenty-five games, but it's a new season. Why not win three straight?"

Winning just one looked doubtful as quarterfinal opponent Bloomington Kennedy led 3–1 after one period.

Drawing from the Rochester experience, Hill-Murray scored four consecutive goals for a 5–3 lead. Kennedy tied the game with less than two minutes remaining, but Curella's third goal clinched a 6–5 victory.

Though thrilled with the comeback, Skrypek wasn't comfortable with junior goaltender Tim Galash's play, so he switched to senior Mike Schwietz for the remainder of the tournament.

Schwietz, who had made nine prior starts that season, stopped twenty-five shots in a 3–1 semifinal victory against Henry Sibley. Horvath scored twice without shooting.

"I was passing to Follmer, and the puck went off their defenseman's skate," Horvath said. "On the second one, they shot it in their own net, and I was the closest."

Once again, Skrypek led an undefeated team to the championship game.

"I tried to portray confidence," Skrypek said. "I didn't bring up the past."

Krois scored twice, and Hill-Murray led 3–2 after two periods. Then Burnsville, a powerful state tournament newcomer, drew even midway through the third period.

Then a huge goal by a small rodent helped Hill-Murray make history.

Nicknamed Rat by teammates, Jim Jirele measured 5 foot 5½ and 145 pounds. He played on the third line, which surrendered Burnsville's first and third goals.

But Skrypek didn't shorten his bench in crunch time. Scott Faust won the faceoff in Burnsville's zone and pushed the puck toward the net. Jirele scurried in and scored with 3:12 remaining.

Hill-Murray's 4–3 victory clinched its first state title in seven tries and the first undefeated season since Edina East in 1974.

Krois and Skrypek finished the job.

"When I skated the trophy toward Skry, the look on his face was worth everything," Krois said.

"It was kind of like something funny came over me," Skrypek said. "I was sad knowing it was over. Hockey is such a team game, and these kids played for each other."

~DL~

Burnsville made its state tournament debut in 1983. Here, Braves players in their Cooperalls make the long walk from the locker rooms to the St. Paul Civic Center ice. Photo courtesy of Kyle Oen/Vintage Minnesota Hockey

Reggie Miracle, the Kentucky-born son of a math professor, moved to Minnesota as a youngster and gravitated toward hockey. He played goalie for the Columbia Heights team that won the 1980 Bantam state title. Three years later, he keyed a quarterfinal upset of defending state champion Edina. Photo by the *St. Paul Pioneer Press*

NAME RECOGNITION

Columbia Heights goaltender Reggie Miracle found stardom with shutout of Edina

His last name was Miracle—perfect for a goaltender who helped his unheralded team to a state tournament.

In 1983, three years after the US Olympic hockey team's Miracle on Ice, Reggie Miracle and Columbia Heights made their state tournament debut and engineered a surprise 2–0 quarterfinal victory against defending state champion Edina.

Much like the Olympic team, the Hylanders were miscast as a bunch of happy-go-lucky rink rats. This Heights team had credentials.

Reaching the state tournament, players said, was expected, considering they were the 1980 Bantam state champions.

Miracle, the Kentucky-born son of a math professor, moved to Minnesota as a youngster. At age nine, he began attending a summer goalie camp run by Warren Strelow, who a few years later served as goalie coach for Herb Brooks and the 1980 Olympic team.

"I practiced hard and memorized everything he said," Miracle said. "And he saw something in me and took me under his wing."

KSTP Channel 5 televised the 1980 Bantam state championship game.

"Warren turned on the game, sees me, and calls Herb and says, 'This is one of my students,'" Miracle said. "Later, Herb sent me an autographed picture of the 1980 Olympic team with a letter that said, 'Congratulations. You are the future of American hockey.' It was overwhelming."

Less overwhelming was Miracle's high school résumé. He didn't play as a sophomore and split time as a junior. As a senior, the 5-foot-9, 160-pound Miracle served as one of three team captains.

"He got pulled a few times during the season," said Tom Palkowski, a senior wing. "But he had a confidence about him."

Heights players entered the state tournament on a high after their Section 2 final upset of Cloquet. Down 4–2 in the third period, Columbia Heights had forced overtime with two shorthanded goals.

Facing Edina? Piece of cake.

"Being a blue-collar town and playing against Edina got our juices flowing," Palkowski said.

Miracle felt something special, too.

"I got up the morning of the Edina game and thought, 'This is it. You're on TV. People don't know you, and this is a chance for them to see what you can do,'" Miracle said.

He stopped all twenty-nine Edina shots and earned the only shutout of his high school career. Miracle credited his teammates—sort of.

"We were so afraid of Edina's offense, we played better defensively," Miracle said. "I've worked a lot harder than that for our team."

The Hylanders' semifinal with Burnsville was tied 2–2 midway through the third period. But a Dave MacNulty penalty shot got past Miracle and left the injury-ravaged Hylanders reeling. Two empty-net goals sealed the outcome.

Miracle made thirty-five saves, the same number he made in a loss in the third-place game.

But little Columbia Heights and its aptly named goaltender beating mighty Edina remains an irresistible tournament memory.

~DL~

HURTING HORNET

INJURED MARTY NANNE EMERGED AS EDINA'S SIX MILLION DOLLAR MAN

DATES	LOCATION	ATTENDANCE	CHAMPIONSHIP
MARCH 8–10	ST. PAUL CIVIC CENTER	100,160	EDINA 4, BLOOMINGTON KENNEDY 2

 Ed Zins, assistant coach to Edina's Willard Ikola for twenty years, guided St. Cloud Apollo to its first tourney berth in his fourth year as the Eagles' head coach.

LIFE COULDN'T HAVE BEEN much sweeter for Marty Nanne in the spring of 1984 as he eagerly made preparations for the most anticipated three days of his hockey career.

Nanne's dad, Lou, had been broadcasting the state tournament since before Marty was born. Now, Marty was going to play in the event that had been so cherished by his family over the years. Heck, he might even win a championship.

That's about as far as Marty dared dream. Images of scoring title-winning goals weren't scrolling endlessly in his head. A grinding, third-line wing, the 5-foot-10 Nanne, an Edina junior, wasn't much of a scoring threat. But he possessed speed, tenacity, and a good feel for the game.

"In all my career, I was never a goal scorer," Nanne said. "But I knew how to get the puck to the guys who were."

Nanne's father had played for the Minnesota North Stars for ten seasons, mostly as a heady, tough, hardworking defenseman. Lou, a grocer's son who grew up in the steel-mill town of Sault Ste. Marie, Ontario, would sacrifice life and limbs if it meant earning a victory, and Marty inherited that slice of DNA.

Two days before the start of the tournament, the Nanne household was buzzing with nervous energy and excitement, Marty headed off to practice and impending doom. A collision with defenseman Steve Vellner sent him crashing to the ice, where he landed awkwardly on his right shoulder. Instantly, he knew something was wrong.

"It was a Grade 2 separation," Nanne said. "I wasn't going to play."

Lou Nanne had endured a litany of scrapes, bumps, and bruises in his NHL career. He had played through more serious injuries, too. Dozens of them. Lou needed just four words to make his point to his dejected son: "No pain, no gain."

Backed by his dad, Marty insisted on playing. "It would have been devastating if I hadn't."

The Nannes scrambled to make an emergency appointment with Dan Rowe, the doctor who made prosthetic legs for Marty's older brother Michael.

"Lou got me in there," Marty said, "and [Rowe] made me a shoulder brace, this plastic and foam thing. I had it probably within five or six hours."

Next, it was off to see Richard "Doc" Rose, the longtime Minnesota North Stars trainer and equipment manager. Lou Nanne was the North Stars' general manager at the time (a young Marty loved to hide within earshot when Lou was negotiating player trades), giving the Nannes access to Rose and the team's training-room resources. Marty was hooked to a transcutaneous electrical nerve stimulation (TENS) device that pumped electric current into his aching shoulder. Ultrasound was used to treat the pain, too. For good measure, Rose gave Marty a cortisone shot.

"I did everything in my ability to play," said Marty, who, despite all the treatment, still couldn't raise his right arm above his shoulder.

Tethered to a portable TENS unit in the locker room, his bulky custom brace at his side, Marty resembled a cross between the Six Million Dollar Man and Mad Max as he geared up for the Hornets' state tournament quarterfinal against Roseau.

The treatment worked. Nanne, playing on a line with senior wing Jerry Kaehler and sophomore center Peter Hankinson, proved healthy enough to score a goal and notch two assists in a 7–0 rout of the Rams.

However, his tournament life was in jeopardy again in the semifinals against Hibbing. And the scare had nothing to do with injury.

Nanne's line was deployed after a second-period power-play goal by Paul Ranheim put the Hornets ahead 3–1. Edina coach Willard Ikola demanded his teams play an up-tempo style that required quick shifts, thirty-five to forty-five seconds at most. Hankinson and Kaehler departed after a burst of forty seconds or so. Nanne stayed on the ice. Ikola went ballistic.

"Willard was usually pretty quiet on the bench. He didn't say much," Hankinson said. "Not that time. He was screaming as loud as he could scream for Marty to get off the ice."

Indeed, Ikola's bellowing can be heard in replays of the TV broadcast. Nanne, meanwhile, was focused on the puck. Ranheim was on his knees behind the Hibbing net when he found Nanne alone in the slot. Nanne, who had been on the ice for 1:21, found pay dirt to make it 4–1 and avert an almost certain benching.

"He shoots it, and it goes in," Ikola said. "So I say, 'Aw hell, Nanne, stay out there as long as you want.'"

"You have to be able to laugh, too."

Teammates chuckled as Nanne finally returned to the bench.

"I told him, 'If you didn't score, you were done, dude,'" said junior defenseman Jeff Johnson. "Ike was pissed."

Edina beat Hibbing 5–1, and Nanne, who had scored four goals during the entire regular season, now had two in as many tournament games.

Awaiting in the championship was Bloomington Kennedy and its irrepressible scoring duo of Dallas Miller and Dan Tousignant. The Hornets led 2–0 in the second period when Miller was hauled down by Greg Dornbach on a breakaway and awarded a penalty shot. Miller converted, and Jeff Jungwirth scored late in the session to knot the score at two.

There's no telling how Lou Nanne managed to keep his composure early in the third period when Marty deflected a pass from Hankinson on Eagles goaltender Bruce Wilson, then popped the rebound over Wilson's outstretched leg.

"A good effort by Nanne as he gets his own rebound, just persevered, and puts it behind Wilson," a remarkably calm Lou said as the goal was replayed.

Marty, who was tackled, then piled on by jubilant teammates after scoring, was shown grimacing after picking himself off the ice and readjusting his shoulder padding.

Ranheim scored later in the period, an insurance goal in the Hornets' 4–2 victory. But it was Nanne's goal that held up as the game-winner.

In the end, Lou's words rang true.

No pain, no gain.

~LRN~

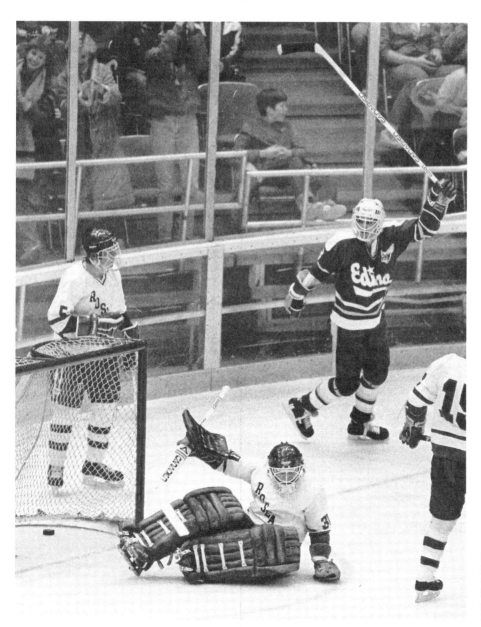

Edina's Marty Nanne flourished as a goal scorer in the 1984 state tournament despite playing with a separated shoulder. He scored a goal in each of the three games, including this one against Roseau in the quarterfinals. Photo by Darlene Pfister/*Minneapolis Star Tribune*

SWEET LOU
TV analyst Lou Nanne's "mind-boggling" five decades of tourney broadcasting

Nerves turned to nausea, and Lou Nanne's championship game status was questionable at best.

Nanne began working as a state tournament TV analyst in 1964, when he was twenty-two and just out of college, taking to the job as naturally as a puck sliding on freshly flooded ice. Twenty years later, the man who claims to have conducted the first interview on a working Zamboni, stashed pro wrestler André the Giant in the crowd for staged between-period sound bites, and killed unexpectedly long breaks in the action by chatting on air with garrulous governor Wendell Anderson was ready to declare himself physically unable to perform.

Nanne's son, Marty, was playing in the 1984 state championship game for Edina, and the obsessive-compulsive Lou (he's openly talked about his obsessive-compulsive disorder for years) struggled mightily with the magnitude of the moment. He said he was so nervous he considered sitting out his color-commentary duties that night.

"That was the absolute worst I've ever been," Lou told reporters after Marty scored the winning goal in the Hornets' 4–2 victory against Bloomington Kennedy. "My wife convinced me to do it because Marty is superstitious like me, and if I didn't, that would have changed things."

Lou's grandsons Louie and Tyler also won titles with the Hornets (Lou in 2010 and Tyler in 2013 and 2014).

"I worked the Stanley Cup, the Olympics, everything there is to do in hockey, but broadcasting my son's and grandsons' games are the toughest games I have ever had to do," Nanne said. "First of all, you want them to do well and their teams to win, but you have to do it professionally, in an unbiased way.

"But your insides are dying."

A native of Sault Ste. Marie, Ontario,

Nanne (nicknamed "Sweet Lou from the Soo") starred at the University of Minnesota for legendary coach John Mariucci. He then played mostly as a defenseman in an NHL career that spanned a decade—645 regular-season games from 1967 to 1978, all of them with the Minnesota North Stars. He spent another ten years as the North Stars' wheeling-and-dealing general manager.

His schedule with the North Stars occasionally conflicted with the state tournament, and he was absent in the late 1960s and again in the early and late 1970s when road games kept him away. Still, his longevity and on-air role make him the tournament's best-known icon. Now a sales manager at RBC Global Asset Management, Nanne has a voice so recognizable that when he makes phone calls to Minnesota businesses, he often hears "Hello, Mr. Nanne" before getting a chance to introduce himself.

These days, Nanne only does the color commentary for the tournament's Class 2A games. That's a light load compared to the days at the St. Paul Civic Center, when he would hustle up and down several flights of stairs from the broadcast booth to the ice level dozens of times a day, conducting as many as fifty-five interviews.

"It was a long way up to the press box," Nanne said.

When the tournament was split into two classes—or tiers—in 1992, Nanne's workload doubled to fourteen games in four days. That was too much, even for the man whose love for the event is unsurpassed.

"There was a time when he was becoming a little free with his speech," Marty said about his dad, who tries not to be too critical of the players. "He went back to just doing the double-A games, thank god."

In 1967, Lou Nanne (left) already was three years and dozens of interviews into his five-decade career as a state tournament broadcaster. Photo courtesy of the Minnesota Historical Society

Lou Nanne has witnessed many of the tournament's greatest moments, Apple Valley's epic 5–4 five-overtime semifinal victory over Duluth East in 1996 among them.

"That was the best game they have ever had in the state tournament," Nanne said. "That was incredible. Not only because it went so long. The goaltenders were magnificent. Both teams had unbelievable scoring chances. Just amazing."

As Nanne's broadcasting career extends into multiple overtimes, his statistics are staggering. He's worked for five TV stations representing pretty much every letter in the alphabet (WTCN, KSTP, WCCO, KMSP, KSTC), worked at all five venues that have hosted the state tourney, and called approximately 435 games.

Mind-boggling, to borrow one of Nanne's favorite expressions.

He's not sure when it will end. He recently welcomed his first great-grandchild into the family, a boy, and who knows? Maybe Nanne will stick around long enough to broadcast his tournament games, too.

"Maybe," he said with a laugh.

~LRN~

FIGHT OF THEIR LIVES

SURVIVOR COACH, PRACTICE SKIRMISHES MADE BURNSVILLE TOUGH TO BEAT

DATES	LOCATION	ATTENDANCE	CHAMPIONSHIP
MARCH 7–9	ST. PAUL CIVIC CENTER	103,096	BURNSVILLE 4, HILL-MURRAY 3

Did you know? Inaugural Mr. Hockey Award winner Tom Chorske and his Minneapolis Southwest teammates played a mock game against Robbinsdale Armstrong at the Civic Center two days before the tournament so the WCCO-TV crew could test its equipment.

CHILLS OVERCAME Burnsville hockey coach Tom Osiecki and tears fell as his son Mark, a junior defenseman, received a state championship medal after ultimate victory in 1985.

The emotions were due to the father's long journey from program architect to parental target to, finally, champion.

A petition to remove Osiecki, signed by thirteen parents, had made the rounds in the spring of 1981.

"People asked my parents to sign when I was a first-year Squirt," said Scott Bloom, future varsity standout.

Osiecki's family suffered. Mark, then a seventh-grader sub-jected to negative comments about his father, began avoiding the varsity games he once enjoyed. Home life wasn't much fun, either, since the stress caused family squabbles.

The petition reached the school board. Osiecki's Lake Conference coaching peers, including Edina's Willard Ikola and Bloomington Jefferson's Tom Saterdalen, attended to show their support.

"They probably saved my job," Osiecki said.

Osiecki stayed. But the coach who had started Burnsville's program in 1966 didn't stay the same. Turmoil taught important lessons.

In 1981, Burnsville coach Tom Osiecki faced a petition calling for his removal, but he persevered and, just four years later, led his team to a state title. Appreciative players carry Osiecki to the microphone at a post-tournament reception at Burnsville High School. Photo by Joe Rossi/*St. Paul Pioneer Press*

"I was aloof; I coached from a distance," Osiecki said. "I tried to get closer to the kids after that."

Soon, Osiecki's teams began challenging the likes of Edina and Bloomington Jefferson for supremacy. Burnsville's inaugural state tournament appearance in 1983 ended with a championship game loss to Hill-Murray.

Then, in 1984–85, Burnsville's unmatched depth of skill conquered the hockey world. Osiecki didn't match forward lines or defensive pairings—he rotated five-man units named after the school's colors.

BLACK	GOLD	WHITE
Forwards John Borrell, Herm Finnegan, and Kelly Ramswick; defensemen Mike Luckraft and Kevin Schrader	Forwards Scott Bloom, Don Granato, and Steve Ferrera; defensemen Mark Osiecki and Scott Schulze	Forwards Scott Branson, Kevin Featherstone, and Mike Travalent; defensemen Kurt Hammond and Steve Treichel

All that talent and only one puck brought out Burnsville's best.

"Practices were insane," said Matt Larson, a junior forward sidelined by a shoulder injury much of the season.

"If someone wasn't in a fight at practice daily, something was wrong," Mark Osiecki said. "There were times I was kicked out of practice. Probably because my dad was making an example of me."

Nine players boasted state tournament experience. Granato, a senior transfer from a Chicago-based AAA team, dazzled new teammates.

"He was right-handed, and one day in practice he's coming down the left side," Larson said. "The puck comes his way for a one-timer, and he spins, opens his hips, and rips a shot.

"We're all going, 'What was that?' The rest of the year, we tried to emulate that move."

Senior goaltender Kevin Gorg, whom Tom Osiecki had known since the youngster called play-by-play during street hockey games, arrived from the junior varsity. A broken collarbone had derailed Gorg's sophomore season, and he spent his junior year catching up. He entered the state tournament allowing just 1.7 goals per game.

His on-ice debut at the St. Paul Civic Center was delayed, however.

That's because Bloomington Jefferson and Minnetonka pushed the evening session's first quarterfinal to a third overtime. Burnsville (22–1–1) and Bemidji (22–1) waited. And waited. And waited.

But Gorg held up just fine thanks to Herb Brooks, on-site as a television analyst. Brooks knew the young man's father, Ken Gorg, who was the golf pro at Faribault Country Club.

"Herb was at his desk near the locker room," Kevin Gorg said. "He calls me over, and we talked hockey—anything but my upcoming game. He kept me laughing."

Brooks shared about Jim Craig, his 1980 Miracle on Ice goalie, and playing after a considerable delay at the 1955 state tournament. Brooks and St. Paul Johnson waited to start their quarterfinal game until after nine overtimes elapsed in the Minneapolis South/Thief River Falls game.

Officials suspended the Jefferson/Minnetonka game until Friday morning. At 11:06 PM, Burnsville and Bemidji started. Two Finnegan goals helped secure a 5–3 victory.

Jefferson/Minnetonka resumed at 9 AM, and the Jaguars completed a 4–3 victory in the only suspended tournament game before or since.

That meant Burnsville could avenge its only loss of the season. Publicly, Tom Osiecki said the 3–1 loss to cap the regular season paid dividends. However, Mark said, "That night, he put his foot through the basement door."

The semifinal against Jefferson began about twelve hours after the Jaguars' morning action, and they went ahead 1–0. But four unanswered Burnsville goals brought a 4–1 victory. Bloom's second-period goal held up as the game-winner.

Championship game opponent Hill-Murray was no stranger. The Pioneers had capped a perfect 1983 season against Burnsville. A year later, Burnsville edged them in the consolation round.

Their third consecutive state tournament meeting was tied 2–2 at the first intermission. Goals from Finnegan and Bloom negated Hill-Murray leads.

Luckraft's power-play goal put Burnsville ahead 3–2 after two periods. But Hill-Murray drew even just thirty-two seconds into the third period, and the teams played without another goal until the final minute.

Then the puck found Bloom at the Hill-Murray blue line.

Bloom hailed from Eagan, which bordered Burnsville to the west and did not yet have its own high school. He joined Burnsville's youth ranks "because that's who you wanted to play for." Bloom was a phenom, scoring 105 goals one season at the Squirt level.

Gorg said, "His wrist shot was harder than his slapshot. He dented my breezers in practice."

Bloom's biggest shots came in the biggest spots, byproducts of an unflappable persona.

"You couldn't rattle the guy because he never made the moment too big," Larson said.

Bloom corralled the puck and headed for the net with only one defenseman to beat.

"I don't think I was thinking goal, just get a shot on goal," Bloom said.

Just inside the right circle, Bloom cut left, fired a wrist shot, and dented the Pioneers' hearts. They broke when the game ended twenty-seven seconds later.

Burnsville had arrived as state champions. Against the odds, the Osieckis were there to share the moment.

"It was pretty special because of what my dad and our family went through," Mark Osiecki said. "We stuck it out."

~DL~

EYE OF THE TIGER

MOTIVATIONAL SONG PUT BURNSVILLE IN PROPER PREGAME FRAME OF MIND

DATES	LOCATION	ATTENDANCE	CHAMPIONSHIP
MARCH 6–8	ST. PAUL CIVIC CENTER	100,824	BURNSVILLE 4, HILL-MURRAY 1

139

 Bemidji big man George Pelawa (6 foot 3, 245 pounds) played in his second and final state tournament in 1986. He went on to win the Mr. Hockey Award and was chosen number sixteen overall by Calgary in the NHL draft but was killed in an automobile accident in August.

AFTER BURNSVILLE EDGED Hill-Murray in the 1985 state championship game, the two heavyweights next met in late December of that year at the Met Center Hockey Classic.

Down 6–1 after two periods, Burnsville got hot and scored four consecutive goals.

"We were all over them," Burnsville coach Tom Osiecki said. "And then they got one of our guys for a necklace."

During games, senior forward Matt Larson always wore a gold chain, a gift from his grandmother to bring him good health. Doing so risked an illegal equipment penalty in the same way driving five miles per hour over the posted speed limit risks getting pulled over. In other words, Larson wasn't alone, and, because of that, officials rarely enforced the rule.

Then Hill-Murray's Steve Rohlik, on orders from his coach, Terry Skrypek, "went over to the ref and pointed toward me," Larson said. "I have no mouthguard in, so I'm thinking that's what they're talking about. I said to Bloomer, 'Give me yours.'"

In one of the most selfless acts in team sports history, Burnsville star forward Scott Bloom made the handoff.

Biting down on the borrowed apparatus should have been punishment enough for Larson. But no, officials assessed a minor penalty for the gold chain.

"We were furious," Larson said.

Tom Quinlan scored on the power play for his fifth goal of the game and a 7–5 Hill-Murray victory.

Afterward, Skrypek apologized and vowed he "would never do that against a team again."

Nevertheless, Larson said, "That whole deal became a catalyst for our team."

Larson had quarterbacked the football team to a Prep Bowl state title in the fall wearing number 22 in honor of Boston College quarterback Doug Flutie. Switching to hockey took time. Larson, one of seven hockey players returning from the 1985 hockey team, personified the defending champions' slow start. Burnsville had lost one game the previous season. The Hill-Murray loss dropped Burnsville to 4–3.

Osiecki tweaked his forward lines, putting Bloom with Lance Werness and Jon McDermott. Despite no previous state tournament experience, the unit of Rob Granato, John Sundby,

and Dan Brettschneider performed well. As did the line of Larson, Steve Ferrera, and Brad Hendrickson, the latter a converted defenseman.

Still, Burnsville's strength came from stalwart defensemen Mark Osiecki, Scott Schulze, and Steve Treichel and from newcomer Marc Linsenman.

Osiecki, a 6-foot-2, 195-pound center on the football field, was "a classic defensive defenseman," his father said. "He blocked a lot of shots, and that becomes contagious. To this day, he thinks he should have been a goalie."

Called Ozzie by teammates, Osiecki was "the fourth- or fifth-best D as a Bantam," his father said. "He didn't make varsity when he was a sophomore, and my wife was mad at me. But he was a guy who had to battle."

That sort of urgency defines playoff hockey. To ensure all players brought the requisite passion and focus, Tom Osiecki used the same motivational song throughout Burnsville's 1980s heyday: "Eye of the Tiger," the theme from the movie *Rocky III*.

On the first day of practice for the Section 1 playoffs, coaches drew a filled-in gold circle surrounded by a black letter H on the shooting side of players' sticks. The H reminded players to play with their heads and their hearts, its curved edges around the gold dot designed to resemble an eye.

Coach Osiecki raised the bar on game days. The moment he concluded his pregame speech, a student manager pressed play on the stereo, and "Eye of the Tiger" filled the room.

"Heads would drop," Larson said. "I looked up one time and saw heads bobbing and feet tapping. Then Coach O would hit the door open hard to kind of startle you, and off to the ice we would go. I get chills now just talking about it."

The day the music almost died was February 28, 1986. Student manager Pete Heunisch forgot the cassette tape and called around until he found someone to purchase a replacement. The tape reached the Met Center in time for the Region 1 final. Burnsville defeated Rochester Mayo, and the defending champions returned to the state tournament.

An unspectacular 17–5–1 record, however, made Burnsville an underdog.

Bloom, who had scored the game-winning goals in the

Burnsville's Scott Bloom (left) and Jon McDermott celebrate a second consecutive state championship at Hill-Murray's expense. Bloom scored a hat trick in the quarterfinals against South St. Paul and then netted two goals in the title game, rounding out a ten-point tournament performance. Photo by Rob Levine/*Minneapolis Star Tribune*

previous year's semifinal and title games, opened the 1986 quarterfinals with a hat trick and two assists in a 7–4 victory against South St. Paul.

The real MVP, however, was Burnsville assistant coach Bill McCarthy. Before the game, an unknown Civic Center arena worker mistakenly sharpened several players' skate blades at a forty-five-degree angle instead of ninety. Turning would have been impossible.

McCarthy, the older brother of North Stars left wing Tom McCarthy, put his sporting-goods store experience to good use. Puck drop was delayed twenty-five minutes as he re-sharpened fourteen pairs of skates.

There was drama in the semifinals, too, as Duluth Denfeld goaltender Robb Stauber helped the Hunters to a 1–0 lead after two periods. But Burnsville rallied for a 3–1 victory and a rematch against Hill-Murray.

Not since International Falls and St. Paul Johnson in 1963 and 1964 had the same two teams met in consecutive finals.

"We were the underdogs from south of the river," Mark Osiecki said. "We fed off that."

The gold chain incident added to players' motivation.

Rohlik put the Pioneers ahead 1–0 at the first intermission, but goals from Larson and Bloom gave Burnsville a 2–1 edge after two periods.

Skrypek would later praise Mark Osiecki, who played through a sternum injury suffered in the quarterfinal, for seemingly blocking as many shots as goalie Tom Dennis. Hill-Murray outshot Burnsville 23–21.

In the final period, McDermott tallied his third tournament goal. Fittingly, Bloom touched off the celebration with an empty-net goal in the final minute. His fifth goal and tenth point of the tournament "put a stamp on his high school career," Mark Osiecki said.

Tom Osiecki savored the fast-approaching 4–1 victory by turning "toward Hill-Murray's bench and saying, 'Where's the chain now?'"

Actually, Larson said, "I still wear it today."

~DL~

REVENGE IN ST. PAUL

KENNEDY GOALIE'S QUEST FOR REDEMPTION TURNED PERSONAL WITH REFRIGERATOR REMINDER

DATES	LOCATION	ATTENDANCE	CHAMPIONSHIP
MARCH 12–14	ST. PAUL CIVIC CENTER	100,215	BLOOMINGTON KENNEDY 4, BURNSVILLE 1

Did you know? Runner-up Burnsville became the first team to reach three consecutive championship games since Edina East (1977–79).

ON CHRISTMAS EVE 1986, visions of a fluke overtime goal danced in the head of Bloomington Kennedy senior goalie Chris Lind.

The night before, Lind's number-one-ranked Eagles had lost 4–3 to number-two Greenway after a puck caromed off the end boards and into the slot for a rebound goal.

A seething Lind clipped the *Star Tribune* headline "Greenway downs top-ranked Kennedy" and pasted it to a sheet of paper. In thick blue letters below, he wrote "Revenge in St. Paul" and put the paper on the refrigerator.

"I stared at it every morning before school eating breakfast for about ten weeks," Lind said.

Kennedy coach Jerry Peterson knew challenges brought forth Lind's best. The veteran coach also knew his team possessed superior talent, speed, and depth. Complacency was his only fear.

So when Lind came into preseason practices thinking the goalie position was his because, he said, "I had played in big games with these guys before and won," Peterson relegated him to third string. Lind, who had quit football to focus on hockey, didn't dress for the season opener and decided to quit hockey.

"I said, 'I'm done,'" Lind said. "But about nine of my teammates came to my house and told me that can't happen. So, I sucked it up and was the water boy for the first game.

"Jerry put me in my place. After that game, he sat me down in his office and said, 'I'll let you work back in.' I said, 'If I play, I won't lose.'"

Peterson's actions and Lind's reaction proved contagious.

"That situation brought us closer as a team," said Jason Miller, a star senior forward. "I didn't like the decision, but Jerry held us accountable. I know it put a little fire in me."

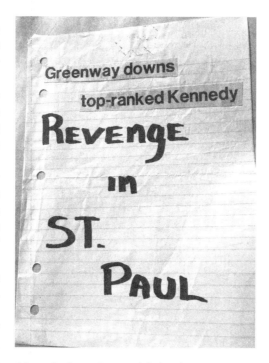

A December loss to Greenway left Bloomington Kennedy goalie Chris Lind seething, so he created this reminder, put it on his refrigerator, and "stared at it every morning before school . . . for about ten weeks." He got his revenge in the state tournament semifinals. Photo courtesy of Chris Lind

The championship quest that players called Mission '87 began with the 1982 closing of Bloomington Lincoln High School.

As Squirts, Lincoln players Joe Decker, Steve Cronkhite, Tom Hanson, Kevin Kalli, Kent Landreth, John Manuel, and Thane Vennix had joined forces with Kennedy youth standouts Lind, Miller, Mike Parent, Chad Pittelkow, and Mark Wallinga.

As Bantams, they beat Greenway for the 1984 state championship.

As the 1986–87 season arrived, so did two additional key players. Senior forward Pat McGowan, whose father, Ed, was a former Kennedy assistant, transferred from Robbinsdale Cooper High School. And senior defenseman Marko Kreus, the captain of Finland's junior national team, arrived as a foreign exchange student.

The Eagles were loaded.

A humbled Lind started the third regular-season game and earned a 6–0 shutout victory against crosstown rival Jefferson.

"There was never any talk of him as the number-three goalie from then on," Decker said. "Thane was more consistent. Chris could be great."

Peterson rotated his talented goalies. Vennix played next against Robbinsdale Armstrong, Lind faced Greenway, and so on. The duo represented Kennedy's overpowering depth.

Up front, Miller centered the top line with Decker, a fellow Mr. Hockey finalist, at wing. In twenty-six games, Miller posted a school record forty-two assists. Decker scored thirty-seven goals.

"He was so good at finding you," Decker said. "My job was to get open and shoot."

Pittelkow, the other wing, scored timely goals and was "the

best backchecker I've seen in my life," assistant coach Mark Hultgren said.

Hanson, McGowan, and Wallinga formed a potent second line. The third line got hot in the Region 5 final. Dave Stansberry tallied a hat trick and Dan Bauer added a goal in an 8–0 rout of Jefferson—which had beat Kennedy in the past two finals.

For Decker, finally reaching the St. Paul Civic Center left an impression.

"The rink was egg shaped," Decker said. "No real corners. The goal lines were back, and there was very little room behind the net. But with the clear boards and the lights, I don't think I've played anywhere that felt more like you were on a stage."

Miller commanded that stage, notching a hat trick in a 7–3 quarterfinal victory against South St. Paul. Number-one Kennedy advanced to a semifinal showdown against number-two Greenway.

Lind, the starting goalie, took the ice and saw his brother, Dave, holding the "Revenge in St. Paul" paper. Their mother, Carole, had thought to bring it to the game, but she could not hold it after separating her shoulder in a fall at the Civic Center during Thursday's quarterfinal game.

"I just about flipped," Lind said. "It rang through to me that I had been sitting with that loss for about two months. I wasn't going to lose again."

Miller and Decker goals built a 2–0 lead just six minutes into the game. Ken Gernander countered with an incredible short-handed goal. Miller made it 3–1 less than thirty seconds later.

Mr. Hockey Award recipient Kris Miller cut the Raiders' deficit to one in the third period, but Kreus clinched the 4–2 victory with an empty-net goal.

That meant a fourth game with back-to-back defending champion Burnsville. And for the first time all season, Peterson chose Lind for back-to-back starts.

"Coming off the ice after the semifinals, he said, 'You're playing tomorrow,'" said Lind, who stopped twenty-two Greenway shots. "I said, 'Yeah, I figured that.'"

Neither Lind's cool under fire nor the Eagles' 24–1 record assuaged Peterson's fears. His one-loss 1976 team had fallen in the state tournament quarterfinals. His 1984 team had over-achieved all the way to a runner-up finish. Anything short of the 1987 championship would be a massive disappointment.

So Peterson stayed behind on Saturday as the team headed back to Bloomington for lunch at Burger King.

"I was worried my nervousness would rub off," Peterson said.

Burnsville showed a champion's pride by going ahead 1–0 just 1:16 into the title game. But goals from McGowan, Miller, and Decker gave Kennedy a 3–1 lead at first intermission. Pittelkow filled the empty net late and solidified a 4–1 victory.

"We worked together for ten years, and we stuck together the whole way," said Lind, who made eleven of his twenty-one saves during the third period. "Mission accomplished."

~DL~

Bloomington Kennedy goaltender Chris Lind allowed Burnsville's first shot past him in the championship game. But he settled in, stopping all twenty-one ensuing shots in a 4–1 victory. Not bad for a young man who almost quit the team after sitting the first game. Photo courtesy of the Minnesota Historical Society

ATTACK OF THE CLONES

NAMELESS, FACELESS EDINA CAME AT OPPONENTS IN HIGH-SPEED WAVES

DATES	LOCATION	ATTENDANCE	CHAMPIONSHIP
MARCH 10–12	ST. PAUL CIVIC CENTER	98,718	EDINA 5, HILL-MURRAY 3

Did you know? Hill-Murray sophomore Craig Johnson didn't score in the tournament; his claim to fame came later when he was a key piece in a trade that sent Wayne Gretzky from the Los Angeles Kings to the St. Louis Blues. Johnson played seven seasons for the Kings.

LARRY OLIMB was up to his eyeballs in Edina green, with no relief in sight. Nameless, faceless, and relentless, the Hornets were like a platoon of clones beamed in from some distant, ice-covered planet, programmed for fast skating and pristine puck movement.

"There wasn't a noticeable difference, from my perspective at least, from who was out there for them," Olimb, a superb senior defenseman and Mr. Hockey Award winner, said about the Warriors' 1988 state semifinal against Edina. "Every other team had a top line and maybe a second line that was a step slower. Not those guys."

Edina coach Willard Ikola had come to the same conclusion a month earlier, after star forward Tom Nevers suffered a broken wrist in practice. With Nevers, a sophomore and the team's runaway scoring leader, out for the season, the veteran coach took a long, hard look at his lineup.

"Everybody looked about the same," Ikola said. "So we started playing four lines."

Ikola, in his thirtieth season coaching the Hornets, brought his sixteenth team to the state tournament in 1988. Starting in the early 1970s, when tournament rosters were expanded from fifteen to seventeen players, Ikola almost always had given his spare forwards and extra defensemen spot duty, deploying them at least a couple of times a period. Ikola believed the method promoted team unity and optimized his preferred high-tempo style.

But he had never rolled four forward lines and three sets of defensemen as religiously as he did with his now superstar-less team. Even the power-play and penalty-killing units were mostly next-man-up affairs.

"If there was a penalty, we'd just say, 'You two guys kill it,'" Ikola said. "It didn't matter who was out there."

Nevers's injury forced Edina's players to recalibrate their collective mindset, too. They held a players-only meeting at captain Rob Copeland's house.

"That meeting came right as we were kind of falling apart," junior goaltender Matt Bertram said. "It was kind of like, 'OK, we've lost Tom—how are we going to do this?'"

Added Copeland: "A lot of the time you have a superstar like that and you wait for him to take over the game. If we were down by a goal, we'd all just think to ourselves, 'Well, no problem. Tommy is good for two.' When he got hurt, we were like, 'Who is going to score for us now?'"

A consensus was reached. From now on, *everyone* needed to make meaningful contributions.

"We said we needed to play together, use our depth, and work hard, or it wasn't going to happen," Bertram said.

Ikola delivered the same message, albeit with a heavier touch. With Nevers out, the playoffs approaching, and the team limping along with five losses (unheard of for an Ikola squad), the state's winningest coach at the time held one of his infamous no-puck practices.

It became obvious trouble was afoot when Bertram and backup goaltender Andy Jones were dispatched to the junior varsity practice on an adjacent rink. The remaining Hornets made a weak attempt to stave off the impending ninety minutes of death.

"We made sure somebody got out before the coaches and dumped the pucks out so they would be spread all over the ice," said Mike Terwilliger, a junior defenseman. "For some reason we thought that might change his mind."

Instead, Terwilliger watched a steadfast Ikola "on his hands and knees in the net putting pucks in the bag, and we are slowly skating around the rink in circles. We knew what was coming, so it seemed like it took an eternity."

Added Noel Rahn, a junior forward: "There were a few guys that didn't know if they really wanted to play hockey anymore after that skate."

The Hornets, unified and fully Ikola-ized, didn't lose again. They won their three Section 6 playoff games by a combined score of 14–2, then opened the state tournament with a 3–2 victory over Cretin–Derham Hall.

Olimb and Chad Erickson, the Warriors' star goaltender and a Mr. Hockey finalist, awaited in the semifinals. The television broadcast buildup included mentions of Warroad's enrollment of 206 students compared to more than 1,600 at Edina, the estimate that sixteen thousand St. Paul Civic Center fans would be cheering for Warroad compared to one thousand sup-

144

Edina's John McCoy (left) celebrates his first-period goal in a 1988 double-overtime semifinal victory against Warroad. Photo by Bruce Bisping/*Minneapolis Star Tribune*

porting Edina, and the obligatory David versus Goliath reference, with a twist.

"But David here tonight is undefeated," longtime state tournament analyst Lou Nanne quipped. "And Goliath already has five losses."

Most Edina players had never seen Olimb, having only heard stories of a mythical player from the Canadian border who never left the ice, played every position (including goalie!), and stood 8 feet tall.

"Then we found out he could do all the things we heard he could," Bertram said. "It seemed like he would go from left D to right D to center to wing."

The broadcast crew used a stopwatch to track Larry Legend's ice time. Through two periods, he played 22:30 out of a possible thirty minutes.

The game stretched into overtime, then another extra period. Junior forward Mike Hiniker scored the winner in a 2–1 triumph. Edina's depth had proven too much for the exhausted Warriors.

"There wasn't an opportunity to take a break, so to speak,"

Olimb said. "There were no times when their fastest guys weren't out there and it would be a little easier to break out or make a play."

Edina senior forward Rob Morris scored his third and fourth goals of the season in a 5–3 championship game victory against Hill-Murray. Bertram did not face a shot on goal in the second period.

The Hornets finished with ten goals in the tournament, eight of them by different players.

"That's how you win a championship," Rahn said.

The title was the eighth and last of Ikola's thirty-three-year career. He was one of Minnesota's most recognizable figures thanks in part to his iconic brown tweed houndstooth cap aptly nicknamed Champ.

Ikola's last championship ranked as one of his most unexpected delights.

"We had a lot of teams with better players," Ikola said. "But I'll be damned if they didn't win it."

~*LRN*~

FINISHING TOUCH

SCORING MACHINE CHRIS TUCKER RESURFACED JUST IN TIME FOR BLOOMINGTON JEFFERSON

DATES	LOCATION	ATTENDANCE	CHAMPIONSHIP
MARCH 2–4	ST. PAUL CIVIC CENTER	95,356	BLOOMINGTON JEFFERSON 5, ROCHESTER JOHN MARSHALL 4 (OT)

Did you know? Edina junior forward Chad Hardie scored twice in the consolation championship game despite playing with a broken bone in his left foot.

Bloomington Jefferson's Sean Rice tallied a quarterfinal hat trick and kept a hot hand with two goals in the first period of the semifinals. Rice gave "endless energy," assistant coach John Bianchi said. "He was full throttle all the time." Photo by John Doman/*St. Paul Pioneer Press*

TWO OF THE MOST dynamic players in program history, forward Jeff Saterdalen and defenseman Tom Pederson, led one-loss Bloomington Jefferson to the 1988 state tournament.

"We thought we were going to win it all," defenseman Kelly Hultgren said. "But it was a two-man show, and if they weren't going, it was debilitating."

Saterdalen and Pederson each scored in the semifinals, but Hill-Murray's depth overwhelmed the Jaguars in a 6–3 victory.

Fast-forward about one year. Wary of high-scoring linemates Tony Bianchi and Chris Tucker being shut down on the same night, coach Tom Saterdalen made changes before the section playoffs.

Tucker, the left wing on the first line, traded places with second-line center Sean Rice.

Bianchi recalled "a few mumbles" were soon silenced as he, Rice, and Tucker adjusted on the fly. They returned to the state tournament and punished opponents.

Rice had posted just one assist in the 1988 state tournament. One year later, he recorded a hat trick and two assists in a 7–2 quarterfinal victory against Warroad.

"There was a lot of one-touch passing, and I'd watch the tape and say, 'Wow, I was part of it,'" Rice said. "We were unstoppable in that game."

Growing up in north Minneapolis, Rice saw hockey's recession in terms of numbers and quality. He wanted out—either by enrolling at Fridley-based private school Totino-Grace or by moving from Minneapolis altogether.

As a seventh-grader, he attended an Edina/Jefferson game. The Jaguars won, and Rice was sold. However, the transition wasn't easy.

"Hockey was a little hard to break into," Rice said. "I had to prove myself in that organization."

Rice adjusted and made friends with future varsity teammates Hultgren and Jason Schwartz. Rice gave "endless energy," assistant coach John Bianchi said. "He was full throttle all the time."

Staying hot in the semifinals, Rice scored two goals in a 7–3 victory against International Falls.

Meanwhile, diminutive senior Tony Bianchi (5 foot 6, 155 pounds) became the Broncos' target.

146

Bloomington Jefferson's Chris Tucker completed a hat trick while becoming just the sixth player to clinch a title game in overtime. He unloaded a slapshot from just inside Rochester John Marshall's blue line and beat the goaltender to deliver the Jaguars' second championship. Photo courtesy of Kyle Oen/Vintage Minnesota Hockey

"I heard one of their players say, 'I'm going to get that little prick,'" Bianchi said. "I thought, 'This is great,' because if they're trying to kill me, Rice will be open."

Bianchi didn't fit the archetype of a prolific playmaker. But he graduated with program records for assists (107) and points (164).

"Tony was never the best skater, and he wasn't the biggest," Rice said. "But he was smart, he saw the ice, and he understood the game."

Like older brother Steve, a key figure on the Jaguars' 1981 state championship team, Tony was a winner. When then freshman Tony was inserted into the starting lineup in 1985–86, Jefferson won eleven consecutive games.

"He was a total team player who was just as good at both ends," Hultgren said.

"Tony was calm and thoughtful," said John Bianchi, his father. "He was always around the big plays."

Winning a state title had been Tony's mission ever since he attended the 1981 state tournament as the team's stick boy. He worked hard to make it happen. Yet accomplishing the feat left him awestruck.

"The team was better than I thought it could be," Tony said. "We overachieved. I overachieved."

The opposite was true of Tucker. He entered the state tournament with thirty-seven goals, good for the Jaguars' program record. But he managed just one goal in the first two blowouts.

Paging Chris Tucker. Please come to the Civic Center and pick up your game.

"There was a lot of pressure on me to score goals," Tucker said. "I hadn't produced as much in the first couple games, but there was also tight coverage on me."

Making matters worse, Saterdalen believed Tucker wasn't giving an honest effort. Saterdalen benched him for the final two minutes of the semifinal. Exasperated, Saterdalen asked John Bianchi to find a way to connect with the young man.

Bianchi and Tucker met at about 2 PM on Saturday in a hallway at the team's Sheraton Midway hotel.

"I told him, 'Unload and go play,'" Bianchi said. "Because when he unloaded, look out."

The five-minute talk ended with a hug.

"I do remember him helping rebuild my confidence," Tucker said. "There was more to give."

Jefferson needed Tucker's best against a physical Rochester John Marshall team. The Rockets eliminated top-ranked Edina 4–2 in the quarterfinals and downed Duluth Denfeld 2–1 in the semifinals.

"They were big," Rice said. "With Warroad and International Falls there was no intimidation factor, but we knew with John Marshall we were in for a game."

Bianchi, Rice, and wing Dave Dahlberg absorbed the Rockets' defensive focus. So Tucker took advantage. He scored, and the Jaguars led 2–1. But two Doug Zmolek goals staked John Marshall to a 3–2 lead after two periods.

Tucker's second goal tied the game. Then Jeff Fogarty's second goal gave the Rockets a 4–3 lead with less than five minutes remaining.

Bianchi answered just thirty-three seconds later on the power play.

"Tucker got it to the net, and I was there on the weak side," Bianchi said. "It was probably the worst goal I scored all year but the most meaningful."

In overtime, Rice took a penalty and left the box just as Zmolek blasted a puck toward the net. But a glove save from Jefferson goalie Derek Anderson prevented a Zmolek hat trick and a Rockets victory.

"It was a Hail Mary save," Anderson said. "I couldn't believe I had it."

Tucker's line was next up.

"I remember thinking, 'It would be kind of cool to score an overtime goal,'" Tucker said.

A pass from Jesse Carlson gave Tucker the puck in the neutral zone with room to skate. He unloaded a slapshot from just inside the Rockets' blue line and beat the goaltender. Tucker completed the hat trick and became just the sixth player to clinch a championship in overtime.

"We were a team that could shoot the puck, and he was a finisher," Tony Bianchi said.

Winning the championship "was as gratifying as you can get," Bianchi said. "We were less talented than the previous year, but we were meaner, tougher, and grittier. We wouldn't back down."

~DL~

IRON FIST

ROSEAU DISCIPLINARIAN DEAN BLAIS MADE INTENTIONS CLEAR FROM FIRST PRACTICE

DATES	LOCATION	ATTENDANCE	CHAMPIONSHIP
MARCH 8–10	ST. PAUL CIVIC CENTER	97,718	ROSEAU 3, GRAND RAPIDS 1

Did you know? This was the first all-northern championship since International Falls had beaten Grand Rapids 3–2 in 1972.

THE FIRST PRACTICE of the season had just ended when Dean Blais summoned Billy Lund into a back room at Roseau's Memorial Arena. Blais was Roseau's new head coach. Lund was the town's beloved goal-scoring sensation.

This wasn't a lighthearted meet and greet. Blais, as Lund was about to learn, didn't do soft and cuddly. A former standout at International Falls and the University of Minnesota, Blais had played for coaching legends such as Larry Ross, Herb Brooks, and Bob Johnson. Like his mentors, he demanded discipline, hard work, and attention to detail.

In Lund's case, Blais required one more thing.

"He told me, 'You are cutting your hair down to helmet length. Have it done by practice tomorrow, otherwise you aren't skating,'" Lund said. "I had been growing it out for two years for the state tournament, and I was trying to beg and plead to not have it cut."

Blais's orders weren't up for debate. Lund got up early and had his hair cut the next morning before school. He was on the ice for practice that afternoon.

And so began the Rams' 1989–90 season.

After spending nine years as an assistant coach under Gino Gasparini at the University of North Dakota, Blais was looking to lead his own team. He had been a runner-up for several Division I college head coaching jobs before accepting the position in Roseau.

"I figured this has got to be the time to find out if I am head-coaching material," Blais said. "I wanted to go to a good high school team."

Blais got his wish. Roseau's group of seniors had been collecting state championships with regularity since they were Pee Wees. Only Grand Rapids was a consistently worthy competitor. As Bantams, Grand Rapids beat Roseau in the Minnesota Amateur Hockey Association state championship game. Roseau returned the favor a few weeks later in the state VFW title game.

With all that youth success came the ultimate in expectations. Roseau, a Canadian-border town with a population of about 2,500, beat archrival Warroad—smaller, with 1,400 people, and located twenty-two miles to the east—twice in the

First-year Roseau coach Dean Blais was at times tough with players and parents while leading the Rams to the 1990 state championship. Photo by Richard Sennott/*Minneapolis Star Tribune*

1988–89 regular season, then lost to the hated Warriors by a goal in the sectional championship. The defeat cost Rams coach Gary Hokanson his job.

"In Roseau, you can lose some games, but you can't lose to Warroad," Blais said.

Under Blais, the Rams won their first nine games, including a 9–0 romp over Warroad, before falling to Grand Forks Red River 4–2. Blais wasn't pleased. Not with the loss nor with what he deemed as a player's disrespectful interaction with the team's bus driver on the ride home.

The next day's practice was held in the least desirable of the town's three indoor rinks, known then as the Dome because the ice sheet was covered by an inflatable bubble.

"As soon as we heard we were practicing in the Dome, we knew what was coming," said Dana Gunderson, a senior defenseman.

The Rams practiced for two hours. All skating and conditioning. No pucks.

"[Blais] was so pissed off at us he was biting his lip, and he was biting it so hard it started to bleed," Gunderson said.

Blais wasn't done delivering messages. Just after Christmas, he heard rumblings that parents of some of the players weren't happy with the way the team was being run. They were questioning line combinations, individuals' ice time, and other coaching tactics. Blais called a parents-only meeting—he labeled it "a tune-up"—in the Rams' locker room. Parents were told to sit in front of their sons' locker stalls.

"It was basically an ass-kicking," said Terry Gotziaman, Roseau's principal and athletic director for twenty-eight years. Gotziaman, also the father of first-line winger Chris Gotziaman, had hired Blais and attended the meeting, knowing beforehand what it would entail.

"He told everyone, 'If I hear one more word about any of this that's been going on, your son is done,'" Gotziaman said. "From then on, there wasn't a whisper about anything."

Winning helped foster harmony. The Rams lost just once more, 4–3 on the road to number-one Grand Rapids. Roseau, ranked number two, then romped through the sectional playoffs, beating its three foes by a combined 24–3.

With an enrollment of 250, Roseau was making its then record twenty-fifth state tournament appearance and gunning for its fifth title (and first since 1961). The Rams dispatched White Bear Lake 5–1 in the quarterfinals. The 5-foot-9 Lund, the

Roseau's Mike Huglen (18) watches as a shot gets by Grand Rapids goaltender Chad Huson during the 1990 championship game.
Photo by Regene Radniecki/*Minneapolis Star Tribune*

state's top scorer with thirty-six goals and forty-seven assists, was held without a goal as linemates Gotziaman (goal and assist) and Chris Hites (two goals) shouldered the scoring load.

Despite a handful of prime chances, Lund was held scoreless again in the semifinals, when Roseau outmuscled big and bruising Minnetonka 5–2 behind two goals from Jamie Byfuglien, a light-scoring defenseman.

Grand Rapids, featuring future NHLers Kelly Fairchild, Chris Marinucci, Jeff Nielsen, and Kirk Nielsen, awaited in the championship.

As expected, the first all-northern school title game since 1972 was hotly contested. The score was tied 1–1 after two periods. Blais made one final demand in the locker room before the third.

"I said, 'We need a big play,'" Blais said. "I looked around the room and said, 'Hey, Hedlund, you are the guy who can do this.'"

Blais chose Todd Hedlund, a second-line winger headed to the University of Wisconsin, because he had been playing well, and "He wasn't Billy Lund. [Hedlund] was probably our fourth- or fifth-best guy," Blais said. "Sometimes you need a little prodding."

Hedlund, of course, followed orders, scoring the game-winning goal 1:56 into the third on a blistering slapshot from just inside the blue line.

The Rams' eventual 3–1 victory added another chapter, crafted in large part by Blais's iron fist, to the town's incredible hockey lore.

"From day one with him," said Lund, who did not score in the tournament, "we knew what our goal was at the end of the year."

~*LRN*~

149

TV cameras captured the celebration from close range after Roseau beat Grand Rapids 3–1 to win the 1990 state title.
Photo by Regene Radniecki/*Minneapolis Star Tribune*

LOVABLE RODENTS
"Rink Rat" T-shirts a popular fixture in tournament backdrop

Whether as a player (twice), a coach (four times), or a fan, Derrick Brown has attended every state tournament since 1994. Each time, he picks up a "Minnesota's Rink Rats" T-shirt, a keepsake he considers "an iconic symbol of the state tournament."

Shirts are created for both classes of the tournament. The design is the same: eight rats, seven standing and one sitting, each donning a qualifying team's jersey. The shirts debuted in 1990 and delighted state tournament goers.

Three former high school hockey players are behind them: Mike Curti, the artist; Paul Deutsch, the printer; and Mark Hultgren, the distributor.

Hultgren played on Minneapolis Roosevelt's 1978 state tournament team and later served as assistant coach for 1987 state champion Bloomington Kennedy, when he created T-shirts featuring rats representing the other

seven tournament teams in the talons and beak of an eagle, Kennedy's mascot. He later enlisted Deutsch, a former Roosevelt teammate, and Curti to help produce shirts with a wider appeal that could be sold to revive the dormant tournament-eve team banquet.

Deutsch, too, wanted to create a tournament memento beyond a program.

"I was at a poker game with some high school buddies, and we started talking about who else was at the 1978 tournament," Deutsch said. "I thought, 'People should have a way to help them remember.'"

Why rink rats? It's a term of endearment for hockey players who grew up playing on ponds and flooded rinks. Curti, a third-string goalie on Kennedy's 1976 tournament team, drew design inspiration from the rodents in the animated films *Cinderella* and *The Secret of NIMH*.

"They paid me $250," Curti said. "I should have asked for twenty-five cents per shirt."

Hultgren emails the coaches of all sixteen teams that reach the section final in each class and asks them to provide a picture of their jersey, a shirt order number, and which rat they would prefer.

For many years, the lone sitting rat was considered cursed because the team represented didn't perform well.

Production begins Friday evening once the tournament fields are set, and shirts are distributed to schools on Saturday afternoon. Each school receives $4 per shirt; the rest offsets banquet expenses. Shirts for the public are ready Sunday afternoon.

Deutsch said early on, shirts were sold on the street from a file cabinet on a dolly. They had to stay a thousand feet from the Civic Center and have a permit through the city of St. Paul.

In recent years, basketball, volleyball, and wrestling shirts were created. But "Hockey is number one," Hultgren said. "If I tell people what I do, I say, 'Rink Rat shirts.' We're hockey guys."

Fan cherish the shirts, with some even making quilts out of them. When it comes to Rink Rat–related items, however, Brown owns the pièce de résistance: a six-foot cardboard replica of the rat wearing Luverne's red jersey on the 2014 T-shirt.

His request for the item was granted after Luverne, located in extreme southwestern Minnesota, sold a record six-hundred-plus shirts before its state tournament debut. Brown kept the life-sized rat in his social studies room at the school.

"There was a line of people to take pictures with it," said Brown, who in 2019 coached St. Cloud Cathedral to the Class 1A state title.

~DL~

Three former high school hockey players— Mike Curti, Paul Deutsch, and Mark Hultgren—are behind the Rink Rats T-shirts, a tradition since 1990. Modeling the 2019 shirt is Delano's Kory Dunnigan. Photo by L. R. Nelson/Legacy.Hockey

TWIN ENGINES

STROBEL TWINS PROPELLED HILL-MURRAY TO LAST SINGLE-CLASS TITLE

DATES	LOCATION	ATTENDANCE	CHAMPIONSHIP
MARCH 7–9	ST. PAUL CIVIC CENTER	99,507	HILL-MURRAY 5, DULUTH EAST 3

 Sophomore center Ryan Meade reached the state tournament with Bloomington Kennedy like his father, Mike, had with Greenway in 1967 and 1968.

WHEN A DECEMBER SCRIMMAGE brought Hill-Murray to St. Paul Johnson's Phalen Arena, a few visiting players voiced disdain for the surroundings and the overall area of town.

"There were some comments made about the East Side that offended Mark and me," Pioneers wing Mike Strobel said. "We said, 'We're the East Siders you're talking about.'"

The identical twins were products of those blue-collar, fiercely proud neighborhoods and had played East Side and later Johnson Area youth hockey through ninth grade. Both were 6 feet and 185 pounds. Mark, older by ten minutes, and Mike brought talent and toughness to the rink and hardened the Pioneers' resolve.

After straightening out their mostly suburban-raised fellow players, the Strobels offered advice about facing their former youth-hockey teammates: "They hate you, so you better tighten your helmet straps."

Sure enough, Mike said, "There was a brawl in the first ten minutes."

Hill-Murray would fight its way to an unlikely 1991 state championship, the last single-class version of the tournament started in 1945.

How unlikely?

The Pioneers allowed eighty-nine goals, the most in school history.

The team ranked ninth in the final Associated Press state poll.

No Hill-Murray player finished among the top fifteen scorers in the Twin Cities Suburban Conference.

Reason for optimism remained, however. Whatever its flaws, this team was a collection of contributors. Too many times the previous season, players had gotten caught up watching the mastery of forward Craig Johnson.

Depth carried the team when injury repeatedly knocked.

Hill-Murray senior forward Mike Strobel loses his helmet in a tussle with a St. Paul Johnson player during the Pioneers' 7–1 victory in their state tournament quarterfinal matchup. Photo by Brian Peterson/*Minneapolis Star Tribune*

Hill-Murray defenseman Mark Strobel scores on St. Paul Johnson goalie and former youth-hockey teammate Ron Bookler. His goal gave the Pioneers a 3–0 first period lead en route to a 7–1 victory. Photo by Joe Rossi/*St. Paul Pioneer Press*

Deep thigh bruises. Bruised collarbones. Separated shoulders. Coach Jeff Whisler didn't have a healthy lineup the first three-quarters of the season.

"We had to persevere," said Mike Strobel, who missed eight games with a separated shoulder. He and Mark spoke often to Steve "Moose" Younghans, their Johnson Area Bantam coach, for encouragement.

"Moose told us, 'Hang in there. You're the leaders. Once the team gets on your backs, who knows what you can do,'" Mike said.

"Those two guys willed that state championship," Younghans said. "They were incredibly competitive, maybe to a fault. But that's the way I trained 'em."

Mark Strobel wore the captain's C on his jersey, and Mike donned an A as one of the alternate captains—patches earned through adversity. As sophomores, they had been cut after varsity tryouts by Whisler, who was married to their sister, Dawn. Though Whisler used to change the boys' diapers, he would not change his coaching philosophy.

"My whole career, I've done what I felt was best for the team," Whisler said.

Though stung by the decision and ready to transfer to St. Paul Johnson, the twins buried their pride and remained at Hill-Murray. They made the big club as juniors and hoped to remain linemates. Then Whisler moved Mark, a wing, to defense.

Mark didn't want to leave Mike, the opposite wing, but he took to his new position like a veteran.

"I needed a D-man, and from the minute it happened, he showed he could carry the puck out of our zone," Whisler said.

Teammate Jim Young called Mark the team's "emotional leader," while Mike "led by example. He'd go hit the biggest guy on the other team."

The Pioneers began the Section 3 playoffs with a 17–2 thrashing of Brooklyn Center. A similar result against Forest Lake seemed inevitable as Hill-Murray stormed to a 5–0 lead less than four minutes into the second period. But the Rangers rallied, scoring five consecutive goals to force overtime. Young scored in the second overtime for a 6–5 escape.

The semifinals brought number-one-ranked Park of Cottage Grove. A hat trick by Jeff Hasselman seemed to be the difference for Hill-Murray until Park tied the game with half a hiccup remaining in regulation. Official time of goal: 15:00 of the third period. Mark Strobel buried the game-winner in overtime for a 4–3 upset.

The championship game at the Met Center in Bloomington brought the third Hill-Murray/White Bear Lake showdown of the season. The rivals split the first two games. In the decisive third meeting, a Brian Bonin goal put the Bears ahead 3–0 about four minutes into the second period.

The twins answered, first Mike and then Mark, before

the period was over. Then Mark tied the game in the third period.

For the second time in three games, Young tallied the game-winning goal. The hero role belied Young's modest hockey upbringing. He never played traveling hockey in Roseville. He never played varsity until his senior year. His preseason dream? Get a point in a game to see his name in a newspaper box score.

Whisler rattled off Young's intangibles: Hardworking. Loyal. Always positive. Team oriented. Couldn't skate backward. Nevertheless, Whisler entrusted Young to take a late faceoff in the Pioneers' zone against Bonin, and Young won.

"Every championship team needs a guy like Jim Young," Mike Strobel said.

Hill-Murray entered the final one-class state tournament with six losses, more than any previous state champion. Technically. In 1981, Bloomington Jefferson had finished 17–8–1, but six of those losses were forfeited victories.

Pioneers players drew encouragement from their 11–2 record in one-goal games and clutch playoff performances. They believed they were peaking at the right time. A 7–1 quarterfinal blowout of St. Paul Johnson provided proof.

Johnson's previous state tournament appearance in 1984 had featured a quarterfinal upset of defending champion Hill-Murray. Several of those Governors' younger brothers were now on the 1991 team. But they could not re-create the magic.

Behind 6–0 after two periods, the Johnson players who weren't arguing in the locker room were sulking. A surprise visit from the East Side's favorite hockey son helped restore purpose.

"I'm sitting at my stall with my head in my hands, and I can hear some commotion," said Jeremy Hackman, junior defenseman. "Then I hear the door slam and a voice yell, 'Sit the [expletive] down and shut the [expletive] up.'"

Hackman glanced up and saw Herb Brooks.

"He looked around and said, 'We're all East Siders here. Arguing is not going to accomplish anything. Play hard in the third period, and get ready for tomorrow,'" Hackman said. "Getting chastised by Herb was cool and intimidating at the same time. And he was 100 percent right. We were feeling sorry for ourselves."

The Strobels helped dismantle a team loaded with many of their former youth teammates. Governors senior defenseman Erik Boxmeyer visited the Strobel house just down the street before the twins' last two sectional playoffs games and wished them well.

Another visitor, this one unknown and unwelcome, dropped by the Strobel house during Thursday's quarterfinal.

"Our house got robbed," Mike said. "I remember silverware thrown everywhere. I think the message was 'You guys should be at Johnson.'"

Mark wasn't so sure it was personal.

"There were a few more break-ins on our block," he said. "They probably figured not many people would be at home during the game."

Hard feelings toward the Strobels, however, were real.

"There was one drunk Johnson dad who called us prima donnas on the elevator after the game," Mike said. "We had played youth hockey with his son."

Grand Rapids, runner-up at the 1990 state tournament, came next. Hill-Murray had lost to the Halloween Machine in five previous state tournament meetings dating back to 1975, but an 11–3 romp soothed those years of disappointment. Matt Mauer scored twice, and Mark Strobel netted a hat trick. Hill-Murray's seven goals in the second period tied a state tournament record.

Later Friday evening, players on the Catholic-school team received "a dispensation from the archbishop to eat prime rib at Hillcrest Golf Course during Lent," Mike Strobel said.

During televised player introductions before Saturday's championship game against Duluth East, Mike Strobel looked at the camera and said, "Hi, Boxy," to acknowledge an injured friend. Boxmeyer was hospitalized with a lacerated kidney suffered on a hit in the consolation game against Bloomington Kennedy.

Then the teams lined up for "The Star-Spangled Banner." Junior goalie Kevin Powell, jersey number 1, took his customary spot on the far right with teammates to his left in ascending numerical order. But Hasselman, number 9, and Brad Meehan, number 16, stood immediately to Powell's left because . . . well, because of hockey superstition.

Maybe that explains how Hill-Murray became the first team to come back from a two-goal deficit and win the championship game.

Derek Locker's second goal of the game put the Greyhounds ahead 3–1 in the second period, but a Mike Strobel power-play goal cut the Hill-Murray deficit to one at second intermission.

"That game was a war," Mark Strobel said. "They were very physical."

The Strobels rallied teammates with a tag-team speech. Bottom line: stay in the locker room if you don't think we can win.

"We demanded that guys give the best of themselves," Mark said.

"My brother and I were raised to be leaders," Mike said.

The pep talk was more than words. Mike scored the go-ahead goal in a 5–3 victory.

Later in the evening, the Strobels drove to Younghans's house to thank their always loyal Bantam coach.

For Whisler, named the coach of the year by his peers, the championship healed past tournament wounds. As a Hill-Murray forward, Whisler had lost to Grand Rapids in the 1975 and 1976 semifinals. In 1987–88, Whisler's first season as the Pioneers' head coach, the team had fallen in the championship game to Edina.

"You're only as good as your players, and that 1991 team was a real team," Whisler said.

~DL~

TRADITION IN TRANSITION

Hill-Murray coach Jeff Whisler stepped off the ice a champion and stepped right into the political fray regarding the future of the state tournament.

He approached Governor Arne Carlson and said, "Leave it a one-class tournament."

Earlier that day, the hockey coaches' association had met to determine its next course of action in a two-year struggle with the Minnesota State High School League (MSHSL) on how to best mold future state tournaments.

Where did this divide begin?

As far back as the 1970s, two hockey coaches, Brooklyn Center's George Larson and Chisholm's Herb Sellars, noticed the many high schools whose chances of making the tournament were akin to a Zamboni's likelihood of winning a drag race.

Smaller communities lacked the resources to compete against the traditional powers in the postseason. Give those student-athletes hope, a fairer fight, Larson and Sellars decreed. Give them their own tournament.

But the MSHSL really didn't listen. Not even when its own ad hoc committee polled hockey coaches in 1982 and found sixty who supported the concept versus forty opposed. Coaches at schools with Class 1A–level enrollments voted 23–2 in favor.

But school principals and superintendents were opposed. And season-ticket holders, also polled for some reason, voted 1,505 to 468 against. Finally, the MSHSL board of directors voted 5–3 to "take no further action on the two-class hockey questions."

Larson and Sellars didn't stop. In the late 1980s, the duo found an audience for their two-class proposal in state Representative Jerry Janezich (DFL-Chisholm). Janezich's brother Richard was Brooklyn Center's principal.

A two-class tournament bill was sponsored by Janezich in the House and Senator Ron Dicklich (DFL-Hibbing) in the Senate, though neither was crazy about meddling in high school sports.

"My intent was never to legislate," Janezich said at the time. "I think you have to create an awareness of the problem."

In April 1989, Larson testified be-

GIVE THOSE STUDENT-ATHLETES HOPE, A FAIRER FIGHT.... GIVE THEM THEIR OWN TOURNAMENT.

fore a Minnesota House of Representatives subcommittee—further than he had previously gotten in his quest.

A few weeks later, language inserted into a $1.1 billion spending bill ordered the MSHSL to create a two-class tournament. Governor Rudy Perpich's signature made it a law in May 1989.

"I was surprised at the amount of people we had to battle for this," Larson said. "The high school league, the media, the coaches, the fans, and the public."

Perpich said he acted in the name of increased student-athlete participation. And he wasn't alone. His staff contacted 107 of the 143 schools playing hockey and found similar numbers as the MSHSL committee did: 67 coaches in support of a two-class tournament and 40 against.

Some coaches were opposed because they didn't like the notion of

government interlopers. Others were afraid to diminish the tournament's grand tradition.

But the law required action. Rather than working together, the hockey coaches' association and MSHSL faced off.

In January 1990, an MSHSL task force proposed a two-class system based on school enrollment and a four-day tournament played at one site—a precursor to the modern-day format.

But the coaches' association pushed for a format based on a program's success more than school enrollment. And they demanded the two tournaments be played on different dates at different sites to protect the big-school tournament's tradition.

Both sides found common ground in getting their debate out of lawmakers' hands. In March 1990, they worked together to get the bill repealed and agreed to partner going forward.

On April 24, 1991, the two-tier tournament was born, but Larson and Sellars were not proud parents handing out cigars.

Two-tier seeding went like this: coaches in the state's eight geographic sections ranked the teams' regular-season performances and put the top eight from each section in Tier I. The schools with lesser records were placed in Tier II.

The tier formula, where success outweighs enrollment, didn't meet the duo's original goal. Small-school programs with strong teams remained in danger of missing out.

"It's still a big mess because it fails to address the problems of small schools with excellent programs not being able to go anywhere," Sellars said at the time.

The new-look 1992 tournament didn't energize longtime fans, either. T-shirts sold a year earlier captured public sentiment: "Farewell Tour: Single Class" and, more pointedly, "Puck 2-Tier Hockey."

Still, the inaugural Tier I bracket looked strong, led by preseason favorite Bloomington Jefferson. Fellow suburban Twin Cities programs Blaine and Eden Prairie were promising newcomers, along with Moorhead.

By comparison, Tier II looked like a consolation bracket. Two teams, New Ulm (8–16–1) and Rosemount (4–20–1), didn't appear worthy. Mahtomedi and Greenway were both 13–12.

Fans voted with their feet. On championship Saturday, Greenway beat Rosemount 6–1 in a matinee at the Target Center in Minneapolis before 6,683 fans. That evening, Jefferson bested Moorhead 6–3 in front of a St. Paul Civic Center audience of 14,340.

Reported total attendance for the two tournaments was 117,563. But the 90,370 who saw the Tier I tournament, home to the state's top eight teams, was the lowest amount for the big show since 1975.

The two-tier tournament wasn't expected to last beyond its two-year trial run. Indeed, on February 24, 1993, the MSHSL board of directors voted it out of existence. Beginning with the 1993–94 season, hockey would adhere to the two-class system used in other sports.

A little less than three weeks later, an Eveleth-Gilbert team with a 14–14 record won the 1993 Tier II championship, its first state title since John Mayasich had last graced the ice in 1951. Tier, schmier, said victorious Golden Bears coach Robert "Bobo" Kochevar.

"Eveleth people went wild," he said. "Ex-Evelethians came to the games all decked out in their memorabilia."

Larson and Sellars, meanwhile, were glad to see two classes replace the two-tier format. The 1994 tournaments, with all winner's-bracket games in both Class 1A and 2A played at the Civic Center, fit their vision.

Class 2A included heavyweights Bloomington Jefferson and Moorhead, while Class 1A included eight smaller-school programs from the Twin Cities and beyond—none with more than nine losses.

"I'm happy with the way it turned out," Sellars said. "They've never asked me to hand out a trophy, but that's OK. It's about more kids getting to enjoy the state tournament."

Whisler, initially opposed to a two-class tournament, came around. He guided Mahtomedi to the 1992 Tier II tournament—the program's first state

ON APRIL 24, 1991, THE TWO-TIER TOURNAMENT WAS BORN.

tournament appearance—and made the Class 1A field in 1994 and 1997.

"Mahtomedi wouldn't have gotten out of Region 3 the way things used to be set up," Whisler said. "Without another tournament, those kids would never have had that experience. And you ask the kids and they'll tell you: it's as special."

Whisler wasn't alone in his changed views. John Bartz, a longtime tournament official who became the MSHSL's associate director in charge of the tournament, said in 1989, "The big school versus small school sweetheart would go down the tubes, and I don't think [two tournaments] would be as prestigious."

Looking back almost thirty years later, Bartz said, "I enjoyed the one-class tournament, but I understood those who were looking for more participation—and I lost some friends over it."

Smaller-school magic still exists

despite initial fears to the contrary. Roseau won it all in 1999 and 2007. Grand Rapids did likewise in 2017.

Meanwhile, in Class 1A, competitive programs with talented players have room to shine. Johnny Pohl and Red Wing. Ben Hanowski and Little Falls. Blake Wheeler and Breck. None of those programs reached a state tournament before 1992.

Growing hockey communities such as Litchfield/Dassel-Cokato and Luverne energized their youth programs with state tournament runs.

"I was always for it," said longtime Edina coach Willard Ikola. "With two tournaments, maybe you get more kids playing hockey and get more rinks built."

Others embraced Class 1A as a way to avoid extinction. Consider the 1991 state tournament bracket: of the eight teams, seven now have Class 1A enrollments. And a sobering reality hit three programs. Johnson is one of two remaining St. Paul Public School programs. Richfield survives as a co-op program. And Bloomington Kennedy draws fewer skaters than it once cut. Playing in Class 1A gives them a more realistic postseason chance.

Without two tournaments, perhaps tiny Warroad never wins a title. Maybe East Grand Forks never becomes back-to-back champion.

Its equilibrium found, the two-class tournament continued through the eightieth year in 2024 and sees no end on the horizon.

But many who reached the state tournament before the expansion era, well, they consider themselves extra lucky.

"Some of us still joke that we're the reigning one-class champion," said Jim Young of Hill-Murray.

~*DL*~

THE MODERN DAY: 1992–TODAY

The value of the state tournament experience, along with imbalances in population and resources within the metro area and in relation to the rest of the state, brought change in the early 1990s. Hotly contested change. A second tournament was formed, and the split arrangement was known for two years as Tier I and II and then as Class 1A and 2A. Purists scoffed. Emerging and struggling programs rejoiced. The event temporarily departed St. Paul for Minneapolis in 1999 and 2000 as the Civic Center was razed and the Xcel Energy Center was built on the same land. The magic and the passion found their way inside the new building, though. And tournament crowds are as robust as ever, annually surpassing 100,000 fans.

Edina's Peter Colby clinched the 2019 Class 2A title with an overtime goal against Eden Prairie. He then mimicked his NHL idol Patrick Kane's "heartbreaker" celebration, busting his arms wide from his chest as he slid on his knees toward the Hornets' student section. Photo by Tim Kolehmainen/ Breakdown Sports Media

DEFENSE RESTS

LOADED D CORPS SET BLOOMINGTON JEFFERSON APART

DATES	LOCATION	ATTENDANCE	TIER I CHAMPIONSHIP:
MARCH 11–14	ST. PAUL CIVIC CENTER [TIER I; TIER II QUARTERFINALS] TARGET CENTER, MINNEAPOLIS [TIER II SEMIFINALS, CHAMPIONSHIP]	117,563	BLOOMINGTON JEFFERSON 6, MOORHEAD 3 **TIER II CHAMPIONSHIP:** GREENWAY 6, ROSEMOUNT 1

 Cambridge sophomore forward Jason Hall scored the first Tier II tournament goal.

DROPPING THE Battle of Bloomington to crosstown rival Kennedy in the 1991 Section 5 title game pained Jefferson coach Tom Saterdalen.

There were the overjoyed Eagles, state tournament bound. And there were his sullen Jaguars, beginning the offseason a week earlier than desired.

"We were bummed," Saterdalen said. "Then at one point, [assistant coach John] Bianchi hits my shoulder and says, 'Don't worry. Better days are ahead.'"

Saterdalen looked up and saw the players' parents packed together among the Met Center crowd. The message came through. If the parents were united, it was safe to assume their sons were, too.

"They didn't care who the star was, and they had expectations of their kids," Saterdalen said.

So did voters, who made Jefferson number one going into the 1991–92 season. The maturation of players two years removed from a 53–1 Bantam season meant these Jaguars were loaded. Before the season's first game, Saterdalen proclaimed the group the most skilled he had coached at Jefferson.

The five seniors eagerly made room.

"No question the younger guys were elite," said Dan Trebil, a senior defenseman. "On that team, there wasn't a seniority thing. Everyone hung out. There was no jealousy or animosity."

Trebil put the team first throughout his prep career. As a sophomore, he accepted Saterdalen moving him from forward to defense.

"I was brought up to not question coaches about anything," Trebil said. "I was initially worried, but I settled in. My strength was passing anyway. I had a knack for making a good first pass."

Saterdalen hoped a strong athlete such as Trebil would bolster the blue line. Trebil did better yet, becoming the leader of the state's best defensive corps.

Six future Division I defensemen dotted the roster: Dusty Anderson, Mike Crowley, Tim Krug, Brian LaFleur, Cory Peterson, and Trebil. Lineup tinkering midseason moved Krug to wing and Scott Hohag to defense.

"That was one of the few seasons I played all six defensemen," Saterdalen said.

The group made an impression on foes and teammates alike.

"A lot of teams would like two of those guys," said Joe Bianchi, a sophomore forward. "We had six. Playing against them in practice—it sucked. You'd struggle just to get a good shot three on one, let alone score."

Junior forward Cort Lundeen said, "We didn't have two of the same player. Dusty was the best penalty killer. Cory was the best open-ice hitter. Dan made the best first pass. Crowley was a stud. LaFleur thought he was a forward. Hohag was nuts. We called him the Undertaker; it was literally written on his stick. He would try to run the goaltender—from defense."

Junior forward Nick Checco said, "Hohag and I collided in practice, and he dented my mask. I went back to wearing an Itech [clear shield] after that."

"I'm glad Hohag was my partner," Trebil said.

Up front, Bianchi centered Lundeen and junior Matt Jones. Checco centered Krug and sophomore Joe Pankratz on another line.

Krug's grit meshed with the forwards' skills.

"He was big, strong, and worked out hard," Joe Bianchi said. "He probably had 3 percent body fat."

Senior Brandon Johnson centered a rotation of sophomore Ian Petersen, junior Tim McDonald, and junior Jon De St. Hubert.

The 1991–92 season brought the newly adopted two-tier state tournament, but the road there remained the same. Jefferson faced Kennedy with a state tournament appearance at stake.

This time, the Jaguars celebrated a 5–1 victory on the Met Center ice. Three juniors and a sophomore scored the goals. But the victory was for Jefferson's senior quintet.

"There were probably better players on JV," Lundeen said. "But the senior group had toughness, and they worked hard. It started with them."

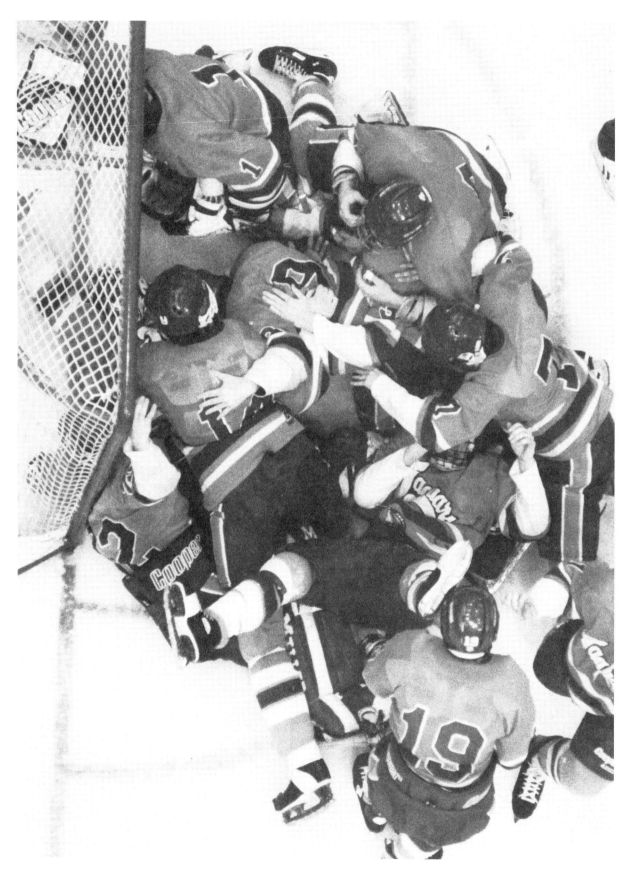

Victorious Bloomington Jefferson skaters mob goalie Randy Koeppl after downing Moorhead 6-3 in the inaugural Tier I state championship game. Koeppl finished with nineteen saves. Photo by John Doman/*St. Paul Pioneer Press*

Advancing to the Civic Center was a new experience for these Jaguars. Checco made sure to absorb the moment.

"Running out there the first time, it was like, 'This is it,'" Checco said. "It was a goal ever since when I was a kid and my mom would get me out of school to watch at home. It was like a holiday. Being there definitely lived up to my expectations. It was really bright on the ice, and those clear boards—that's what it's all about."

The Tier I quarterfinals brought Eden Prairie. Jefferson ruined the Eagles' debut with a 7–1 victory. Bianchi scored once each period for a hat trick.

But while Eden Prairie was a breeze, semifinal opponent Cloquet/Esko/Carlton took the Jaguars' breath away.

"That was one of the most physical games I played in my high school career," Bianchi said.

"Jesse Bertogliat hit me harder than anyone ever hit me," Crowley said.

More than intimidators, the Lumberjacks led 4–2 just forty-two seconds into the third period.

"We were like, 'What the hell?'" Joe Bianchi said. "We didn't have that happen to us. This game was our toughest test, and we had to continue to believe."

Lundeen said, "I was puking right through my mask near the end of the game. I was exhausted. Then ten seconds later, Checco scores."

Checco tied the game 4–4 with fifty-one seconds remaining in regulation.

"LaFleur comes up and says to me, 'Checco, I love you.'" Overtime.

McDonald's game-winning goal capped his hat trick in style.

"He was one of the great kids," Saterdalen said of McDonald, who was killed in a helicopter crash in 2019 at age forty-four.

Title game opponent Moorhead was new to the state tournament. But not to Jefferson. The Spuds had gotten the Jaguars' attention earlier in the season with a strong scrimmage performance.

In the final, Jefferson turned a 2–2 second-period stalemate into a footnote. The Jaguars pumped in four goals, including three in a row from Bianchi.

Jefferson won 6–3 to claim its third state title and first since 1989. The defense finished with ten shutouts and a paltry thirty-eight goals allowed in twenty-eight games.

Speaking of numbers, Saterdalen afterward said, "Now I know why you had us rated number one at the start of the year."

~DL~

Bloomington Jefferson defenseman Scott Hohag (17), a converted forward, brought a physical presence to the blue line. Teammates called him the Undertaker. Photo courtesy of Tom Saterdalen

SINGLE-DIGIT SALUTE

COACH'S PRODDING PUSHED NICK CHECCO TO BRINK, JEFFERSON OVER THE TOP

DATES	LOCATION	ATTENDANCE	TIER I CHAMPIONSHIP
MARCH 10–13	ST. PAUL CIVIC CENTER [TIER I; TIER II QUARTERFINALS] TARGET CENTER, MINNEAPOLIS [TIER II SEMIFINALS, CHAMPIONSHIP]	107,030	BLOOMINGTON JEFFERSON 4, HILL-MURRAY 0 **TIER II CHAMPIONSHIP** EVELETH-GILBERT 3, LAKE OF THE WOODS 2 [2 OT]

Did you know? Cloquet/Esko/Carlton teammates Jamie Langenbrunner and Sergei Petrov tied for first in tournament scoring with thirteen points each.

BLOOMINGTON JEFFERSON coach Tom Saterdalen's provocations became more than senior Nick Checco could stand.

In mid-January 1993, the season midpoint for a team pre-ordained to go undefeated, the Jaguars faced a solid Apple Valley squad.

But the Eagles were like every other team: so far behind Jefferson that Saterdalen knew he couldn't motivate players through fear of loss. Instead, he used players against one another to get the desired effect.

Saterdalen needled Checco, the team's first-line center and the best of the Jaguars' six Division I–bound forwards, after his line allowed a first-period goal by the Eagles' leading scorer, Graham Lomen.

"Joe Bianchi is outplaying you," Saterdalen said, referring to

Emotions flow from Bloomington Jefferson seniors Jon De St. Hubert (left) and Nick Checco (right) after the Jaguars captured back-to-back Tier I state championships. A fiery competitor with jets strapped to his skates, Checco centered one of the best teams in high school hockey history. Photo by the *Star Tribune,* courtesy of Kyle Oen/Vintage Minnesota Hockey

Jefferson's second-line center, whose line managed to contain Lomen.

Saterdalen hurled similar jabs at Checco again in the second period as Lomen beat his line for another goal. Checco was furious.

Late in the second period, Checco and the penalty-killing unit readied for a faceoff.

Rip me? I'll show you.

"Nick wins the draw, goes through Lomen's legs, goes down and scored top shelf," Saterdalen remembered. "Then he turned around and gave me the middle finger. The bench erupted."

"Looking back, I wish I would never have done that," Checco said. "But [Saterdalen] laughs about it now. Sats always got the best out of you. He challenged me and got me wanting to prove him wrong."

All that talent. All that pride. All that competitiveness. Other teams didn't stand a chance. Jefferson finished 28–0 and became the first undefeated state champion since the 1983 Hill-Murray Pioneers.

The Mall of America in Bloomington, home to more than three hundred retail stores, opened in August 1992. Jefferson's megateam, featuring eleven future Division I college players, hit the ice a few months later. Both left observers in awe.

Jefferson beat all but one opponent by at least three goals. The Jaguars won by five or more goals an incredible eighteen times. Behind 1–0 after the first period in its opening game, Jefferson never trailed after a period again.

"My only team that wasn't lucky," Saterdalen said.

The Jaguars returned thirteen players from the 1992 Tier I state championship team. Such depth made them too big to fail.

Case in point: Mild shoulder separations forced Bianchi and Checco to miss a late-December game against Grand Rapids. No problem. Wings Cort Lundeen and Matt Jones took the center spots, and both recorded hat tricks in a 12–2 blowout.

A week later, Jefferson blasted Moorhead 7–2. Afterward, Spuds coach Terry Cullen raved, "There is no question that they could beat some small-college teams."

The apex of Jefferson's dynasty, the 1993 team combined all the best parts of Saterdalen's preparation and motivation, assistant coach John Bianchi's big heart and competitive streak, and the discipline instilled by youth coach Greg Trebil.

Trebil's zero tolerance for cutting corners and insistence on puck movement and team play became Jaguar hallmarks.

"All the parents and players were afraid of him," defenseman Mike Crowley said. "He influenced this group maybe more than anyone. Most of us would have rather had an assist than a goal, and that came from him."

Crowley led a defense that permitted just thirty goals in twenty-eight games—still the program record. Fellow blue liners Dusty Anderson, Brian LaFleur, and Cory Peterson became a nearly unbeatable foursome.

Keeping his team accountable from within, Saterdalen taxed his defensemen with thirty pushups for each goal allowed in practice. He rarely collected.

Checco said at the time, "We go three on two at them, and maybe once a week they might get beat."

That speaks volumes because Jefferson lit up teams all season. Jones and Bianchi tied for the team lead with twenty-three goals. Checco and Ian Petersen each scored twenty-two. Lundeen (eighteen) and Tim McDonald (thirteen) came next, followed by Crowley and Jon De St. Hubert (twelve each).

To stem the carnage, Saterdalen often benched his top guys in the third period. They packed snacks for their viewing pleasure.

"We'd sneak food and candy in our breezers," Crowley said.

For sophomore forward Mark Parrish, a varsity newcomer, third periods were go time.

"We couldn't wait," Parrish said. "We'd get double-shifted a lot because we'd come back to the bench and the older guys would laugh and tell us to get back out there."

On a team of stars, Checco stood apart. His raw speed drew raves.

"Checco could glide faster than I skated," Lundeen said.

"When he turned it on, he left people in the dust who I knew were fast," Parrish said.

Checco impressed Parrish in other ways,

Brian LaFleur (9), part of Bloomington Jefferson's embarrassment of blue line riches, helped the Jaguars permit a paltry thirty goals in twenty-eight games—still the program record. Photo courtesy of Tom Saterdalen

Bloomington Jefferson forward Tim McDonald made the state tournament semifinals his showcase. He tallied five goals in 1992, including a hat trick and the game-winning goal in overtime, and added a pair of goals in the 1993 semis against Elk River. Here he scores on Cloquet/Esko/Carlton Lumberjacks goalie Dutch Barrett. Photo by Mike Thill/*Let's Play Hockey*

too. He sometimes bought the underclassman lunch and provided rides to and from practice.

"He's the reason I switched to number 21 my last two years of high school," Parrish said. "He was an incredible captain. He was soft-spoken, but his Italian side came out every now and then."

Jefferson's state tournament run began with Apple Valley. Whatever bad blood the teams had accrued in their first two meetings showed itself in fourteen combined penalties. But a physical game failed to rattle the Jaguars in a 6–2 victory.

Another rematch awaited. Bloomington Jefferson defeated Elk River 4–1 in December but trailed 1–0 in the semifinals. For twenty-four seconds. McDonald and Checco each scored in the first period and each added a second goal in a second 4–1 victory.

Only Hill-Murray remained. Jefferson made the Pioneers a

green-and-white speed bump on its way to history. Bianchi, Petersen, Checco, and Crowley each scored in the 4–0 victory, and senior goalie Randy Koeppl earned his twenty-third victory of the season.

"Guys were pretty emotional going into the third period because we knew we were going to win," Crowley said. "Joe [Bianchi] and I had always played with the '93 class growing up, so that was more emotional for us."

Checco finished as the first Mr. Hockey Award recipient from a championship team.

"It could have gone to any senior on that team," Checco said. "Winning [Mr. Hockey] really didn't add anything to that season. Winning a championship with my friends meant more."

~DL~

FROM THE MOUTHS OF JAGS

JEFFERSON'S RUN TO THIRD STRAIGHT TITLE, IN PLAYERS' WORDS

DATES	LOCATION	ATTENDANCE	CLASS 2A CHAMPIONSHIP
MARCH 9–12	ST. PAUL CIVIC CENTER	112,846	BLOOMINGTON JEFFERSON 3, MOORHEAD 1
			CLASS 1A CHAMPIONSHIP
			WARROAD 5, HIBBING 3

 In its tenth state tournament appearance since 1948, tradition-rich Warroad captured its first championship.

BLOOMINGTON JEFFERSON had iced a team in 1992–93 widely considered the best in Minnesota high school hockey history.

Two returning standouts, forward Joe Bianchi and defenseman Mike Crowley, plus several key contributors, found that maintaining the Jaguars' dominance in 1993–94 wasn't easy—despite a 26–1–1 record.

Here's their journey to a third consecutive state championship in the words of players from the team and others who knew them well.

Follow-Up Pressure — *The 1993–94 Jaguars sought to become the first program to three-peat since International Falls (1964–66). Only five regulars returned.*

MARK PARRISH (junior forward): There was always an expectation to follow in the older guys' footsteps. It was Jaguar pride. And I was excited as all hell to see if I could help carry the torch as well as they did.

MIKE CROWLEY (senior defenseman): We weren't as great; we had to earn it. There was pressure because you're judged on how you do as a senior.

TOBY PETERSEN (freshman forward): Expectations were to win another state tournament.

TOM SATERDALEN (head coach, *Star Tribune* interview, 1993): We're not going to go undefeated [again] this year. If I had to make a bet, I would put $100 to $10 we'd lose.

Streak Ends — *Jefferson, ranked number one in Class 2A, rode a sixty-game unbeaten streak (58–0–2) into an early January game at the Blake School. The Bears, ranked number four in Class 1A, pulled the 3–2 upset.*

PARRISH: If we had a lead, we wouldn't lose it. Against Blake, we couldn't get it.

DEREK CAMUEL (senior forward): We were devastated.

PETERSEN: It made us stronger in the end.

Crowley the Great — *Defenseman Crowley finished the season with a program-record seventy-seven points. He capped the season by earning the Mr. Hockey Award.*

SATERDALEN (*Star Tribune* interview, 1994): I have never coached a better defenseman than Mike Crowley.

JOE BIANCHI (senior forward): [Crowley] jumped one or two levels from junior year to senior year. He forced puck carriers into bad positions. On offense, he could break the puck out himself, carry, distribute—and shoot it.

CORT LUNDEEN (1993 graduate): He didn't shoot it enough. I only saw him get beat once—against Roseville and "Bullet" Bobby Dustin.

CROWLEY: On my first varsity shift, freshman year, Bobby Dustin goes through my legs and scores.

As a freshman, Crowley was humbled off the ice, too.

CROWLEY: Jesse Carlson gave me a swirly every day. I started just walking to the toilet versus getting carried there. At least it was a clean toilet.

A Natural Scorer — *Bianchi, who joined Crowley for all three of the Jaguars' 1990s championships, tallied seventy-four points as a senior. He was the last of three brothers who all wore number 15, scored big goals, and won state titles.*

LUNDEEN: Joey was a prick. He'd slash you. All of his goals were scored within five feet of the net.

PARRISH: He'd just give you a look like "Go there," and then the puck would be on your tape.

Bloomington Jefferson's Mike Crowley, the greatest high school defenseman of his era, moves the puck past Moorhead forward Troy Bagne in the 1994 Class 2A championship game. "Everything you want in a hockey player, Crowley had," said Jefferson forward Nick Checco, who won two championships with Crowley. Photo by Marlin Levison/*Minneapolis Star Tribune*

Fans of Bloomington Jefferson's early-1990s dynasty saw tenacious forward Joe Bianchi often doing his best work around the net. Bianchi, seen here pressuring Osseo goalie Matt Jeffers in the 1994 Class 2A quarterfinals, holds the program record with 168 career points. Photo by Jerry Holt/*Minneapolis Star Tribune*

PETERSEN: He was a natural goal scorer from the time I'd watch Jefferson games on cable-access TV to when we were on the same bench.

JOHN BIANCHI (assistant coach): He has the [Jefferson] career scoring record [168 points]. He beat his brother, Tony, for the honor. Nice kid, huh?

Coach Bianchi's Big Save — *Jefferson won the Section 5 title and earned a state tournament spot. But after-school shenanigans almost cost several players their chance.*

CAMUEL: We're waiting for our bus to take us from school to practice. We're bored, so we get snowballs ready to throw at our bus. And Jimmy, the driver, is running late, so we're waiting and waiting. Then this other car comes rolling around, and we just let the snowballs go. Well, the lady gets out just livid.

SATERDALEN: She drove a Cadillac.

CAMUEL: She goes and tells the principal how disrespectful the hockey team is. Sats is beyond upset. He tells Mr. Bianchi, "I don't know if we want them coming to the state tournament with us." And Mr. Bianchi says, "Let me handle it."

So we're on the bus, and then Sats and Mr. Bianchi have us get off. Sats lines us up and says, "If you don't confess to who did this, I'll skate you to death or not take you to the state tournament. So if it was you, raise your hand." Our two student managers' hands go up right away. We figure Mr. Bianchi must have had a chat with them.

JOHN BIANCHI: I can't say for sure, but I probably did. But then in the summer, that lady saw me as I'm working in my garden. She drives up, and I'm thinking, "What the hell is the matter now?" She gets out, and she's got her hands on her hips and says, "Thank you for taking care of those kids."

Three-Peat Complete — *Jefferson's three state tournament opponents—Osseo, Duluth East, and Moorhead—pushed back hard. The Jaguars edged Osseo 1–0 despite outshooting the Orioles 40–18, then fought off Duluth East for a 2–1 victory.*

JOE BIANCHI: Duluth East was tough. They were willing to lay it all out there. We couldn't get separation from them.

Jefferson advanced to face Moorhead in the championship game for the second time in three seasons. Jaguars senior goalie Jeff Heil was the difference in a 3–1 victory.

PARRISH: Who was that no-name guy from Moorhead? Oh yeah, Matt Cullen. Jeff stopped him point-blank. Without Jeff, there wouldn't have been a three-peat.

Parrish tied the game 1–1. Camuel tallied the game-winning goal in the third period.

CAMUEL: In tryouts my junior year, I had to go against Checco, [Matt] Jones, and [Tim] McDonald. It was cutthroat, the most physical tryout I ever experienced. They were basically beating the hell out of us in scrimmages. But I think Sats did that to find out who wouldn't back down.

Sats would always say, "You never know who the hero is going to be." That stuck with me.

~DL~

Motivator. Strategist. Technician. Tom Saterdalen ensured his Bloomington Jefferson teams always came ready to play. The Jaguars won five state titles from 1981 to 1994 with Saterdalen and assistant coach John Bianchi behind the bench. Photo by Mike Thill/*Let's Play Hockey*

ONCE, TWICE, THREE TIMES A LEGEND

AMAZING TRIO OF HAT TRICKS FOR DULUTH EAST'S DAVE SPEHAR SET UP BY TRUSTED SIDEKICK

DATES	LOCATION	ATTENDANCE	CLASS 2A CHAMPIONSHIP
MARCH 8–11	ST. PAUL CIVIC CENTER	116,870	DULUTH EAST 5, MOORHEAD 3
			CLASS 1A CHAMPIONSHIP
			INTERNATIONAL FALLS 3, TOTINO-GRACE 2

167

 International Falls ended a twenty-three-year championship drought on Jon Austin's goal with 17.3 seconds remaining.

ONCE THE CENTER on Duluth East's explosive top line, Chris Locker found himself the odd man out when practices began his junior season.

An unselfish passer on the ice, Locker kept doing selfish, stupid things that kept him off the ice. Twice busted for underage drinking as a sophomore, Locker ended his season due to an academic suspension before the Section 7 championship game.

The Greyhounds still qualified for the state tournament and took third, but Locker's absence irked star right wing Dave Spehar. And the hard feelings lingered.

During the first practices of the 1994–95 season, Spehar showed no interest in pairing with Locker, his classmate and, for six successful seasons, his linemate.

"Dude, I want to kill you," Spehar said he told Locker. "I'm still pissed at you. I want to play with you, just not now."

Locker understood.

"I had to build a lot of trust back with my teammates," he said.

But Spehar knew he couldn't stay mad for long. Undeniable chemistry made him and Locker unstoppable. They entered the 1995 state tournament ranked number one and two in state scoring. Spehar, the finisher, posted forty-nine goals. Locker, the playmaker, tallied fifty-two assists.

Beyond their whopping point totals was the manner in which Locker and Spehar did their damage. Permitted to use his keen anticipation, Spehar would slip behind defensemen and look for a long pass. Locker could oblige. A style some teams bad-mouthed as cherry-picking became a weapon.

"Locker had uncanny vision and made passes no one else saw," said Dylan Mills, then a sophomore defenseman. "Spee thought the game a little differently and better than anyone else. And he could catch passes better than anybody I'd seen."

Mills said the 5-foot-9, 175-pound Spehar "was definitely not floating."

Locker and Spehar dominated prep hockey's premier event, though Spehar is best remembered for tallying three-goal performances all three nights.

Number-four Duluth East readied for a quarterfinal showdown with number-one Bloomington Jefferson—the three-time defending state champions.

In December, the Greyhounds and Jaguars had scrimmaged to a 5–5 tie. The prior meeting gave Jefferson coach Tom Saterdalen ideas for stopping Locker and Spehar. But three days of game planning with four future Division I defensemen proved insufficient.

Locker and Spehar shredded the Jaguars' scouting report just 1:23 into the game. A sixty-foot pass from Locker found Spehar between two Jaguars at the far blue line. With only goalie Jake Bullard to beat, Spehar went right and scored his fiftieth goal of the season.

Spehar struck again about five minutes later, corralling a Jefferson turnover just inside the Greyhounds' blue line and going on the attack as a three-on-one advantage developed.

Turning as if to pass, Spehar instead snapped off a quick shot and put the puck past Bullard.

"I think I heard the goalie say, 'Oh my god,'" Locker said. "That shot epitomized Dave. You hear about a goal scorer's goal—that was a legend's goal."

Down 2–0, Jefferson went on the power play but failed to score. Just as Jefferson's man advantage ended, Spehar pursued the puck along the wall. A pinching Jaguars defenseman arrived first, but Spehar instinctively bolted toward the now-vacated space beyond the blue line.

Good thing, because teammate Cullen Flaherty gained possession of the puck and immediately fired a sixty-foot pass to Spehar. Once again, Spehar cashed in on a breakaway.

Time of death for the Bloomington Jefferson dynasty read 9:28 of the first period.

Spehar's hat trick was the story of Duluth East's 5–0 victory. But senior goalie Cade Ledingham's eighteen-save shutout became a compelling subplot.

A stalwart in net much of the season, Ledingham suffered a psychological blow when coach Mike Randolph started sophomore Kyle Kolquist for the Section 7 semifinals and championship game.

Then Randolph started Ledingham against Jefferson "because of the way he played against them in the scrimmage," and the captain handled the pressure with aplomb.

Upon their return to the Embassy Suites hotel on the east end of downtown St. Paul, the Greyhounds were hailed as conquering heroes by parents and Duluth East fans—even tournament attendees with no skin in the game.

"I'm the last one off the bus, and Spehar and Locker come back to tell me, 'You won't believe it in there, Coach,'" Randolph said.

Spehar remembered, "Every railing was full, and everyone was giving us a standing ovation, cheering. There was an electricity."

An entrepreneurial businessman came by the hotel Friday morning with freshly printed white T-shirts that read, "Duluth East 5, Bloomington Jefferson 0. Any questions?"

One, actually.

Randolph pondered his team's mental state before the semifinal against Edina. He worried an emotional victory against Jefferson might have left his troops flat. To ensure a spark, Randolph started his senior line of Ryan Engle, Matt Meier, and Dan Zabukover.

"I told them, 'If you score, we're going to win,'" Randolph said.

Just fifteen seconds into the game, the trio accustomed to playing strong defense came through. Zabukover dumped the puck into the Edina zone, and a hustling Engle gained possession. He sent the puck behind the goal toward Meier but stayed in pursuit. All that work paid off as the puck came free and Engle scored.

Goals from Spehar and Dave Almquist staked Duluth East to a 3–0 lead. When Edina cut its deficit to 3–1, Spehar answered with more highlight-reel fodder. Moving as the puck was dropped, Spehar received a pass from Locker and rifled a slapshot into the far side of the net for a 4–1 lead.

Spehar said, "[Locker] had a different internal clock. He didn't wait the extra second and a half. I could find the seams, but if that puck isn't delivered, I might as well be drinking a soda and having a hot dog."

Spehar later completed the hat trick in a 6–2 romp, driving to the net and diving to get his stick on a Locker pass.

Randolph enjoyed another memorable postgame moment.

"I met Herb Brooks after that game," he said. "We went to a bar in his old neighborhood. He told me that he loved the way we stretched the rink."

Locker and Spehar fueled the vertical attack. Products of Duluth outdoor rinks—Lower Chester and Glen Avon, respectively—they overwhelmed opponents after becoming Pee Wee linemates. In 1990–91, Locker said, "Spee scored 176 goals that season, and I had 100 goals and 180-some assists. Together, we had 480-some points."

Locker recalled their Pee Wee team led 9–0 in the third period of an afternoon regional playoff game in Chisholm when the opposing coach suggested running time. He wanted the Duluth youngsters to get home and watch the Greyhounds' Section 2 championship game against Cloquet at the Duluth Entertainment and Convention Center.

"We could barely get in the arena," Locker said. "I looked around and couldn't see stairs anywhere."

Locker's visions for his own high school career were cemented watching older brother Derek skate to a 3–2 overtime victory that propelled the Greyhounds to their first state tournament appearance in sixteen years.

Randolph knew the two up-and-coming scoring demons could take his program even higher and wasn't about to change their style.

"So many coaches try to make every player fit into a mold," said Randolph, a playmaking center who won three consecutive Catholic hockey tournament championships (1967–69) with Duluth Cathedral. "We want to let the players be free to develop as much as they can."

Randolph's willingness to let players express themselves was a big reason Spehar approached him before the 1995 championship game against Moorhead and said, "I don't care if we win or lose tonight—you're the greatest coach a player could have."

Facing Moorhead meant a return engagement with forward Matt Cullen. The teams had scrimmaged before the season, and Randolph hailed Cullen as "the best two-way player we've seen. He's not only skilled, he's the toughest and meanest guy to play against, and he has the softest hands."

Spehar struck first with a power-play goal on assists from Matt Mathias and Locker. Cullen answered with two goals. Then Locker's first tournament goal tied the score 2–2 in the second period.

Moorhead, eager to win a title after finishing second in 1992 and 1994, went ahead 3–2 in the third period on a Joel Jamison goal from Cullen. Just forty seconds later, Duluth East junior Ted Suihkonen tied the game 3–3.

Suihkonen, who had transferred from Virginia before the season, and Zabukover, a transfer from Duluth Central, added depth to the forward lines. Their arrival bothered Spehar, however, because it meant his friends Mark Anderson and Pat Miner were cut from varsity. Both stayed on as student managers.

After what Spehar called "a feeling-out process," both Suihkonen and Zabukover became two of the boys.

When Suihkonen scored, "Spee turns to [Randolph] on the bench and goes, 'About frickin' time,'" Mills said.

"I meant it out of endearment," Spehar said. "That goal may have been the biggest goal of the state tournament."

But far from the most memorable.

A Spehar breakaway, sprung by a long Locker pass from deep in the Duluth East zone, was stopped short as Spuds defenseman Rory Kortan tripped him up from behind.

"I thought we were going on the power play," Locker said. "Then the crowd erupted."

Officials called a penalty shot.

"This is going to be as exciting as it gets," television analyst Lou Nanne said.

"I have never had a penalty shot against me," Moorhead goalie Jason Gregoire said. "All I was thinking was, 'Stop the puck.' I didn't care who was shooting the shot."

Dave Spehar ranks among the legends against which all future state tournament stars are compared. He tallied hat tricks in all three tournament games as Duluth East won the 1995 Class 2A title. As if that weren't enough, Spehar also scored on this penalty shot against Moorhead in the championship game. Photo by Duane Braley/*Minneapolis Star Tribune*

Randolph cared a great deal. He considered Spehar to be "the greatest scorer in Minnesota," so when Spehar sought Randolph's advice, "Go bury it," was the reply.

Randolph had no doubt.

"Mike said on the bench, 'When he scores, let him have his time. Let him enjoy this,'" Mathias said. "The confidence Mike had was incredible."

Starting from the Greyhounds blue line, Spehar gathered the puck at the red line and headed toward the Moorhead goal. The baby-faced sniper wore number 33 in honor of his favorite player, Patrick Roy—who just happened to be a goalie.

Gregoire, also number 33, readied for the showdown.

"My coaches told me before the game about all the moves he has," Gregoire said. "I was going through them in my head before the penalty shot."

Aware the right-handed Spehar often finished from his forehand, Gregoire took the proper precautions.

"When I started to go right, he was playing me that way," Spehar said.

Spehar countered on the fly, moving the puck from his forehand to backhand and sliding the puck past Gregoire.

"I guess I was a little surprised he went to his backhand," Gregoire said. "That's not that high of a percentage shot, but it worked."

Whatever questions remained about who owned this tourna-

ment disappeared. An ecstatic Spehar headed back up the ice, sliding on his right knee as he pumped both arms in celebration of the sixth successful penalty shot in state tournament history.

"It's the first time he's gone left all year," Randolph said. "We've been trying to get him to do that. But he buries the puck in the net every time, and that makes it hard to convince him he's doing anything wrong."

Spehar wasn't finished. He stuffed the puck home from close range later in the third period for his third hat trick in as many games.

"Three hat tricks in three games—what more could you want?" Randolph said. "That's what dreams are made of."

And champions. A 5–3 victory gave Duluth East its first state title since 1960.

Spehar finished tops in the state with fifty-eight goals and 102 points. Locker's ninety-two points, including fifty-nine assists, ranked second. Locker assisted on six of Spehar's nine tournament goals.

"It was a very, very special time with a special group of teammates that grew up together," Spehar said. "You were expected to win when you put on a Duluth East jersey. It culminated with a wonderful experience at the state tournament."

~DL~

LADIES FIRST

Farmington forward Amber Hegland never thought of self as trailblazer

Amber Hegland became the first girl to play in the boys' state high school hockey tournament, hitting the ice with her Farmington teammates March 9, 1994, and making the event's fiftieth running truly historic.

The buzz wore off two and a half minutes into the game when Mahtomedi's Todd George lowered the boom.

"It was my first shift," said Hegland, a senior third-line center. "I had the puck. They were fast, and chances are I had my head down and wasn't ready."

Lying on the ice moments after the clean, hard check along the boards, Hegland thought of her mother's lone hockey rule.

No matter what, always get up.

Suzan Hegland couldn't squelch Amber's love for hockey if she wanted to, even if it was an era when few girls grew up playing. She put Amber in dance lessons. Before the final recital, Amber smiled bigger than ever knowing that dance would soon be out of her life. The ice is where Amber longed to be, skating outside with her future varsity teammates.

Now they had reached their state tournament dream together and Hegland wasn't about to quit.

She got up and dealt with it, just like she shrugged off the ceaseless questions leading into the game about her unique accomplishment. Girls' hockey became a sanctioned high school sport in the 1994–95 season, which tempers Hegland's view of herself as a trailblazer.

"Even as I reflect back now, not that it wasn't important, I guess, to be the first female to play in the state tournament," Hegland said, "but being there with my teammates is still what means the most."

She later coached girls' hockey at Wayzata with Larry Olimb, whom Hegland emulated after watching him play with Warroad in the 1987 and 1988 state tournaments.

Television brought Hegland and the tournament into a house on St. Paul's East Side, where Amy Murphy was summoned to the living room.

"My brother was watching the Farmington/Mahtomedi game on TV and yelled for me, 'Amy, you've got to see this,'" she said. "I thought it was so cool."

In 1994, Farmington senior Amber Hegland made history as the first female player to compete in the boys' state hockey tournament. A third-line center, Hegland suffered a clean, hard check on her first shift but kept playing. Photo by Bruce Bisping/*Minneapolis Star Tribune*

A goalie in St. Paul Johnson–area youth hockey, Murphy said, "All of us grew up calling the state tournament the Show. I wrote 'The Show' on the wall inside my closet and listed all the things I was doing to get there."

Watching Hegland meant Murphy's early-morning workouts; summer goalie camps with Warren Strelow, goalie coach for the 1980 Olympic team; and her own indomitable spirit could bring a similar result.

Unlike Hegland, who said she received no flak from opponents or community members, Murphy said she endured sexist comments. She drew strength from her male teammates, but when that wasn't enough, she never let on.

"I always had to have thick skin," she said. "If my feelings were hurt or I had to cry, I dealt with that when I got home."

Murphy received occasional playing time her junior season, highlighted by playing the third period of the Governors' 1995 Class 2A state tournament consolation game.

"My knees were shaking so hard," said Murphy, a 5-foot-2 goalie listed as 5-foot-7 in game programs.

She watched her team battle White Bear Lake players she knew from summer hockey. Bears senior Whitey Schwartzbauer offered his support of Murphy, yelling toward Johnson's bench, "Put Amy in!"

Murphy stopped the only two shots she faced in the Governors' 6–1 loss. She played for Wes Barrette's East Side Midget team as a senior, but making "the Show" remains a cherished memory.

"I wanted to be out there," she said. "I'd worked for it."

~DL~

Her knees shaking inside her leg pads, junior goalie Amy Murphy played the third period of St. Paul Johnson's 1995 Class 2A state tournament consolation game. She became just the second female player to participate in the boys' hockey state tournament. Photo courtesy of Amy Murphy

THE GAME

FIVE-OVERTIME THRILLER BETWEEN DULUTH EAST AND APPLE VALLEY AS GOOD AS IT GETS

172

DATES	LOCATION	ATTENDANCE	CLASS 2A CHAMPIONSHIP
MARCH 6–9	ST. PAUL CIVIC CENTER	115,235	APPLE VALLEY 3, EDINA 2
			CLASS 1A CHAMPIONSHIP
			WARROAD 10, RED WING 3

 Breck junior forward Jon Maruk, whose father, Dennis, played for the Minnesota North Stars, finished with two goals and three assists as the Mustangs took third in Class 1A.

WELL PAST MIDNIGHT, Rick Larsen pulled his Pontiac Grand Prix into the garage at his Eagan home. He shut off the engine, opened the driver side door, and realized he had a huge problem.

His legs wouldn't work. They had cramped up on the ride home from the St. Paul Civic Center, where Larsen had just officiated the longest state tournament game ever played. The five-overtime tour de force had lasted a record 93:12. Apple Valley won 5–4 over Duluth East at 1:39 AM.

Far from the stadium lights and the buzz of the crowd, Larsen rolled out of his car and onto the garage floor. He crawled into the house and labored into bed, relieved to have not woken wife Deb and their two young daughters in the middle of the night. Then Deb rolled over. The clock on their nightstand read 2:45 AM.

"She says, 'I told you not to go to the bar after the game,'" Larsen said. "I said, 'Obviously you didn't watch the game.' She shut it off after the first period."

Anyone who checked out early missed the defining tournament game of its era.

The pace, superb: neither offensively gifted team held anything back. The quality, sublime: defending champion Duluth East and a one-loss Apple Valley team would send a combined eighteen players to Division I college hockey programs. The star, Apple Valley's Karl Goehring: the 5-foot-6½, 150-pound goaltender stopped a state tournament record sixty-five shots.

The game was a smaller, colder, granola-less Woodstock—everyone says they were there. Those who actually were there experienced something special.

"I have never been in a hockey rink to this day with that energy," said Dave Spehar, Duluth East forward. "Wasn't just loud. Wasn't just a great game. It was an out-of-body experience. And I never think about it, really. Never talk about it. After that day, I kind of left it where it ended. But it was something."

Spehar was the main attraction, thanks to the three hat tricks he had racked up in as many games during the Greyhounds' 1995 title run. An extraordinary finisher, Spehar raised his profile with a four-goal performance in Thursday's quarter-final against Blaine.

No more of that, thought the Apple Valley coaching staff. During a team meeting Friday morning, coach Larry Hendrickson wrote Spehar's number 33 on the board, circled it, and told players, "There's one god, and it sure as hell isn't Dave Spehar."

Hendrickson instructed his top two centermen, Chris Sikich and Erik Westrum, to hassle, harangue, and hound the mighty Greyhound.

"Larry told us to chop him on the laces as hard as we could when the refs weren't looking," Westrum said.

Spehar wasn't fazed. Everyone had wanted a piece of the 5-foot-9, 175-pound wing all season.

"I grew up in the 218," Spehar said, referencing northern Minnesota's area code. "I didn't feel it when I was out there."

Apple Valley led 2–1 in the second period as efforts to slow Spehar and, in turn, Spehar's grit were put on full display.

Larry Hendrickson, one of the game's most intense yet colorful coaches, directed Apple Valley to a 5–4 victory against Duluth East in the 1996 semifinals. The five-overtime game ranks among the most memorable in state tournament history. Photo courtesy of Vince Muzik

Spehar and Sikich jostled for the puck behind the Apple Valley net and both fell. Spehar popped Sikich in the chin, then got up and kept battling for the biscuit.

Eagles senior defenseman Matt Skogstad arrived and got knocked back by Spehar's shove in the chest. Then Skogstad, who measured 6 foot 2 and 185 pounds, blasted Spehar to the ice. The two exchanged words near their benches.

Physical play gave way to individual skill in the third period. Duluth East center Chris Locker, feared for his ability to spring Spehar for scoring chances, tied the game with a shorthanded goal.

Later in the same Apple Valley power play, Westrum gave the Eagles a 3–2 lead.

Duluth East fans, who held a "#33 Mr. Hockey" banner in support of Spehar, finally saw their main man score. Spehar received the puck on the end line, skated around the Apple Valley net, turned, and fired. Tie game.

Spehar's goal came against Apple Valley's third line, so Hendrickson, sporting a bomber jacket the same color brown as his team's jerseys, benched them for the night.

Spehar was too much for most lines to handle. He tallied a hat trick in five of his six state tournament games as a junior and senior. Only Apple Valley held him to one goal.

Meanwhile, Westrum stole a pass behind the Duluth East net and buried a backhand shot. The tremendous individual effort gave him a hat trick and his team a 4–3 lead.

Color analyst Lou Nanne's call remains burned in Westrum's memory: "This kid is having the night of his life."

"That's what you dream about," said Westrum, whose father, Pat, a former University of Minnesota captain, served as the Eagles' assistant coach.

Glen Sonmor said Pat, whom he coached with the Gophers and the St. Paul Fighting Saints, "was as tough as nails, and as competitive as a player can get."

The father passed those traits to his son.

"He knocked over the Parcheesi board if he lost," said Pat, a defenseman who reached the 1966 state tournament with Minneapolis Roosevelt.

The younger Westrum grew to be a skilled forward, leading all Apple Valley players with four state tournament goals.

"Of all the guys I've been around, if I need a goal late in a game, he's at the top of the list," said Paul Ostby, Apple Valley's volunteer goaltender coach. "He's got an unbelievable will."

Spehar was no slouch in clutch moments, either.

Less than one minute remained in regulation as Apple Valley defenseman Aaron Dwyer mishandled a puck in his zone. Spehar stole the puck, continued behind the net, and drew the attention of Goehring and three additional Eagles. They didn't see Locker driving to the net. Spehar did.

Overtime.

How many goaltenders become legends in a 5–4 game? The question drew a knowing chuckle from Goehring.

"It's not what most goaltenders dream of," he said.

Going into his senior season, Goehring knew his state tournament dreams came down to beating Bloomington Jefferson.

The focus of Apple Valley's defensive game plan, Dave Spehar couldn't work his hat trick magic. But he remained dangerous, passing to Chris Locker for the goal that forced overtime. Photo by Mike Thill/*Let's Play Hockey*

In the 1995 Class 2A, Section 5 championship game, Goehring allowed five goals on eighteen Jefferson shots. Hendrickson pulled Goehring midway through the third period. After the season, the coach took Goehring aside.

"He knew how disappointed I was, but we chatted, and he lifted me up," Goehring said. "I took away from it that he was proud of me for the overall season I'd had. That helped kick-start me getting ready for the 1996 season."

Three games in, however, Jefferson beat the Eagles 3–2, and Goehring found himself at odds with Westrum.

During practice that week, Westrum whiffed on a puck, and Goehring chirped, "Nice shot."

Already agitated by Goehring's play against Jefferson, Westrum fired a puck at Goehring and caught him square on the chin.

"I wanted to know if he was for real," Westrum said. "I needed to know he wouldn't fold emotionally or physically."

Challenge accepted.

"I was like, 'That's how it's going to be? Let's go,'" Goehring said. "As a smaller guy, I had to bring it and couldn't be intimidated."

Westrum said, "That's when I knew he and I were on the same page."

Apple Valley beat Jefferson 2–1 in a section final rematch, and Goehring stopped a breakaway in overtime.

Goehring and Westrum ended up as state tournament roommates.

"There's a fiery competitor in both of us," Goehring said. "We pushed each other."

As overtime play ensued, Goehring and his counterpart, Duluth East's Kyle Kolquist, were left exposed as their coaches eschewed conservative play.

First overtime: Goehring made a pad save to stop Spehar at close range. Westrum corralled the puck and made an end-to-end rush thwarted only by Kolquist's poke check.

Second overtime: Game officials likely missed Duluth East's game-winning goal when Matt Latour tipped a Dylan

174

Mills slapshot past Goehring and under the crossbar. Latour instantly raised his stick, but officials did not signal goal. As the linesman positioned at the red line, Larsen said, "If asked, there was no way I could say yes." Television replay showed the puck went in before quickly caroming out. Unfortunately for the Greyhounds, video review at state tournament games wouldn't begin until a decade later.

Third overtime: The mounting pressure began affecting Goehring. After the third extra session, Ostby came to the locker room and found his intense yet introverted goalie on the brink of collapse.

"I felt like I couldn't go on after so many shots," Goehring said. "I was near tears."

Ostby, who had played goalie and later coached the position at the University of Minnesota, helped soothe the frazzled youngster.

"He was super anxious and just wanted to get the game over with," Ostby said. "Karl had a tendency to get ahead of himself. I remember talking briefly and saying, 'Slow down, relax.'

"Goalie is not about being tough. It's about being good in your head."

Goehring credited Ostby for helping refocus him.

The officiating crew of Larsen and referees Bill Mason and Mike Riley, meanwhile, were enjoying their extended evening.

"I remember us saying how we had one of those great high school hockey games on our hands," said Larsen, a senior defenseman on St. Paul Johnson's 1984 state tournament team. "I remember drinking a lot of water, too."

Fourth overtime: Goehring's sixty-second save of the evening broke the twenty-six-year-old tournament record. Notified over the public address system, the enthralled crowd—many of the 16,934 remained—rose to applaud.

Goehring's and Kolquist's saves in the fourth overtime (seventeen and ten, respectively) were a testament to all the players' stamina and spirit.

Fifth overtime: The game's final faceoff took place in the Duluth East zone to Kolquist's left. Larsen threw down the puck with his left hand.

Sikich won the draw, but the puck got batted around. Larsen skated backward toward the blue line, just behind Dwyer, as the Eagles' Jeff Przytarski pursued the puck behind the Greyhounds net.

Przytarski sent a backhand pass toward the slot, and the puck hopped away from Sikich out toward Dwyer, just beyond the faceoff circle. In the final seconds of regulation, Dwyer had hesitated and lost. This time, he drew back his stick and swung at the moving puck.

Moments later, Kolquist sat motionless in his crease as Dwyer skated the length of the ice with arms held aloft.

"I got good wood on it, let it go, and luckily it went in," he said. "I'm glad it was a good goal, not cheesy."

That brought little consolation for Duluth East. Later that morning, the team met in an Embassy Suites conference room. Randolph stood to speak but produced more tears than words.

Locker lightened the mood during the meeting with officials before the third-place game.

"One of them said, 'Any questions?'" Locker recalled. "I raised my hand and asked, 'Do all goals scored count today?'"

On Saturday night, Apple Valley regrouped to beat Edina 3–2 for the championship. Junior forward Aaron Fredrickson, benched with the third line against Duluth East, scored a goal and assisted on the game-winner.

The Edina game is overshadowed by the Duluth East marathon in the same way the Miracle on Ice in 1980 made the Americans' gold medal–clinching game against Finland an afterthought.

Westrum said, "Ninety-nine out of a hundred people think we beat Duluth East for the championship."

At the Westrums' later Saturday evening, Hendrickson placed a long-distance phone call to his son Darby, then playing for the Toronto Maple Leafs. Westrum listened on another phone.

As a Minneapolis Washburn player, Larry had lost in the 1959 state tournament championship game. Same result in 1976 as Richfield's coach. He coached three seasons at Apple Valley in the early 1980s, then returned for a second stint in 1994, finally winning the elusive title.

"Darby said, 'Dad, I'm so proud of you. You've been waiting for this for a long time,'" Westrum recalled. "For Larry, plus my dad, and all the time and effort they put in—it was special."

~DL~

Apple Valley senior Karl Goehring stopped a tournament-record sixty-five shots as the Eagles ousted defending Class 2A state champion Duluth East in five overtimes. Photo by Mike Thill/*Let's Play Hockey*

The St. Paul Civic Center scoreboard provides some hint to the five-overtime madness that just ended below. Period: 8. Shots: a whopping 69 for Duluth East to 54 for Apple Valley. Photo courtesy of Vince Muzik

TRADITION!

GOALIE JEFF HALL DETERMINED TO END EDINA'S LONG TITLE DROUGHT

DATES	LOCATION	ATTENDANCE	CLASS 2A CHAMPIONSHIP
MARCH 5-8	ST. PAUL CIVIC CENTER	111,800	EDINA 1, DULUTH EAST 0

CLASS 1A CHAMPIONSHIP
RED WING 4, WARROAD 3

 Proctor senior forward Dom Talarico tied the state tournament record for most assists in a game with six.

EDINA JUNIOR GOALTENDER Jeff Hall, the first player introduced before the 1997 Class 2A championship game, skated up to the television camera in the traditional pregame introductions and made his intentions known with a single word.

"Tradition," said Hall, his penetrating eyes locked in a six-second stare.

Before each home game, Hall, in his first season on varsity, scanned the row of eight state championship banners hanging in Braemar Arena. On the left, 1969. On the right, 1988. During those twenty seasons, the Hornets' faithful never had to wait more than four years to cheer another title team.

Nine bannerless seasons later, Hall felt an obligation—no, a duty—to restore Edina's greatness.

"I would think, 'This is wrong,'" Hall said. "The tradition was not what it used to be, and it pissed me off because it mattered a lot to me."

Coach Bart Larson helped create Edina's tradition as an assistant to the legendary Willard Ikola. The pair won a title in 1971, then the school district opened a second high school, Edina West. Larson took the Cougars' head coaching job, while Ikola remained at the legacy school, renamed Edina East.

Larson led Edina West to its lone state tournament appearance in 1981 before the schools merged in 1981–82 due to low enrollment at Edina East. Administrators selected Ikola as head coach. Larson didn't want to lose his teaching seniority and stayed on as an assistant. The old friends won titles in 1982, 1984, and 1988.

Ikola stepped down in 1991, and Larson took over. In 1995, his Hornets placed third at state. The next season brought a runner-up finish. There was only one place left to go.

"We had T-shirts made before each of those seasons," forward Ben Stafford said. "They were black with green writing on the chest. Sophomore year, it just had the dates of the state tournament. Junior year, it had the time and date of the championship game. Senior year, it had the same thing, plus it said something about being in a good mood."

The success of Stafford and Dan Carlson, sophomores on the 1995 team, got Hall's attention. A drummer with friends outside hockey circles, Hall rededicated himself to his sport.

"Carlson and Stafford were bound for glory, and I had to help them," Hall said. "They were a grade ahead of me, but I remember thinking, 'These guys are going to need me to step up.' They inspired me."

Stafford joked, "I wish I had a three-year plan when I was fourteen."

Classmates since elementary school, Carlson and Stafford dominated as senior linemates. Carlson, a wing, and Stafford, a center, combined for more than 130 points.

Second-line center Peter Fitzgerald said Carlson possessed "a quiet confidence. He would not be outworked in practices or games."

As for Stafford, Fitzgerald said, "Bart told me, 'I don't think Stafford made a mental mistake in three years playing for me.'"

"Both of them were soft-spoken hard workers who we all tried to keep up with," Hall said. "It's easy to thrive in that environment."

The vibe changed during a late-season showdown with Duluth East. The top-ranked and unbeaten Greyhounds made a February 11 visit to number-two Edina.

Outplaying Edina from the start, Duluth East cruised to a 5–2 victory.

"They sort of kicked our butts," Larson said.

"They were the better team that night, and we knew we had to get better," Carlson said.

Edina regrouped to win the Class 2A, Section 6 title. The Hornets returned to the state tournament and opened against Henry Sibley.

A 3–0 victory brought Hall, a 5-foot-9 standup goaltender, his first complete-game shutout. Larson had pulled Hall late in the Hornets' three previous shutouts to give the backup a few minutes of action.

Semifinal opponent Hill-Murray, meanwhile, scored seventy-two seconds into the game. Racehorse hockey ensued as Edina led 3–2 after one period. The Pioneers tied the game 4–4 by the second intermission.

In overtime, Hall stopped several breakaway chances by Hill-Murray's Brandon Sampair. Hall's improbable saves inspired the teammates who had once inspired him.

"That gave us confidence," Carlson said. "We said, 'OK, Jeff's there. Now we need to figure out a way to win.'"

In the third overtime, defenseman Sam Cornelius fired a long rebound home for a 5–4 victory at 12:37 AM Saturday.

The championship game later that day meant a rematch with undefeated Duluth East. A different Edina game plan brought the desired result.

"The way they dominated us [in February], we knew we couldn't play the same way," Carlson said. "We knew we had to be more conservative."

The teams combined for seven shots in the first period. But one good shot was all Edina needed.

Stafford won a faceoff in the Duluth East zone and sent the puck back to Carlson, who fired from the top of the circle and scored.

"I definitely felt right from the start that it wasn't going to be 5–2," Stafford said. "There was more room on the ice. They weren't as suffocating as they were at Braemar."

Duluth East pressed for the equalizer. But Edina's 1–0 lead held after two periods.

"We gained more confidence with every minute that went by knowing there was more pressure on them," Fitzgerald said.

Four of the Greyhounds' previous six state tournament goals had come in the third period. But the tying goal never came Saturday night. Hall stopped all twenty Greyhound shots.

"Jeff played the tournament of his life, which is what you need when the margins are so narrow," Carlson said.

Hall and his teammates bolstered Edina's tradition by beating the state's stingiest team—Duluth East had allowed just thirty-three goals in twenty-eight contests—at its own game.

"To beat the best defensive team in a defensive struggle made it that much sweeter," Hall said.

Larson had a championship of his own.

"This is unbelievable when you've coached so long," Larson said afterward, adding that Ikola called "and congratulated me on adding one more [championship] to the eight the school has."

~DL~

With a goal in the first period, Edina's Dan Carlson unknowingly provided all the offense his team would need to upset previously undefeated Duluth East 1-0 in the Class 2A state championship game. In this photo, Carlson is going hard to the net in a 3-0 quarterfinal victory against Henry Sibley. Photo by Bruce Bisping/*Minneapolis Star Tribune*

SOUTHERN CHARM

Gas station mishap proved Red Wing superstar was mere mortal despite on-ice dominance

A strange tugging sensation got Johnny Pohl's attention as he pulled his blue Toyota Camry away from the gas station. But he was in a hurry to get to school and let it go.

He was running behind, so a few minutes earlier, he had hastened the refueling process by inserting the nozzle into the gas tank opening and going inside the station with a blank check signed by his mother. When the pump shut off, he wrote the check and bolted.

Back on the road, Pohl noticed the citizens of Red Wing were especially friendly that morning. They honked. They gestured. They waved. Pohl, a sophomore in his first year as a licensed driver, waved back.

Then it occurred to him— he had probably left the gas tank door open. Pohl looked in the side mirror and saw an open gas tank door. And the nozzle still attached. And the hose, slithering in the breeze.

That's not good, he thought. He stopped by his father's house and hid the nozzle and hose behind a wood pile in the garage. When Pohl arrived at school, a classmate told him, "Dude, I saw an idiot driving with a hose hanging out of his gas tank."

Pohl recalled, "And this is how naïve I was: I honestly thought, 'Wow, I guess I wasn't the only one.'"

On the ice, there was only one Johnny Pohl. As a junior in 1996–97, the prolific centerman led the Wingers to a 28–0 season and the Class 1A state championship.

He finished the season with fifty-four goals and fifty-seven assists. As a senior, he became the first Class 1A recipient of the Mr. Hockey Award. And he graduated as the state's all-time leading scorer (378 points). But the state championship remains his greatest accomplishment.

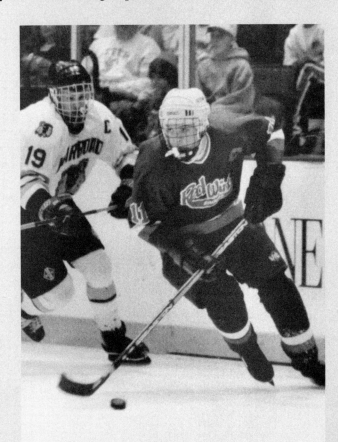

Star center Johnny Pohl and Red Wing legitimized the addition of a second tournament class for smaller schools. "For us to not only get there, but to win it, showed other programs, especially in southern Minnesota, they at least have a chance," Pohl said. Photo by Mike Thill/*Let's Play Hockey*

Red Wing legitimized the addition of a second tournament class for smaller schools, still a sore subject three years into its existence.

"Class 1A is designed for the Red Wings or Warroads of the world who can't consistently compete with Edina and Wayzata," Pohl said.

Red Wing, located fifty miles southeast of St. Paul, brought representation from an unlikely area.

"For us to not only get there but to win it showed other programs, especially in southern Minnesota, they at least have a chance," Pohl said.

Red Wing built a rivalry with Warroad from the start. The Warriors beat the state tournament newcomers 7–2 in the 1995 third-place game; a year later, Warroad smoked the Wingers 10–3 in the championship game.

In 1996–97, greater depth and an ability to handle more physical play earned the Wingers a title game rematch with Warroad.

Mark Pohl, Johnny's younger brother and a passenger in that blue Camry, tallied a shorthanded goal. Then Johnny scored. A power-play goal from Tom Moore catapulted Red Wing to a 3–0 lead after one period.

Warroad cut its deficit to 3–2 at second intermission. But a Mark Bang goal just 1:22 into the third period put Red Wing ahead to stay in a historic 4–3 victory.

"In the grand scheme of things, it wouldn't have mattered who we beat in the championship game," Johnny Pohl said. "But for it to be the team that destroyed us the year before was sweet."

~DL~

ODE TO THE 218

GUERILLA SUMMER WORKOUT TACTICS PAID BIG DIVIDENDS FOR DULUTH EAST

DATES	LOCATION	ATTENDANCE	CLASS 2A CHAMPIONSHIP
MARCH 4–7	ST. PAUL CIVIC CENTER	116,155	DULUTH EAST 3, ANOKA 1
			CLASS 1A CHAMPIONSHIP
			EVELETH-GILBERT 4, HERMANTOWN 2

Did you know? Craig Homola, an outstanding Eveleth player in the mid-1970s and an all-American at Vermont, coached Eveleth-Gilbert to the state title.

SUMMER HOCKEY WORKOUTS for standout Duluth East defenseman Nick Angell often meant traveling no farther than his one-stall garage.

Old carpet mounted to some two-by-fours provided a target. Pucks were fired off a plastic mat coated with furniture polish.

"It was a 218 shooting gallery," Angell said, nodding to the northland's area code. "There was nothing pretty about it."

When Angell was a Pee Wee, his father, Brad, wore a mitt for catching pucks. That ended when Angell became a Bantam.

"I let a shot go by his head, and he didn't move," Angell said. "He took the glove off, threw it, and went to the kitchen."

About two miles away, goaltender Adam Coole spent summers in the backyard wearing full pads—even skates—and maneuvering on a wood platform while older brother Ryan and others peppered him with shots.

Other days, as many as thirty middle schoolers met to play hockey on inline skates in the parking lot at Lutheran Church of the Good Shepherd.

Senior captain Adam Coole anchored Duluth East in goal in 1998. In the 1970s, his father, Clarke, had also played goalie and served as Duluth East's team captain. A backup for two seasons, the younger Coole made the most of his only season as a starter. Photo by Jerry Holt/*Minneapolis Star Tribune*

"Guys would get stitches," defenseman Patrick Finnegan said.

Summer blood and sweat prepared the boys for long winter seasons. Duluth East captured the 1995 state championship, then placed third and second the next two seasons. In 1997–98, the Greyhounds took the number-one ranking into the season and planned to still hold it in March.

"We felt only one result was going to be acceptable with that team," Coole said. "We all rallied behind that. Sometimes a team will accomplish what it aspires to do."

A 5–0 start with zero goals allowed signaled Duluth East's intentions to the other teams. Then trouble surfaced on and off the ice. Grand Rapids handed the Greyhounds a 7–5 loss, and eligibility concerns benched senior wing Rheese Carlson.

Carlson had played his junior season in the United States Hockey League but returned home a month before his senior season to join younger brother Ross, a sophomore wing. Duluth East administrators misinterpreted Minnesota State High School League bylaws, and Carlson, after playing the first two games, missed the next seven pending an investigation.

In mid-January, the MSHSL reinstated Carlson but changed the Greyhounds' first two victories, in which Carlson had played, to forfeit losses.

Carlson ended the season with twenty goals and a spot on the Associated Press All-State team with Angell, Coole, and Finnegan.

Angell, a senior, and Finnegan, a junior, made Duluth East special. Both were gifted offensive players. The booming shot Angell had honed in his rudimentary garage gallery became his trademark. Finnegan, who had arrived from nearby Virginia in middle school, scored twenty goals and boasted speed and stickhandling comparable to Bloomington Jefferson great Mike Crowley.

Angell and Finnegan were their team's versions of Chris Locker and Dave Spehar.

"They were the two best [defensemen] in the state," Coole said. "[Coach Mike] Randolph was very wise to give them a lot of latitude."

Senior captain Coole anchored the team. In the 1970s, his father, Clarke, had also played goalie and served as Duluth East's team captain.

A backup for two seasons to Kyle Kolquist, Coole made the most of his only season as a starter. Kolquist had won the 1997 Frank Brimsek Award as the state's top senior goalie. Coole won in 1998.

"Adam was the best captain I ever had," Randolph said twenty years later. "There were times I was about to head into the locker room and I wouldn't because I'd hear him talking and I wouldn't have anything to add."

"That's some of the highest praise I've ever received," Coole said.

Duluth East closed the regular season with a 6–5 comeback victory against Anoka, allowed one goal in three Section 7 playoff games, and took the number-one ranking into the state tournament.

"Adam gave a speech before we left Duluth and said how it would be unacceptable if we don't come home with a championship," Finnegan said. "We put an enormous amount of pressure on ourselves."

Pressure points existed throughout the first two games. Duluth East led quarterfinal opponent Hastings 5–4 after two periods. Finnegan, penalized for roughing, watched as the game's final seconds ticked away. Hastings pulled its goalie for an extra attacker while Angell lay face down on the ice courtesy of a slapshot off his right ankle. Coole's save with two seconds remaining prevented overtime.

Next up: second-ranked Bloomington Jefferson, whose youth teams had owned Duluth East for years.

"That was our state title game," said Angell, who played on a modified skate to accommodate his swollen ankle.

Randolph paired Angell and Finnegan later in the game to generate offense, and they delivered. The teams were deadlocked 1–1 midway through the third period when Finnegan corralled a loose puck in the offensive zone and got two Jaguars to bite on his shot fake. They slid past Finnegan, who then sent the puck toward the opposite circle for a waiting Angell.

"If he misses from there . . ." Finnegan thought. No worries. Angell's blast was true.

"I saw the puck hit his stick, and I heard a thud in the back of the net," Finnegan said. "It was that fast."

Jefferson rallied to force overtime, which Kevin Oswald ended with his second goal of the night and the biggest of his twenty-five that season.

"In the locker room, you'd've thought we won the Stanley Cup," Coole said. "The leaders shut that party down. We said, 'Think about going to Duluth on Sunday with no trophy.' That shut everybody up."

In the Anoka rematch, goals from Gabe Taggart (his twentieth of the season) and Ross Carlson put the Greyhounds ahead 2–1 at second intermission. Coole stopped all eight shots he faced in the third period, and Rheese Carlson assisted on Chad Roberg's goal—the last state tournament goal scored at the Civic Center. The building was soon demolished to make way for the Xcel Energy Center.

"That was the only group I played with in high school that accomplished the shared goal we set out to achieve," Coole said. "We're yoked for life."

~DL~

CHAIN GANG

NO WEAK LINKS IN ROSEAU TEAM PLAYING FOR BELOVED SKATING COACH

DATES	LOCATION	ATTENDANCE	CLASS 2A CHAMPIONSHIP
MARCH 3–6	TARGET CENTER, MINNEAPOLIS	106,307	ROSEAU 4, HASTINGS 0
			CLASS 1A CHAMPIONSHIP BENILDE–ST. MARGARET'S 4, EAST GRAND FORKS 2

CHAIN GANG

NO WEAK LINKS IN ROSEAU TEAM PLAYING FOR BELOVED SKATING COACH

DATES	LOCATION	ATTENDANCE	CLASS 2A CHAMPIONSHIP
MARCH 3–6	TARGET CENTER, MINNEAPOLIS	106,307	ROSEAU 4, HASTINGS 0
			CLASS 1A CHAMPIONSHIP BENILDE–ST. MARGARET'S 4, EAST GRAND FORKS 2

 *Did you know?* Benilde–St. Margaret's junior forward Troy Riddle opened with a hat trick and finished with seven goals as he led the Red Knights to the Class 1A championship. Riddle, a fourth-round NHL draft pick by the St. Louis Blues, scored eighty-two goals playing for the University of Minnesota and spent seven seasons playing professionally in the United States, Europe, and Asia.

THE PREGAME RITUAL was called "linking up." Josh Olson took it upon himself to ensure the process was completed in an efficient, timely fashion.

"He had an army sergeant's voice," said Phil Larson, Roseau's senior captain in 1998–99, "and very colorful language."

Olson was a big dude—6 foot 3 and 215 pounds of pure intimidation. On a team loaded with oak trees masquerading as hockey players (half the roster topped out at 6 feet or more), Olson, a senior forward, towered above as a sequoia.

When Olson barked, "What time is it?" (with more than a few expletives sprinkled in), the Rams snapped to attention. Time to link up.

Early in the season, on the orders of coach Bruce Olson (no relation to Josh), every player was given a chain link and told to keep it with them at all times. At home. At school. Around town. Get caught without your link, and you contributed a dollar to the pot.

On game nights, the links were screwed together, twenty

Roseau co-captains Phil Larson (left) and Paul Baumgartner signaled the Rams' season-ending status after they beat Hastings 4–0 in the 1999 championship game. Photo by Mike Thill/*Let's Play Hockey*

of them for all the players plus three more from the coaching staff. In the Rams' locker room at Roseau's Memorial Arena, the chain was hung from a nail pounded into a beam near the door.

"We'd touch it for good luck on the way out," said Jake Brandt, the Rams' senior goaltender.

Bruce Olson, a Roseau native in his eighth season as the Rams' coach, was a master of anticipating and solving problems. If the team struggled with a certain skill or system in a game, by the next practice he had a drill prepared to address the weakness. If parents were creating disharmony, Olson would seek them out and clear the air.

"One of the problems we had conceded with that team—it had a lot of personalities," said Jim Lundbohm, one of Olson's assistants. "When they were coming through as Bantams, it

got to be almost a competition of who would be the MVP of each tournament. With the parents, it was like, 'My son could have had it.' 'No, my son should have had it.'

"One of the things we wanted to do was turn it into a team concept."

Undefeated and anointed the number-one team in the state's big-school rankings early in the season, Roseau celebrated the honor with a 6–3 loss to Greenway on a road trip to the Iron Range. A lackluster overtime victory over Hibbing followed the next day.

After returning home, Olson, worried the season might be unraveling, pulled Larson and fellow senior captain Paul Baumgartner aside. Olson explained his idea for creating a chain that would represent the team's strength in its togetherness.

Roseau's Mike Klema (16) led all 1999 tournament scorers with seven goals, including four in the quarterfinals against Holy Angels and goaltender Justin Eddy.
Photo by Mike Thill/*Let's Play Hockey*

He sent the pair out to buy the links, then had them sell their teammates on the concept.

"It sounded kind of silly at first," Larson said. "But the more that we spoke about it ourselves, the more we said, 'Hey, this can work. This can be something that unifies the team.'"

Roseau, opting to play in the big-school version of the two-class playoff system despite an enrollment of 339 (the smallest in Class 2A), had won twenty-three straight games when it faced St. Cloud Apollo in the Section 8AA final.

The Rams dedicated their push for the school's sixth state title to Nancy Burggraf, the town's iconic sixty-eight-year-old power-skating instructor, who was battling cancer. For decades, Roseau youth players had grown up adoring the 5-foot-3, 110-pound spitfire. This group was no exception.

Call it divine intervention or just plain luck, but Roseau beat Apollo in double overtime on junior defenseman Josh Grahn's first goal of the year. Minutes earlier, Apollo star Chris Harrington rang a shot off the intersection of the right post and crossbar.

"We needed some puck luck that night," Brandt said. "And we got it."

With Burggraf watching from her hospital room bed, Roseau opened the state tournament with a 4–2 victory against Rochester Mayo. Third-period goals by Josh Olson and senior Mike Klema secured the triumph.

"A couple of goals were the kind that I never let in," said Brandt, who made fourteen saves and was bitterly disappointed in his play.

Roseau romped past Holy Angels 6–2 in the semifinals behind a four-goal Klema outburst, but again Brandt was critical of his nineteen-save performance.

"I felt like the team really bailed me out the first couple of games," he said. "I felt like I owed them one."

Brandt's biggest test awaited in the championship. Hastings boasted two of the state's most prolific all-time scoring threats in seniors Dan Welch and Jeff Taffe.

Welch was named the state's Associated Press Player of the Year. Taffe would later earn the Mr. Hockey Award as the state's top senior. The duo shared the *Minneapolis Star Tribune*'s Metro Player of the Year honors.

In the quarterfinals, Welch scored twice in the final forty-one seconds—his second goal coming with 0.2 seconds remaining—as Hastings stunned Blaine 7–6. The Raiders needed two overtimes the next night to get past Elk River in the semifinals.

Against Roseau, Hastings showed no signs of a semifinal hangover. The Raiders peppered Brandt with eleven first-period shots—including six in the first 2:30—as the puck rarely left Roseau's end. The Rams needed 7:44 to get their first shot on goal.

"[Brandt] made some huge stops," said Klema, who scored his tournament-best seventh goal in the second period.

Klema's goal came twenty-three seconds after Olson had opened the scoring. Roseau dominated the final two periods, outshooting Hastings 14–8 and getting two more goals in the third in a 4–0 victory that bookended the decade with state titles for the school (which had also been champion in 1990).

Olson's kick-starting the victory, Brandt's finding redemption, and Klema's hot hand were mere footnotes. Remember, this was a team thing for them, and they had one final piece of business.

With the trophy in the forefront, they huddled in front of a TV camera and shouted in unison a message to their proud and gravely ill skating coach: "This is for you, Nancy!"

~*LRN*~

MIND GAMES

ELABORATE "TOUR" HELPED FRAGILE BLAINE REBOUND FROM CRUSHING DEFEAT

DATES	LOCATION	ATTENDANCE	CLASS 2A CHAMPIONSHIP
MARCH 8–11	TARGET CENTER, MINNEAPOLIS	106,918	BLAINE 6, DULUTH EAST 0
			CLASS 1A CHAMPIONSHIP
			BRECK SCHOOL 3, WARROAD 2

Did you know? Class 1A entrant Sauk Rapids–Rice featured freshman forward Nathan Raduns, who would play four seasons for St. Cloud State and appear in one game for the Philadelphia Flyers in 2008–09.

BLAINE CO-HEAD COACH Steve Larson, long fascinated by the psychology that drives top athletes and championship teams, tried an unusual tactic to boost his squad's confidence and focus before the 2000 playoffs.

"We rented a coach bus," Larson said. "All we told the guys was, 'We are going on a little tour.'"

After brief stops at the Champlin Park Ice Forum, site of the early rounds of the playoffs, and the State Fairgrounds Coliseum in St. Paul, host of the section's championship game, the Bengals cruised into downtown Minneapolis. Target Center was home to the NBA's Minnesota Timberwolves and, for two seasons, the state tournament. As they reached the service-entrance side of the building, an oversized door opened, allowing the bus to plunge deep inside the arena.

"I don't know how he pulled that off," senior forward Brandon Bochenski said.

Players were led to the same locker room they had occupied in the 1999 state tournament quarterfinals. The returners all silently gravitated to the same seats they had taken the previous year when they suffered a devastating loss to Hastings. In one of the most dramatic comebacks in state tournament history, the Raiders had scored twice in the final forty-one seconds—including the winner with 0.2 seconds showing on the clock—to rally for a 7–6 victory.

"That was the most heartbreaking game of my life," Bochenski said.

Larson, hoping to cap the tour with a poignant moment, walked up to Matt Hendricks, the team's senior captain

In the tournament's second year at Minneapolis's Target Center, Duluth East and Blaine line up for the national anthem before the start of the Class 2A championship game. Photo by Mike Thill/*Let's Play Hockey*

Captain Matt Hendricks was a multisport athlete and a team leader for Blaine. Here he wheels around the net in an attempt to score on Duluth East goaltender Dan Hoene in the 2000 title game. Photo by Mike Thill/*Let's Play Hockey*

and inspirational leader, and said, "Matt, what are you thinking?"

"He was sitting on his bench, rocking back and forth," Larson said. "You could see emotions were welling up inside of him. He said something to the effect of 'Never again. That will not happen this year.'"

Hendricks was the alpha on a Blaine hockey team loaded with star multisport athletes hell-bent on winning. He was also the quarterback of the football team that matched up against future Major League Baseball star Joe Mauer's Cretin–Derham Hall squad in the 1999 Class 5A playoffs. (Blaine lost 29–21.)

Ten of Blaine's hockey players had suited up for the football team. In hockey, like in football, they all followed Hendricks's lead.

According to Larson, Blaine's hockey team had had issues in previous years with "kids using chemical stuff." In a meeting before the 1999–2000 season, he proposed to the team that, in an effort to discourage continued rule-breaking, they double all of the state high school league penalties for those same violations.

"That's when Matt stood up and said, 'Do we have to do that?'" Larson said. "He said, 'Can't we just kick somebody off the team if they get into that?'"

Larson put Hendricks's proposal to a vote. "Everybody agreed, and that was our rule," Larson said.

Hendricks separated both shoulders early in the season, missing six games. Although still not fully healed, he returned to bolster a Bengals team that relied heavily on just two forward lines, both of which ranked among the state's best.

"He was just a warrior," Bochenski said. "He would just run through walls. He was a guy that you wanted in the trenches."

If Hendricks provided the grit, Bochenski supplied the guile. More than once, Bochenski left teammates and coaches in awe after scoring goals in seemingly impossible ways.

"Probably the purest goal-scoring player I have ever coached," Larson said.

Added Hendricks: "I remember one time he broke his stick

and came to the bench to get a new one on the fly. He ended up with a left-handed stick even though he was righty, and he still scored on that shift."

Featuring two more speedy, high-scoring forwards in Matt Moore and Trevor Frischmon as well as workhorse defensemen Scott Foyt and Scott Romfo and standout goaltender Steve Witkowski, the Bengals went 18–5–2 in the regular season, a season-ending loss to section rival Elk River serving as a startling jolt of reality. The 7–1 dismantling at the hands of the Elks, the state's number-one-ranked team, was so lopsided that few outsiders gave the Bengals a puncher's chance of reaching the state tournament.

"We weren't too high on ourselves after that game," Hendricks said.

Even parents of Bengals players were brimming with pessimism.

"We lost that last game to Elk River, and some of the parents on our hockey team planned the team's banquet before the state tournament was even over," Larson said. "I said, 'What are you doing? We haven't even started the playoffs.'

"I made them push the date back."

The expected section final showdown between Elk River and Blaine never materialized. Osseo shocked the Elks 5–4 in the semifinals.

"You need a lucky bounce or two in the playoffs, and I think our lucky bounce was Elk River getting beat by Osseo," said Hendricks, who, like Bochenski, was a future NHLer.

Blaine cruised past Osseo 6–2 in the section final to earn a return trip to Target Center, where they met, of all teams, Hastings in the semifinals. Hendricks scored twice in the first period en route to Blaine's 4–3 victory. The Bengals led 4–2 when Andy Hartung scored with five seconds left, not enough time for the Raiders to duplicate their comeback magic of the previous year.

Taking advantage of the extra breaks in the action to accommodate television commercials, Larson leaned heavily on his top eight players. Bochenski and Adam Holmgren played on a line centered by Moore. Hendricks centered Frischmon and Chad Smith.

On defense, Foyt and Romfo, a converted forward, logged as much ice time as they could stomach. They alternated long shifts with short breaks, signaling to Larson when they were ready to return to the ice.

In an anticlimactic finale, Moore and Frischmon each scored twice, and Witkowski made twenty-one saves as the Bengals routed Duluth East 6–0 in the championship.

"I think we had that killer instinct," Bochenski said. "When we got the lead, we would step on teams' throats. The floodgates just opened [against Duluth East].

"That game was over before it even started."

~LRN~

THE VENUES

In 2001, the Xcel Energy Center in downtown St. Paul became the fifth Twin Cities–area venue to serve as the home of the boys' state hockey tournament. Each of the five brought its own distinctive flavor to the event.

The St. Paul Auditorium, shown here during the 1966 state tournament and renamed the Roy Wilkins Auditorium in 1985, held more than seven thousand fans by the end of its twenty-four-year run as the tournament's home. Photo courtesy of the Minnesota Historical Society

ST. PAUL AUDITORIUM

LOCATION	YEAR OPENED	TOURNAMENT YEARS	SEATING CAPACITY
DOWNTOWN ST. PAUL	1932	1945–1968	7,000-PLUS

PROS

The Auditorium was the first St. Paul arena to have artificial ice. The seating capacity was massive compared to what was available in the limited number of other indoor arenas around the state. The downtown St. Paul location made for easy access to multiple nearby hotels, restaurants, department stores, and shops.

CONS

A cloud of smoke hung perpetually above the fans puffing on cigars and cigarettes. The unpainted ice typically was black for the first few games before slowly turning white through scarring from players' skates. There were just two main locker rooms, neither of which could be described as plush.

Canvas walls erected behind the players' benches and in front of the stands served as two additional dressing areas.

COMMENTS

The perfect choice to host the early years of the state tournament, the Auditorium simply became too small for the event and its surging popularity.

QUOTES

"Our locker room was like an old army tent they erected right outside the boards."
—Bobby Krieger, Edina

"They had some canvas locker rooms. No [bathrooms]; you had to go into some other locker room to take a leak."
—Willard Ikola, Eveleth

TRIVIA

The building still exists as a multipurpose arena renamed the Roy Wilkins Auditorium. Legendary artists such as the Grateful Dead, Bruce Springsteen, Bob Dylan, and Guns N' Roses have played there. So did the University of Minnesota hockey team from the 1930s to the 1950s.

The Metropolitan Sports Center in Bloomington held more than fourteen thousand fans for state tournament games, double the capacity of the St. Paul Auditorium. Photo by the *St. Paul Pioneer Press,* courtesy of the Minnesota Historical Society

METROPOLITAN SPORTS CENTER

LOCATION	YEAR OPENED	TOURNAMENT YEARS	SEATING CAPACITY
BLOOMINGTON	1967	1969–1975	14,400

PROS

The Met had double the seating capacity of the old St. Paul Auditorium. Sight lines, seating, lighting, locker rooms, and a fast ice surface all combined to make it one of the finest arenas in the NHL. Above-average concession food for the time period included, tacos, fried chicken, and rare roast beef. Ample parking.

CONS

Sprawling suburban Bloomington lacked the cozy feel and variety of dining and shopping options of downtown St. Paul. Players often complained about the suffocating heat at ice level.

COMMENTS

The Met was billed as the greatest arena in the nation when it was built, and it might have been. It provided a great home for the tournament, even if the location wasn't ideal.

QUOTES

"It was fancy. State of the art."
—Bobby Krieger, Edina

"That was the hottest place we've ever played in."
—Denny Tetu, South St. Paul coach

TRIVIA

The Met's green, gold, and white seats were installed in random color patterns by accident—the initial plans called for seats of matching colors to be placed together in single-color sections. The building was demolished on December 13, 1994, after North Stars owner Norm Green moved the franchise to Dallas.

The St. Paul Civic Center's clear boards and spiderweb ceiling made it a state tournament venue unlike any other. Photo by the *Minneapolis Star Tribune,* courtesy of the Minnesota Historical Society

ST. PAUL CIVIC CENTER

LOCATION	YEAR OPENED	TOURNAMENT YEARS	SEATING CAPACITY
DOWNTOWN ST. PAUL	1973	1976–1998	16,000

PROS

The rink's distinctive clear Plexiglas boards gave the building a one-of-a-kind feel. The spiderweb ceiling (white support beams spanning from the outside edges of the building all met in the middle) only added to the charm. And it was located in the heart of downtown St. Paul with all its amenities.

CONS

A gradual pitch meant nosebleed seats were far from the action.

COMMENTS

Weird, quirky, and altogether different from any other arena in the state—or the world, for that matter—the Civic Center was the ideal venue for the golden years of the nation's most distinctive high school tournament.

QUOTES

"I remember it was a long tunnel from the locker room to the ice, so it felt like you'd be walking for a while. Then, finally, the arena would come into view. You could see how high the seats were and how bright the lights were. It felt like you'd finally arrived."
—Adam Coole,
Duluth East

"Everybody always asks me about those boards, how weird it was. Well, it wasn't all that different, other than you could look down and see what kind of shoes guys were wearing."
—Noel Rahn,
Edina

TRIVIA

Billy Joel, Madonna, Elton John, Aerosmith, and KISS were Civic Center regulars. Eric Clapton played the final concert there. Renamed RiverCentre in the mid-1990s, it was torn down in 1998 to make way for the Xcel Energy Center (today a conference center also named RiverCentre adjoins the Xcel).

Target Center in Minneapolis was the location of the 1992 and 1993 Tier II title games. The arena later served as a temporary home to the 1999 and 2000 Class 1A and 2A tournaments while the Xcel Energy Center in St. Paul was under construction. Photo by Mike Thill/*Let's Play Hockey*

TARGET CENTER

LOCATION	YEAR OPENED	TOURNAMENT YEARS	SEATING CAPACITY
DOWNTOWN MINNEAPOLIS	1990	1992–1993 [TIER II SEMIFINALS AND CHAMPIONSHIP] 1999–2000	17,500

PROS

Target Center held more fans than the Civic Center, and the downtown Minneapolis location offered easy access to nearby hotels and eateries.

CONS

Minneapolis couldn't match St. Paul's rich tradition as tournament host. The hockey setup felt like an afterthought. Ice conditions were not always ideal.

COMMENTS

Though great for basketball and a nice building that has been updated several times, it never has caught on as a home for hockey.

QUOTES

"The first two games, we got the locker rooms that were built for basketball players. The showerheads were for guys who stood 7 feet. The lockers were that tall, too."
—Phil Larson, Roseau

"I don't think anybody was complaining about playing there. But it just didn't have that same state tournament smell [as the St. Paul Civic Center]."
—Matt Hendricks, Blaine

TRIVIA

Target Center hosted six neutral-site games during the 1993–94 NHL season. The IHL's Minnesota Moose played several home games there in the mid-1990s. A $140 million renovation was completed in 2017.

Lakeville North and Duluth East line up for the national anthem before the start of the 2015 Class 2A state championship game at the Xcel Energy Center in downtown St. Paul. "The X" began hosting the state tournament in 2000. Photo by Brendan Meier, licensed under the terms of the GNU Free Documentation License, CC BY 2.0

XCEL ENERGY CENTER

LOCATION	YEAR OPENED	TOURNAMENT YEARS	SEATING CAPACITY
DOWNTOWN ST. PAUL	2000	2001–PRESENT	17,954

PROS
Back in its original home of downtown St. Paul, the tournament continues in a venue built as a monument to the "State nf Hockey." Jerseys from every high school in Minnesota hang on the wall in multiple concourses. Steeply pitched seats put fans on top of the action.

CONS
Hard to think of any.

COMMENTS
This venue, with all its modern amenities and nods to the state's rich hockey history, is a fantastic fit for the tourney's modern era.

QUOTES
"We went from having a picnic table in our home rink's locker room to leather sofas and fridges stocked with Gatorade. We kind of felt like we were kings."
—Ben Gustafson, Elk River

"When you are fifteen years old and playing in front of eighteen thousand people at the Xcel, it is hard to think that anything could be better than that."
—Jared Hummel, Holy Angels

TRIVIA
In 2015, a crowd of 21,609 attended the state Class 2A semifinals, setting a record for most fans to attend an indoor hockey game in the state. The press box is named in honor of Al Shaver, the "Voice of the North Stars," who also called state tournament games in the late 1970s and early '80s.

TEAM OF DESTINY

TRAGIC DEATH BOOSTED SENSE OF TOGETHERNESS FOR COMMITTED ELK RIVER

DATES	LOCATION	ATTENDANCE	CLASS 2A CHAMPIONSHIP
MARCH 7–10	XCEL ENERGY CENTER, ST. PAUL	111,273	ELK RIVER 8, MOORHEAD 1
			CLASS 1A CHAMPIONSHIP
			BENILDE–ST. MARGARET'S 2, ROCHESTER LOURDES 1

191

 Small school Greenway, opting to play in the big-school class, had all three of its games go to overtime as the Raiders, led by high-scoring forwards Gino Guyer and Andy Sertich, finished third.

THE INSTANT Tony Sarsland wheeled his car into the Elk River Ice Arena parking lot, he knew something was wrong. Tragically wrong.

Sarsland, the Elk River coach, was in the midst of his game-day routine. As usual, he had arrived at the rink early, expecting to watch the junior varsity game between his Elks and Osseo. Instead, he saw groups of somber players, parents, and fans huddled together outside the entrance. They were talking in hushed tones. Tears were flowing.

"They told me Trevor Stewart had come home from school and found that his brother had killed himself," Sarsland said. "I said, 'Where's Trevor?' Somebody told me they had seen him walking down School Street. So now I go looking for him."

The defining moment in Elk River's 2000–01 season came that frigid January 18 night, when Sarsland pulled his car up next to Stewart, rolled down the window, and told the Elks' star forward to get in. Stewart ignored the order and kept walking.

"I said, 'Trevor, if you have any respect for Coach Sarsland, you are going to get in the car,'" Sarsland said.

Elk River's scoring standout and emotional leader Trevor Stewart (left) and goalie Brent Solei celebrate their 2001 state championship win over Moorhead. Photo by Jeff Wheeler/ *Minneapolis Star Tribune*

Finally, the distraught Stewart swung the door open and climbed into the passenger seat.

"He was in pretty rough shape," Sarsland said. "He kept saying, 'Coach, why did I have to find him?' What are you going to say in a situation like that? Then, it was like God put the words in my mouth, and I said, 'The Lord knew you were the only one strong enough in the family to handle it.'"

Stewart remembers Sarsland's words and, just as much, his silence.

"I basically cried on his shoulder for a half hour or so," Stewart said. "I was in a state of shock."

Before becoming stepbrothers, Stewart and Clint Martin had forged their friendship in the fourth grade when they played on the same baseball team. That's also when Martin's mother, Edie, and Stewart's dad, Greg, started their relationship. Edie and Greg got married when the boys were high school freshmen. Friends became brothers, and Stewart cheered on Martin when he won the state Class 3A wrestling championship at 135 pounds as a sophomore. A week later, Martin was Stewart's biggest fan when the Elks finished third at the state Class 2A tournament.

"It seemed like he was on top of the world," Stewart said a few weeks after Martin's death. "No one saw it coming."

A team that had spent its summers playing roller hockey from dawn to dusk in the parking lot at Elk River's Solid Rock Church now congregated daily at Stewart's house.

"That was something that hung over us the rest of the season," said Nate Droogsma, a senior forward. "It was never really spoken about as a motivation. But we all knew Clint, and he was a great kid."

Sarsland played the role of eternal optimist that season, even though the Elks had been stunned in the 2000 section semifinals by Osseo in one of the biggest upsets in state playoff history: the number-one-ranked Elks lost 5–4 in two overtimes after racing to a 4–0 lead in the first six minutes. That Elk River team, led by future Mr. Hockey Award winner and NHLer Paul Martin, Clint's first cousin, was so loaded with talent it seemed a foregone conclusion it would win the section and, most likely, the school's first state title.

"We were so good it was ridiculous," Sarsland said. "But we weren't as committed as we needed to be."

If that team couldn't even make a section title game, what was Sarsland thinking when, essentially, he guaranteed a state championship for the next year's group?

"I told my players before the season, 'If you will commit to me for a little under four months—totally commit—we are going to win the championship,'" Sarsland said.

This wasn't some motivational ploy dreamed up by the veteran coach.

"I honestly felt that way," he said.

Adversity, then tragedy, greeted the Elks at every turn. Before the season, high-scoring forward Kelly Plude had surgery on his left knee in the spring but wasn't cleared to play until September because of a staph infection in his back. In early February, he was diagnosed with mononucleosis.

Martin's death left Stewart, who had had offseason shoulder surgery, so shaken he didn't sleep regularly for weeks.

"I went to the emergency room one time," Stewart said. "I had gone seventy-two hours without sleeping. I think I passed out just from exhaustion."

"Destiny" became the Elks' rallying cry. They reached the state tournament with a 26–1–1 record and the state's number-one ranking. Elk River beat Eastview 3–1 in the quarterfinals, a game in which goaltender Dustin Hall faced just seven shots (one in the final period).

Stewart, wearing a chain with an angel carved into a penny (a gift from Edie), scored Elk River's final three goals in a 4–3 semifinal triumph over Hastings.

"I just got the puck in the right spots," said Stewart, known more as the playmaker on the Elks' number-one line, which also included Plude and Joel Hanson.

Longtime nemesis Moorhead awaited in the championship. In 1994, the Spuds, fueled by future NHLers Matt Cullen and Ryan Kraft, had outlasted Elk River 4–3 in four overtimes in an epic Section 8 title game in St. Cloud.

"We weren't going to let them beat us again," Sarsland said.

Plude had a hat trick as the Elks' top line accounted for five goals in an 8–1 rout of the Spuds. The seven-goal margin of victory remains tied as the largest in a title game.

"Everything went our way," Droogsma said.

The joyous Elks returned to their locker room whooping and laughing. There, in the background, lost among the hugs and high fives, was the whiteboard on which Sarsland had listed the team's three goals for the game.

As a final note, the coach known for his trademark cowboy boots had spelled out one last thing in big, bold, underlined letters before the Elks hit the ice.

D-E-S-T-I-N-Y.

~LRN~

ANGELS AND DEMONS

BOO BIRDS SERENADED HOLY ANGELS' ALL-STARS TO BIG-SCHOOL CROWN

DATES	LOCATION	ATTENDANCE	CLASS 2A CHAMPIONSHIP
MARCH 6–9	XCEL ENERGY CENTER, ST. PAUL	108,524	HOLY ANGELS 4, HILL-MURRAY 2
			CLASS 1A CHAMPIONSHIP
			TOTINO-GRACE 3, RED WING 2

 Tournament ticket holders were treated to bonus hockey, as period lengths were extended from fifteen to seventeen minutes starting in the 2001–02 season.

THE BOOS THUNDERED down in bursts, as if cannons loaded with low-pitched, high-decibel disapproval were intermittently being fired iceward.

The pregame announcement of Holy Angels' starting lineup had triggered the jeers. And any penalties, real or perceived, committed by the Stars really stoked the massive Xcel Energy Center crowd's disapproval.

BOOOOOOOOOOO!

Holy Angels was playing Roseville in the big-school semifinals of the 2002 state tournament, and it didn't take an abacus, NASA mathematician, or liquid-cooled supercomputer to calculate that an overwhelming majority of fans were in favor of Roseville.

"It was jam-packed, nineteen thousand people," said Jack Hillen, a Holy Angels sophomore defenseman that season. "I guarantee you only our small student-body section and our parents were rooting for us."

Holy Angels, with controversial and ultrasuccessful coach Greg Trebil at the helm, had risen from small-school hockey afterthought to Class 2A giant killer in just a few seasons. Luring high-end players from Twin Cities outskirts such as Maple Grove to the north, New Prague to the south, and all points in between, the Stars couldn't have been more aptly named.

Trebil's reputation as an innovator, taskmaster, and winner was a big part of the draw. As a coach in Bloomington's youth system for fifteen years, he went 538–73–30 and led one Pee Wee and three Bantam teams to state championships. All three of his sons played on state championship high school teams at Bloomington Jefferson (Greg in 1989, Dan in 1992, and Ryan in 1994).

Trebil left for Holy Angels, a private Catholic school in neighboring Richfield, in the summer of 1996. Four of his Bloomington Bantams joined him, thus creating a rift with longtime friend Tom Saterdalen, the legendary Jefferson head coach who won five state championships. By 1999, Holy Angels, a small school (585 students in 2002) opting up to play in the big class, was making its first state tournament appearance.

"I had heard about his coaching pedigree," Mike Taylor, a sophomore forward in 1992, said about Trebil. "I grew up watching his sons at the U of M. The name was synonymous with hockey."

Added Jimmy Kilpatrick: "He just had this aura about him."

Allegations of recruiting swirled around Trebil almost from the start of his tenure at Holy Angels, and in 2000, the Minnesota State High School League concluded one of the most thorough investigations it had ever conducted. No recruiting violations were found, although Trebil was ruled to have made two relatively minor violations. He was fined $500 and put on probation for a year.

Meanwhile, the Holy Angels hockey machine kept churning. The Stars entered the 2002 state tournament with a 23–4–1 record and riding a seventeen-game winning streak. Two of the losses came on an East Coast road trip to longtime New England powers Boston Catholic Memorial (3–2) and Rhode Island's Mount St. Charles Academy (2–1).

A 5–2 quarterfinal rout of Cloquet set up Holy Angels' Saturday-night semifinal showdown with Roseville, a one-loss team anointed as the pretournament favorite.

"I remember sitting up in the stands and scouting Roseville," said Guy Olson, Trebil's longtime assistant. "Greg and I looked at each other and said, 'They have slow D.' We just smiled."

Holy Angels' offense was predicated on quickness and rat-a-tat puck movement. The Stars' forwards weren't big, but their lack of size had never been an issue. You can't hit what you can't catch.

Kilpatrick, a junior forward from New Prague, centered an explosive top line that included the team's top scorer in senior Tyler Howells and insanely creative and competitive junior Kevin Rollwagen. Faceoff specialist Kevin Huck, a junior, centered a second line that included sophomore Matt Kaiser and senior Dan Kronick. There was little to no drop-off in talent on the third line, which had senior Kevin Krmpotich, also a soccer standout, centering Taylor and junior Erik Heltne.

Dan Kronick of Holy Angels reaches high with his stick to deflect the puck past Hill-Murray goalie Tony Ciro and tie the score at one in the first period of the 2002 championship game. Photo by Marlin Levison/*Minneapolis Star Tribune*

"We asked Krmpotich to center the third line so we could get our lines more even," Olson said. "He said, 'Sure, whatever.' He would have played first or second line on any team in the state."

Kronick was Holy Angels' leading scorer with seven goals and fourteen points when he shattered his left ankle in a December 20 game against Eastview. He had surgery the next day. Doctors told him he was done for the season, but he returned weeks earlier than expected and scored a clutch goal in a double-overtime section semifinal victory over Eastview.

Against Roseville, Kronick, a St. Paul kid who wore number 19, emerged as public enemy number one. He scored four goals, all of them highlight-reel worthy, in the 6–3 triumph.

The boos gave way to . . . nothing.

"We scored, and it was just silence," said Hillen, a Minnetonka native who would play eight seasons in the NHL.

Hill-Murray, a Catholic school located in Maplewood, squashed the delicious possibility of a championship grudge-fest between Trebil and Saterdalen, the latter of whom was coaching in his final season, by routing Bloomington Jefferson 5–0 in the other semifinal.

The first private-school-versus-private-school matchup in single-class, Tier I, or big-school history brought mostly apathy from the crowd, portions of which began chanting "*Pub-lic schools! Pub-lic schools!*"

Hill-Murray fans were quick to respond, reminding neutral observers their teams had been eliminated: "*You're not heeeere! You're not heeeere!*"

"It seemed like most of the crowd wanted both teams to lose because they hated private schools so much," Hillen said.

Nothing short of a victory would satisfy Holy Angels' senior mainstays. Howells, Krmpotich, and Kronick all scored against the Pioneers (Kronick his sixth goal of the tourney). The final goal in the 4–2 triumph came from Rollwagen with 4:13 remaining on a brilliant individual effort.

"Rollwagen . . . what a goal," Trebil told reporters. "He's not a real big kid. But he has a heart as big as this state."

Trebil could have been describing his entire team—a team that was now more than just a collection of stars.

Despite the crowd's objections, it was a group of champions.

~LRN~

MIRACLE MAN
Holy Angels defenseman and future *Miracle* actor Joe Cure a unique leader

Barriball. Frazee. Hagemo. Hillen. Hengen. Johnson. Taylor.

Some of the biggest names in Minnesota high school hockey, future Division I college standouts and first-round NHL draft picks among them, were rolling through Holy Angels with regularity from the late 1990s into the mid-2000s.

Then there was Joe Cure.

In terms of his hockey skills, the best that could be said about Cure was that he knew his limitations.

"He wasn't the most talented guy," said Guy Olson, an assistant coach during Holy Angels' run of five state tournament appearances in seven years that netted the Richfield-based Catholic school two titles. "He would be the first to tell you that. That is one of the reasons why he was so successful and gave us so much."

Cure was a senior during the 2001–02 season, which began with an influx of fuzzy-cheeked phenoms on defense. Freshman Jared Hummel had been a standout Bantam in Eagan. Fellow freshman Nate Hagemo arrived with a hockey bag full of accolades out of Edina. Sophomore Jack Hillen, maybe the best of the young guns, came straight out of Minnetonka with a truckload of talent.

Cure played defense, too. It only figured that, with so many new kids hungry to get a regular shift, he wouldn't be particularly welcoming. Ice time has its limitations, too.

Instead, Hummel said, "He was the one who took all three of us under his wing. He helped us adjust to varsity hockey."

After school, Cure gave the young pups rides to practice. He'd drive some of them home, too. When Hummel's skates and hockey gloves were stolen, Cure was determined to find the culprit.

"Joe jumped in and was super angry," Hummel said. "He tried to figure out who did it and why they did it. It was like he felt personally obligated to fix it."

In a program that pulled hotshot players from all corners of the Twin Cities, Cure, a Bloomington native, was the glue that kept the team together. Heck, his personality was so magnetic he brought the entire *school* together.

Joe Cure (right) poses during the filming of *Miracle* with actor Noah Emmerich, who portrayed Team USA assistant coach Craig Patrick. Cure played Mike Ramsey in the 2004 movie. Photo courtesy of *Let's Play Hockey*

"He had the heart and the leadership," said Mike Taylor, a sophomore in 2001–02. "He was also a jokester who could keep things light."

State tournament box scores from Holy Angels' run to the 2002 championship list Cure's name twice. He took penalties for cross-checking and holding in the semifinals against Roseville.

"One time, he was helping us in one of our summer-league clinics with the younger kids," Olson said about Cure. "We were working on breaking the puck out. One of the things we started to do was have the kids just get it out of the zone off the glass. At that point, Joe just pops in and says, 'I know all about that, right, Coach?'

"He didn't have very good hands, but he was big and strong. He would do anything for the team."

Cure's interests extended far beyond hockey. He was involved in the school's theater program and convinced other members of the hockey team to join him in trying out for the school's spring musical.

"He got the acting bug," Olson said.

Cure was just a few years out of high school when, with no professional acting experience, he auditioned for the 2004 movie *Miracle*, about Team USA's victory over the Soviet Union en route to the gold medal at the 1980 Winter Olympics in Lake Placid. He got the part of defenseman Mike Ramsey, the youngest player on the team. Cure's big moment in the movie comes when combustible head coach Herb Brooks (played by Kurt Russell) bursts into the locker room during the team's opening game at the Olympics.

Says an incensed Brooks: "This is unbelievable. You guys are playing like this is some throwaway game up in Rochester. Who are we playing, Rammer?"

Ramsey: "Sweden."

Brooks: "Yeah. You're damn right—Sweden! In the Olympics!"

Being in the movie left a lasting impression on Cure. "The story of *Miracle* is truly a love story about twenty young boys coming together and taking on the world. . . . Being a part of *Miracle* forever changed the way I view the Olympics," he said in a 2014 interview with the Minnesota-based magazine *Let's Play Hockey*.

In November 2011 Cure, just thirty-one, died in an accident in his adopted home state of Montana when the car he was driving hit a patch of ice and rolled violently.

"He didn't wear a [captain's] letter, but he was great as a leader, a team guy," Hillen said. "Boy that hurt when he died."

~LRN~

BAND OF BROTHERS

NO SACRIFICE TOO BIG FOR ANOKA'S GRITTY, HARD-HITTING GROUP

DATES	LOCATION	ATTENDANCE	CLASS 2A CHAMPIONSHIP
MARCH 5–8	XCEL ENERGY CENTER, ST. PAUL	115,524	ANOKA 3, ROSEVILLE 1
			CLASS 1A CHAMPIONSHIP
			WARROAD 3, SIMLEY 1

 Holy Angels freshman defenseman Erik Johnson didn't register a point, but his big score came later. In 2006, the St. Louis Blues made him the first Minnesotan selected with the first overall pick in the NHL draft.

ANOKA HAD JUST knocked off defending champion Holy Angels in the semifinals of the 2003 state tournament, and jubilant Tornadoes players were spilling off the bench and onto the ice in a tidal wave of maroon and white.

Among the players grinning and whooping and acting like mad men was junior defenseman Joe Ganser, dressed in full gear from his head to his . . . ankles.

"Watch the replay of the celebration," said Sean Fish, a senior co-captain that season. "All of a sudden you will see a kid running out in his Doc Martens because he doesn't have his skates."

A few hours earlier, panic had spread through the Anoka locker room. Derek Johnson, a senior who played on Anoka's top defense pairing, was about to tug on his skates for warmups when he noticed the steel in one of his blades was broken—cracked clean through. The skate was unusable until a replacement blade could be installed, a labor-intensive and time-consuming process back in the early 2000s.

"We were wondering what we could do to get a hold of the kid's dad to get them fixed," Anoka coach Todd Manthey said. "But then, where do you go to fix it?"

Plan after plan was discussed and then discarded, and just when it seemed certain Johnson was destined to be a healthy scratch, Ganser, the team's fifth or sixth defenseman, spoke up.

"Ganser said, 'I have the same size skate. Same model, too. He can wear mine.'" Manthey said. "It was 100 percent his idea. Pretty unselfish."

A day earlier, Ben Hendrick had scored a most improbable goal off a faceoff from his knees with 17.1 seconds remaining to give Anoka a 4–3 lead over Duluth East. The Tornadoes' leading scorer then benched himself for the closing seconds of the victory.

"Benny comes off the ice and says, 'Hey, put Fish out there. He's a better defensive center than I am,'" Manthey said. "That's the kind of team we had."

With seventeen players returning from the previous season, thirteen of them seniors, there was a sense among Ano-

ka's coaches and players this could be the program's last best chance for its first state title.

"We were a senior-dominated team that kind of realized this was it," said Manthey, who had been coaching many of those seniors, his son Tim among them, since they were Squirts rising through the youth hockey ranks.

Todd Manthey grew up in Anoka and was quarterback of the football team and high-scoring triggerman of the hockey team. He married Tami Hartje, sister of Todd Hartje, another mid-1980s Anoka hockey star.

"Cut us, and we bleed maroon," Manthey said.

The Manthey family received an outpouring of community support in the heart of the 2002–03 season, including food, clothes, and gifts, when their house burned down three days before Christmas. Two days later, Tami was driving the family's 2000 Chrysler Concorde when it was rear-ended. The car was totaled.

The Mantheys' run of bad luck had started earlier that fall, when Tim was hit while running out of bounds in Anoka's first football game of the season. His leg was broken in two places. He returned in time for the hockey season but needed a few weeks to ramp up to full speed.

As Manthey, the Tornadoes' top defenseman, was rounding into top form, the rest of the team was doing the same. Holy Angels, the private school program that was drawing elite talent from all over the metro, traveled north from Richfield and deep into the epicenter of the northern suburbs' blue-collar belt. The midseason scrimmage at Anoka Ice Arena consisted of two forty-five-minute halves. Holy Angels, all speed and skill and flash and panache, controlled the first half.

Anoka ramped up its intensity in the second half, leading to more physical play. Eyebrows raised as the Tornadoes dominated long stretches.

"We thought, 'Hey, we can play with these guys,'" Todd Manthey said.

The Tornadoes had speed, they had grit, and they liked to

hit. Forward Andrew Johnson was the epitome of toughness and tenacity, in the same mold as fellow forward Zach Nelson, a middle linebacker on Anoka's football team. They flanked Hendrick, the scoring machine who had hat tricks in four consecutive games during the regular season and was a pit bull in the corners.

And that wasn't even Anoka's most physical line.

Twin brothers Andy and Aaron LaHoud had moved to the school district from Irondale when they were in the eighth grade, immediately adopting Fish as a member of the family. The trio formed a forward unit nicknamed the Triplets, a joke playing off the size difference between the massive LaHouds (6 foot 2, 200 pounds) and the diminutive Fish (5 foot 6, 130).

"They had shirts made up that said 'Bro 1,' 'Bro 2,' and 'Bro 3,'" Fish said.

Andy LaHoud wore jersey number 21, Aaron number 22, and Fish number 23.

"They had a little bit of skill," Todd Manthey said about the LaHouds, "but they were more physical than finesse."

Anoka put them and the rest of its bangers to good use in the tournament semifinals against Holy Angels. The team escaped with a 2–1 upset victory after scoring on its first two shots; the Stars managed just fourteen shots.

"We were bigger than a lot of teams, and we used that to our advantage," Tim Manthey said. "I remember watching the highlight tapes from the tournament, and they said we had something like thirty-some hits against Holy Angels."

Anoka rallied from a 1–0 deficit after the first period to beat Roseville 3–1 in the title game. The clinching goal came midway through the third after Tim Manthey's point shot on a power play deflected in off Craig Chapman, Anoka's third-line center, who was the team's third-leading scorer and a power-play regular.

"The winning goal goes in off Chappy's butt," Fish said, adding that goaltender Kyle Olstad made a brilliant save on the next shift to preserve Anoka's one-goal lead (Derek Johnson added an empty-net goal in the final minute). "That's just the way we were—everybody contributed.

"We were a band of brothers."

~LRN~

Anoka's Craig Chapman deflected the puck past Roseville goalie Jerad Kaufmann in the third period for what proved to be the winning goal in the Tornadoes' 3–1 victory in the 2003 championship game. Photo by Bruce Bisping/*Minneapolis Star Tribune*

MARCH SICKNESS
Breck star's annual bout with "flu" allowed him to skip school, watch idols

Blake Wheeler considered it ironic that, as a youngster, he always developed the state tournament flu.

Wink, wink.

Watching the likes of Johnny Pohl of Red Wing, Troy Riddle of Benilde–St. Margaret's, and Dave Spehar of Duluth East provided the cure. Years later, he would join them as a state champion and a Minnesota Gopher—and he surpassed them as a top NHL draft pick.

Those accomplishments seemed distant when Wheeler arrived as a sophomore at the Breck School in Golden Valley. He stood about 6 foot 4 but only began to fill out his frame and find the consistent form that made him the Bantam player of the year in Wayzata's youth ranks.

"He was a little clumsy," Mustangs coach Wally Chapman said. "He wasn't a 'Coach, put me in the game' guy at the start. But toward the end of that first season, he realized hockey could be a career for him. Then you saw him with a leg over the boards anytime we got a power play."

As a junior, Wheeler earned two state championships during the 2003–04 school year, the first of them as a tight end with seven receptions for 147 yards in the Mustangs' Class 2A Prep Bowl victory.

Football was nice and all, but "the hockey tournament was the one I grew up dreaming about," he said.

Wheeler played most of the season at right wing on Breck's first line with Robbie Dee and Dustin Fulton. All three were talented. But Wheeler earned a different sort of attention.

In January, NHL Central Scouting ranked him number forty-six among North American skaters and tops among high school players. Every NHL team sent representatives to a Breck game at least once. First-round draft pick projections swirled.

But Wheeler stayed focused on the state tournament. When he arrived, he was sick—and not the kind of sick that would keep him home from school.

Wheeler tallied a hat trick in a 10–1 quarterfinal rout of Albert Lea. In the semifinals, South St. Paul's Alex Stalock, a future NHL goaltender, made thirty-eight saves and kept the Packers close in a 3–2 loss to Wheeler's Mustangs.

"To this day, it was one of the best performances I ever saw," said Wheeler, who assisted on all three goals.

He regained the scoring touch with a second-period hat trick in the championship game. Breck crushed Orono 7–2 for the title.

"Going out for the third period, we knew we had it in hand," Wheeler said. "It was a pretty special feeling."

And Wheeler was a pretty special player. He finished the season with one hundred points on forty-five goals in thirty games and was drafted fifth overall by the Phoenix Coyotes in June.

~DL~

Forward Blake Wheeler led Breck to the 2004 Class 1A state title with one hundred points (forty-five goals) in thirty games. Photo by Marlin Levison/*Minneapolis Star Tribune*

MR. ZERO

CENTENNIAL GOALIE GREGG STUTZ'S THREE STRAIGHT SHUTOUTS REMAIN AN UNMATCHED FEAT

DATES	LOCATION	ATTENDANCE	CLASS 2A CHAMPIONSHIP
MARCH 10–13	XCEL ENERGY CENTER, ST. PAUL	120,114	CENTENNIAL 1, MOORHEAD 0
			CLASS 1A CHAMPIONSHIP
			BRECK SCHOOL 7, ORONO 2

Did you know? Duluth East's wild 7–4 victory over Wayzata in the Class 2A third-place game set or tied multiple records, including Duluth East's five power-play goals and its four power-play goals in a single period (the third). The teams combined for seven power-play goals, another record.

THREE GAMES, three straight shutouts.

With each passing season, Centennial's one-of-a kind state tournament feat becomes incrementally more remarkable.

The Cougars, with senior Gregg Stutz tending goal as if he were a grizzly protecting its cubs, soared into a never-before-reached echelon during the 2004 state tournament. Centennial, making its first tourney appearance, shut out Holy Angels 2–0, Wayzata 3–0, and Moorhead 1–0 for its only title.

No team had ever registered back-to-back-to-back tournament shutouts before. No team has done it since.

"You don't really realize what an incredible accomplishment it was in the moment," said R. J. Anderson, a junior defenseman in 2003–04.

The feat is so unique it wouldn't be outlandish for Stutz, Anderson, and the rest of the Cougars to copy a page out of the playbook of the 1972 Miami Dolphins, the only team to win

Centennial goalie Gregg Stutz became the first—and, to date, only—goalie to record three straight state tournament shutouts.
Photo by Sherri LaRose/*St. Paul Pioneer Press*

the Super Bowl with a perfect season. A handful of Dolphins players gather yearly and pop the cork for a low-key celebration when the last undefeated NFL team suffers its first loss of the season.

Although it would make for a juicy tale, the Cougars don't reunite each year in early March to break out the champagne and stogies after the last unscored-upon state tournament team surrenders its first goal. Not that Anderson is opposed to the notion.

"Keep the champagne coming," he said with a laugh.

The first bottle would go to Stutz. The goaltender with the distinctive metallic silver mask (nicknamed the "chrome dome" by teammates) was flawless in the three tournament games with a combined fifty-three saves, the most incredible of which not only seemed to defy the laws of physics but remains a source of contention today.

"I saw the puck go past the line and raised my stick," Mike Taylor, Holy Angels' leading scorer in 2003–04, said about his power-play one-timer that sent the puck rocketing toward the goal line at precisely the same moment Stutz's left leg pad flashed through the crease.

"It was definitely a goal," said Guy Olson, a Holy Angels assistant coach that season. "His pad was all the way in the net when he stopped it."

The view is different from Centennial's vantage point.

"I should have blocked the pass [through the crease] in the first place," Stutz said. "But I feel like my foot did get there in time. I'm 90 percent sure it was a save, with a 10 percent chance it was a goal."

"No, it wasn't in," Anderson said. "It didn't count, did it?"

Amazing, and controversial, as it was, Stutz's save of the game, tournament, and lifetime wasn't so extraordinary to Centennial's players. With Stutz, the impossible was simply part of his routine.

"He was always the clutchest guy in the biggest of moments," said Tim Ornell, a senior forward in 2004. "He was kind of the rare Michael Jordan type of character in that way."

Stutz had been in goal three years earlier when Centennial won the state Bantam A championship 1–0 over White Bear Lake. And in 2003–04, the Cougars started the season with three straight shutouts. An incredible run of five straight shutouts came later.

"In the bigger games, I seemed to kind of lock in a little more," Stutz said. "It's hard to explain it. I liked being in front of the bigger crowds."

Centennial, ranked number one in the state for most of the season, suffered an early loss to Edina and then went unbeaten the rest of the way, finishing with a twenty-seven-game win streak and 30–1 record. The Cougars scored an incredible 255 goals and allowed just 33.

Curiously, Stutz, who insisted on pregame meals of orange juice and spaghetti and would allow only assistant coach Andy Marshall to assist him with his pregame stretching routine, was barely an afterthought entering the state tournament. He wasn't among the four goalies picked to the *Star Tribune*'s All-Metro first, second, or third teams. He wasn't a consideration for the Frank Brimsek Award, which goes to the state's top senior goaltender. Stutz was a late addition to the *St. Paul Pioneer Press*'s All-State team, released after the state tournament, only because of his championship series brilliance.

"We had a lot of firepower on our team," Ornell said about the repeated Stutz snubs. "Who are you going to notice?"

Senior forward Tom Gorowsky was impossible to miss. A 6-foot, 200-pound package of equal parts power and finesse, Gorowsky led the state with eighty-five points in the regular season. Anderson had one of the greatest offensive seasons for a defenseman in state history, amassing an incredible eighty-two points heading into the state tournament. Both were named to the *Star Tribune*'s All-Metro first team, with Gorowsky, who later was named Mr. Hockey, selected as the Metro Player of the Year.

By the championship game, however, Stutz was the talk of the state. On a team that suddenly had become offensively challenged—Gorowsky was playing with a hernia and torn knee ligaments, and high-scoring sophomore forward Ryan Flynn suffered a shoulder injury in the semifinals and did not play in the championship—Stutz's excellence would again be crucial. He made fifteen saves against Moorhead, among the best of which was a glove-hand stab of a Chris VandeVelde wrister in the first period that kept the score knotted at zero.

Mike Montgomery scored the lone goal in the second period, drilling home a rising shot while sailing down the right wing, his long blond hair flowing out his helmet.

Gorowsky was presented with the championship trophy during the postgame award ceremony but instantly passed it off to Stutz, who dashed straight toward the Centennial cheering section and, surrounded by his teammates, slammed himself and the trophy against the Plexiglas.

"For a bunch of guys who grew up playing together since they were Mites," Stutz said, "you couldn't ask for a better ending."

~LRN~

BOOM!

WARROAD'S T. J. OSHIE AND TOTINO-GRACE'S ROB HOODY CLASHED WITH DRAMATIC EFFECT

DATES	LOCATION	ATTENDANCE	CLASS 2A CHAMPIONSHIP
MARCH 2–5	XCEL ENERGY CENTER, ST. PAUL	123,809	HOLY ANGELS 6, MOORHEAD 4
			CLASS 1A CHAMPIONSHIP
			WARROAD 4, TOTINO-GRACE 3 (2 OT)

Did you know? Eighth-grader Jordan Schroeder wasn't just occupying a roster spot and warming the bench for Class 1A entrant St. Thomas Academy. The elusive forward scored two goals and added three assists in a performance that made him the youngest player ever named to the all-tournament team.

TELEVISION CAMERAS were rolling and boom mics were swaying in the Warroad locker room as a grinning T. J. Oshie, resplendent in dress shirt, tie, and freshly bleached blond hairdo, put on a dazzling display of hand-eye coordination by masterfully juggling a Wiffle ball off the blade and handle of his hockey stick.

Minutes later, as opening puck drop approached, Totino-Grace players sat deadly silent and still in their nearby Xcel Energy Center locker room as coach Mark Loahr gave a fire-and-brimstone pregame speech that reached a crescendo: "And this is the kind of game, right here, where you are going to have to go out there and, maybe literally, get your nose bloody."

Totino-Grace center Rob Hoody wasn't the type of player who needed much pregame inspiration. He played the same every shift, every situation. No exceptions. Which is to say he attacked the opposition like a tiger presented with a freshly cut pork chop. Still, this was the state Class 1A championship game, and Hoody's already maxed-out compete level was now in the stratosphere thanks to Loahr's speech and the grand (nineteen-thousand-capacity NHL arena) stage.

"I remember it was the morning of the game and me thinking it was my job to shadow this guy everyone in the world is watching," Hoody said. "I was amped."

"This guy" would be Timothy Leif Oshie (T. J. stands for Timothy Jr.), Warroad's starting center. Oshie was a rare talent, even by tradition-rich Warroad's standards. He had amassed ninety-eight points heading into the title game, and his every move was being examined by hordes of NHL scouts who coveted his athleticism, hockey IQ, work ethic, and feisty style of play.

Looking back, with the fire-breathing Hoody on one side of the opening faceoff and the do-anything-to-win Oshie on the other, fireworks were inevitable.

Sure enough, before the puck could even hit the ice to start the game, BOOM, Hoody plowed straight ahead into Oshie, then pitchforked the Warroad superstar to the ice. For good

measure, as Oshie tried to get up, BOOM, Hoody was there again to cross check him in the back.

Seconds later, Oshie was digging for the puck in a corner when in rushed Hoody. Again, he had Oshie in his sights. This time, Oshie was ready. He delivered a preemptive shoulder into the onrushing Hoody.

BOOM.

"I was face-planted in the corner," Hoody said. "I guess I got what I deserved.

"After that, I remember saying to myself, right then and there, 'We have our [expletive] hockey game. This is going to be insane.'"

And so began one of the greatest championship games in state tournament history. Hoody and Oshie would meet several more times with dramatic and bone-jarring effect, and—speaking of drama—both players had key roles in the double-overtime goal that would end what to that point was the longest title game in state tournament history.

Warroad entered the 2005 Class 1A championship with an unbeaten record (28–0–2) and a roster filled with names right out of the who's who of Warriors hockey: Boucha, Marvin, Krahn, Olimb.

"There was a lot of hockey blood on that team," Warroad co–head coach Albert Hasbargen said.

Ties to Warroad's fabulous 1969 state runner-up team were numerous. Senior wing Kyle Krahn, sophomore center Aaron Marvin, and junior defenseman J. P. Boucha all had famous fathers (Frank Krahn, Mike Marvin, and Henry Boucha) who played starring roles for the 1969 Warriors squad that lost the one-class state title game in overtime to Edina. Senior defenseman and co-captain Kyle Hardwick was the grandson of Dick Roberts, Warroad's coach in 1969 and, before that, a star Warriors player in his own right in the years (early to mid-1940s) just before the founding of the state tournament.

Oshie came from hockey blood, too. His great-uncle Max Oshie led Warroad to the 1948 state title game as a senior and

Warroad's T. J. Oshie (right) got the better of this confrontation with Totino-Grace superpest Rob Hoody. Photo by Scott A. Schneider/*Let's Play Hockey*

been a toss-up who spent more time at the arena.

"He was at the rink all the time; he just loved the sport," Hasbargen said. "In fact, there were a lot of times when he would be at the rink when he wasn't supposed to be at the rink."

Hasbargen said it wasn't uncommon for him to open the building in the morning and see the ice, which he had left in pristine condition after resurfacing it and locking up for the night, all carved up.

Oshie.

"I don't how he was getting in there, but I knew somebody was letting him in there," Hasbargen said.

Said Oshie: "We might have had a key we weren't supposed to have."

Warroad's superb class of seniors tasted success at every level. As Bantams, they played in both the VFW and Minnesota Hockey state tournaments, a rare achievement for even the largest of Minnesota's youth programs. The arrival of Oshie only bolstered an already winning lineup, and the Warriors won the state Class 1A championship in 2003 with several of its eight sophomores making heavy contributions (Oshie was named to the all-tournament team). The Warriors were unceremoniously bounced from title contention in 2004 with a 2–1 overtime loss to Orono in the state tournament quarterfinals.

The hangover from that loss carried into the summer, when rumors of top players such as Kyle Hardwick, Eric Olimb, and Josh Brodeen, among others, leaving school early to play in the United States Hockey League or other junior-level leagues were rampant.

Oshie said there was even talk he was headed to southern Minnesota and Shattuck–St. Mary's, the private school hockey factory in Faribault with alumni that include the likes of NHL superstar Sidney Crosby.

"I remember me and Kyle getting together that summer," Oshie said. "He said, 'Hey, are you going to go?' I said, 'I don't know, I don't really want to. Are you going to go?' We both said, 'No, let's stay and go win a championship.'"

Added Hardwick: "Our whole mission that year was to come back and take care of unfinished business because we lost the year before."

Totino-Grace, a private high school located just north of Minneapolis in Fridley, couldn't match Warroad's unbeaten record, high-end talent, or rich hockey tradition. The school was founded in 1966, more than two decades after Warroad had established its storied program. The Eagles won a state Class 1A title in 2002 and had finished as runner-up in 1995. Despite a lineup loaded with talented seniors, Totino-Grace started the

is best known for scoring what is believed to be a single-game state record twelve goals in a January 6, 1948, matchup against Thief River Falls. Oshie's grandfather, Alvin "Buster" Oshie, was another standout player for Warroad in the late 1940s.

Those family ties, along with years of incessant coaxing from Henry Boucha, T. J.'s second cousin, led to Oshie finally moving with his father from Everett, Washington, to Warroad for his sophomore season.

"Instantly, I fell in love with the town, fell in love with the guys," Oshie said. "Back in Washington, in the ninth grade, I was the only kid in the school of twelve hundred kids who not only played hockey but probably who knew how to skate. I was spending three hours, minimum, in the car each day just getting back and forth from practice.

"It was a really cool thing in Warroad, having all the ice you wanted for free."

Hasbargen managed Warroad's hockey arena, which was built in 1993 for $3.5 million, has 1,454 theater-style seats (a capacity nearly equaling the northern Minnesota town's population of about 1,700), and is named the Gardens. As the high school coach and rink manager, it was easy for Hasbargen to monitor Oshie's daily activities, since it might have

BLONDS HAVE MORE FUN
Warroad's tournament success seemingly hinged on power of bleach

Players who wore odd numbers were required to become blonds. The even-numbered guy had to dye their hair black.

The bumblebee look not only matched Warroad's uniform colors but also appeased the team's moms heading into the 2005 state tournament.

"Some of the moms on the team wouldn't let their kids go blond," said T. J. Oshie, a senior co-captain that season. "So half the guys would go black, and half the guys would go blond."

Back when Warroad made the state tournament in 2003, all the Warriors' players, in a show of team unity, style, and goofiness, bleached their hair blond. Warroad won the state Class 1A title that year.

The Warriors reached state again in 2004. No hair was colored. Warroad lost in the quarterfinals.

Back at the state tournament in 2005, Warroad players weren't going to make the same mistake.

"We tried to make it so every other player, when they called their name and they skated out to the blue line, had a different color," Oshie said.

Warroad's "blonds"—Oshie among them—presented a wide range of shades, from platinum to dirty to pumpkin-esque.

"You could tell the guys who got it done by their mom or their mom's hairstylist and the guys who did it themselves," said Kyle Hardwick, a senior defenseman and co-captain. "The ones who did it themselves ended up with an orange-ish color."

Oshie had a big edge over most of his teammates in terms of being well coiffed. His mom, Tina, was a hairdresser who owned a high-end salon in the Everett, Washington, area.

"She was in town for sectionals [in 2003], and I think it might have even been her idea," Oshie said. "She ended up doing a lot of the guys' hair. A lot of the more professional-looking platinum dye jobs, I imagine it was Mom who did those."

Other teams have tried the blond look for the state tournament, with fleeting success. Blaine, a tournament qualifier for six straight years starting in the mid-2000s, took a shining to the bleached look. The Bengals never advanced past the semifinals in that stretch.

Mahtomedi reached the state tournament in 2009, 2010, 2015, and 2017. Each time the Zephyrs went as blonds. They never reached a title game, either.

In 2018, Mahtomedi coach Jeff Poeschl instituted a strict no-bleach policy. "We're here to play hockey," he said when asked about the break in tradition.

The Zephyrs, as nonblonds, lost in overtime to eventual small-school champion Orono in the semifinals.

It's worth noting that Warroad, back as blonds [well, at least half the players], won the state championship again in 2005.

~LRN~

Warroad players dyed their hair blond and black in a display of team spirit—and a stab at good luck—before the 2005 Class 1A tournament, which ended with them celebrating a double-overtime win over Totino-Grace in the championship. Photo by Richard Tsong-Taatarii/*Minneapolis Star Tribune*

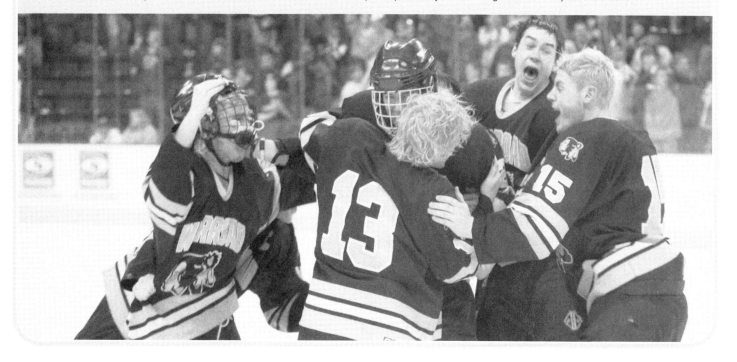

Goaltender Dave Norling and defenseman Brett Miller (left) helped lead a tight Totino-Grace defense in 2005. Here they drop to the ice to block a shot from Warroad's Ben Bengston in the Class 1A championship game. Photo by Mike Thill/*Let's Play Hockey*

2004–05 season with a 2–3 record punctuated by a 6–0 shellacking at the hands of section rival Breck.

Senior goaltender Dave Norling wasn't pleased with the poor start, much less his play against Breck. He saw firsthand the team's talent every day in practice. The potential was there for greatness, Norling thought, fueling his frustration. He wasn't shy about expressing his feelings.

"I personally stopped everyone and said, 'Hey, guys, we've got to figure this out,'" Norling said. "After that, something just clicked."

Erik Bredesen, a defensive back, and Joe Bennek, the back-up quarterback, were top forwards who missed the start of the hockey season as Totino-Grace's football team rolled to a state championship. An early-season injury to first-line wing Dan Malone, as pure a skater and scorer as the Eagles had, also contributed to the slow start.

After the loss to Breck, and with all his best players now in the lineup, Loahr adjusted the team's top forward lines. Hoody, a lifelong winger, moved to center between Bredesen and Malone, both of whom had played center most of their careers. All three accepted their new roles without complaint.

"You can have the best group of players, but if they don't get

along and don't want to work together, you ain't going to win anything," Loahr said. "But these guys, they were willing to do what we asked them to do."

With the defensive-minded Bennek anchoring the second line, the continued maturation at defense of hulking 6-foot-3, 210-pound Brian Schack (a converted forward who emerged as a power-play sniper), and superb play of fellow defensemen Brett Miller and Aaron Mathison, the Eagles had all but erected a brick wall in front of Norling and fellow goaltender Andy Houdek.

Totino-Grace shut out four of its next five opponents after the embarrassing loss to Breck. Defense became a source of pride. The Eagles' running count of goals against was posted in the locker room. They allowed no more than three in any game as they reeled off twenty-five straight victories (allowing twenty-four goals in those games) heading into the championship showdown with Warroad.

The Warriors were heavy favorites, but there was no shortage of confidence among the Eagles.

"When you are on a twenty-five-game win streak, you know you are not going to lose," said Bennek, who took Loahr's pre-game speech to heart and broke his nose against Warroad.

"Never once did it cross my mind that we were going to lose that championship game."

As emphasized by Hoody on the opening shift, Totino-Grace had no intention of handing the championship to Warroad. Each team held the lead at least once during three regulation periods that offered more twists and turns than a ride at Six Flags.

Most often, Hoody and Oshie were at the center of the action. In a span of about four minutes in the third period alone:

- Hoody blasted a shot off the crossbar, the puck bouncing straight forward and down before skidding between Mark Thiele's legs on its way back out of the crease.

- Oshie stole the puck from Brett Miller at center ice and, catching Totino-Grace on a line change, raced in on a partial breakaway. Oshie tried unsuccessfully to fire the puck through Norling's legs. "I came out and challenged him and prayed to god he shot," Norling said, "because I knew if he made a move I was done." Breakaways were Oshie's specialty. He would convince Warroad's goaltenders to stay after practice to work on them, stopping only when Hasbargen backed the Zamboni out on the ice.

- BOOM. Oshie hammered an unsuspecting Hoody with a hard hit in the corner, sending the Totino-Grace superpest to the ice and Oshie to the penalty box for elbowing.

- Hoody scored from the top of the slot on a quick snapshot midway through the third period. The goal broke a 1–1 tie and ignited a run of four goals in a span of 6:05.

Totino-Grace sophomore Tony McDonald ended the scoring flurry and forced overtime with his deflection in the slot with 2:56 left in the third that tied the score at four.

And then the fun really started.

With less than two minutes left in the first overtime, Warroad players raised their hands in celebration as Ben Bengston swatted the puck behind Norling. But the puck never crossed the goal line, and Norling alertly reached behind his back and swept it out of harm's way. The final minute of the period saw Hoody slam Olimb into the end boards, then race to the other end and cross-check Oshie a couple of times in front of the Eagles' net.

Confusion reigned early in the second overtime when Warroad's Andy Brandt flung his stick against the boards in disgust after a Bredesen shot slipped behind goaltender Mark Thiele. But the puck had hit the right goalpost and slid forward toward the backside of Thiele, who sat on it to end the threat.

"I think I made it to center ice celebrating before I realized it wasn't a goal," Norling said.

As the second overtime continued, the defenses loosened. Scoring chances came in rapid-fire succession: a one-timer by Olimb from the point and rebound that Oshie scooped and sent over the glass, a quick shot from close range by McDonald that was stopped by a sprawling Thiele, another save by Thiele on a hard shot from Malone, a sprawling Norling stopping Bengston on a breakaway by tossing his stick aside, then diving and throwing both hands at the oncoming puck.

Oshie was the trailer on the Bengston breakaway, and as he dug for the rebound at the side of the net, in came Hoody. BOOM. Oshie was sent airborne before sprawling face first onto the ice. This time, it was Hoody who was sent to the penalty box.

"I had a lot of penalty minutes, not that I am proud of that," said Hoody, who stood 5 foot 9 and weighed in at about 170. "But if you look at the penalties, they weren't for hooking and tripping. They weren't lazy penalties. I was a little rough. I'd like to think that I set the mentality that 'Hey, if you are going to go into the corner against us, you are going to get hit.'"

Totino-Grace coaches and players, to a man, never have criticized Hoody for his untimely penalty.

Totino-Grace's Dave Norling makes a sprawling save on a breakaway attempt by Warroad's Ben Bengston during the second overtime of the title game. Photo by Scott A. Schneider/*Let's Play Hockey*

206

"He probably crossed the line a few too many times that game," Bennek said. "But that's just the way he played."

With Hoody watching from the penalty box, Totino-Grace had a golden opportunity to end the marathon game when Malone stole the puck from Hardwick and raced to the other end on a two-on-one. Malone elected to shoot, and his stick snapped, the blade hitting Thiele's leg pads as the puck skidded wide right.

As Warroad's power play continued, a faceoff was set in the Totino-Grace end to the right of Norling. In the overtime periods, Warroad was playing mostly two lines to Totino-Grace's three. In an attempt to give his forwards a few more seconds of rest, Hasbargen started making late personnel changes, exchanging one forward for another at the last possible moment. On this occasion, he pulled Brodeen off the ice for Marvin, the sophomore sensation who centered the Warriors' second line.

Marvin lined up at left wing, directly in front of Norling. Oshie, who had been winning faceoffs all afternoon by pulling the puck back to his defensemen, had a moment of inspiration as he glided in for the draw against Malone.

"I kind of had this flash of this memory when I was in Spokane, Washington, when I was in Pee Wees," Oshie said. "We were in the semis of a big tournament, and I pushed it forward through the other guy, and I scored high glove right off the faceoff.

"I just wanted to try it again."

Oshie didn't execute his plan as he had hoped. He did chip the puck forward past Malone, but it slid too far. As Oshie tried to reach for it, Norling skated out of the crease and shoved his stick at the puck.

"I could see the play developing, and I saw the puck laying there," Norling said. "I thought my only play was to try to poke it away from Oshie. I missed, and he got there first."

A diving Oshie swatted at the puck just ahead of Norling,

sending it through the slot—between two Totino-Grace defenders and onto a wide-open Marvin's stick. Marvin only needed to deposit the puck into an open net, a routine play but hardly a gimme, given the circumstances.

"I had no idea that was coming," Marvin said. "If you watch the replay, I was basically just standing there watching. But that was classic T. J. He used to do that in other situations, tap it by the guy and basically just dance around him."

Looking back, Marvin is relieved he didn't have time to overthink his game-winning shot.

"They say with deer hunters, sometimes it is easier to shoot if you don't know the deer is coming," Marvin said. "Not having time to think was probably a big advantage."

The goal, securing Warroad's 5–4 victory and the only unbeaten season in the program's history, touched off a wildly unorchestrated celebration. Warriors players leaping off the bench and onto the ice didn't know whether to mob Marvin, Thiele, or the nearest black-and-gold jersey. So they did all three.

"It was crazy," said Oshie, who went on to achieve Olympic stardom and win a Stanley Cup with the Washington Capitals. "I've watched the video of that celebration, and I remember at one point I am kind of getting up from a pile, and you can see I am just looking around. I didn't know what to do. I didn't know who to hug or where to go.

"I was lost in the excitement."

Bennek, the bloodied Eagles captain who had his nose reset after the game, said, "There were a lot of tears shed. I don't think it was so much because we lost on that stage. I think it was just guys being upset because we were done.

"It was that close knit of a group."

~LRN~

Totino-Grace defenseman Brent Miller (left) and goaltender Dave Norling were overcome by emotion after losing the 2005 Class 1A championship game 4–3 in double overtime to Warroad. Photo by Scott A. Schneider/*Let's Play Hockey*

FORGOTTEN MISFIT

Virginia spent decades trying to climb out of neighboring Eveleth's shadow

FINALLY!

Blue Devils advance to first-ever state tournament, topping Hibbing to win Section 7A Championship

Three-goal third period lifts Virginia/MIB to 5-3 victory over rival Bluejackets; five different players score as balance, depth once again pays off

By BRIAN MILLER
Staff Writer

DULUTH—Virginia, your wait is over. Your Blue Devils are finally going to the state hockey tournament.

Thanks to a never-say-die mentality and an explosive three-goal third period, the Virginia/Mountain Iron-Buhl boys' hockey team rallied to down Hibbing 5-3 in the Section 7A Championship Game before a packed, electric DECC in Duluth Wednesday.

As the final horn sounded, the Blue Devils piled on goaltender Logan Hoche, who stopped 23 shots in the victory, behind their net in jubilation.

"Forget a monkey, this is like getting King Kong off (Virginia's) back," said Kyle Altobelli, who netted what proved to be the game-winner in the third.

"I never had a doubt in my mind we were going to come back and win this game. This is an unbelievable feeling."

Added standout senior Matt Niskanen, "I'm speechless. It feels great. This team proved it had the character and guts to do this. This is for the whole town of Virginia and the great players and teams they've had over the years that never had this opportunity.

"This is everything I've ever dreamed of. We did it together. This was a total team effort tonight. Hibbing had their time. This is our time."

Trailing 3-2 after the Bluejackets scored a pair of goals in the first 2:01 of the second period, the Blue Devils returned the favor to Hibbing, which had rallied from a one-goal deficit in upset Virginia/MI-B in last year's section semifinals. The two-time defending section champion Bluejackets also eliminated the Blue Devils two seasons ago.

Virginia players huddled in celebration of the long-suffering program's first section title—which sent the Blue Devils to their inaugural state tournament. Photo by Mark Sauer/*Mesabi Tribune*

Eveleth great Willard Ikola was visiting his hometown long after the Golden Bears' hockey dynasty had faded and found himself in a bar listening to lubricated locals discussing the decline.

"One of them said, 'When the Eveleth boys went and married Virginia girls, that's what screwed up Eveleth hockey—all the mixed marriages with Virginia,'" Ikola recalled.

Poor Virginia. Just six miles north of Eveleth on Highway 53 but years behind in hockey. The Blue Devils' dormant high school program restarted in 1954–55, by which time Eveleth owned five state championships. Miners Memorial Arena was built in 1957, thirty-five years after the Eveleth Hippodrome.

The breakthrough just wouldn't come. Not in 1975, despite being ranked number one and featuring studs such as Keith Hendrickson. And not in section final appearances in 1991 and 1998.

In 2004–05, Hendrickson coached a promising Virginia/Mountain Iron-Buhl team led by senior defenseman Matt Niskanen and bolstered by seven freshmen and sophomores.

A mix of old and new started with the top line of senior wings Kyle Altobelli and Devin Ceglar centered by freshman Nico Sacchetti.

Niskanen, the lone Mountain Iron student on the hockey roster, quarterbacked the Rangers to the football state tournament in the fall of 2004. He brought those intangibles to the ice for the combined hockey program.

Maybe this would be the team, Hendrickson thought.

"As a player that never made it, it kind of haunted me," Hendrickson said. "But I didn't want to use that as motivation because I didn't want to put undue pressure on the kids."

Facing Hibbing in the Class 1A, Section 7 final was motivation enough. The Bluejackets had ended Virginia/Mountain Iron-Buhl's past two seasons in the semifinals.

Two Bluejackets goals in the second period gave them a 3–2 lead.

"It was 'Oh crap, here we go again,'" Niskanen said. "But the ninth- and tenth-graders hadn't been through that, so it didn't seem like they had any doubt. We went out and played our best period of the year."

Virginia/Mountain Iron-Buhl rallied for a 5–3 victory, earning a team from the Queen City of the North a hockey state tournament trip fifty years in the making.

"I don't remember thinking there was a curse," Niskanen said. "But it was a frickin' mountain. And we finally did it."

Hendrickson received 350 cards and emails after the Hibbing victory. And several fans raised a toast in the Blue Devils' honor.

"There was a time in those days that if you went downtown, you didn't have to pay for a drink," Hendrickson said.

The Blue Devils lost both games in St. Paul, but Niskanen said, "Anyone who grows up here wants to play Division I college hockey and play in the NHL. But the first goal is they want to go to state before they move on. It's one of the coolest things ever."

Old grudges gave way to reality in 2020–21, when Eveleth and Virginia merged and became Rock Ridge High School. Their athletics teams are called the Wolverines.

Hendrickson described the consolidation as "a sign of the times" on the Iron Range, where mining and related jobs are no longer plentiful and populations have dwindled. He believes "the priority should be education" and supports the new school.

But a twinge of sadness remains.

"Yeah, it's sentimental, emotional," Hendrickson said. "It's not a question of right or wrong. It's just a feeling you get. Those rivalries were a big part of the tradition."

~DL~

CAPTAIN CONFIDENCE

CORVIN KIEGER CRETIN–DERHAM HALL'S ETERNAL OPTIMIST

DATES	LOCATION	ATTENDANCE	CLASS 2A CHAMPIONSHIP
MARCH 8–11	XCEL ENERGY CENTER, ST. PAUL	125,201	CRETIN–DERHAM HALL 7, GRAND RAPIDS 0
			CLASS 1A CHAMPIONSHIP
			ST. THOMAS ACADEMY 4, DULUTH MARSHALL 3

Did you know? Instant replay was used to review goals, or potential goals, for the first time in the 2006 championship.

IT'S A GREAT DAY TO BE A RAIDER.

That's what Corvin Kieger told his teammates, his coaches, and anyone else willing to listen.

He said it over and over and over again.

It's a great day to be a Raider.

The occasion was the state Class 2A championship game. The opponent was Grand Rapids, the legendary program from the northern reaches of the state. Tradition was on Grand Rapids' side; the Thunderhawks had more state championships (three) than Cretin–Derham Hall had state tournament appearances (two).

Yet Kieger, a senior defenseman, was convinced Saturday, March 11, 2006, would be a good day for the Raiders. Correction: make that a *great* day.

"That was his slogan that day," Cretin–Derham Hall coach Jim O'Neill said. "He kept saying it, and we believed it."

Kieger was the Raiders' leader. He kept the team loose. He kept the team focused. He organized the off-ice gatherings. He made everyone, no matter their role, feel important. He always knew just what to say and when to say it.

"He's the best captain I have ever had in any sport," said O'Neill, who was the Raiders' head hockey coach for thirty years and head baseball coach for eighteen. "He had such a good read on the guys on the team and the pulse of how we were feeling."

The Raiders were a relaxed bunch that championship Saturday. Kieger remembers the movie *Armageddon* playing on the TV monitors in the locker room before the game. The campy Bruce Willis and Ben Affleck flick that pits a group of misfit oil drillers turned astronauts against an asteroid "the size of Texas" racing toward Earth wasn't so much a metaphor for the Raiders and their Herculean task that night as it was a light-hearted diversion.

"It was whimsical, but at the same time it had that whole serious save-the-world story," Kieger said.

How loose were the Raiders? Among other activities, Kieger, senior forward Ben Kinne, and junior defenseman Ryan McDonagh engaged in a "hydration contest" before the game.

"I think he just did a great job of keeping everybody calm and relaxed and not getting tensed up and trying to do too much," McDonagh said about Kieger, who was also a baseball star. "Everything was so positive with him. He was a huge reason why our team continued to gain confidence."

On the ice for warmups, the Raiders looked up at the massive Xcel Energy Center crowd and couldn't help but notice the fans were clad mostly in Grand Rapids orange. Dating back to the late 1960s, public schools from the north almost always had been the tournament's fan favorites, especially when competing against a metro program. Metro private schools received even less support. This was no exception.

"Holy cow, was there orange in that arena," Kieger said. "If nine out of ten weren't wearing orange . . . I don't know what the numbers were."

Just as Kieger was assessing the size of the pro-Thunderhawks crowd, he felt a tap on his breezers. It was Kinne.

"Corvin, we are going to shut up sixteen thousand people tonight," Kinne said.

Kieger, the eternal optimist, drank in the comment with a huge grin. That's what he liked to hear.

It's a great day to be a Raider.

Before private schools were allowed in the state tournament, and long before merging with the all-girls school Derham Hall in 1987, Cretin had been something of a hockey power. An all-boys Catholic school located five miles southwest of downtown St. Paul, Cretin won eleven private school state championships from 1949 through 1963.

More recently, Cretin–Derham Hall had become a destination school for elite football and baseball players. Major League Baseball Hall of Famer Paul Molitor played for the Raiders, as did three-time American League batting champion Joe Mauer and NFL quarterbacks Steve Walsh and Chris Weinke. With so much talent streaming through those programs, Cretin, and

RIGHT: Captain Corvin Kieger provided leadership and inspiration for Cretin–Derham Hall heading into the 2006 Class 2A championship game. Here he celebrates his third-period goal during the 7–0 rout of Grand Rapids. Photo by Bruce Bisping/*Minneapolis Star Tribune*

BELOW: Cretin–Derham Hall forward Chris Hickey (7) scored the opening goal in all three of the Raiders' 2006 state tournament games and finished with an event-best six in all. Photo by Mike Thill/*Let's Play Hockey*

later Cretin–Derham Hall, became a perennial state power in football (appearing in seven big-school championships and winning titles in 1999 and 2009) and baseball (winning eleven state titles between 1981 and 2007).

Hockey talent didn't flock to the school like the top-end athletes in the other major sports, however, and O'Neill's teams typically consisted of athletes who were football and baseball phenoms first, serviceable hockey players second.

There was one notable exception to that rule in 2006, when twelve baseball players dotted the hockey team's lineup. McDonagh's superior athleticism (he's the nephew of Walsh, an NFL quarterback for ten seasons) made him a standout in football, baseball, and hockey. But he gave up football after his sophomore season as it became more and more apparent that hockey was the sport that would take him the furthest.

"When he skated, his skates made a different sound than everyone else's," O'Neill said, adding that he had never seen a player who could move laterally as quickly or smoothly as McDonagh. "I'm sure the scouts noticed that, too."

The 6-foot-1, 195-pound McDonagh already had committed to play collegiately at Wisconsin by the end of his junior season when he was named to the *Minneapolis Star Tribune's* All-Metro first team. More than a smooth, powerful skater, McDonagh, who would be a first-round NHL draft pick in 2007, possessed an uncanny ability to read the ice, then anticipate and create plays. His competitiveness, even in practice, was off the charts.

"He's the kind of guy if you beat him once, you remembered it because he is as competitive as you are," said Chris Hickey, a hard-driven goal scorer and one of the few players who could match McDonagh's will to win.

McDonagh and Hickey, the Raiders' top scorer, made each other—and their teammates—better every day with one-on-one battles so intense their massive, ice-shaking collisions threatened to break the tectonic plates deep underneath St. Paul's Highland Arena, their home rink.

"He was one of the most competitive kids I ever played with at the high school level," McDonagh said about Hickey, a running back on the football team. "Practice was an all-out battle with him when you were defending him in drills."

Naturally, McDonagh and Hickey welcomed the Raiders' attempt to beef up their schedule for the 2005–06 season. Cretin–Derham Hall, for years a member of the milquetoast St. Paul City Conference, applied for membership in nine other conferences in a quest to consistently play tougher teams in all sports. The Raiders were rejected by all nine leagues and placed in the Suburban East Conference by the Minnesota State High School League.

"As a new team in the conference, it helped us play with a chip on our shoulder," McDonagh said.

The Raiders, playing then powerhouse programs such as White Bear Lake, Roseville, and Woodbury twice each, won the Suburban East with a 14–2 record.

"Night in and night out, there were no easy games," said Kinne. "I don't remember us blowing out anybody. Every game was a tight game. I think that is what really helped us.

"Even going into the third period of that state championship game, we knew how to win those tight games."

Grand Rapids, led by high-scoring forward and future first-round NHL draft pick Patrick White, stunned heavily favored Hill-Murray 3–2 in the semifinals to reach the championship. The loss was just the second of the year for the Pioneers.

The other pretournament favorite was Blaine, which rode a twenty-two-game unbeaten streak into its semifinal against Cretin–Derham Hall. Hickey, who had opened the scoring and finished with two goals (bringing him to thirty-three on the season) in a 5–2 quarterfinal triumph over Eagan, repeated the feat with a first-goal, two-goal effort in a 4–2 win over the Bengals in an exceptionally physical game.

"The biggest hit was one on me," Kieger said. "It was a line change, and I thought I had breakaway coming down the right side. I had a really good breakaway move that I never got to use, and I was thinking about that when Ricky Doriott, their 6-foot-5 defenseman, stepped into me.

"Man, I didn't have a chance."

Kieger played the rest of the tournament with a broken rib.

After two dominating periods, including yet another game-opening goal from Hickey and one from McDonagh, the Raiders led Grand Rapids 2–0. The Thunderhawks had managed just a combined six shots compared to twenty-two for the Raiders through two periods, yet O'Neill was in an uneasy mood in the locker room before the third.

"We were dominating the game, and it was only 2–0," he said. "They get one [goal], and it changes everything."

So O'Neill asked for a volunteer. "We need a big goal. Who's got it?" he said.

Kieger was a defenseman known for his smart, steady, physical play. Not for his goal scoring. But remember, he had a good feeling about this day, this game. He had a good feeling about the third period, too.

"I said, 'Coach, I got this,'" Kieger said.

Less than three minutes into the third period, Kieger, who rarely rushed the puck, took off down the side boards and into the Grand Rapids end. He fought off a check and whipped a bad-angle shot at the net. Somehow, the puck squirted past Thunderhawks goaltender Reidar Jensen and into the goal.

Kieger was so excited he didn't wait for his teammates to gather for a celebration, instead opting to race up the ice and zoom past the Cretin–Derham Hall bench.

"I pretty much had to go straight to O'Neill and tell him I told him so," Kieger said.

Energized by their leader, the Raiders scored three more goals in the next 4:31. Kinne added one to make it 4–0, then big Joe Bonfe, the hulking but light-scoring defenseman, freight-trained a Grand Rapids player to the ice seconds before heading off on a most improbable end-to-end rush and goal. It was just the fourth goal of the season for the 6-foot-3, 220-pound Bonfe, and the Raiders led 5–0 early in the third period.

Cretin-Derham Hall players bring their celebration—and Class 2A championship trophy—to their fans after winning the 2006 title. Photo by Mike Thill/*Let's Play Hockey*

The game, effectively, was over.

"He was my defense partner, and I had seen him put big hits on a lot of kids," McDonagh said about Bonfe. "But that one was by far the biggest. I think that goal buried any kind of will Grand Rapids had in them, any kind of hope."

Hickey scored his second goal of the game and sixth of the tournament (the most by any player that year), and McDonagh added a goal late in the third to complete the 7–0 triumph. Grand Rapids mustered just two shots on goal in the final period, eight for the game. The margin of victory remains tied for the largest in a championship game, matching International Falls' 7–0 win over Bloomington in 1965, Warroad's 10–3 win over Red Wing in 1996, and Elk River's 8–1 win over Moorhead in 2001.

After the game clock hit zero, after the traditional helmet-glove-and-stick-toss mayhem, Raiders players started to collect their gear and their thoughts. O'Neill, who watched his players celebrate from the bench, had tears in his eyes as Kieger glided up and gave his coach a hug. The rest of the Raiders followed suit.

"He was a special kid, mature beyond his years," O'Neill said about his captain. "We were lucky to have him."

The Raiders went to their high school gymnasium after the game for a celebration with their parents and fans. Afterward, O'Neill told his players they were welcome to come over to his house, within walking distance of the school, for pizza and more camaraderie.

"All twenty guys showed up," O'Neill said. "I'll never forget that."

The Raiders ate their pizza and, late into the night, watched the championship game they had just played in, roaring with excitement yet again when Kieger scored his goal.

"Someone had taped the game," McDonagh said. "But we really didn't even need to watch the video. We could have replayed every minute in our heads."

Turns out Kieger had been right all along.

It had been a great day to be a Raider.

~*LRN*~

OLIVER'S TWIST

COACH'S LATE-SEASON GOALTENDING CHANGE RANKLED SOME ROSEAU RESIDENTS

DATES	LOCATION	ATTENDANCE	CLASS 2A CHAMPIONSHIP
MARCH 7–10	XCEL ENERGY CENTER, ST. PAUL	124,348	ROSEAU 5, GRAND RAPIDS 1
			CLASS 1A CHAMPIONSHIP
			HERMANTOWN 4, DULUTH MARSHALL 1

 Hermantown, a Duluth suburb playing in its sixth state tournament, capped a 29-0-1 season with its first state title.

BORN IN WINNIPEG, Manitoba, Scott Oliver grew up playing junior hockey, then coaching for sixteen years at the University of Minnesota Crookston. He thought he had experienced passionate hockey.

Then he became varsity head coach at Roseau.

So revered is the opportunity to play for Roseau's high school, no youth teams are permitted to don the school's green and white.

To earn a framed picture on the Wall of Fame inside Memorial Arena, players must be collegiate all-Americans, national team members, Olympians, or NHL players. There are thirty-two so far. Trophy cases below offer tributes to seven state champions, the pinnacle of thirty-four tournament appearances.

Decades of hockey tradition from a town of about 2,500 people.

The tiny town with giant hockey expectations fit Oliver like a baked skate when he arrived in the spring of 2003. In his second season (2004–05), he coached sons of former NHL players Aaron Broten and Butsy Erickson. That season's Bantam team, coached by Broten, included Oliver's own son, Nick.

Yep, Oliver loved his job—even when folks questioned his decisions.

"I'm at the grocery store filling my cart, saying hello to some people," Oliver said. "Then I notice this lady refusing to look at me or acknowledge me. I'm thinking, 'Do I have a cold sore or something?' I find out later she is the aunt of our third-string goalie. You're not going to make everyone happy."

Oliver, who in 2006 directed the Rams to their first state tournament appearance in six seasons, said he "didn't have to reinvent the culture or the program."

But refining was needed. Oliver instilled some of the same values he had used to coach Glyndon-Felton's football team to the Class C title in 1985.

"We became more disciplined, grittier," said Oliver, who played linebacker in the Canadian Football League with the Winnipeg Blue Bombers and Toronto Argonauts. "We played harder, tougher."

Oliver's approach meshed with sophomore defenseman Aaron Ness. A 150-pound dynamo, Ness impressed teammates with quick feet, offensive skills, and competitive zeal.

"I hated practicing against him because if you beat him once, he got so mad," said Tyler Landman, then a sophomore forward.

Roseau began the 2006–07 season with state championship aspirations. Chances cannot be wasted when you're opting up to Class 2A and some schools' enrollment numbers are larger than your town's population.

"We wanted to do something special," Ness said. "We were all focused on winning."

Setting lineups and selling players on their roles wasn't easy for Oliver, who said, "Everyone in Roseau thinks they are the next Division I college or NHL player."

Oliver's most scrutinized move came late in the season.

The Rams lost just twice all season—both times against Moorhead. With a likely showdown against the Spuds in the Section 8 playoffs drawing close, Oliver changed goaltenders.

Sophomore Mike Lee started the regular season finale against Grand Rapids and earned a 3–1 victory despite his Rams being outshot 45–40. The performance solidified Lee as the playoff starter. Senior Alex Bjerk, the state tournament starter a year earlier, became the backup.

"It was a pretty controversial decision in a small town," Nick Oliver said.

Bjerk was in goal for both Moorhead losses, and Scott Oliver felt "we had to adjust. Sometimes players play differently in front of a different goalie."

Lee brought athletic ability and smarts, having played quarterback in football and shortstop in baseball. And he "loved having it on his shoulders."

"He had a calm presence," Landman said. "When he was in the net, guys played well."

Sure enough, a trip to St. Paul went through Moorhead. This time, Bjerk rooted Lee on from the bench as Roseau prevailed 1–0.

To create more compelling semifinal matchups, the 2007

state tournament was the first to seed the top four teams. Roseau earned the number-two seed and faced newcomer Woodbury in Thursday's first quarterfinal.

Down 1–0 early, Roseau pulled away for a 7–2 victory. Ness assisted on the first three goals. Nick Oliver, one year removed from watching the state tournament from the seats, scored twice.

Roseau was the only seeded team to survive the quarterfinals.

"Whatever hockey gods there are were with us that weekend," Lee said.

Rochester Century came next. A Dustin Moser shorthanded goal followed by a Kurt Weston power-play tally made it 2–0 at first intermission. Lee stopped all but one of Century's thirteen third-period shots in a 3–1 victory.

Roseau would face Grand Rapids in a rare all-northern final. But first, something bigger than hockey beckoned.

On Saturday morning, Scott Oliver and his wife, Denise, attended a funeral for their twenty-five-year-old nephew Chad Allen, a marine sergeant killed in February in Iraq. He was laid to rest in Maple Lake, about an hour northwest of the Twin Cities. Nick Oliver made the quiet drive with his parents.

"I realized how fortunate I was to be playing a game with the reality of war around you," Nick Oliver said.

Upon their return, father and son focused on hockey. Scott Oliver wore a button on his jacket during the game in tribute to his fallen nephew.

Roseau gained control of the title game and led 2–0 after two periods. Then Landman scored twice in the third period, during which Lee made eleven of his twenty-eight saves.

Hockey-mad Roseau celebrated a 5–1 victory and its first state title in eight years.

Players hadn't just added to the Rams' tradition. They had benefited from it during Wednesday-night "Rams versus Lambs" pickup games, organized by Billy Lund (class of 1990) and featuring fellow state champions Derrick Byfuglien and Phil Lund (both class of 1999).

Landman said the old-timers would "hook you and hold you. It was competitive. They beat us most of the time."

Losers kept the "Lambs" title for a week. But each side won the other's respect.

"Before we left for the state tournament, they shook our hands and said 'Good luck,'" Landman said.

"Those games helped push us over the top," Lee said.

~DL~

Ryan Larsen's rebound goal staked Roseau to a 1-0 first-period lead in the Class 2A state championship game, much to the dismay of Grand Rapids defenseman Corey Kosak and goalie Reidar Jensen—and Thunderhawk fans. Photo by Sherri LaRose-Chiglo/*St. Paul Pioneer Press*

CLIQUES FINALLY CLICK

"CLIQUEY" HILL-MURRAY PROVED IT COULD PUT DIFFERENCES ASIDE FOR BIGGER GOAL

DATES	LOCATION	ATTENDANCE	CLASS 2A CHAMPIONSHIP
MARCH 5–8	XCEL ENERGY CENTER ST. PAUL	129,643	HILL-MURRAY 3, EDINA 0
			CLASS 1A CHAMPIONSHIP
			ST. THOMAS ACADEMY 5, DULUTH MARSHALL 1

 Defenseman Joe Gleason scored Edina's first tournament goal on an assist from goalie Derrick Caschetta.

SCRIMMAGES on the final two Fridays in July 2007 brought the heat to Hill-Murray's summer workouts. The captains divided players in grades ten to twelve into two teams and got after it.

"Most games in the summer, it's like, 'Guys, it's OK to hit a little bit,'" head coach Bill Lechner said. "That group took it more serious. They were on a mission."

Skill. Size. Toughness. A little mean. The performances left Lechner and assistant coach Pat Schafhauser in agreement.

"We looked at each other and said, 'We're going to be pretty good,'" Schafhauser said.

Not that anybody else noticed. Edina and Roseau used up all the buzz during the 2007–08 season.

Edina boasted "the Brothers," a group of longtime youth-hockey teammates supplemented by the return of prodigal son Anders Lee from St. Thomas Academy. Lee and fellow forwards Zach Budish and Marshall Everson formed the Hornets' unstoppable first line.

Defending champion Roseau, led by brilliant offensive-defenseman Aaron Ness, went undefeated in the regular season and garnered weekly stories in the nationally distributed *Hockey News* magazine.

Hill-Murray players harrumphed. *We can play with them. And we can beat them.* A two-word reply from their coaches became the season motto: "Prove it."

First, the Pioneers had to prove they could get along. Despite returning ten forwards and six defensemen, Hill-Murray was no band of brothers to start.

"It was a cliquey team," said Joe Phillippi, senior goalie. "There were about three different groups. But toward the end of the season, we put it aside and put what we wanted first."

A mid-January locker room blowout cleared the air.

"We could hear them, and there was about a ten- to fifteen-minute verbal argument," Lechner said. "We listened and heard the captains grab the situation."

Lechner and Schafhauser intervened to ensure the matter was settled, but they felt an important moment had arrived.

Phillippi and fellow senior captains Ryan Furne and Bo Dolan asserted themselves.

"We had some guys who didn't like their role," Dolan said. "But we said, 'Guys, it's not that hard. Show up and play hard. Table everything else.'"

Dolan backed his words with action. He requested the coaches pair him with fellow defenseman Dan Sova, a youth-hockey rival, to better the team.

"They were not best buds, but they were good teammates," Schafhauser said. "We could put them out there against anybody."

Down the stretch, Hill-Murray won eleven, tied once, and lost none. Awarded the number-four seed for the state tournament, the Pioneers opened against newcomer Lakeville South.

"That was the scariest game," Dolan said. "It's tough to find your feet when you step onto the ice at eighteen years old in front of eighteen thousand people."

A 3–0 victory meant a showdown with number-one Roseau and hopefully, as far as Phillippi was concerned, more action. He stopped all eighteen Lakeville South shots, then put a shot across Roseau's bow.

"I want a lot of shots from them," Phillippi told reporters. "I like stepping up in big games."

"I saw that in the paper and covered my eyes," Schafhauser said. "That was Flipper."

"I thought that quote showed his determination," Sova said.

Phillippi had plenty of help. Tournament darling Roseau, pride of northern Minnesota, had bugged the Pioneers all season. The Pioneers were ready.

"I looked around the locker room, and everybody was into it," Phillippi said. "It was like a pack of dogs."

And Ness was wearing Milk-Bone breezers.

"We knew if we got into Ness's head by being physical that they would fold," Sova said.

Ness, who measured 5 foot 10, 155 pounds, couldn't find much open ice. That's because wherever he went, the wing on his side and the center rolled toward him. More than installing a game plan, Hill-Murray coaches fostered a mindset.

"We said, 'When he's on the ice, go step on him. Go after

Hill-Murray goaltender Joe Phillippi took the sting out of the Edina Hornets' offense in a 3–0 victory in the Class 2A championship game. Phillippi, stopping this Anders Lee shot, anchored a defense that permitted just four goals in six postseason games. Photo by Bruce Bisping/*Minneapolis Star Tribune*

him—legally,'" Lechner said. "We were betting on the refs letting them play."

Hill-Murray stormed to a 2–0 lead.

"No one ever tried to do that to us," Ness said. "We couldn't adapt fast enough."

Moments after the horn sounded to end the first period, Isaac Kohls cross-checked Ness in the back.

"We weren't proud he did it, but I think anyone standing there would have been cross-checked," Dolan said. "This was our game."

Phillippi stopped thirty-four shots, and Hill-Murray won 6–2. Having spoiled a highly anticipated Edina/Roseau matchup, Pioneer coaches went to work finishing the job. They broke down video of the victory against Roseau until 3 AM. About four hours of sleep later, Lechner rose and began studying video of number-two Edina's semifinal victory.

Saturday's jersey color helped get players emotionally ready.

Black jerseys had been unveiled earlier in the season to commemorate twenty-five years since the 1982–83 Pioneers had won the program's first of two state tournament championships. Lechner was an assistant coach for the undefeated squad.

The Edina game marked the sixth time Hill-Murray wore the special third jerseys. And the Pioneers were 5–0 in them, including the Roseau upset.

"Those jerseys were almost their own pregame speech," Lechner said.

"In your head, it was almost like, 'This has to be a win,'" Furne said.

Furne helped Hill-Murray jump on Edina. He scored his fourth and fifth goals of the tournament, the latter with one second remaining in the first period.

On the back end, Dolan and Sova helped blank Edina's big line with another sterling defensive effort. The Pioneers permitted just four goals in six postseason games and never trailed.

"Dudes were selling out, blocking shots and clearing rebounds," Phillippi said.

Edina outshot Hill-Murray 31–26, but no puck beat Phillippi.

Hill-Murray won 3–0 and claimed its first state title since 1991.

"After we beat Edina, we went from ecstatic to tears," Dolan said. "I was sobbing because it was over. We did it, and we wouldn't have it any other way.

"There weren't any superstars. It was a collective effort. There truly wasn't a guy we could've done without," Dolan said.

The team later received white long-sleeved shirts that said it all: "Proved it."

~DL~

There were rumors that Eden Prairie star defenseman Nick Leddy might bolt to play elsewhere prior to the 2008–09 season. Instead, the team co-captain helped the school to its first championship, scoring a goal in each of the Eagles' three tournament games in 2009. Photo by Tim Kolehmainen/Breakdown Sports Media

ALL FOR ONE

NICK LEDDY HELPED UNIFY EDEN PRAIRIE'S RARE MIX OF SOPHOMORES, SENIORS

DATES	LOCATION	ATTENDANCE	CLASS 2A CHAMPIONSHIP
MARCH 11–14	XCEL ENERGY CENTER, ST. PAUL	116,690	EDEN PRAIRIE 3, MOORHEAD 0
			CLASS 1A CHAMPIONSHIP
			BRECK SCHOOL 7, WARROAD 3

 *Did you know?* *Sports Illustrated* hockey writer Michael Farber covered the tournament for the first time and wrote an article titled "Be True to Your School" about Edina's group of seniors.

STICKS AND ELBOWS were getting high. Tempers were running short. A meaningless summertime scrimmage might as well have been a bundle of dynamite.

And the fuse had been lit.

"Those summer games are hard to ref sometimes," Eden Prairie coach Lee Smith said. "And this thing got out of hand."

Smith's Eagles were scrimmaging Blaine in summer 2008. Both teams were considered state title contenders and, even with the start of the season months away, eager to establish their bona fides.

"Somebody took a cheap shot at [Kyle Rau], and everybody came to his defense," Smith said. "We had six guys in our penalty box, and Blaine maybe had seven."

Eden Prairie entered that summer as a team facing a potentially Grand Canyon–sized divide. Half the roster consisted of sophomores (a whopping ten of them) coming off a second straight state Bantam championship. The other half was made up of juniors and seniors who had suffered a disappointing 6–5 section semifinal loss to Benilde–St. Margaret's the previous season.

Parents were split, too. The Eagles had an open assistant coaching position, and battle lines were drawn on who should fill it. Some thought Smith, who had taken three teams to state but never reached a title game in his sixteen seasons, should hire Chris LaCombe, then a highly successful Eden Prairie youth coach. Others backed Ty Eigner, who had served as the head coach at Rosemount and Brainerd and earned section coach of the year honors while leading both programs.

Smith settled on Eigner. Feelings were hurt. Three top players left the program—two to play junior hockey in the United States Hockey League and another for Faribault-based Shattuck–St. Mary's.

Rumors circulated that defenseman Nick Leddy, a projected high-round NHL draft pick and top contender to win the state's Mr. Hockey Award, was on his way out, too. Leddy had received multiple offers to play elsewhere his senior season, including an invitation to join some of the nation's best players

in his age group as part of USA Hockey's National Team Development Program.

Much to the relief of his coaches and teammates, Leddy insisted he was staying.

He played in the scrimmage against Blaine and was one of the veterans who came to Rau's defense.

"Right there, you could see there wasn't a seniors-this or sophomores-that mentality," Smith said. "That little situation really showed that these kids really cared about each other and wanted to play for each other."

Added Leddy: "There are times when a team comes together. Maybe that was a specific moment where we all kind of decided we were one."

Leddy's loyalty was tested yet again during tryouts. Several of his buddies, seniors who were top scorers and key contributors from the previous season, were cut.

"I think there was a little bit of a shock at first," said Leddy, who joined senior Joe McQuillan and junior Mike Erickson as captains. "There were a lot of the kids in my grade that weren't chosen, and I think that was a little surprising. But I think as we started going through our season, we could see how special our group was."

Sophomores Curt Rau (Kyle's twin brother) and Dan Molenaar backed Leddy as key defensemen.

Kyle Rau, an undersized scoring phenom as a youth player, was paired with rugged 6-foot-2, 190-pound senior Taylor Wolfe and junior Mitch Rogge on an instantly effective forward line.

"We just had amazing chemistry that you can't describe, really; it just happens," Wolfe said about his linemates. "When guys just click, they click."

Seniors Jordan Hoffman and Mattson "Mad Dog" Gravelle, defensive stalwarts who emerged as ace penalty killers, were joined by sophomore Jack McCartan on yet another effective Eagles line.

Wolfe's willingness to serve as the 5-foot-7 Kyle Rau's de facto bodyguard, and Hoffman and Gravelle's unselfishness in embracing defense-first roles, contributed to the team's unshakable all-for-one mentality.

But it was Leddy's brilliance as a defenseman (Smith gave him the green light to rush the puck any time he desired) that armed Eden Prairie with a weapon no team could match.

"He is probably the best skater I have ever played with and against," Wolfe said about Leddy. "He's just a very strong human being from the waist down."

Leddy's mind for the game was as superior as his stride.

"He was so fast with the puck he would think the game in different ways than everybody else," Wolfe said. "The amount of times in Bantams and in high school I would see him make a stretch pass to the far blue to spring someone on a breakaway had to be in the hundreds."

The Eagles, having settled on sophomore Andrew Ford as their starting goaltender, won fifteen straight games to end the regular season as they compiled a 25–3 record. They tied a state tournament record with their ten sophomores on the roster and boasted the state's number-one ranking. Erickson scored in overtime to lift Eden Prairie past defending champion Hill-Murray 3–2 to open the quarterfinals.

The Eagles weren't shy about celebrating again later that night when, while eating a pasta dinner, they watched the television broadcast of top-seeded Edina, featuring the likes of Anders Lee, Marshall Everson, and Connor Gaarder, suffering a shocking 5–2 loss to Moorhead.

However, a familiar and none-too-friendly foe awaited in the semifinals: Blaine. Trash talk carried over from that summer scrimmage and reached a fever pitch when the Bengals surged to a 2–0 first-period lead and began chirping R-rated comments as they skated past the Eden Prairie bench. The Eagles rallied with a second-period goal from Wolfe and got two more from Kyle Rau in the third en route to a 4–2 victory.

Other than an early Moorhead goal that was disallowed after video review, there was little drama in Eden Prairie's 3–0 dismantling of the Spuds in the championship. Ford finished with twenty-eight saves, and Leddy, who a day later would be named Mr. Hockey, notched his third goal of the tournament.

"To win the first state championship in Eden Prairie history . . ." Leddy said. "It was more surreal than anything."

~LRN~

Eden Prairie's Kyle Rau (7), Nick Leddy (3), Taylor Wolfe (8), and Dan Molenaar (17) surround goaltender Andrew Ford after the Eagles won the 2009 state championship. Photo by Helen Nelson/Legacy.Hockey

218

HORSE MANURE

MOTIVATED BY ARCHRIVAL, EDINA SNIFFED OUT CHAMPIONSHIP

DATES	LOCATION	ATTENDANCE	CLASS 2A CHAMPIONSHIP
MARCH 10–13	XCEL ENERGY CENTER, ST. PAUL	118,934	EDINA 4, MINNETONKA 2
			CLASS 1A CHAMPIONSHIP
			BRECK SCHOOL 2, HERMANTOWN 1

 At 5:40 PM Thursday, Jean Johnson became fan number five million to pass through the gates at the boys' hockey state tournament.

FREAKING MINNETONKA . . .

Edina despised losing to the Skippers, yet that's all the Hornets kept doing in 2010. First, a 3–2 loss in the Schwan Cup Gold Division championship game played January 1 at Xcel Energy Center.

Next, a 7–1 whitewashing on January 23 at Pagel Arena. Edina coach Curt Giles said that in the postgame handshake line, a Minnetonka player actually said his Hornets were horsesh . . . um, manure, and then threw Giles's hand aside.

The insult failed to stir Edina. Back home on February 11 at Braemar Arena for their third crack at Minnetonka, the Hornets fell behind 4–0 after one period. Players braced for Giles's worst.

"We all came into the locker room essentially depressed and expecting Curt to hand it to us," senior forward Blake Chapman said. "But he just said, 'You have two choices: come out flat and let it happen again or chip away. If you want to do the first thing, take off your gear because what's the point?'"

Finally, something clicked. Edina rallied for a 5–4 overtime victory and gave the top-ranked Skippers their first loss.

"It was almost personal after the first period—more than hockey," Chapman said.

Edina won its next six games and captured the Class 2A, Section 2 title. The Hornets received the number-two state tournament seed behind Minnetonka, still the overwhelming favorite.

It's a tricky thing being the team no one expects to lose. Edina had carried that status in 2008 until getting shut out in the championship game. And the Hornets had been the number-one tournament seed in 2009 before getting bounced in the quarterfinals.

Those teams added to the picture gallery of Division I college players in the Braemar Arena lobby but couldn't supplement the nine state tournament championship banners hanging above the West Rink.

Though far from horse manure, the 2010 team didn't seem capable of claiming the program's first state championship in thirteen years.

"We had no one committed to a college program, nobody with NHL interest, no expectations to live up to," senior Steven Fogarty said.

Not so for Giles, still without a state championship in his eleventh season. Just a few years earlier, unhappy parents had petitioned to remove him.

Failures reinforced the importance of depth. The 2010 group had it. And Giles intended to use it.

"The two years before, we played our top guys to death at the state tournament," Giles said. "We had to find character players who would accept their roles. And I couldn't be afraid to use them. If you're trying to win every minute of every game all year, you're going to wear out."

Instead, Edina wore down opponents. Fogarty's twenty-one goals and forty points led the team. But Charlie Taft (thirty points), Michael Sit (also thirty), Jake Sampson (twenty-eight), Ryan Cutshall (twenty-four), Brett Stolpestad (eighteen), and Chapman (sixteen) could shine on any shift. And forwards Jon Cote and Joey Kopp crunched opposing players with fervor.

Goaltender Connor Girard earned the postseason nod after spending much of the season splitting time with John Ankeny.

"When we got down 4–0 in that third Minnetonka game, I thought we might lose 12–0," Giles said. "I asked Connor if he wanted out, and he said, 'No, I'm fine.' I think that's the only time I heard him speak. But he wanted to battle."

Edina opened state tournament play against Roseau and trailed 2–1 in the second period. Then Chapman, crashing the net, pushed a rebound past the goaltender.

"One of our coaches said that goal changed the atmosphere on the bench from there," said Chapman, whose father, Wally, skated to the 1982 state championship with Edina.

Seven different players and all four lines scored in Edina's 7–3 victory. Two goals for the first line, three for the second line, and one each from the third and fourth lines.

No Edina player scored more than one goal in any of the three tournament games.

Stolpestad, whose father, Dave, played on the 1971 St. Paul Johnson team that lost in the semifinals to Edina, ended up with the game-winning goal against Roseau.

"Technically," Brett said. "But I'll take it."

A 2–0 semifinal victory against Apple Valley featured Taft's sixth shorthanded goal of the season and an amazing Girard glove save.

Good fortune continued for the Hornets as Friday's nightcap, Minnetonka versus Hill-Murray, lasted four overtimes. Minnetonka won 2–1 at 12:22 AM, and Edina players were pumped for the rematch.

"We had something special with Tonka," Stolpestad said.

Before the game, Giles reminded his guys, "They had one loss this season—and to who? That means we can do it again."

Minnetonka's elite defensemen—Troy Hesketh, Justin Holl, and Andrew Prochno—set the Skippers apart. In the championship game, Edina took them apart.

Hesketh's clearing attempt hit Fogarty, and two passes later, Cutshall scored just twenty-six seconds into the game. Stolpestad made it 3–0 in the second period by beating Prochno to a loose puck.

"To take advantage of their miscues or to burn them, that told us these guys aren't invincible," Fogarty said.

Edina led 4–0 at second intermission. But Prochno scored twice within the first two minutes of the third period. The

Edina forward Brett Stolpestad, who personified the unheralded but unrelenting Hornets, scored the game-winning goals in the 2010 quarterfinal and championship games. Photo by Tim Kolehmainen/Breakdown Sports Media

Hornets worried their comeback from a 4–0 deficit, the victory that ignited their stretch run, could be turned on its head.

"I thought, 'No flipping way,'" Stolpestad said.

Giles said, "You could see that big blue wave, but our kids buckled down, and that high-powered team never got a sniff after that."

Edina prevailed 4–2. Once again, Stolpestad got the game-winning goal.

Technically.

"I'll take it," said Stolpestad, who couldn't make a Bantam A team before joining the high school ranks.

These players that Giles called mutts in the locker room and clowns at the postgame news conference were state champions who took him along for his first title ride.

"To this day, it's still my biggest hockey accomplishment," Fogarty said eight years later. "To do it against the number-one team was surreal. I was happy for Curt. And the city deserved it."

~DL~

Edina's Michael Sit fired home a puck that had bounced off the end boards and into the slot for a 2–0 lead in the second period of the Class 2A championship game. The Hornets went on to defeat favored Minnetonka 4–2 and claim their first title since 1997. Photo by Helen Nelson/SportsEngine

TO STAY OR NOT TO STAY

FROM BEGINNING TO END, KYLE RAU AT CENTER OF EDEN PRAIRIE'S HIGH DRAMA

DATES	LOCATION	ATTENDANCE	CLASS 2A CHAMPIONSHIP
MARCH 9–12	XCEL ENERGY CENTER, ST. PAUL	116,662	EDEN PRAIRIE 3, DULUTH EAST 2 (3 OT)
			CLASS 1A CHAMPIONSHIP ST. THOMAS ACADEMY 5, HERMANTOWN 4 (OT)

 St. Thomas Academy tied a tournament record for most goals in a period with seven in the first period of a 13–2 quarterfinal romp over New Ulm.

KYLE RAU WAS GONE. Checked out. Done.

On the eve of the opening day of tryouts, the biggest name in high school hockey called his coach and texted his teammates. He told them he would be playing the 2010–11 season for the Sioux Falls Stampede of the United States Hockey League.

Rau, committed to play his college hockey at Minnesota, was hardly convincing as he tried to sell shell-shocked Eden Prairie coach Lee Smith on the merits of the decision. Players leaving high school early for other opportunities wasn't a new phenomenon, but a decision to stay or go never had created so much drama.

"The feeling I got was Kyle didn't want to do it," said Smith, who endured "a pretty rough, sleepless night."

Des Shavlik, Rau's lifelong friend and longtime linemate, didn't take the news well.

"I was very selfishly pissed off," said Shavlik, who had missed his junior season with a torn Achilles tendon. "I was thinking, 'I can't believe this.'"

Shavlik's anger failed to subside the next day, when he kept his distance from Rau in the classrooms and hallways of Eden Prairie High.

"I didn't say anything to him all day," Shavlik said. "Two or three times during the day my mom texted me and was like, 'Have you wished Kyle good luck yet?' I was like, 'Nope, nope.' 'Have you wished Kyle good luck yet?' 'Nope, nope.'

"Finally, whenever it was, after that first day of tryouts, I sent him a text saying, 'Good luck this year.' And then he immediately called me and said, 'I'm staying.'"

Rau's reversal didn't come because of an impassioned speech from Smith or any of his Eagles teammates. His parents and three brothers, including twin Curt, didn't stage a last-ditch intervention. There was no epiphany.

After a fitful night of sleep, Rau, projected as an early-round NHL draft pick, reversed his decision.

"Something wasn't right," Rau said. "I slept on it, then woke up in the morning and decided I wanted to stay."

And with that, the state's balance of power again tipped in Eden Prairie's favor. The Eagles, with ten seniors returning

Kyle Rau nearly didn't play his final season for Eden Prairie, having the option to join the junior ranks for the 2010–11 season. Instead, he helped lead the Eagles to an emotional and exhausting triple-overtime victory over Duluth East to win the 2011 Class 2A state championship. Photo by Helen Nelson/SportsEngine

from its 2009 championship team, joined defending champion Edina as the preseason favorites to win the 2011 state title.

Rau, a key cog on the Eagles' 2009 championship team as a sophomore, scored forty goals and had forty-one assists in twenty-eight games as a junior in 2009–10. That season ended with a 7–2 section final drubbing at the hands of Minnetonka.

As a senior, Rau was the preseason favorite to win Minnesota's 2011 Mr. Hockey Award. He stood just 5 foot 7 and had been told all his life he was too small to excel at hockey's highest levels. As a result, he played with a Zamboni-sized chip on his shoulder.

"He had been hearing from outsiders, 'Oh, he's not going to make it at Pee Wees,'" Shavlik said. "Oh, he's not going to make it at Bantams. He's not going to make it at the high school level. He's not going to make it in juniors. He's not going to make it in college.

"You just heard it time and time again. I think that fueled him to prove everyone wrong."

Eden Prairie's seniors got their first taste of tournament success as nine- and ten-year-old Squirts, winning the thirty-two-team Fargo Invitational. They won a state title as second-year Pee Wees and captured back-to-back state championships as Bantams. As sophomores in 2009, they beat Moorhead 3–0 for the state Class 2A title. Four seasons, four straight state championships.

"I think early on, it was just really instilled in all of us that nothing is just going to come to you," Shavlik said. "You are only as good as you want to be."

As they grew older, the inseparable Eagles spent much of their off-ice time at Eden Prairie's Staring Lake Park, pushing through grueling workouts, then playing beach volleyball and soccer, among other sports. When they felt the urge to play hockey, they called the nearby Velocity Ice Center. As luck would have it, Noel Rahn, their old Pee Wee coach, owned the facility that offered a three-on-three-sized ice sheet and spacious workout room.

"[Rahn] was like, 'Alright, come on over,'" Shavlik said. "There would be twelve or fifteen of us, and we would go play three on three for an hour and a half."

High-scoring defenseman Dan Molenaar, who played his senior season on balky hips that would both require surgery a week after the state tournament, organized many of the team outings.

"Molenaar for sure was our vocal leader, off the ice and on the ice," Curt Rau said. "He was the guy you could count on for that."

Eden Prairie's cast of characters included another set of supremely skilled senior twins. Forwards Mark and David Rath were top scorers and fierce competitors.

"They were good at everything," Shavlik said. "And if they were on two different teams, it was all-out war."

The Eagles were loaded with win-or-die seniors. Rugged defenseman Nick Seeler played as though he would rather chew razor blades than allow a goal. He routinely used excessive force to clear pucks and bodies from the front of the Eagles' net.

"Seeler was the guy you wanted to have on your team," Curt Rau said. "You never wanted to be playing against him."

Smooth-skating winger Luc Gerdes possessed the lethal combination of top-end speed and a scorer's touch. He was second only to Kyle Rau in scoring as a senior, racking up twenty-nine goals and twenty-eight assists.

Bruising forward Jack McCartan was blessed with impressive size (6 foot 1, 215 pounds) and impeccable bloodlines (he was the grandson of the gold medal–winning 1960 US Olympic goalie of the same name).

223

Kyle Rau's headfirst slide and poke at the puck resulted in a bank shot off the post and into the net off Duluth East defenseman Andrew Kerr's (3) skate to secure Eden Prairie's triple-overtime victory in 2011. Photo by Helen Nelson/SportsEngine

224

Goaltender Andrew Ford left Eden Prairie for Breck as a freshman, but he returned after a semester and became a three-year varsity mainstay.

"He was serious when he needed to be serious," Shavlik said about Ford. "And when he didn't need to be serious, when he wasn't playing, he was the guy with his phone on the bench."

The Eagles posted an 18–5–2 regular-season record, four of the losses coming against state tournament entrants. After pounding Lakeville North 5–0 in the quarterfinals, Eden Prairie avenged one of those regular-season setbacks with a 5–1 semifinal rout of Eagan, setting up a championship matchup with Duluth East.

Duluth East reached the state tournament with a 2–1 overtime victory over Grand Rapids. The "Cardiac" Greyhounds engineered two more overtime triumphs, 4–3 over White Bear Lake in double OT and 2–1 over Edina, to reach the title game.

"By the time we got to that game, I felt like we were playing on house money," Duluth East's Nate Repensky said about the championship. "Because it wasn't our year to quote-unquote 'win,' because we were so young."

The Greyhounds had defeated Eden Prairie 4–3 in overtime in Duluth in mid-January, and they held leads of 1–0 and 2–1 in the rematch. David Rath's goal with 2:56 remaining in regulation tied the score at two and pushed the game into overtime.

Eden Prairie's Kyle Rau races along the glass as teammates, including Nick Seeler (11) give chase after Rau scored in triple overtime to lift the Eagles past Duluth East. Rau and Seeler both have gone on to play for the Minnesota Wild. Photo by Helen Nelson/SportsEngine

Rau, who had scored forty goals in thirty games, was held mostly in check by Duluth East's suffocating defensive corps led by junior Repensky, sophomore Meirs Moore, and a previously unheralded sophomore by the name of Andrew Kerr. As the game stretched into a second overtime, and then a third, the 5-foot-8, 160-pound Kerr repeatedly dished out devastating hits, two of them leaving Kyle Rau in a heap on the ice.

"Obviously you had to be aware when he was out there; he's their best player," Kerr said about Rau. "Before the game, I kind of had the mentality where I was going to make it as hard as I can on him."

Rau welcomed the physical play.

"I remember getting hit a lot more than normal," he said. "That's the kind of stuff I like. It got me fired up."

Prime scoring chances, which had been a rarity in regulation, all but dried up in the overtimes. With time winding down in the second overtime, it was stunning, then, for Smith to see Duluth East force a turnover near center ice, then quickly roar into the Eden Prairie zone.

Smith was even more deflated when he saw it was the Greyhounds' magical all-junior forward line of Trevor Olson (who had scored both Greyhound goals), Jake Randolph, and Dom Toninato racing toward Ford.

"They've got their top line going in on a three-on-one, and I was honestly getting down off the bench to go shake [Duluth East coach Mike Randolph's] hand," Smith said. "Somehow, they didn't score. I bounced right back up on the bench, thinking, 'Maybe this is our night.'"

The score remained 2–2 heading into a third overtime as the game set the mark for the longest championship in the tournament's history (it had an elapsed time of 80:43 and remains the lone triple-overtime title game).

Legs weakened. Lungs burned. Play started to slow. Shavlik had the puck but no energy early in the third overtime. So he whipped a knee-high pass up to Curt Rau and headed to the bench. Rau batted the puck down with his stick, then carried it over the Duluth East blue line and unloaded a slapshot at Greyhounds goaltender JoJo Jeanetta.

"I knew we were tired and changing," Rau said. "I just wanted to get the puck in, get it deep. Try to hit the net so it doesn't wrap out."

Rau's blast sailed into Jeanetta's leg pads, but the goaltender didn't squeeze them together quite in time, and the puck squirted through. As it dribbled into the crease, suddenly, there was a red-and-white flash streaking in from the blue line just as a Duluth East defender partially whiffed on his

Duluth East's Andrew Kerr (left) and Dom Toninato bow their heads in dejection after losing the 2011 championship game. Photo by Helen Nelson/SportsEngine

clearing attempt. The Eden Prairie player got a piece of the puck as he rocketed toward the net in a headfirst slide. The puck hit the left goalpost, then came straight back into the crease, where it caromed off the Duluth East defender's skate and back into the net.

Goal. Mayhem. Confusion.

Eden Prairie players launched themselves from the bench and ripped off their helmets as they raced to mob their hero. It all happened in a blink of an eye. The winning sequence was so fast, fans filling the Xcel Energy Center looked at each other and wondered aloud, "Who scored the goal?"

Ten days earlier, Kyle Rau had scored in double overtime as Eden Prairie outlasted Wayzata in a section final.

Upon further review, there could be only one goal scorer in a triple-overtime championship.

"If we needed a big goal, more often than not he was on the end of it," Curt Rau said about his brother.

The Duluth East defender? Andrew Kerr.

"I didn't get all of it clearing it, and that would have saved it," Kerr said. "I was very upset with myself for not making that play. I never really have gotten over it, honestly."

Thrilled as he was with the goal, and battered as was after all the body blows, Kyle Rau said he felt bad for Kerr, Jeanetta, and the Greyhounds.

"Everyone is so tired, I felt like it was going to have to be a fluky one," he said.

Rau was in the locker room getting his bloody chin bandaged when Mike Randolph entered and delivered some choice words for the Eagles. He thanked them for declining opportunities to play elsewhere, sticking with high school hockey, and being part of one of the greatest games in state championship history.

"Pretty classy," Rau said.

~LRN~

THE SMOKERS' DOORS

Free admission into tournament for neighborhood kids required quickness and timing

A trio of St. Paul twelve-year-olds were so infatuated with the state tournament they made a secret pact to skip school and attend the opening day of the 1979 event, consequences be damned.

To them, the event was Christmas, Halloween, and the Fourth of July all rolled into one.

"That first weekend of March was always like a holiday for us," Dan Beaudette said.

They hatched the plan while playing after-school boot hockey on the tennis courts in their Highland Park neighborhood. There wasn't a lot of sophistication involved in the caper, which hinged entirely on sneaking into the St. Paul Civic Center through what the kids called "the smokers' doors."

They agreed to meet the next day and get themselves on the Grand Avenue bus to downtown St. Paul. The secret plan went public as soon as Dan Kovarik got home and spilled his guts.

"I am honest to a fault," he said. "So I went to my parents the night before and told them what we were going to do."

Then came the interrogation.

"They said, 'Do you have any tickets?'" Kovarik said. "I said, 'No, we don't have any tickets.' They said, 'Do you have any money?' I said, 'No, we don't have any money.' They said, 'Do you have a ride?' I said, 'Yeah, we are going to take the bus.'

"Then, and I can't believe it to this day, they said, 'Great. Have fun.'"

The next day, Kovarik, Beaudette, and buddy Steve Ambel took the bus as planned, jumping off not far from the Civic Center. One of the massive circular building's main entrances was at the intersection of West Sev-

enth Street and Kellogg Boulevard. A few hundred feet to the east, down Kellogg, was a bank of exit-only doors.

The smokers' doors.

Between periods and in the breaks between games the doors would burst open, and out would come the smokers. They would either prop open the doors or leave someone stationed inside, ready to reopen them when they heard knocking. Security personnel were tasked with keeping non-ticket holders, like St. Paul's rink rats, from sneaking inside.

"But they weren't stationed just at those doors," Kovarik said. "They had half a rink where they were kind of patrolling back and forth and walking around."

Kovarik said it was too obvious, and risky, to stand directly in front of the doors. Security guards would quickly spot the kids and shoo them away. But if you stood far enough back and stayed patient . . .

"Smokers were never in a hurry, and they would prop those doors open, and we would just go running in them," Kovarik said.

Once inside, they would marvel at the skill of the players—Roseau's Neal Broten, Columbia Heights' Reggie Miracle, and the Lecy brothers from Rochester John Marshall were among their favorites through the years — as well as the sounds from the pep bands, the array of school colors, and the smells wafting from the concession stands. Sometimes, they would sneak down through the bleachers and into the bowels of the building, where the locker rooms were housed, to get a closer look at the players and coaches. They liked plopping into the seats intended for

the cheerleaders, who never sat down anyway.

"We knew every inch of that building," Kovarik said

Kovarik went on to play high school hockey at Cretin-Derham Hall, but he never played in the tournament. His passion for the event only grew over the years, however, and after playing at Saint Mary's University in Winona, Minnesota, he devised a new plan that would not only get him into the tournament but put him at center stage.

"It's the reason I got into officiating, to work the state tournament," Kovarik said.

Three decades after his smokers'-doors escapades, and long after the old Civic Center was demolished to make way for the more luxurious Xcel Energy Center, Kovarik developed a reputation as one of the state's top high school hockey officials.

"He's reffed many, many of our games and has always done a wonderful job," said Jim O'Neill, the former Cretin-Derham Hall coach who had Kovarik as a player. "He's always under control no matter how tough things get, no matter how frantic coaches get. That's probably how he has lasted so long and done such a good job."

Kovarik was chosen to work the 2011 big-school state championship game between Eden Prairie and Duluth East, considered one of the greatest state title games in the tournament's history. Kovarik and referee partner Joe Harris called just three penalties in a game that went to three overtimes (Eden Prairie won 3–2) and remains the longest championship in the tournament's history—80:43 of elapsed time.

St. Paul native Dan Kovarik, a fan of the state tournament since his grade school days sneaking into the old St. Paul Civic Center, worked the 2011 championship game as a referee. Photo by Helen Nelson/SportsEngine

Kovarik and Harris's work drew praise from the players, too.

"They were very consistent, so you knew what they were going to call and not call," said Duluth East defenseman Andrew Kerr, a sophomore who dished out numerous crushing hits on Eden Prairie star Kyle Rau. "That's all you can ask for."

Kovarik was stunned to receive an email from Duluth East coach Mike Randolph after the tournament. "Uh-oh, this can't be good," Kovarik thought when he saw who had sent the message. But the email was not what he expected. "He thanked us for working [the game]. That just does

not happen in high school sports, particularly with the losing coach."

The next year, Kovarik was wandering through the *Let's Play Hockey* Expo, an all-things-hockey marketplace set up adjacent to the Xcel Energy Center during the tournament, when he saw a mural depicting the opening ceremonies of the 2011 Class AA championship game. With a view from the upper reaches of the arena, it showed Kovarik standing at center ice with the other on-ice officials. The trio is sandwiched between the players lining each blue line and flanked by the teams' cheerleaders.

"I was in awe," Kovarik said about

the mural. "It looked so cool. That game had been so incredible, and there I was at center ice."

Kovarik tracked down a poster that showed the same scene, and to this day it hangs in his basement. Kovarik placed a detail from the poster art, the part showing him with the other on-ice officials, atop his Facebook page.

All of which is further testimony to the passion a St. Paul rink rat for life has for the tournament.

"I don't know if the words 'love affair' are strong enough," he said.

~LRN~

BEL13VE

GRANT BESSE'S RECORD-SETTING TITLE GAME PERFORMANCE INSPIRED BY PARALYZED TEAMMATE JACK JABLONSKI

DATES	LOCATION	ATTENDANCE	CLASS 2A CHAMPIONSHIP
MARCH 7–10	XCEL ENERGY CENTER, ST. PAUL	123,615	BENILDE–ST. MARGARET'S 5, HILL-MURRAY 1
			CLASS 1A CHAMPIONSHIP
			ST. THOMAS ACADEMY 5, HERMANTOWN 1

 Maple Grove made its state tournament debut after dethroning six-time defending section champion Blaine.

JACK JABLONSKI grew accustomed to attention as word of his spinal-cord injury spread through the local media and on to foreign countries and even Hollywood.

Felled by an illegal check from behind in a junior varsity game on December 30, 2011, Jablonski, a sophomore at Benilde–St. Margaret's, suffered two fractured vertebrae and a severed spinal cord. He lost the use of his legs and a promising hockey career.

His story triggered a flood of support. Prayers and well-wishes via tweets (#jabs) and messages on CaringBridge and Facebook numbered in the thousands. Some came from England and Australia.

Hockey royalty such as Zdeno Chara, Phil Housley, Mikko Koivu, and Lou Nanne offered heartfelt messages, as did sports broadcaster Bob Costas, NFL legends Dan Marino and Roger Staubach, and even actor Steve Carell. Pop star Taylor Swift sent a personalized, autographed photo. Jablonski's room at Hennepin County Medical Center featured enough signed professional jerseys to make memorabilia collectors salivate.

Jablonski became the face of a game some decried as becoming too violent and reckless. He also represented hope and courage.

A similar dichotomy existed among his Red Knights teammates, who wore Jablonski's jersey number, 13, as a patch on their jerseys and a sticker on the backs of their helmets. Their season had been just ten games along when Jablonski's tragedy struck. Would a fallen teammate sink their season? Or would they pull together?

Jablonski, who made seven varsity appearances and notched two assists before his injury, made clear his intentions anytime a teammate visited his hospital room. "I was very vocal

about how I didn't want the team to get off track on our goals," he said.

The Red Knights, featuring nine future Division I college players, reached the Class 2A, Section 6 championship game and were within a victory of their first state tournament in four years.

Fast and skilled, Benilde–St. Margaret's used the larger Mariucci Arena ice sheet to its advantage in a 5–1 romp over Minnetonka. Players mobbed together in front of the student section to celebrate. And then, one minute later, the Zamboni entrance opened, and small ramp was laid on the ice.

Jabs was coming out. Whether he wanted to or not.

"[Benilde–St. Margaret's junior varsity coach Chris] McGowan was like, 'Let's get you on the ice.' I was like, 'I'll pass,'"

Sophomore Jack Jablonski's devastating injury in December 2011 became a rallying point for his Benilde-St. Margaret teammates—and generated support from celebrities near and far. Goaltender Anders Jecha honored his injured teammate on the side of his helmet, and the logo featuring Jablonski's jersey number could be found on stickers and buttons. Photo by Adam Crane/SportsEngine

228

said Jablonski, who two games before had started joining the team at the rink. "I wasn't comfortable with the physical condition I was in. I still had my halo. I didn't want to be part of the public atmosphere the way I looked at the time. But he was like, 'You're going to love it. They want you out there.' So I said, 'Let's just go.'"

Fans from Section 2 finalists Burnsville and Edina, along with Minnetonka fans, rose from their seats and joined Benilde–St. Margaret's faithful in a chorus of applause. Goosebumps rose from the skin as Jablonski motored through the handshake line exchanging fist bumps with Minnetonka players.

"It was unbelievable to have everyone stand up once they realized what was going to happen," Jablonski said. "I started tearing up. It was an unbelievable moment."

And the last of its kind. Benilde–St. Margaret's realized the program's state championship dream ten days later with a 5–1 victory against Hill-Murray at the Xcel Energy Center. With Jablonski's story engrossing diehard and casual fans, and even those who weren't hockey fans at all, the state tournament drew its best attendance and television viewership in four years. An unusually large number of fans hung around for the medal ceremony, many to witness Jablonski again motor onto the ice.

They left disappointed.

Before the tournament, Minnesota State High School League officials, on the advice of its legal team and insurance company, deemed the ice off-limits to Jablonski. Still, the Jablonskis pushed for ice access in the hours before the championship game.

But as Jablonski exited the elevator at ice level, six security guards waited, carrying news as cold and hard as the concrete under his wheelchair.

"They're like, 'You're not getting on the ice,'" Jablonski said. "I said, 'Are you kidding me? The last thing you're going to do

is make sure I can't get on the ice? After all this?' Emotions were running so high in a positive direction that it was more just disbelief that this was happening."

The tournament offered surreal moments throughout.

Four teams were awarded seeds, and all four lost in Thursday's quarterfinals, a first in six years of tournament seeding. The evening session started with unheralded Lakeville South knocking out number-one Duluth East, the state's top team all season.

"We had scrimmaged earlier in the year and tied them," said Cougars senior forward Justin Kloos, the 2012 Mr. Hockey Award recipient. "We had zero pressure, and they probably had other things in mind."

In the nightcap, Benilde–St. Margaret's Christian Horn, who along with fellow senior captain Jake Horton helped ensure the emotional well-being of the locker room, scored with 23.9 seconds remaining in a 3–2 upset of number-four seed Edina.

While the Lakeville South upset of Duluth East gave the Red Knights an easier path, they weren't at 100 percent. Center T. J. Moore suffered a shoulder injury against Edina. And Jablonski, who watched Thursday from the suite level and later celebrated with teammates in the locker room, wasn't in the building after waking up Friday with a temperature and no appetite.

Meanwhile, Kloos recalled, the Cougars "celebrated like we won the Stanley Cup" after ousting Duluth East and brought a lot of confidence to the semifinal.

Red Knights coaches, determined not to see their team suffer an emotional collapse, relayed a "win one for me" message from Jablonski before the game.

Wish granted. Junior wing Dan Labosky finished with a hat trick in a 10–1 blowout.

Regarded by some as a Cinderella team galvanized by a fallen teammate, these Red Knights were Ken Pauly's best since the 1999 squad, the first of two teams that had won a Class 1A title. Bigger dreams had led to the program opting up to Class 2A in 2005–06.

"Winning in 2012 put a stamp on our bona fide credentials as one of the top programs in the state," Pauly said. "When you're Class 1A, you can only talk about it."

Should Benilde–St. Margaret's, the surprise sentimental favorite, win the championship game, Pauly knew Jablonski would not join the team on the ice. Pauly and Craig Perry, Minnesota State High School League hockey tournament director, spoke on Saturday before the tournament about the challenges ahead.

"We knew as a league that Jack and his story were going to be part of this tournament," Perry said. "However, I told Ken, 'We get that there's something different with Jack, but this is about all sixteen teams and making it a lifetime memory for them as well.'"

Jack Jablonski watched Benilde–St. Margaret's tournament games from a suite inside the Xcel Energy Center. Joining him are (from left) family friend Lisa Collins, mother Leslie, and brother Max. Photo by Helen Nelson/SportsEngine

Pauly said, "I was sympathetic to that. But at the end of the day, there was no getting around" Jablonski as a massive storyline. Jablonski watched from a suite and was welcome in the team locker room before and after each game.

Then, on Saturday afternoon, Pauly said Perry approached him and said, "Ken, we need help. The Jablonskis are insistent on going on the ice." Flustered, Pauly said he "was trying to deliver the league company line" when "Mike Jablonski told me, 'We'll handle it.'"

"I looked at Craig and said, 'I'm out,'" Pauly said. "There was great tension in the room." Mike Jablonski said he couldn't recall specifics.

During Saturday's championship game preview show on Channel 45, longtime local sports broadcaster Joe Schmit said of the state tournament, "Legends are made here. Mayasich, Brooks, Broten, Antonovich, Spehar. Will there be another one tonight?"

Yes, and his name was Grant Besse.

He started fast, popping two first-period goals against Hill-Murray. Despite entering the state tournament with forty-four goals and a verbal commitment to play at Wisconsin, Besse was not considered a big-game performer.

"It's funny because in the section quarterfinals all four years, I got a hat trick or more," he said. "But I had no goals in the semifinals or section finals."

Goaltender Justin Quale also emerged. Suspended for the first six weeks of the season for disciplinary reasons, Quale drew Pauly's praise at first intermission for negating solid Pioneer chances.

The second period showcased what Benilde–St. Margaret's defenseman Jonah Johnson meant to his team. Hill-Murray forward Conrad Sampair, who scored both goals in a 2–1 semifinal victory against Moorhead, carried the puck deep into Red Knights territory before Johnson crushed him along the end boards.

Johnson, a senior transfer from Hill-Murray, sent a message that his new team wouldn't cower under the wrecking-ball presence of Pioneer defenseman Blake Heinrich.

"He gave us experience and a grit factor," Pauly said. "He stepped right up, and it kind of emboldened our guys a little bit."

High school hockey took a radical shift after Jablonski's injury. In an unprecedented midyear change, the MSHSL began imposing tougher penalties for three of hockey's most dangerous infractions. Starting in mid-January, players called for a check from behind, boarding, or head contact received at least a five-minute

major penalty. Approval by the National Federation of State High School Associations came barely two weeks after Jablonski's injury—the boldest action by far amid other recent calls to make youth hockey safer. League executive director Dave Stead said never in his twenty-six years with the league had such a major change been approved so quickly and implemented midseason.

Play along the boards became less reckless. But hockey is a fast, physical, and emotional game, and safety cannot be legislated. A reminder came in the second period as a flying Besse crashed hard into the end boards behind the Hill-Murray goal and remained on the ice for several minutes. Pauly saw Besse go into the boards feet first and knew in his logical mind there was no danger of another catastrophic Jablonski-type injury. Try telling that to the emotional part of his brain, however.

"I was panicked, like, 'Oh my god,'" Pauly said.

Besse skated off and resumed his record night.

Junior forward Jake Guentzel, the trigger man on Hill-Murray's top power-play unit, would later become a catalyst for Pittsburgh's 2016–17 Stanley Cup run. But in this title game, he struggled. He sent a shot off Horn, who collected the puck. Besse took off, and Horn hit him with a pass at the red line. Breakaway. Now, Besse thought, what to do, what to do?

"Normally I just shoot it," he said. "But I saw the goalie was pretty far out, and I knew I had some speed going, so I tried to beat him to the post."

A backhand flip into the net validated Besse's approach and gave him fifty goals for the season. Benilde–St. Margaret's led 3–0 with just 1:39 to go in the second period. Now a notable tournament player, Besse skated on toward legendary status.

Dogged Hill-Murray wasn't acquiescing. Forward Zach LaValle scored on the power play to cut the Pioneers' deficit to 3–1 in the third period. Then a chippy game—seventeen penalties were called, including two for unsportsmanlike conduct—got the better of Horton. He speared a Hill-Murray player and was ejected. In addition, the Red Knights faced a five-minute Pioneer power play.

"I could feel that dread, that sense that it was slipping away," Pauly said. "We had struggled with this even before Jabs got injured, the question of 'Can we maintain our composure?'"

When play resumed, the Red Knights got a big bounce. A shot on goal caromed out past Hill-Murray attackers in the slot and to Besse. Off he went. This time, he just ripped a shot over John Dugas and sent the goalie's water bottle into orbit. Benilde–St.

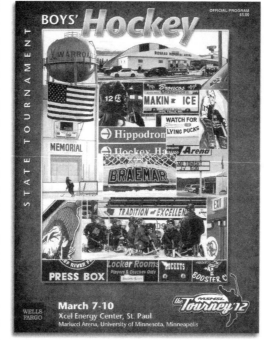

Margaret's took control at 4–1 with nine minutes remaining.

"To me, that was the dagger. They had hope, and we got it back," Besse said. "It was probably my favorite of the five goals."

The celebration wasn't. Besse skated past teammates to the faceoff dot at center ice and waited with his arm aloft—a combination of the Chicago Bulls' Michael Jordan holding his jump-shot form against Utah in the 1998 NBA Finals and San Francisco wide receiver Terrell Owens, who in 2000 ran alone to midfield and celebrated on the blue star at Texas Stadium.

"It was a little much," Besse said. "I cringe when I see it."

Members of Hill-Murray's power play can relate. Besse's record fifth goal started with a Pioneers player whiffing on a shot attempt from the faceoff dot in the Red Knights' zone. Besse grabbed the puck, glided down the ice, and sent it home from a few strides inside the blue line.

"I'd like to say I was shooting for that exact spot, but I just tried to put it on net," Besse said. He had eclipsed Eveleth's John Mayasich, who scored four times in the 1951 title game. Afterward, Pauly referenced another of those legends.

"That's a Spehar-type performance," Pauly said in the press conference of Besse's five goals, three shorthanded. "Anyone in high school hockey knows what that means."

Well, almost everyone. Besse later pleaded ignorance regarding Dave Spehar and his three hat tricks in as many nights in the 1995 state tournament.

Benilde–St. Margaret's tumultuous yet triumphant 2011–12 season literally left its mark on Besse. He had "Believe," Jablonski's rallying cry, needled into his left bicep, the first letter made to look like the number 13. Viewed upside down, "Believe" becomes "Forever."

On his left side is the scripture Job 39:19–24, which opens the movie *Secretariat*. Pauly made the passage a season-long purpose statement. Besse committed the last three verses to his body:

> He laughs at fear, afraid of nothing; he does not shy away from the sword.
> The quiver rattles against his side, along with the flashing spear and lance.
> In frenzied excitement he eats up the ground; he cannot stand still when the trumpet sounds.

In the team's yearbook, Pauly wrote, "This fits us perfectly! If the 2011–12 Red Knights could capture just a small part of that fearlessness, then a state title was a realistic goal for this

Grant Besse scored all five of Benilde–St. Margaret's goals—three of them shorthanded—in a 5–1 victory over Hill-Murray during the Class 2A title game. His performance eclipsed the previous single-game championship record of four goals, set by Eveleth's John Mayasich in 1951. Photo by Helen Nelson/SportsEngine

talented team. When I chose that verse, I thought that I was preparing a team to have the confidence to bring their very best to the starting gate before the biggest games of the season. Little did any of us realize exactly what the trumpet sounding would truly come to mean. The trumpet sounded on an event that would have a profound impact on our team forever."

Besse said of the championship season, "I've come to appreciate it more. It's pretty cool to look at what we did, especially considering the circumstances. I mean, how many people were rooting for us because of Jabs? That just shows what an effect he's had on people's lives. He's an inspiration."

As Besse and his teammates collected their medals, the Benilde–St. Margaret's student section chanted, "We want Jabby." Jablonski, who had watched the game while taking intravenous fluids in his family's suite, waited in the locker room. Security was stationed outside to keep him there.

"I'm literally looking at the TV, hearing them chant my name," he recalled.

Pauly scanned the lower arena bowl during the medal ceremony and noticed few empty seats.

"I'm thinking, 'Why are this many people still here?'" he said. "Then it hit me. 'Jack.' And then, 'Where is he?'"

That question, Jablonski said, has come up often through the years. "The next question after you tell them is, 'What were they thinking?'" he said. "I got to spend time in the locker room with the guys and celebrated with them there. It just would have been nice if it was in front of the people that stayed to see it."

On Twitter in the hours after the game, the hashtag #besse trended worldwide, meaning it ranked among the top-ten topics mentioned on the popular social media site. But Besse found his ego checked by none other than Jablonski.

"I heard about the trending stuff on Twitter, but then Jabs goes, 'Who was first?'" Besse said.

The emotional victory led students to gather for an impromptu late-night welcome-home celebration at St. Louis Park Recreation Center, the Red Knights' home rink. Pauly estimated "well over two hundred students," some standing atop parked cars, cheering as the team bus arrived. Some didn't stop there.

"There was a swarm of kids running at the bus and shaking it," Besse said. "You felt like a celebrity."

Questions about Jablonski's absence didn't stop, either. Stead issued a statement two days later acknowledging the league had been fielding inquiries about Jablonski. Stead noted that Jablonski was not part of the team's official roster and that "championship medals are awarded to each member of the team, team managers and coaches. A school can also request additional medals for players, and we accommodate all teams in all sports."

Stead also said the league's catastrophic injury insurance policy might have been jeopardized "if an accident of any type would have occurred."

But following the 1997 Class 2A championship game and trophy presentation, Edina's Ben Peyton, injured in a Junior Gold game that season and in a wheelchair, had been rolled onto the ice by cheerleaders to celebrate with his victorious friends.

In retrospect, Pauly wishes he would have been more adamant about getting Jablonski involved. The missed opportunity lingers.

"It was just so wrong that he wasn't there," Pauly said. "But that's what a bureaucracy does. It doesn't recognize the moment."

"It's not the most important thing to me in the world," Jablonski said. "But it sure would have been a hell of an end to a story and to the year."

~DL~

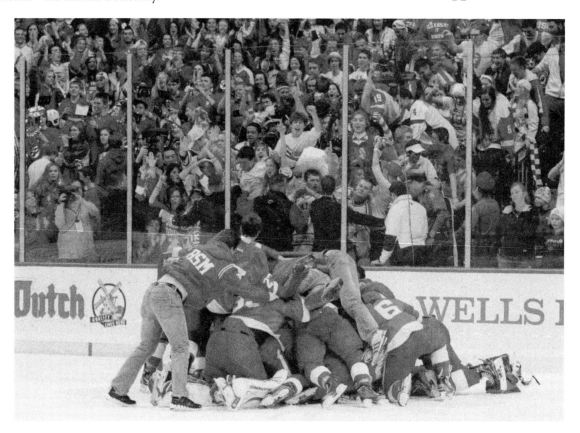

Benilde-St. Margaret's celebrated on ice after capturing the program's first Class 2A state championship and third state title overall. An unusually large crowd stayed for the medal ceremony. The only thing missing, many tournament-goers felt, was a Jack Jablonski appearance. Minnesota State High School League officials, citing insurance liability, barred Jablonski from motoring his wheelchair onto the ice. Photo by Adam Crane/SportsEngine

"THE NOTHING MOVE"

GRINDER ANTHONY WALSH'S UNLIKELY BREAKAWAY GOAL CLINCHED EDINA TITLE

DATES	LOCATION	ATTENDANCE	CLASS 2A CHAMPIONSHIP
MARCH 6–9	XCEL ENERGY CENTER, ST. PAUL	116,051	EDINA 4, HILL-MURRAY 2
			CLASS 1A CHAMPIONSHIP
			ST. THOMAS ACADEMY 5, HERMANTOWN 4

 *Did you know?* Marshall junior goalie Mason Campion recorded fifty-eight saves in the consolation semi-finals, a regulation-game record. He posted twenty-eight saves in the second period.

A GREEN-AND-WHITE flash mob enveloped Edina forward Anthony Walsh along the boards to celebrate his championship game goal.

Then, as the four players who huddled around Walsh began dispersing, defenseman Matt Nelson offered another hug and pat on the helmet. The moment was about a half dozen years in the making.

As seventh-graders, Nelson and Walsh, along with forwards Dan Labosky and T. J. Moore and defenseman Parker Reno, had keyed Edina's Pee Wee A state championship run. Their onslaught resumed as second-year Bantams until three of the ninth-graders earned varsity spots.

Reno stayed at Edina and won the 2010 state championship. Labosky and Moore headed to Benilde–St. Margaret's and captured the 2012 title as juniors.

High school success proved elusive for Nelson and Walsh. They were among the final Edina varsity cuts as freshmen. As sophomores, they reached the state tournament and placed fourth. As juniors, the duo lost both state tournament games.

Senior year became their last shot at glory.

"We were the only two off that amazing, destined group to not win yet," Walsh said.

"Losing again," said Nelson, "wasn't an option."

As two of the team's ten seniors, Nelson, who committed to Princeton, and Walsh, a third-liner, embodied a team that excited coach Curt Giles.

"State tournament teams have to be physical and strong and play hard," Giles said. "We had that and a capability to score goals."

These Hornets also had an attitude.

"We pushed them during the year, and they'd look at you like, 'Knock yourself out,'" Giles said.

"We said to the coaches, 'If you think this will get us there, throw it at us. We're tough. We can take it,'" Walsh said.

Confidence waned in February. Giles benched his first line as Cretin–Derham Hall built a 3–0 lead in the second period. Walsh scored twice as he and the third line tied the game. The Hornets escaped with a 4–3 overtime victory.

Edina won its next game 2–0 at Hopkins on goals in the last two minutes. But a flat performance the first forty-nine minutes irked Giles. Afterward, players were instructed to take their equipment home. Their new Braemar Arena locker room was off-limits until Giles deemed their efforts worthy.

"Most of the kids we get have high skill levels, and a lot of that comes naturally," Giles said. "If you can get them to compete all the time with that skill level, then you're doing something."

Section 2 playoff semifinal opponent Bloomington Jefferson demanded everything Edina could muster. The underdog Jaguars led 4–3 early in the third period, and Hornets junior forward Miguel Fidler had enough.

Giles said Fidler "stood up on the bench and yelled, 'We will not lose this game!'"

Backing his words, Fidler tied the game 4–4 with less than five minutes remaining.

Then, with overtime forty-nine seconds away, Nelson scored for the first time in more than a month. His fourth goal of the season won the game.

"That's still the biggest goal I ever scored," Nelson said.

Three of the four forward lines each contributed a goal in the 3–2 section final victory against Burnsville.

The state tournament brought Edina the number-three seed and quarterfinal opponent Lakeville North. The talented top line led the way in a 9–3 rout.

Regular-season tinkering by Giles moved wing Andy Jordahl off the top line, which sent center Connor Hurley and wing Dylan Malmquist into a funk. They missed all the little things Jordahl did well.

"Jordahl was fine alone, but the other two struggled," Giles said. "When we put them back together, they took off."

Number-two seed Duluth East, the Hornets' semifinal opponent, previously thumped them in a 4–1 December victory.

"Curt was so mad at me the first time we played them," Walsh said. "He said, 'You are getting manhandled.' I couldn't let that happen again."

The tougher team, Giles said, would win the rematch.

234

Teammates since youth hockey, Edina's Anthony Walsh (left) and Matt Nelson (right) overcame years of big-game frustration by winning the 2013 Class 2A championship. Nelson played sound defense throughout the tournament, and Walsh tallied a breakaway goal in the championship game. Photo by Adam Crane/SportsEngine

"We challenged our kids to finish every single check," Giles said. "And they were relentless."

Edina battled throughout a 3–2 victory.

"It was a north/south bloodbath," Nelson said. "Every shift meant so much, and it made for good hockey. That was really the biggest game of the tournament for us."

Title game foe Hill-Murray provided Edina another redemption opportunity. On January 5, the Pioneers edged the injury-ravaged Hornets 2–1 in overtime.

Full-strength Edina proved too much. Number-one seed Hill-Murray struck first, but the 1–0 advantage didn't last.

Racing into the Pioneers' zone, Malmquist maneuvered around Hill-Murray goaltender John Dugas's outstretched leg and scored his team-leading twenty-third goal of the season. Earlier on that same Hornets power play, Dugas slid across the crease and stoned Malmquist.

Two Cullen Munson goals bumped Edina's lead to 3–1 early in the second period. Then Walsh made the game's defining play.

Walsh blocked a Hill-Murray shot from the point, corralled the puck, and dashed down the middle of the ice toward the Pioneers' goal.

In the title game a year earlier, Benilde–St. Margaret's sniper Grant Besse scored two of his five goals on breakaways. Fans thinking Walsh might mimic Besse's deft backhand move or send a laser under the crossbar instead got . . . nothing.

Walsh barely handled the puck but coaxed Dugas into creating an opening and slid his seventh goal of the season underneath.

"That's called 'The Nothing Move,'" Walsh said. "You move your stick but then you just go five-hole."

Senior forwards Dan Hinueber and Tim Spicola arrived first to congratulate Walsh. Then Nelson and Tyler Nanne.

"Matt came over and hugged me," Walsh said. "I think he was happier for me than I was for myself."

Nelson said, "He's a third-line guy who I felt worked harder than anyone. To see it finally pay off was special."

The goal put Edina in control. A 4–2 victory made it official. Nelson and Walsh ensured their youth hockey quintet didn't come up two high school rings short.

"We were not going to leave St. Paul without a championship," Walsh said.

~DL~

235

LEFT: Hermantown coach Bruce Plante was hopping mad each time his small, outstate public school program lost a Class 1A state championship game to metro-area private school St. Thomas Academy. Photo by Tim Kolehmainen/Breakdown Sports Media. RIGHT: St. Thomas Academy co-head coach Greg Vannelli addressed the media after Hermantown coach Bruce Plante blasted the private school for remaining among the smaller schools by enrollment. "It was like we were illegitimate," Vannelli said after his team beat Hermantown in the Class 1A title game for the third year in a row. Photo by Adam Crane/SportsEngine

THE HEIGHT OF LUNACY

Rivalry between Hermantown and St. Thomas Academy went off the rails in 2013

Here comes Hermantown head coach Bruce Plante, red faced and spewing righteous indignation.

It's 2013, and the St. Thomas Academy Cadets, metro-area private schoolers who Plante says have zero business in the Class 1A state tournament, just won their third consecutive small-school title at Hermantown's expense.

The game is over. But Plante is far from finished. He walks almost the width of the ice to berate an official for putting St. Thomas Academy on the power play late in regulation and then missing the headlock applied to one of his guys on the sequence during which the Cadets scored the game-winning goal.

"It wasn't a discussion," Plante said afterward. "It was a comment. Or two. Or five."

Never afraid to speak his mind throughout more than two decades coaching Hermantown, Plante appears to be unhinged. This rivalry,

both north versus south and public versus private, reaches the height of its lunacy.

"I'm watching this bizarre behavior and can't believe it's happening," Cadets co-head coach Greg Vannelli recalled. "I told my athletic director, 'If I did that, I'd be blasted for it. I'd probably lose my job.' But whatever he did, he could get away with it. It was like he was untouchable."

Minnesota State High School League hockey tournament postgame press conferences begin with the losing coach and selected players. Here comes Plante, walking to the stage past a full house that includes more than double the typical media presence, Hermantown's activities director, and, making a rare appearance, MSHSL executive director Dave Stead.

"I saw the heavy hitters," Plante said. "They were worried what I'd say."

After blowing a 3–0 lead in the 2011 title game

and losing in overtime, Plante lamented St. Thomas Academy, an all-boys private school in Mendota Heights, was "a double-A team playing single-A hockey."

He pronounced his guys as "public school champs" after getting walloped by the Cadets 5–1 in 2012.

This time, after blowing a 4–2 lead after two periods in a 5–4 loss, he finishes player introductions with "ZIP code 55811," the location of his small suburban-Duluth town.

The gripes from there lacked their usual bite and occasional profanities. But Vannelli knew from experience that following Plante was a tough draw.

"They always went first, so he set up this circumstance where I had to defend our program versus honoring our players," Vannelli said.

Looking back, Plante said, "It was never personal, though it sounded like it at the time. But your kids are bawling. They're hurting. You're hurting. Then they drag you in there and you're still pissed off. I probably said some things I wish I hadn't. But I know a lot of coaches felt the way I did."

Public school champs? ZIP code 55811?

"I guess I don't regret those things," Plante said.

Vannelli felt Plante did his own teams a disservice.

"We thought he was our best ammunition. He was convincing his team they couldn't beat us," Vannelli said. "He had a couple teams that were better than ours. We got the breaks."

Plante snorted.

"That's BS. We were never better than them," Plante said. "They were always deeper and stronger. But we played with passion. And those were pretty great games. Some of those games were the best we played all season."

Hermantown lost the next two Class 1A championship games, running its futility streak to six. The Hawks finally won in 2016 and 2017, Plante's final season.

But after 2013, Plante never faced St. Thomas Academy, which opted-up to Class 2A beginning with the 2013–14 season. The move fulfilled Plante's wishes yet ended a colorful era in Class 1A hockey.

~DL~

E-DYNASTY REBORN

BIG-GAME TRACKER MIGUEL FIDLER ROSE TO CHALLENGE AS EDINA'S METTLE TESTED

DATES	LOCATION	ATTENDANCE	CLASS 2A CHAMPIONSHIP
MARCH 5–8	XCEL ENERGY CENTER, ST. PAUL	118,249	EDINA 8, LAKEVILLE NORTH 2

CLASS 1A CHAMPIONSHIP
EAST GRAND FORKS 7, HERMANTOWN 3

Did you know? Gary Thorne, a television broadcaster who did play-by-play at the Stanley Cup Finals, Winter Olympics, and World Series, called the state tournament action.

WHO'S AFRAID OF the big, bad Wolff? Edina's whole team, apparently.

That's what coach Curt Giles discovered when his defending state champions lost 2–1 in early December at Eagan.

"We were tip-toeing around," Giles said. "The whole game we were like that. And we're a big, strong team. So us coaches were going, 'What happened?'"

Giles asked players afterward and learned the reason: Eagan's Nick Wolff. The 6-foot-4, 205-pound defenseman could move. And hit.

"He terrorized our kids all the way up through youth hockey," Giles said. "They didn't want to go anywhere near him."

Senior forward Miguel Fidler said, "He was a killer. You heard some of our guys say, 'If he's out there, I'm getting off,' or, 'Don't pass me the puck if he's out there.' And Nick knew kids were afraid of him. He'd hit you and scream, and you'd think, 'What is this psychopath doing?'"

Curt Giles was never the fastest or most skilled defenseman during his NHL career, but he survived by playing a relentless style. He coached Edina as he played, demanding consistent effort and treating bench players no differently than goal scorers. The payoff: four state championships. Photo by Tim Kolehmainen/Breakdown Sports Media

Frightening as Wolff was, Edina players only saw him once or twice a season. They faced Giles, another intimidating defenseman, every day. Giles stood 5 foot 8 but became a two-time all-American at Minnesota Duluth and a fourteen-year NHL veteran. As a coach, he demanded the same consistent effort that fueled his playing career.

"He's really about hard work and being a good person off the ice," said Dylan Malmquist, one of the team captains.

Off the ice, Giles was a tough person to spot in Edina. The affluent Minneapolis suburb demands success. The school district's motto is "Defining Excellence."

Hockey is the most revered sport at a high school with more than 180 state champions. When Giles's teams won in 2010 and 2013, the pressure only increased. Going into 2013–14, fans saw ten players back to defend the title and expected them to repeat.

"There are a lot of ghosts there," Eden Prairie coach Lee Smith said. "Curt is being evaluated by a lot of people who played in that community."

Giles avoided the chatter by going for walks with his wife, Mary Pat, around Lake Harriet, just over the border in southwest Minneapolis. The couple would also grocery shop at odd hours. Getting access to Curt's cell phone number? Indiana Jones had an easier time getting the Ark of the Covenant.

Giles could accept the nuisances so long as players skated with purpose. If not, he would get an honest day's work by other means.

The season's low point came in mid-January. A listless 6–1 loss at Hill-Murray had players fearing the consequences on a silent forty-minute bus ride back to Braemar Arena.

"When Curt is mad, you don't speak or even look at him," Fidler said. "We parked at the arena, and Curt turned around and said, 'Be on the ice in five minutes. We're working on our power play.' One of the sophomores said, 'That doesn't sound too bad.' But one of the seniors said, 'We're not working on the power play, buddy.'"

In the rush not to be late, one player borrowed a shin pad. Another gave up trying to find socks and went without. As Giles saw it, his players' ragtag appearances fit their performances.

He skated his team hard to counteract the entitlement that had led to its blowout loss.

"I wouldn't accept their lack of effort," Giles said. "We went in thinking we were better than we were. We showed nobody respect."

Afterward, Fidler waited outside for his mother's arrival. Giles approached.

"Tough day?" the coach asked.

"Yep," Fidler said.

The next ten minutes, the two didn't speak another word.

Edina didn't lose another game, winning its last thirteen in a row.

In retrospect, Fidler said, "I'm glad it happened."

Earning the number-one state tournament seed, Edina turned quarterfinal opponent Stillwater to rubble in a 6–1 victory. Senior co-captain Tyler Nanne set a state tournament record by scoring three of his four goals on the power play.

A rematch with Eagan boogeyman Nick Wolff came next.

"We had to go after him, get in his way, chip him and aggravate him," said Giles, who asked Fidler to make a stand. A skilled player who tallied twenty goals and thirty assists as a senior, Fidler was equally valued for playing with an edge typically not associated with Edina kids.

"Giles told me, 'You've got to go toe to toe with him,'" Fidler said. "I had to prove a point, and we had a good battle."

Wolff, a Mr. Hockey Award finalist, threw some big checks and logged a ton of ice time. But with Fidler standing up to the big fella, the Hornets were inspired to take a hit to make play. Malmquist scored twice, and Garrett Wait added a goal in the 3–1 victory.

Lakeville North, the final obstacle in Edina's road to a repeat title, fought well for seventeen minutes. The Panthers endured back-to-back overtime games yet trailed only 3–2 after the first period.

But three goals in a span of 4:17 from Fidler, Parker Mismash, and Kieffer Bellows gave Edina a 6–2 lead at second intermission.

"That was probably the best game we played the entire season," Malmquist said. "We were fast and skilled, just ripping pucks on net."

"It was like the Hill-Murray game in reverse," Fidler said. "We could feel everything going our way. We knew we were going to destroy 'em."

Edina won 8–2 with six different players scoring. The top three forward lines each chipped in at least two goals.

"It was real tough to pick this team, but the coaches didn't miss," Nanne said in the press conference. "Everyone contributed."

The victory cemented a dynasty—three titles in five years. The Hornets were the first program in the large-school class to win back-to-back championships since Bloomington Jefferson had won three consecutive crowns from 1992 to 1994.

Arriving back at Braemar Arena, players ran onto the ice without skates and savored their final evening as teammates.

"Winning with this group was just as incredible, especially watching the guys not on the team the year before," Malmquist said.

"It was so good to leave my high school career with the title," Fidler said.

~DL~

237

Miguel Fidler was a skilled player who tallied twenty goals and thirty assists as a senior, but he was equally valued for playing with an edge typically not associated with Edina kids. Fidler scored twice and assisted on another goal as the Hornets crushed Lakeville North 8-2 in the Class 2A championship game. Photo by Tim Kolehmainen/ Breakdown Sports Media

VISION QUEST

LAKEVILLE NORTH ENVISIONED UNDEFEATED SEASON, THEN MADE IT HAPPEN

DATES	LOCATION	ATTENDANCE	CLASS 2A CHAMPIONSHIP
MARCH 4–7	XCEL ENERGY CENTER, ST. PAUL	123,067	LAKEVILLE NORTH 4, DULUTH EAST 1

CLASS 2A CHAMPIONSHIP — LAKEVILLE NORTH 4, DULUTH EAST 1

CLASS 1A CHAMPIONSHIP — EAST GRAND FORKS 5, HERMANTOWN 4 (OT)

Did you know? Corey Millen returned to the state tournament for the first time in thirty-three years, this time as a fan—without crutches. Millen scored forty-six goals in eighteen games as a senior, propelling Cloquet to its first state tournament in 1982. A broken ankle, however, made him the most significant nonparticipant in the event's history.

LAKEVILLE NORTH COACH Trent Eigner made no attempt to humble himself before the hockey gods. Before the 2014–15 season, Eigner challenged his stacked squad to go undefeated.

31–0.

"I felt I had a group that understood the magnitude of the opportunity," Eigner said. "The premise of going undefeated was to set the bar really high."

A loaded lineup featured six Division I–committed players backed by a supporting cast that had taken second at the previous state tournament.

Still, athletes believe that anticipating great outcomes creates bad karma. A baseball pitcher nearing a no-hitter isn't approached by teammates on the bench. National Hockey League players seldom touch the conference trophy.

But Eigner? Pfft. He gave players an A-plus grade long before they took the final exam.

And these Panthers did have it all. Senior twin brothers Jack and Nick Poehling, along with sophomore brother Ryan, formed a dynamic top line. One NHL scout said Henry Enebak, Max Johnson, and Taylor Schneider gave Lakeville North the state's two best lines.

A pair of Jacks on defense, McNeely and Sadek, backed by Angelo Altavilla and Luke Seper, made for a tough hand to beat.

"We all could skate and move the puck and had good heads for the game," McNeely said.

The final piece: junior goaltender Ryan Edquist, who, after Mites, left Lakeville in pursuit of higher-level hockey only to come back needing a regroup.

Edquist did not make the Under-17 US National Team Development Program. That spot went to Jake Oettinger, who as a freshman helped Lakeville North finish second at the 2014 state tournament.

"I definitely felt a little down after not making the NTDP," Edquist said. "But it also gave me the motivation to want to dominate the upcoming season."

"The opportunity to go back to Lakeville North was intrigu-ing," Edquist said. "Knowing what they had coming back, it looked like a special opportunity that was too good to pass up."

Edquist arrived from Shattuck–St. Mary's, the prestigious hockey factory in Faribault. Everyone assumed he would keep Lakeville North solid between the pipes and propel a run back to the championship game.

"I'm sure there were expectations of me," Edquist said. "I know I felt a little pressure."

But an inauspicious season opener at Farmington included five blown leads and a few soft goals. Several teammates doubted their new netminder.

"He goes out and fell over on one of the goals, and we're like, 'Is this our guy?'" Ryan Poehling said.

Edquist said, "There was a lot of hype. It's a big rivalry, and the crowd is rowdy and gets in your head. [Schmitz-Maki Arena] is one of the toughest buildings to play in, and I wasn't as confident."

A Jack Poehling overtime goal ensured a 6–5 victory and preserved big dreams.

"We talk about that all the time," Jack Poehling said. "We lose that game and the whole season is completely different."

Eigner said, "Ryan [Poehling] came to me on the bench while everyone was mobbing Jack and says, 'Eigs, we still have a chance to go undefeated.'"

Nine days later, two-time defending state champion Edina came to Ames Arena for the Panthers' home opener. The Hornets had owned Lakeville North in the past two state tournaments: a 9–3 thrashing in the 2013 quarterfinals and an 8–2 throttling in the 2014 title game.

This time, Lakeville North took control early. Nick Poehling scored twice in a sixty-one-second span in the first period. He later completed the hat trick in a 3–1 victory. Edquist rebounded with a solid twenty-eight-save performance.

"That proved we meant business," McNeely said.

Business was good whenever the Poehling twins were on. And their switches were stuck in the "on" position.

"The twins admittedly played with a chip on their shoulders," Eigner said. "Their aggressive style, which at times bordered on being a bit undisciplined earlier in their careers, was rechanneled toward our goal. This temperament actually was a catalyst for the group, and there was never a doubt who was driving the bus."

Tim Poehling named his sons Nick (first into the world by eight minutes) and Jack in honor of the legendary golfer Jack Nicklaus. Nick's golf-related middle name, Palmer, is the maiden name of his mother, Kris.

The wingers were talented and tough. Jack played with a torn labrum most of his junior year.

The duo became a trio in 2013–14 when Ryan Poehling joined his older brothers as a freshman. The youngster's laid-back approach balanced his brothers' intensity. The new line-mates hit the trifecta when they announced their commitment to St. Cloud State on Twitter at 8:58 PM on February 13, 2014.

Then they teamed up for a goal in the 2014 state tournament quarterfinals against Roseau: Jack from Ryan and Nick.

"The rest of the team does a great job understanding the uniqueness of the situation," Eigner said. "And the work that the brothers do every day in practice far outweighs anything that would distract their teammates."

Minimal hiccups occurred during the 2014–15 regular season. Trailing after the first periods in back-to-back games against Benilde–St. Margaret's and Wayzata, Lakeville North rallied to win each time.

The Panthers trailed for 38:58 all season. That's a little more than two periods.

"As the pressure mounted throughout the season, I enjoyed seeing them handle it the way they did," Eigner said. "You just knew they were going to do it."

Edquist became the force everyone expected. Rattled by a raucous high school hockey crowd on opening night—"You play at Shattuck in front of fifty people," Eigner said—Edquist learned to love the festive environment.

"High school hockey is completely different, and I was excited to experience it," Edquist said. "When you're playing for your school and you've got the band there, it makes the games more meaningful. It's some of the most fun hockey I've ever played."

And some of his best. Edquist finished the season with eight shutouts while stopping 94 percent of shots faced. The student section began a call and response after saves that went, "Eddy says . . . No!"

Lakeville North forward Nick Poehling was selected to the *Star Tribune* All-Metro team in 2015, and he backed up that honor with a stellar performance in the Panthers' tournament semifinal win over Eden Prairie, assisting on three third-period goals to secure a 6–2 triumph. Photo by Tim Kolehmainen/Breakdown Sports Media

240

Lakeville North's Ryan Poehling was diagnosed with mononucleosis in the days leading up to the state tournament. Although he was a liability in the semifinals, he returned to form in the Class 2A championship game, putting the Panthers ahead 1–0 against Duluth East. He goes hard to the net here against the Greyhounds' Gunnar Howg. Photo by Chris Juhn/SportsEngine

"He was so dependable," McNeely said. "Every puck that got dumped in, he set up the puck or passed it. He made it ten times easier for us."

The Panthers won both regular-season meetings with Farmington and drew the Tigers in the Section 1 championship. It was no contest. Enebak netted a hat trick in a 6–1 victory.

Lakeville North dispatched its first twenty-eight foes while also checking egos. Edquist, McNeely, and Nick Poehling were selected to the *Star Tribune* All-Metro team, and none of their talented teammates felt slighted.

"One of the inherent difficulties is there's only one puck," Eigner said. "How do you set up lines so that everybody feels they're contributing their perceived value? That can upset the apple cart, but they stayed well below the red line and that's 100 percent credit to the kids."

Senior goalie Pierce Wilson embodied the team's sacrifices. Edquist's arrival relegated Wilson to just two starts, but he was invaluable behind the scenes.

"He led the postgame locker room dance," Eigner said. "That was his role thirty-one times."

"Pierce Wilson deserves a ton of credit for the way he handled a tough situation," Edquist said. "He kept the whole team in good spirits."

United and unbeaten, Lakeville North earned the state tournament's top seed. The Panthers sought to become the first large-class team to finish undefeated since Bloomington Jefferson in 1993. The number-two seed went to one-loss Edina, aiming for the first large-class three-peat since those same Jaguars did it from 1992 to 1994.

Hockey observers salivated over a potential Panthers/Hornets final.

For Lakeville North, the quarterfinals brought Hill-Murray. The teams were tied 1–1 in the second period when Jack Poehling, incensed by a blown offsides call, went off. He won the ensuing faceoff just outside the Hill-Murray zone and beat three Pioneers before backhanding the puck home.

Another Jack Poehling backhand less than three minutes later—on assists from each brother—gave his team a two-goal lead en route to a 4–1 victory.

The semifinal against Eden Prairie sat tied 2–2 at second intermission. Twice, the Panthers led, but the Eagles fought back each time. Meanwhile, Ryan Poehling was losing an internal battle with his stamina.

A doctor had diagnosed Ryan with mononucleosis earlier in the week and refused to clear him to play in the tournament. The family sought a second opinion, and a third, and Ryan was allowed to resume, provided he adhered to bed rest and intravenous fluids when he wasn't playing.

Mono complications include an enlarged spleen, and Ryan said his almost doubled in size. He wore a flak jacket for added protection.

"I felt like Cam Newton," Ryan joked, referring to the NFL quarterback.

But he was noticeably dragging.

"After the second period, Nick and I were talking about how Ryan was slowing down," Jack Poehling said. "Eigs called us in and said, 'Ryan is playing terrible. I don't think I can play him on your line anymore.'"

The twins didn't hesitate to put the Panthers' brotherhood ahead of their own.

"We said, 'Get rid of him,'" Jack Poehling said.

Ryan Poehling saw action only on the power play in the final period.

"I'm glad they did it," he said. "I couldn't even move that night."

Enter sophomore forward Chaz Dufon. He scored four goals all season before receiving a crunch-time call-up. Eigner inserted Dufon rather than disrupting additional lines.

His team ahead 3–2 on Max Johnson's rebound goal, Dufon made his promotion count. He buried the puck for a two-goal advantage, and the Panthers cruised to a 6–2 victory.

Earlier Friday evening, unseeded Duluth East had shocked Edina and most of Minnesota with a 3–1 upset. A colossal finale and the Panthers' chance at ultimate redemption would not happen.

"Everyone wanted it," Ryan Poehling said. "But we beat Edina earlier, and it's tough to beat a great team twice. I wasn't pissed when they lost."

Lakeville North had edged Duluth East 2–1 on January 13.

Eigner and his assistant coaches on the bench, Jake Enebak and Jake Taylor, knew the Greyhounds played a methodical style. So Panthers coaches instructed players to do likewise.

"We were patient, workmanlike," Eigner said. "We like to run and gun, but our opponent wasn't going to allow it. We had a lot of teams try to shorten the game and try to catch us napping in the third period."

Duluth East coach Mike Randolph had called the Poehlings over after the mid-January game and told them, "You guys need to shoot the puck more."

They listened. All three scored in the rematch.

Nick Poehling intercepted a clearing attempt and fed Ryan for a goal and a 1–0 lead.

Jack Poehling's power-play goal from the blue line made it 2–0 after two periods. Then Angelo Altavilla delivered a clutch goal at 4:11 of the third period.

Committed to play Division I baseball at Nebraska, Altavilla had set the state's single-game record with twelve RBIs as a junior the previous spring. His hockey credentials were solid. His father, Bob Altavilla, was an assistant coach at Apple Valley when the Eagles won the 1996 title. Bob also was on Eigner's staff.

With Duluth East players keyed on him, Nick Poehling spotted Altavilla rushing in from the blue line and slid a pass for him to bury. 3–0 Panthers.

"After that goal, Duluth East had a massive hill to climb because we were really hard to score on," Eigner said.

Nick Poehling later hit the empty net for his first tournament goal and Lakeville North won 4–1 to achieve perfection. 31–0.

"The difference between winning and losing was the character we had," Ryan Poehling said. "We weren't just playing with each other; we were playing for each other."

At the postgame press conference, Randolph, unprompted, said, "It's a credit to those kids that they stuck together. The target was on them all year and they went undefeated. They're a true champion."

~DL~

Lakeville North players and coaches celebrate the fulfillment of their mission. The Panthers finished a perfect 31-0 and became the first large-class team to finish undefeated since Bloomington Jefferson in 1993. Photo by Chris Juhn/SportsEngine

BEST IN FLOW

Fun-intended All-Hockey Hair Team became coveted honor, internet sensation

Luke Seper could gauge the origins of his new Saint Mary's University teammates by the manner in which they inquired about his two greatest hockey exploits.

"The Canadians and North Dakota guys would bring up the state tournament," said Seper, a defenseman on Lakeville North's undefeated 2015 championship team. "One of the guys from Texas asked me, 'Are you the hockey hair guy?'"

That's what YouTube viewership in the hundreds of thousands will get you. And that speaks to the immense popularity of the All-Hockey Hair Team, a post-tournament sideshow turned internet sensation. Since 2011 and with no end in sight, the tournament

isn't complete until Saturday night's "best in flow" showcase.

The top-ten (and beyond) collection of mullets, mops, salads, and "dual exhaust pipes" elevated the importance of looking good for the quarterfinals' helmetless player introductions.

Filming clips of the introductions with his cell phone, a mystery narrator then guided viewers through his selections. Often hilarious, never mean-spirited, the narrator gave these hairdos their due and made social media stars out of players.

Fans loved it. Players aspired to be part of it. Seper started growing out his hair almost two years in advance. But who produced this low-budget classic?

The big reveal came in 2016, when

ESPN and hockey analyst Barry Melrose came to the state tournament and filmed an *E:60* segment called "Minneflowta." The mystery man's identity: John King, a forty-two-year-old marketing executive promoting what he considered "sort of our Minnesota superpowers" of hockey and hockey hair.

King's inaugural All-Hockey Hair Team aired in 2005 on local television but drew little notice. Reviving the concept in 2011 allowed King to tap into an expanded social mediaverse and society's equally growing desire for personal fame.

At the end of the 2014 video, King said he couldn't "imagine what next year will bring. I hope a ponytail."

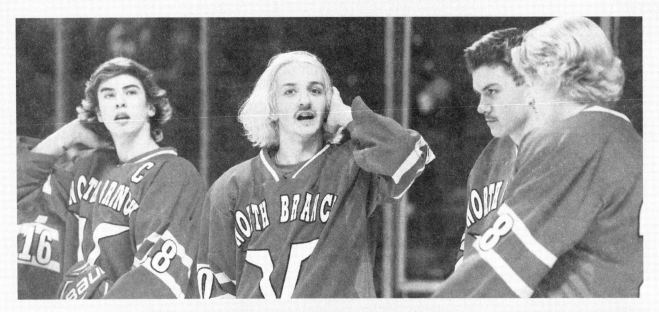

TOP: North Branch made its Class 1A state tournament debut in 2019, but its players sported veteran flow (left to right): Justin Sachs, Kade Koecher, Matt Courtright, and Dawson Johnson. Photo by Tim Kolehmainen/Breakdown Sports Media BOTTOM: New Ulm's Murderer's Row of hockey hair (from left): Shane Esser (14), Teagan Kamm (15), Hunter Hulke (16), and Blake Tauer (18). Photo by Tim Kolehmainen/Breakdown Sports Media LEFT: Luke Seper, Lakeville North's 6-foot-6 defenseman, drew a gasp from the Xcel Energy Center crowd after removing a ponytail band and unfurling his beautiful dark flow during player introductions at a 2015 quarterfinal game. Photo by Mark Hvidsten

Challenge accepted.

"I thought, 'I'll one-up that,'" Seper said.

A year later, Seper drew a gasp from the Xcel Energy Center crowd with his presentation. Already hard to miss at 6 foot 6, Seper skated to where his teammates stood for introductions, removed the ponytail band, and unfurled his beautiful dark flow.

"This kid was like Jimi Hendrix at Woodstock," King said on the video.

"We've never seen anything like it."

Still, King rated Seper second on the top-ten list.

"But when you go to YouTube, I'm the thumbnail image so that's a win in itself," Seper said.

King works with his wife and two children to select the teams. And he uses the videos to raise money for the Hendrickson Foundation, which promotes sled hockey, special hockey, and programs for military veterans.

King announced the 2019 state tournament would be his last. But he changed his mind and kept going with the flow, much to the delight of players.

"I see it as an added event," Seper said. "You're there for the hockey, but why not show off your hair?"

~DL~

HAMMER TIME

RUGGED WAYZATA TRASH-TALKER HANK SORENSEN BELOVED BY TEAMMATES

DATES	LOCATION	ATTENDANCE	CLASS 2A CHAMPIONSHIP
MARCH 2–5	XCEL ENERGY CENTER, ST. PAUL	123,316	WAYZATA 5, EDEN PRAIRIE 3
			CLASS 1A CHAMPIONSHIP HERMANTOWN 5, BRECK SCHOOL 0

 Hermantown ended an unprecedented run of six straight Class A championship game losses with a convincing 5–0 rout of Breck.

OPPONENTS LOATHED Hank Sorensen. Called him cheap, dirty, disrespectful, and dangerous.

A hack.

Unflattering adjectives were affixed to the Wayzata defenseman as easily as stickers slapped on a bumper.

Agitator, instigator, trash-talker.

Teammates saw Sorensen differently. To a man, they loved him.

"He was not just some fourth-line goon out there trying to pick fights," Billy Duma said. "He was the epitome of a guy you want on your team.

"But I would never want to play against that kid."

Nicknamed the Hammer because of his punishing style of play, Sorensen had complexity that made him more than the out-of-control cartoon character on skates so many typecast him to be. As a cornerstone junior during the 2015–16 season, he showed his kinder, gentler side to teammates each day.

"He's someone that you wouldn't expect to be this caring guy, but he was extremely loving of his teammates," goalie Alex Schilling said.

The 6-foot-1, 195-pound Sorensen scored eight goals and added ten assists in the regular season. His sixty-five penalty minutes were more than twice as many as any other player on the team and tied for twelfth most in the state, a testament to his nightly tightrope walk between fair and foul play. But it was Sorensen's zest for playing lockdown defense against opponents' top forwards that set him apart.

"He was the heart and soul of the team," Wayzata coach Pat O'Leary said. "He brought something to the table that you can't coach."

The Trojans were built on depth and defense. After a strong start, they suffered through a midseason tailspin during which they won just one of six games. They pulled out of their funk with a six-game winning streak that included a showdown with rival Eden Prairie. Sorensen's job was to make life miserable for Eagles star Casey Mittelstadt, a future Mr. Hockey Award winner and first-round NHL draft pick.

Wayzata won 4–2. Sorensen scored twice. Mittelstadt, who had scored a hat trick a few weeks earlier in a 4–2 win over the Trojans, managed a single assist.

The late-season momentum extended to the playoffs, and Wayzata might as well have scripted its state tournament quarterfinal matchup, what with Burnsville senior Cade Borchardt having scored hat tricks in all three of Burnsville's section playoff games. The game was set up as another Sorensen Special.

Borchardt opened the scoring late in the first period. But with Sorensen staring him down and roughing him up shift after shift, the Burnsville star was held scoreless the rest of the way in a 3–1 Wayzata triumph.

"It's just common sense," Sorensen said about his eagerness to go toe to toe against the opposition's star players. "It puts the team in a better place to win. If Borchardt doesn't score a hat trick, if their best player doesn't do well, their team doesn't do well."

Wayzata held Stillwater without a goal until the final minute of the third period in a semifinal that ended as a 2–1 Trojans' victory.

It was Hammerin' Hank versus Mighty Casey once again when Wayzata and Eden Prairie met in the championship. The fireworks started early: Sorensen's hit on Mittelstadt on the game's opening shift sent the Eden Prairie star skating gingerly to the bench. The banged-up Mittelstadt was examined briefly by a trainer but didn't miss a shift.

Sorensen was relentless in both his physical play and his verbal jousting.

"I remember one instance sitting at a TV timeout being a little sarcastic with him," Sorensen said about Mittelstadt. "I remember assistant coach Dave Brown said to me, 'Don't poke the bear.' I laid off him a little bit after that. Good memories."

Mittelstadt scored on a first-period power play, and Eden Prairie was leading 3–1 in the second when Sorensen was whistled for a five-minute major penalty for boarding.

"I remember hopping into the penalty box thinking, 'Shoot, this is it,'" Sorensen said. "They are probably going to score a couple of goals. I was kind of down."

Wayzata defenseman Hank Sorensen (right) took on Eden Prairie star Casey Mittelstadt (left) at every opportunity in the 2016 Class 2A title game. Photo by Mark Hvidsten/SportsEngine

O'Leary called a timeout. Wayzata's seniors did most of the talking.

"During that timeout, Amar Batra said, 'I am playing like [expletive]. I have to play better. I apologize. I am going to turn my act around,'" said Duma, a senior co-captain. "I credit a lot of what happened next to him."

Duma forced a turnover and sailed in on a two-on-one with Luke Paterson. Duma finished the passing play, and the short-handed goal pulled the Trojans to within 3–2. With the teams playing four on four after an Eden Prairie penalty, Matt Nelson tied the score at three with seventy seconds left in the second.

"My teammates covered my ass," Sorensen said.

Wayzata got the winning goal from Logan Lindstrand early in the third, and Colin Schmidt clinched the 5–3 victory with an empty-net goal with two seconds remaining.

"It was pretty hard to stop us from winning that third period with all the momentum we had going into it," said Schilling, who finished with thirty saves. "I've never seen a game change that quickly."

During the postgame media session, an intensely disappointed Mittelstadt was asked about Sorensen's tactics. You could all but see the fire coming out of Mittelstadt's nostrils as he downplayed the Hammer's impact.

"I'm not going to change how I play if he's on the ice," Mittelstadt said. "I don't care if I get hacked or slashed. I'm going to keep going to the net."

Sorensen took command in the interview room just as he had on the ice, repeatedly interjecting comments as Lindstrand and Schilling were being asked questions.

"My boy Logan here has been working on that, after practice," Sorensen said about Linstrand's winning shot from the point.

When the conversation turned to Schilling's performance, Sorensen spoke up again in praise, describing the goaltender as a "brick wall."

"Hammer was always up for a good time, and as much as he made enemies on the ice, he made friends off the ice really easily," Schilling said. "I've never met someone like him."

~*LRN*~

In front of their ecstatic fans, Wayzata players dropped everything to celebrate their 2016 state championship. Photo by Mark Hvidsten/SportsEngine

OPPORTUNITY LOST—AND FOUND

GRAND RAPIDS PLAYERS TALKED DISMAYED COACH INTO RETURNING, THEN WON HIM A TITLE

DATES	LOCATION	ATTENDANCE	CLASS 2A CHAMPIONSHIP
MARCH 8–11	XCEL ENERGY CENTER, ST. PAUL	126,255	GRAND RAPIDS 6, MOORHEAD 3
			CLASS 1A CHAMPIONSHIP
			HERMANTOWN 4, MONTICELLO/ANNANDALE/MAPLE LAKE 3 (2 OT)

Did you know? Hermantown senior forward Ryan Sandelin, whose father, Scott, coaches three-time NCAA champion Minnesota Duluth, scored four goals in Hermantown's 6–5 semifinal victory, including the winner with 21.3 seconds left in overtime.

IN LATE MARCH 2016, the entire Grand Rapids hockey team met at its home rink, the Itasca Recreation Association Civic Center, to convince coach Trent Klatt to reconsider his recent resignation.

Klatt, a fourteen-year NHL veteran in his first season as a varsity head coach, had just guided the Thunderhawks to their first state tournament in eleven years. But talented sophomore forward Blake McLaughlin got suspended for a rules violation and missed the tournament.

Players knew McLaughlin's suspension and Klatt's resignation were symptoms of larger problems within the team, though specifics remain private.

Players also knew they possessed the talent to challenge for a Class 2A title but needed Klatt. At the meeting, they spoke less about hockey and more about being accountable young men.

"We had an attitude on our team," McLaughlin said. "That's why [Klatt] left. We had to grow up and take responsibility for our actions."

Forward Micah Miller said, "We had to change some things as a team. We had to be more truthful, obey rules, and not get into trouble."

Klatt listened. A few days later, he came back to coach.

"We knew we could get him back if we said the right things," forward Gavin Hain said. "He wanted to coach us."

Grand Rapids, the lone program on the hockey-proud Iron Range to opt up and play in Class 2A, doesn't have the enrollment numbers to compete annually for a state title.

But the 2016–17 team had what it took. Many of the juniors had won the Bantam AA state championship two years earlier.

A refocused Thunderhawks team featured the dynamic Hain, McLaughlin, and Miller line producing 188 points. Fate united the terrific trio.

Miller, who lived in Remer and began playing youth hockey in Crosby, drove forty-five minutes to and from Grand Rapids throughout high school. He blasted music to stay awake on those predawn trips north on Highway 6 to County Road 63. Sophomore year, he fell asleep and totaled his car.

"It was tough but always worth it," Miller said.

McLaughlin grew up in Elk River and at age ten lost his father, Jon, to a heart attack. His mother met former Grand Rapids hockey standout and recent widower Grant Bischoff, and the two married. Blake, then in middle school, moved north.

Marriage also played a role in Klatt's arrival in Grand Rapids. The former Osseo High School star and his wife, Kelly, bought a house next door to Kelly's twin sister, Kerby. She married former Greenway star Ken Gernander, Trent's University of Minnesota teammate.

The state tournament had always been out of reach for Klatt's late-1980s Osseo teams. Getting there as a coach felt "like I got my second chance," he said.

But the Thunderhawks' 2016 team struggled after learning of McLaughlin's suspension an hour before the team bus left for the state tournament.

"That 100 percent derailed us," Klatt said. "I believe if he played, we would have won. Blake has the ability to win a game at any moment. He's that good, that dynamic."

Grand Rapids fell 6–2 against Eden Prairie in the semifinals and regrouped to finish third.

The team meeting a few weeks later brought both the return of Klatt and a renewed purpose.

"Our core group loved to play King of the Hill," Klatt said. "When they were not on top, they would do anything possible to get to the top."

As the number-four seed for the Section 7 playoffs, Grand Rapids endured two huge tests. Down 3–2 against Elk River in the third period of the semifinals, the Thunderhawks roared back for a 5–3 victory. Hain tallied a hat trick.

Miller's goal in double overtime against Duluth East sent the team back to St. Paul—this time with the entire roster.

Still, Klatt wasn't taking chances with distractions.

"On the way to the Cities, there was a big bucket on the bus to put your phone in," senior defenseman Jack Bowman said.

Grand Rapids, the number-five seed, drew number-four Maple Grove to start. Down 2–0 less than five minutes into

Grand Rapids teammates (from left) John Stampohar, Micah Miller, and Gavin Hain celebrate Miller's goal in the third period of the 2017 Class 2A title game. Miller, Hain, and linemate Blake McLaughlin produced a combined 188 points during the season. Photo by Tim Kolehmainen/Breakdown Sports Media

the game, Grand Rapids rallied for a 6–4 victory. McLaughlin scored twice, including the game-winner.

"I told them, 'You guys are driving me nuts,'" Klatt said.

Another situation nagged Klatt: his goaltenders. Good friends Gabe Holum and Zach Stejskal rotated until Holum suffered a minor injury late in the season.

Stejskal started the final two section games and the state quarterfinal. Holum, however, was healthy for the semifinal against Eden Prairie. And he had beaten the Eagles 3–1 in December. But Klatt stayed with Stejskal.

Grand Rapids wanted this game bad—ever since Eden Prairie's amazing Casey Mittelstadt announced that he was staying for his senior season. The Thunderhawks saw the Eagles during the summer and the regular season and won each time.

"That was huge for our confidence," Miller said. "We weren't intimidated anymore."

Klatt shortened his bench, using television timeouts to keep his top two lines fresh.

"No disrespect to them, but we didn't have three lines we could just roll," Klatt said. "I'm not proud of it. But that was the time to try and win it."

The top line was blanked, but defenseman John Stampohar and forwards Keaghan Graeber and Connor Stefan tallied goals. Stejskal stopped forty-seven shots, including twenty-four in the third period, in a 3–2 upset of number-one seed Eden Prairie.

Players believed they couldn't lose in the championship game against Moorhead despite a 4–0 Spuds victory on February 11. The first time around, Klatt had benched Hain for the night and McLaughlin for a period as punishment for undisciplined play during the previous game against Bemidji.

The top line was intact and magnificent in the rematch.

Hain tallied a hat trick, and the Thunderhawks led 4–2 after two periods. Miller and McLaughlin added goals, the latter an empty-net goal that sent Hain jumping for joy.

A 6–3 victory brought Grand Rapids its first state championship in thirty-seven years.

"It wasn't easy, but these guys took me on a fun ride," Klatt said.

~DL~

Captain Gavin Hain led Grand Rapids with a hat trick in the Class 2A championship game, and he led the postgame celebration by skating the trophy to the Thunderhawks' student section. The 6–3 victory over Moorhead brought Grand Rapids its first state title since 1980. Photo by Tim Kolehmainen/Breakdown Sports Media

GLUE GUY

MATURE BEYOND HIS YEARS, JOE MOLENAAR ENSURED MINNETONKA'S COLLECTIVE MINDSET WAS "RIGHT"

DATES	LOCATION	ATTENDANCE	CLASS 2A CHAMPIONSHIP
MARCH 7–10	XCEL ENERGY CENTER, ST. PAUL	121,389	MINNETONKA 5, DULUTH EAST 2
			CLASS 1A CHAMPIONSHIP
			ORONO 2, ALEXANDRIA 1

Did you know? Edina defenseman Jake Boltmann and Centennial goaltender Travis Allen killed time during a break in the third-place game by passing the puck back and forth, Boltmann setting up Allen for one-timers, much to the crowd's delight.

THE NIGHT BELONGED to Joe Molenaar.

The mosh pits and dog piles, the high fives and fist bumps, the bear hugs and the tears—the Minnetonka senior wasn't just in the middle of them all. He *owned* them.

Molenaar's night? Forget about him setting up first- and second-period goals. How about the pass rocketing in from the blue line—too hot for Molenaar to handle—and caroming off his left skate . . . straight into the net?

"When that one went in, you kind of question whether it is going to be your night or not," longtime Duluth East coach Mike Randolph said about falling behind by two goals early in the third period of the 2018 state championship game.

Randolph's instincts were right. This was Molenaar's night.

Molenaar was among the first on the scene after Matt Koethe scored into an empty net in the final minute. Yep, that was Molenaar diving headfirst like a linebacker onto the stumbling, tumbling, overjoyed Koethe after the goal secured Minnetonka's 5–2 victory and first state title.

The celebrations kept on coming, another after the final horn sounded, another after the Skippers received their championship trophy, and another for an award that could have only gone to Molenaar.

Described alternately as the team's "glue guy," "spoke," and "satellite" by Skippers coach Sean Goldsworthy, Molenaar organized team summer activities, helped the student managers carry stick bags to and from the team bus, and thanked every staff member he could find at visiting arenas for their hospitality.

"My mom and dad always preached that respect for everybody that you are around," Molenaar said.

Molenaar's father, Steve, died in 2011 at the age of forty-five, five months after being diagnosed with cancer. Steve had been the captain of Bloomington Jefferson's 1984 team. Joe was twelve when he lost his father and biggest fan.

"I think with his dad passing at a young age, he was forced to grow and mature quicker than anyone else," fellow senior and

Senior Joe Molenaar provided ample amounts of leadership and goal scoring to help Minnetonka win the 2018 state championship. Photo by Tim Kolehmainen/ Breakdown Sports Media

co-captain Luke Loheit said. "No one else could have handled it better than he did. We all looked up to him for it."

Molenaar had a knack for knowing just what to say and when to say it. If the team was too tight, he'd tell a joke to lighten the mood. If teammates started worrying too much about individual success, he had words for them, too.

"He was acting like a college captain more so than a high school kid," Goldsworthy said. "He understood that if the room wasn't right, we weren't going to win, and his whole objective was to win. Completely selfless."

Goldsworthy said Molenaar, the team's top goal scorer with thirty-one in thirty-one games, was easy to talk to. He said the duo shared a lot of "heart to hearts" during the season. The first-year Minnetonka coach had a lot in common with his co-captain.

Goldsworthy had been co-captain of Minnetonka's 1989–90 team, which finished third at the state tournament. His late father, Bill Goldsworthy, was best known for his "Goldy Shuffle" goal celebrations with the Minnesota North Stars. Bill died in 1996 just as Sean was beginning his coaching career with a brief stint as an assistant at St. John's University.

Sean took over the Minnetonka program in the summer of 2017 after spending a combined twenty-three seasons as player and coach at St. Olaf College in Northfield.

"I would say his biggest strength was relating to the players," Molenaar said about Goldsworthy. "He got to know each one of us on a deeper, personal level. It's not very often where each and every one of the guys loves his coach."

The players all loved Molenaar, too.

Molenaar connected with everyone, from baby-faced, braces-wearing sophomore Bobby Brink to Loheit, 6 foot 1 and 185 chiseled pounds of unadulterated intimidation.

"He was always the guy you could go to when you have a tough decision," Brink said.

Loheit and Brink each centered a high-scoring forward line. And that's where the similarities ended. Brink was to would-be defenders what the Harlem Globetrotters are to the Washington Generals. Which is to say the 5-foot-9 jitterbug, as clever as he was dragster quick, was so dominant at times he was met with what looked like only token, comical resistance.

Loheit loomed at the other end of Minnetonka's royal-blue-and-white spectrum. With his shaved head, bristly facial hair, and hardcore temperament, Loheit might have walked straight out of a Metallica jam session and into the Skippers' locker room. Getting in Loheit's way was like stepping in front of a bullet train. Opposing players called him Psycho. (But not to his face.)

"I always knew that when Loheit was coming to hit me in practice that was a place that I didn't want to be," Brink said.

No matter the Skippers' differences, Molenaar ensured they were a tight bunch. They hung out at the lake, watched movies, lifted weights, and shot pucks—they did most everything as a group.

"We were like a giant family," Molenaar said. "It was so

tough to play that last game knowing we were never going to be together again."

Minnetonka had won back-to-back state Bantam AA titles in 2015 and 2016. Expectations had never been higher for a high school program that had made five previous state tournament appearances—but none since 2010, when the favored Skippers finished second to Edina.

The victory over Duluth East completed a 27–2–2 season. The postgame ceremonies included the announcement of the Class 2A Herb Brooks Award winner that goes to the player who exhibits, among other traits, strong leadership qualities, willingness to sacrifice for the team, integrity, and mental toughness.

Molenaar, the Skippers' "no-brainer" nominee for the award, according to Goldsworthy, was announced the winner.

"It was emotional," said Brink, whose scored a tournament-best five goals despite playing with torn knee cartilage. "Just listening to him give his speech made me tear up."

"When he got his name called, I burst into tears," Loheit said. "I think that was his dad rewarding him for all his hard work.

"He was watching over him."

~LRN~

Minnetonka seniors Joe Molenaar (left) and Andrew Hicks get wrapped up in the joy of winning a state championship after the Skippers defeated Duluth East 5-2 in the 2018 title game. Photo by Tim Kolehmainen/Breakdown Sports Media

PAINTINGS SPEAK VOLUMES

Terrence Fogarty's tourney-inspired art tells story of event's homespun appeal

Generations of hockey players creating art with sticks and pucks on ice inspired Terrence Fogarty to do likewise with brushes and paints on canvas.

Since 1998, the state's signature high school tournament has featured a Fogarty painting on the program cover. Whether depicting fictional rinks, real places such as Mork's Pond, or spot-on renditions of the old St. Paul Civic Center, Fogarty's works carry hockey's spirit.

More than twenty years of revered program covers make Fogarty the Norman Rockwell of Minnesota hockey. While no self-promoter, he sees a connection to the illustrator and painter best known for *Saturday Evening Post* magazine covers.

"That's what I like about his work—it conveys a certain sentiment and stirs certain emotions, as corny as they might be to some," Fogarty said.

Fogarty's hockey art speaks to Tim Poehling, a longtime collector.

"They are a really cool thing that create their own little stories," Poehling said.

And boy, does Poehling have a story.

Fogarty created a historical scrapbook for the 2019 program cover honoring the tournament's seventy-fifth year. The old-time greats received their due: There are portraits of Eveleth's John Mayasich and Warroad's Henry Boucha. Bygone dynasties International Falls and St. Paul Johnson are recognized. And "Champ," the houndstooth hat Willard Ikola wore while coaching Edina/Edina East to eight state championships, is included.

When it came to modern-era greatness, Fogarty sought an item from Poehling to represent Lakeville North. Three of Poehling's sons—Jack, Nick, and Ryan—played key roles on the Panthers' undefeated 2015 state championship team.

But the black helmet used in the painting belonged to youngest son Luke. A permanent connection to Fogarty's work brings Poehling's love for the tournament full circle. In the 1970s, Poehling skipped school to attend the state tournament. He kept those programs and later became a collector.

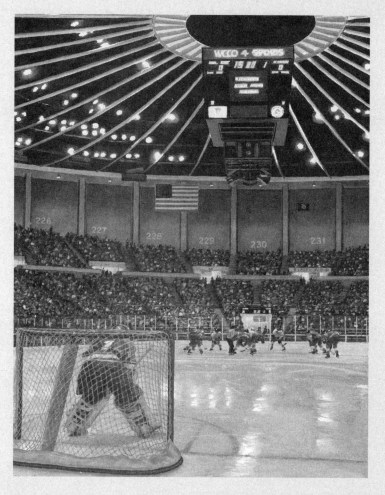

Since 1998, the state's signature high school tournament has featured a Terrence Fogarty painting on the program cover. This particular work, *'91 Final—Hill-Murray versus Duluth East*, was done as a study for the painting *Champions*. Fogarty's works are beloved for carrying hockey's spirit. Image courtesy of Karen and Terrence Fogarty

Fogarty's 1999 cover *Tribute* ranks as a favorite among Fogarty art collectors. The panoramic painting features players donning jerseys of the tournament's best teams, gathered on the ice within the clear boards at the St. Paul Civic Center. There's Rochester John Marshall's red, some Grand Rapids orange, and the maroon of St. Paul Johnson, Fogarty's alma mater.

Fogarty and his wife, Karen, make the four-day tournament their art gallery. Folks drop by their display located on the main concourse, offering praise for the work and sharing their own hockey tournament stories.

Fogarty also started painting covers for the girls' hockey state tournament programs in 1999. He takes great pride in providing both tournaments with additional pageantry.

"It's like getting a part in a good sitcom that does well," Fogarty said. "The great thing about the state tournament and, I suppose, the State Fair, is that they never really change. It's fun to have some things that remain."

~DL~

GOING THE DISTANCE

TWO UNHERALDED SENIORS SECURED EDINA'S THIRTEENTH STATE TITLE

DATES	LOCATION	ATTENDANCE	CLASS 2A CHAMPIONSHIP
MARCH 6–9	XCEL ENERGY CENTER, ST. PAUL	119,813	EDINA 3, EDEN PRAIRIE 2 (OT)
			CLASS 1A CHAMPIONSHIP
			ST. CLOUD CATHEDRAL 5, GREENWAY 2

 Greenway/Nashwauk-Keewatin, less than a decade removed from almost folding due to dwindling numbers, became the tournament's darlings with a stirring run to the championship game.

JOYFUL ON-ICE MOBS bookended Edina's season, each signifying happy conclusions to difficult journeys.

The first one happened November 15, near the Zamboni entrance at Braemar Arena, in honor of Kevin Delaney. The relentless senior had earned a varsity spot, the first time he played on the top team for his age group.

The second came March 9, before a raucous Edina student section at the Xcel Energy Center, to celebrate the Hornets' Class 2A state championship.

Delaney, who took the backroads through Edina's youth system, tallied a goal and an assist in the 3–2 overtime victory against Eden Prairie. Peter Colby, relegated to the third line, scored twice, including the game-winning goal. Together, Colby and Delaney joined Rick Wineberg (1971), Marty Nanne (1984), and Rob Morris (1988) as unlikely heroes to shine for a title-winning Edina team.

Questions persisted about even college-bound studs Jett Jungels and Mason Nevers, who were manhandled by Duluth East in a 2018 state tournament semifinal loss. They were two of the returning Hornets with a salty spoon in their mouths.

"The year before, we thought we had a good chance, but we didn't have the character to be a championship team," Colby said. "This team had that."

Coach Curt Giles only nudged his group at times, like he did as Edina prepared for its first meeting with loathed rival Minnetonka.

The defending state champion Skippers were the stars of *Dream. State.* The season-long, six-part documentary made the target on Minnetonka visible from outer space. Giles saw an opportunity.

"He put one of the episodes on in the locker room that week and was like, 'Look at these guys,'" Delaney said.

Message received.

Trailing 2–1 at Minnetonka's Pagel Activity Center, Edina erupted with four unanswered goals in the third period. The 5–2 victory against the previously undefeated Skippers moved the Hornets to number one.

Delaney contributed to the late barrage with his thirteenth goal of the season, a remarkable output from a player consistently on the wrong side of cuts in youth hockey.

A seat at the big table had always eluded Delaney. Varsity tryouts senior year were his final chance. On Wednesday, Delaney saw several seniors cast aside. He remained. Thursday made it official. Delaney would pull a varsity jersey over his head, an arrival made sweeter by all those detours.

"Every level looks up to varsity, so it was so cool to make it," Delaney said.

"You don't just pick a hockey team on pure talent," Giles said. "You pick on character as well, and he was a kid who fought his whole way through. We've had a couple other players come from somewhere along those lines, but they didn't have as big of an impact."

"Kevin is a good kid and we wanted him on the team," Colby said. "Not too many kids are willing to stick with it."

Teams struggled to stay with Edina for entire games. The Hornets outscored their opponents 70–18 in third periods and overtimes. They used four goals in the third period to beat Benilde–St. Margaret's 5–1 in the Section 6 championship game.

Edina earned the number-one seed for the seventy-fifth state tournament, but Giles kept poking his players. Quarterfinal opponent Moorhead had observers noting the ten-year anniversary of the Spuds' first-round upset of the top-seed Hornets.

"Curt told us to use what people were saying as motivation," said Delaney, who scored in a 4–2 victory.

Senior wing Liam Malmquist's hat trick led Edina's 6–3 semifinal victory against St. Thomas Academy.

A fourth meeting with Lake Conference rival Eden Prairie came next. The invigorated Eagles led 1–0 at first intermission, outshooting Edina 13–5.

"Curt told us, 'You can't wait until the third period to save this thing—do it now,'" Colby said. "Then we go out and get two shots in the second period."

Edina goaltender Louden Hogg, a transfer from Wyoming,

254

limited Eden Prairie to a 1–0 lead after two periods. In the locker room, Edina's seniors rediscovered their urgency.

"It wasn't their night in the first couple periods, but they never quit, they never jumped on each other, they never barked at each other," Giles said afterward. "All they did was make a dedication to themselves in the third period that they were going to change."

Giles also made changes, juggling the six seniors on the top two forward lines. Malmquist moved to the first line with Jungels and Nevers. Colby went up to the second line with Delaney and Brett Chorske.

Delaney and Colby spurred the comeback. Delaney tied the game 1–1 at 5:21, and Colby put Edina ahead 2–1 just twenty-two seconds later. Eden Prairie, no longer the overmatched team of three previous losses to the Hornets, forced overtime.

Colby's speed and tenacity had helped him make all the top youth teams. But being a player who was "never noteworthy" gave an "edge to him," Giles said. Colby led the team with thirty-five penalty minutes.

"I didn't have to be a goal scorer, but I needed to have an edge," said Colby, who totaled just seven goals and five assists heading into the state tournament.

"All year long, he had great opportunities," Giles said. "He could've scored fifteen, eighteen goals. He has a great shot and gets himself in good position, but it never quite happened."

Giles stayed with Colby but didn't picture him as the hero.

"You take a look at those top six kids we had in there at the end against Eden Prairie, and you're not going to say, 'I betcha Colby gets the game-winner,'" Giles said.

But that's exactly who did. A personnel change on the fly sent Colby straight from the bench into the offensive zone. Jungels threaded the puck into the slot, and with Chorske screening the goalie, Colby fired the puck through his teammate's legs.

Exactly fifty years since winning its first state championship, Edina clinched its thirteenth title.

"We had worked so hard all year," Colby said, "and to be in that position, and to come away with it is such a great feeling."

~DL~

Kevin Delaney finally gave Edina life offensively with his game-tying third-period goal in the 2019 Class 2A final. Delaney, who took the backroads through Edina's youth system, tallied a goal and an assist in the 3-2 overtime victory over Eden Prairie. Photo by Tim Kolehmainen/Breakdown Sports Media

HARD TRUTH

MAHTOMEDI SHEDS "SOFT" REPUTATION TO WIN PROGRAM'S FIRST STATE TOURNAMENT TITLE

DATES	LOCATION	ATTENDANCE	CLASS 2A CHAMPIONSHIP
MARCH 4–7	XCEL ENERGY CENTER, ST. PAUL	118,141	HILL-MURRAY 4, EDEN PRAIRIE 1
			CLASS 1A CHAMPIONSHIP
			MAHTOMEDI 3, HERMANTOWN 2 (OT)

Did you know? Hill-Murray senior Charlie Strobel and sophomore Dylan Godbout skated the same championship lane as their families' previous generations did with the 1990–91 Pioneers. Father Mike and uncle Mark Strobel were teammates of father Jason and uncle Brent Godbout.

MANY TALENTED Mahtomedi hockey teams fell short of state tournament success, and coach Jeff Poeschl said the explanation wasn't hard.

The Zephyrs were soft.

Before the 2020 state tournament, Mahtomedi was 0-for-5 in the semifinals. It was always some dang thing.

In 2010, an apparent Mahtomedi goal scored with no time remaining in regulation triggered a massive on-ice celebration. Video review (correctly) overturned the call. Spent emotionally, the Zephyrs lost 7–6 in overtime to Hermantown.

In 2015, East Grand Forks outworked and outhit Mahtomedi into submission. Green Wave coach Tyler Palmiscno called it a "man's game," which his team won 5–2.

The 2018 game against Orono featured a promising Zephyrs' comeback from a 4–0 deficit—yet ended with a 5–4 overtime loss.

A year later, Greenway/Nashwauk-Keewatin pulled a 3–2 overtime upset of the top-seeded Zephyrs. That one really hurt. "I thought that this was the group that would push us over the top," Poeschl said afterward.

As the 2019–20 season started, Poeschl made his intentions clear.

Mahtomedi senior forward Colin Hagstrom was his team's top scorer as a junior with twenty goals. But a broken fibula threatened to derail his senior season and the Zephyrs' chances. He returned and finished his prep career with the overtime winner against Hermantown to secure Mahtomedi's first Class 1A state title after years of semifinals failures. Photo by Tim Kolehmainen/Breakdown Sports Media

Just a sophomore, Ben Dardis gave Mahtomedi the ultimate state tournament ingredient—a hot goaltender. Dardis stopped eighty-seven of ninety-two shots faced for a .946 save percentage on the biggest stage. Photo by Tim Kolehmainen/Breakdown Sports Media

"I told our players, 'We need to name it, to call it what it is. We can't dream of winning a state championship without first winning the semifinal game,'" Poeschl said. "I was tired of giving that speech after losing the semifinal game about how fortunate we still are to be playing in the third-place game."

Poeschl worried the call for renewed urgency might be wasted on subpar skill.

"We weren't loaded," Poeschl said. "We had a good group. But if you watch tape of that team around Christmastime, you would say, 'How in the world would they ever win the state tournament?'"

Mahtomedi got pummeled 9–2 on December 21 at Hermantown, part of what Poeschl called the team's "coma" after losing senior Colin Hagstrom to injury. Hagstrom, the Zephyrs' top scorer as a junior with twenty goals, slammed into the boards and broke the fibula in his left leg on December 10.

However unlikely it seemed at the time, the resulting lineup shifts led to success. Players were forced into new or expanded roles.

Junior JD Metz, a forward through most of youth hockey before switching to defense in high school, moved back to the front halfway through a January 11 game against Hill-Murray.

He assisted on third-period goals by new linemates Nikolai Dulak and Adam Johnson in a 3–2 victory.

The emergence of sophomore defenseman Grant Dardis made moving Metz an option. Dardis worked his way into a regular shift as a top-four defenseman about midway through the season.

Hagstrom assumed a new role as servant leader. He attended every Zephyrs practice and game. He filled water bottles.

"He would have a boot on at practice and be on the ice stick-handling," Johnson said. "He showed how dedicated he was to the team. And we wanted to show how dedicated we were to him."

When Hagstrom returned after thirteen games for a January 28 contest with Stillwater, he joined Dulak and Metz on the top line. Johnson dropped to the second line with fellow juniors Dylan Duckson and Ethan Peterson, giving the Zephyrs two forward units with offensive potency.

"We no longer had to worry whether we had last change," Poeschl said.

And with sophomore Ben Dardis between the pipes, the Zephyrs didn't need to fret about their goaltending.

Dardis, a triplet along with brothers Grant and Jack, earned the starting job as a freshman. He helped the Zephyrs reach the state tournament, finishing his ninth-grade season 13–5–1 with a 1.57 goals-against average, .930 save percentage, and five shutouts. Mahtomedi opened the 2019–20 season with a rare luxury: a seasoned sophomore goalie.

Though he started every game as a sophomore, Dardis was kept honest by Poeschl, a former Hill-Murray goaltender who started for the Pioneers in three state tournaments (1978–80).

Dardis took a 3–1 loss on January 9 against Tartan and fellow sophomore goalie Jack Cashin. Afterward, Poeschl told Dardis, "Cashin outplayed you tonight," to which Dardis replied, "Yes, he did."

Poeschl's challenge proved extra useful when Mahtomedi faced Tartan in the Section 4 semifinals. Dardis stopped all twenty-nine shots faced in a 2–0 victory. He finished the season with seven shutouts.

"It was so satisfying to tell him afterward, 'You outplayed him,'" Poeschl said.

The good feelings vanished as Delano grabbed a 2–0 lead in the state tournament quarterfinals. Not to worry, though, because Mahtomedi exploded with four goals in the third period. All season long, a program scarred by late-game collapses was a consistent closer. Poeschl called it "finishing the sandwich." The Zephyrs outscored foes by a combined 47–21 in third periods.

Another lopsided cumulative statistic took shape during Mahtomedi's state tournament run. Semifinal opponent Warroad, the top seed, outshot the Zephyrs 30–18. But Dardis and goals from five different skaters, including unheralded seniors Billy Buttermore (forward) and Nathan Gruhlke (defense), who only played junior varsity in 2018–19, each scored against the Warriors.

The Zephyrs finally picked the lock on the door to the state tournament title game.

"After the game, we were at Patrick McGovern's, and we saw some alumni who were like, 'I can't believe we're finally going to play for the state championship,'" Gruhlke said.

Next up: Hermantown.

Power-play goals from Metz and Peterson provided a 2–0 Mahtomedi lead early in the second period. The Hawks cut their deficit to 2–1. But the Zephyrs remained on the cusp of a state championship until Aaron Pionk's tying goal with 21.2 seconds remaining in regulation.

Another state tournament, another Mahtomedi collapse, right? Wrong.

"You can read a team, and there was never that feeling of, 'Oh, man, now we don't have a chance,'" Poeschl told the media after the game. "It was: 'All right, let's get after it. We're going to need another goal.'"

Hagstrom, who committed to play lacrosse at Maryland before switching to Notre Dame, made his final hockey game one to remember. He scored at 2:44 of overtime for his hundredth career point and made program history.

"It felt weird," said Hagstrom, a veteran of four state tournaments. "It seemed so hard. Now I was looking at the scoreboard like, 'Wow, we finally figured it out.'"

Once again, Mahtomedi was outshot. This time 42–12. The Zephyrs' twelve shots on goal set a record for the fewest by the winning team in a championship game. The previous mark of fourteen was set in the 1977 Rochester John Marshall upset of Edina East.

Mahtomedi skaters did their best Ben Dardis impressions, blocking twenty-six shots—a combined eleven by Tony Neubeck and Grant Dardis.

"Even guys who don't normally block shots were blocking shots," Ben Dardis said. "That gave us the best chance of beating a team we probably didn't have any business beating."

Poeschl said his team's past overtime losses in the semifinals against Orono and Greenway both came on goals that "started with a shot from the point. If you want to block a shot, you will. But if you don't, you won't. And we looked like flamingos."

The Zephyrs finally put their foot down.

"This was a significant win for our alumni and our community," Poeschl said. "We were no longer the little engine that couldn't."

~*DL*~

SURPRISE APPEARANCE

Hill-Murray junior defenseman Joey Palodichuk missed the game but snuck into the celebration

Joey Palodichuk kept Hill-Murray progressing toward a Class 2A state championship while his health steadily deteriorated.

Then on Saturday, just hours before the title game, the standout junior defenseman made himself an unhealthy scratch. Two days of a cough and a sore throat, plus increasingly swollen eyes and worsening pain on his left torso convinced Palodichuk to see a doctor.

He had mononucleosis.

"My spleen was twice the normal size," Palodichuk said. "The first two games, I was lucky. The doctor said, 'I don't know how you've been playing.'"

Palodichuk, a *Star Tribune* All-Metro third-team selection who had verbally committed to Wisconsin, believed he was done.

"I brought the guys together and said, 'I'm out,'" Palodichuk said. "I told them, 'Play for me and the guy next to you and get the W.'"

Never in eight state tournament championship game appearances (four each as an assistant coach and head coach) had Bill Lechner dealt with this manner of drama. He called the Pioneers together and mustered his own version of analytics.

"I told them, 'Joey is in a tough situation, and he's a big part of what we do,'" Lechner recalled. "I said, 'If everyone plays 5 percent better, we're going to do this.'"

Lechner's confidence was a front. Behind the scenes, the coaching staff scrambled to adjust the special teams. Penalty kill. Power play. They were reminded of the many hats Palodichuk, second on the team with thirty-five assists and third with thirty-nine points, wore with aplomb.

Palodichuk had to wear his helmet to be allowed on the team bench for Saturday's game. He plucked it out of his equipment bag, which team managers Connor Laschinger and Andrew Schlundt had brought—just in case.

Palodichuk traded his on-ice role to play both Pioneers' cheerleader and adviser as the team battled Eden Prairie.

Hill-Murray received the game's first power play and made good on the opportunity. Defenseman Matthew Fleischhacker put his team ahead 1–0, and the Pioneers would never trail or be tied.

Charlie Strobel's second goal of the game bumped Hill-Murray's lead to 4–1 with about six minutes remaining in the third period. Palodichuk had an idea. He slipped off the bench and into the Xcel Energy Center tunnel. He reemerged dressed in his full uniform and skates—right down to the tape on his socks. He took a water bottle and wet his hair to complete the subterfuge. Then he sat with teammates as they all counted down to the on-ice celebration.

Assistant coach Pat Schafhauser, who runs the defense, turned and shot Palodichuk an incredulous look.

"Schaf looked at me like, 'What are you doing?'" Palodichuk said.

Lechner didn't notice until the game went final.

"All of a sudden, we see number 2 go over the boards," he said.

Video shows Palodichuk, in his black Pioneers' jersey, standing near the pile of crazed teammates. Moments later, as players gathered for a picture with the trophy, Palodichuk found a spot in the lower right corner. He finished with two assists in the state tournament and one memorable surprise appearance.

"Of course, I wanted to be playing, but it is what it is," Palodichuk said. "The guys got it done, and I'm still a state champion."

~*DL*~

Initially sidelined for the Class 2A state championship game by a bout of mononucleosis, standout Hill-Murray junior defenseman Joey Palodichuk ended up in uniform on the bench and then celebrating on the ice. Photo by Tim Kolehmainen/Breakdown Sports Media

CONQUERING THE UNKNOWN

EDEN PRAIRIE PERSEVERED THROUGH A SEASON SHORTENED BY COVID-19, A PANDEMIC THAT KEPT ONE STATE TOURNAMENT–QUALIFYING TEAM HOME

DATES	LOCATION	ATTENDANCE	CLASS 2A CHAMPIONSHIP
MARCH 30–APRIL 3	XCEL ENERGY CENTER, ST. PAUL	8,265	EDEN PRAIRIE 2, LAKEVILLE SOUTH 1 (2 OT)
			CLASS 1A CHAMPIONSHIP
			GENTRY ACADEMY 8, DODGE COUNTY 1

 Dodge County junior forward Brody Lamb joined Eveleth's John Mayasich (1950 and 1951) as the only players to tally at least ten state tournament goals.

LEE SMITH PACED the black rubber floor outside Locker Room 2, positioned about halfway down the tunnel between the home team bench and the Minnesota Wild dressing room. His Eden Prairie Eagles were tied 2–2 after the first overtime of the state tournament championship game, and Smith grasped for the right words to lift his tired and reeling team.

Win, and the Eagles triumph in a season reduced to less than three full months by the COVID-19 pandemic. Lose, and they become the first single-class or Class 2A team to fall one game short three consecutive times.

Then Smith considered how five of his team's final eleven games that season went to overtime. The Eagles hadn't lost, going 2–0–2. The veteran coach realized the best words on this Saturday night would not be his own.

Locker Room 2 served as Eden Prairie's base camp back in 2011, when Kyle Rau and company won in triple overtime. And Smith remembered a key moment between the first and second extra periods, when senior forward Jack McCartan stood up and told teammates, "We're going home with the [expletive] trophy."

Smith stopped pacing. He hustled into the room and to a spot about six feet out from the third locker stall on the north wall. He shared his flash of inspiration, telling of McCartan's impromptu speech on this spot. Then Smith offered a challenge. Who would be Jack McCartan at this moment?

"I will," said senior defenseman Mason Langenbrunner. His father, Jamie, was a Cloquet hockey legend who led the Lumberjacks to the 1992 and 1993 Tier I state tournaments, captained the 2010 US Olympic Team, and played on two Stanley Cup championship teams.

Mason Langenbrunner came to Eden Prairie from Cloquet as part of a talented infusion of transfers before the 2019–20 season. Though he lacked longevity as an Eagle, he earned his stripes through a crushing 2020 state tournament championship game defeat against Hill-Murray. And he wanted nothing more than a redemption opportunity.

The 6-foot-3 Langenbrunner, a vocal leader all season, stood and announced, "Boys, we're not leaving without the [expletive] trophy."

Smith's concerns subsided.

"The guys started rallying around him, so I walked out," Smith said. "Emotionally, they were in a good spot."

Since mid-March 2020, few US citizens found themselves in a good spot emotionally as the COVID-19 pandemic prompted massive shutdowns. Those cancellations reached the Minnesota high school sports scene just six days after the conclusion of the boys' high school hockey state tournament.

The boys' and girls' basketball state tournaments were lost. The entire spring sports season was the next casualty. In the following months, daily news reports became dominated by rising death tolls, variants, masking, and social distancing and also by objections to stringent safety measures.

Come fall, football and volleyball were initially canceled by Minnesota State High School League officials before getting cleared to start about two months later than usual. State tournaments for all fall sports, however, were canceled.

Winter sports coaches pondered the fate of their state tournaments. Boys' hockey coaches, constantly trying to keep their best players from leaving for junior leagues throughout the Midwest, were especially concerned. They couldn't give players much assurance of a tournament since the MSHSL didn't even announce tentative tournament plans until mid-November—right about the time youth sports were paused for what turned out to be six weeks.

"If we were going to have a state tournament, then our band was coming back together," Smith said. "As good as Minnesota high school hockey is, it's nothing without the state tournament."

The new year brought renewed hope as winter high school teams were cleared to practice January 4, 2021, and to finally play games ten days later. Players and coaches were forced to adhere to MSHSL and Minnesota Department of Health mandates that face coverings be worn throughout practices and games in basketball and hockey. Ecstatic to play again, resilient players put their passions above the chaos and abnormalities.

Eden Prairie hockey players began the abbreviated season on January 16 with a 6–2 victory at St. Michael–Albertville. But the Eagles' drive to another state tournament championship game wasn't fully set in motion until junior forward Jackson Blake came back.

Similar to Langenbrunner, hockey royalty was in Blake's blood. His father, Jason Blake, led Moorhead to the 1992 Tier I state tournament. He helped North Dakota capture the 1997 NCAA championship and finished his NHL career with one All-Star Game appearance plus 486 points in 871 games.

Jackson Blake played Eden Prairie youth hockey before attending Shattuck–St. Mary's. He arrived via transfer as a sophomore midway through the 2019–20 season. The timing of the move drew MSHSL scrutiny. The league granted Blake varsity eligibility beginning on January 28. Blake finished the partial season with seven goals and twelve assists in thirteen games, and his contributions helped the Eagles reach the state tournament title game.

Blake's junior year took a similar course. Minnesota's pause on youth sports kept Blake in Chicago, competing with his United States Hockey League team, the Steel. He played twenty-one USHL games before returning to Eden Prairie for his debut on January 28 at Buffalo. The Eagles beat the Bison 5–1 as Blake scored once and assisted on three additional goals.

"There were zero excuses at that point," Langenbrunner said. "It was win the championship or bust."

And there would be an opportunity to play for a state title. Winter state tournaments were announced February 4. Hockey champions would be crowned at the Xcel Energy Center per usual—but, for the first time, in April.

Blake's torrid start continued. He averaged 4.2 points per game as Eden Prairie beat five reputable hockey programs by at least three goals each. The top line of Blake as right wing, senior center Carter Batchelder, and senior left wing Drew Holt became the state's most feared unit.

Their dominance appeared lost during a February 16 game against Benilde–St. Margaret's, when Blake crashed into the boards late in the first period. He got up, favoring his left leg. But he began walking in the locker room during intermission and returned to the game midway through the second period.

"I was playing on one leg," Blake said.

X-rays later revealed a broken ankle, and doctors inserted two screws. Praised by Smith for his ability to "stickhandle through anyone," Blake spent the remainder of the season skating through as much pain as he deemed tolerable.

"I know it hurt like hell," Smith said.

Not enough to thwart the mission.

"One of the reasons I came back was to win a championship," Blake said. "I grew up with almost all these guys, and I would sacrifice for any of them."

The Eagles' championship march fell out of step during the Section 2 championship game against Lake Conference rival Minnetonka. The Skippers built a 3–1 second-period lead. Goals from Batchelder and Holt tied the game, which Eden Prairie won 4–3 in overtime. The gut-check game offered a glimpse of the herculean task waiting in St. Paul.

At least the Eagles got to make the trip. On the same Wednesday of Eden Prairie's comeback victory against Minnetonka, Hill-Murray blasted White Bear Lake 5–0 for the Section 4 title. The reigning state tournament champion Pioneers were set to defend their title. At least until the phones started ringing Sunday evening.

Hill-Murray coach Bill Lechner learned a White Bear Lake skater reported a positive COVID-19 test. Minnesota Department of Health and MSHSL protocols at the time required a seven-day quarantine for exposure. That meant Wednesday's quarterfinal against Wayzata could not happen.

Hell-bent on keeping the Minnesota State High School League from enforcing the COVID measure, families of nine Hill-Murray players filed a lawsuit the day before the Wayzata game. The suit and a letter from school officials to hockey families maintain that video review showed Hill-Murray players "had almost no contact with the infected player" from White Bear Lake, and that when contact occurred, all players were wearing masks.

The court did not take action against the MSHSL decision.

Wayzata offered to move the game to Thursday. The MSHSL said no.

Hill-Murray became the first team to qualify for the state tournament and not play. Lechner tried to soften the blow.

Instead of hitting the ice at 11 AM Wednesday at the Xcel Energy Center as the number-two state tournament seed, the Pioneers met about ten miles and emotional light-years away at Aldrich Arena in Maplewood. After the one-hour scrimmage between Team Green and Team White, eight seniors partook in the program's traditional Last Lap. Players skated one at a time at their chosen pace.

Lechner concluded the season telling players, "'I would love to be able to give you guys a magic answer to make this right. If we would have lost on the ice, there's a certain closure—you can at least look in the mirror. In this case, we did nothing wrong.' That's what was frustrating."

The MSHSL had informed Hill-Murray the team could play Wednesday "with eligible student athletes who are not subject to quarantine." But the Pioneers' JV program had already ended its season, and players were scattered to various spring break locations. Plan B worked for Hermantown in Class 1A, however. Heck, one of the Hawks players flew home from vacation in Florida.

Hermantown had beaten Virginia/Mountain Iron–Buhl in the Section 7 semifinal. But two Blue Devils subsequently tested positive for COVID-19. Three Hermantown varsity players who did not see action against the Blue Devils were allowed to play in the state tournament quarterfinal. The remainder of the roster were JV players. The number-one seed Hawks

ABOVE: COVID-19 precautions dictated that only 250 fans were allowed in the Xcel Energy Center for the Wednesday, March 31, quarterfinals. Looser restrictions on indoor gatherings began April 1, which meant 2,300 fans could attend the semifinal round on Friday and the next day's championship games. But several rows of stadium seats remained covered to maintain social distancing between players and the crowd. The few, the proud Eden Prairie supporters cheered their boys after a 6–5 overtime victory against Maple Grove on April 2. Photo by Leila Navidi/*Minneapolis Star Tribune*

LEFT: Eden Prairie, runner-up in the 2019 and 2020 Class 2A state championship games, began its drive toward redemption when junior forward Jackson Blake (43) rejoined the team on January 28. Despite suffering a broken ankle during the shortened season, Blake later scored the game-winning goal in double overtime to ignite a celebration with teammate Tyler Johnson (9). Photo by Alex Kormann/*Minneapolis Star Tribune*

dressed sixteen skaters and two goalies and were dumped 7–3 by Dodge County and six Brody Lamb goals.

"I couldn't be more proud of our program in terms of what we put on the ice tonight in less than twenty-four hours after finding out we had COVID exposure," Hawks coach Patrick Andrews said after Tuesday evening's game.

On Wednesday, several hours after Hill-Murray's bitter-sweet intrasquad scrimmage ended in hugs and hurt feelings, Eden Prairie arrived at the Xcel Energy Center for a state tournament setting best described as just plain weird.

For the first time, team buses entered into the Xcel Energy Center bowels, filled with players already dressed in their hockey gear and wearing masks. Tournament officials came aboard and provided instructions.

Rather than feeling the energy and jitters of hitting the ice with thousands of people in the stands, players felt eerily alone. Student sections were small enough to fit in the penalty box. No student bands performed renditions of their school's fight song. Players exited the ice without a postgame handshake or media session and were quickly ushered out of the building. Journalists called coaches and players for perspective on the games.

Crowds wouldn't touch the typical five-digit numbers because only 250 fans were allowed in the building for the Wednesday, March 31, quarterfinals. Looser restrictions on indoor gatherings began April 1, which meant 2,300 fans could attend the semifinal round on Friday and the next day's championship games.

"We said among ourselves as the tournament stewards, 'We can't screw this up for the Minnesota Wild or our basketball state tournaments,'" said Bob Madison, who was in his first year as an MSHSL associate director in charge of the hockey tournament. "We were one of the first to do something like this, and we wanted to do it well."

At the Holiday Inn across the street from the Xcel Energy Center, Eden Prairie transformed a large conference room into a locker room for the week. No bus rides to and from the west-metro suburb in full gear this time around. The Eagles dropped the puck with St. Thomas Academy at 6:10 PM Wednesday, and hockey finally became the focus.

Five third-period goals, two from Batchelder, fueled a 6–2 Eagles victory. A semifinal game against Maple Grove came next.

"That group had never beaten Maple Grove growing up," Langenbrunner said. "So that semifinal was the Super Bowl."

The game sat tied 2–2 after two periods. A raucous third period came next. The Crimson went ahead 3–2, but leads became only temporary.

Batchelder made it 4–3 Eden Prairie; Maple Grove drew even. Just twelve seconds later, Holt restored a 5–4 Eden Prairie lead.

A mere nine seconds later, Maple Grove tied the score. On the bench, Smith threw a water bottle in disgust. His players were more amused than angry.

"We would score and think, 'Now we're going to hold onto it,'" Langenbrunner said. "And then they would score and it was, 'Ope, we've got to get it back.'"

Overtime would decide who scored the final goal. Langenbrunner broke up a Maple Grove three-on-one opportunity. At the other end, Blake inadvertently knocked himself and Batchelder to the ice on a rush. But Holt ensured the gaffe wouldn't haunt the Eagles. He controlled the puck, buying Batchelder time to get in position for a tap-in.

"I saw Holt and got up as fast as I could," said Batchelder, who completed the hat trick.

Firewagon hockey gave way to a tight, bruising final against undefeated Lakeville South. Forward Cade Ahrenholz and defenseman Jack Malinski were part of the Cougars' mythical Class 6A state championship football team in the fall and brought their physical play to the ice.

Ahrenholz and linemates Cam Boche and Tanner Ludtke helped South play the Eagles to a 1–1 stalemate through regulation and a scoreless first overtime period.

Elevated tension had Smith pacing outside Locker Room 2.

"We were tired and beat up," Smith said. "They weren't afraid of us, and there was fear in our eyes."

Langenbrunner's words gave the boys hope, though not all of them were in need.

Senior defenseman Luke Mittelstadt, a *Star Tribune* All-Metro first team selection, said Blake "was laughing on the bench before the second overtime. He was the least serious person of all time. Then he went out and made another one of the fifty great plays he made that season."

Blake's rebound goal in the second overtime owed to the entire top line. Batchelder head-manned the puck to Holt. His sharp-angle shot caromed off the goaltender's right leg pad, and the puck popped straight into the slot.

"I saw that rebound come out and I saw the defender in front of me," Blake said. "So I just tried to get one quick step away from him."

The snap decision made the difference between a potential blocked shot and a game-winning goal.

Blake wept in celebration, proof that no matter the circumstances, winning a state tournament means the world to players and coaches.

"I was so emotional because that year was crazy," Blake said. "But also because we finally did it, and it was even more exciting because it was with that great group of guys."

~DL~

GOOD COP, BAD COP

ANDOVER'S LARGER-THAN-LIFE CHARACTERS IN COACH MARK MANNEY AND DEFENSEMAN WESTON KNOX PLAYED OFF EACH OTHER PERFECTLY

DATES	LOCATION	ATTENDANCE	CLASS 2A CHAMPIONSHIP
MARCH 9–12	XCEL ENERGY CENTER, ST. PAUL	119,643	ANDOVER 6, MAPLE GROVE 5 (2 OT)
			CLASS 1A CHAMPIONSHIP
			HERMANTOWN 3, WARROAD 2

 Senior forward Alex Bump scored five goals in Prior Lake's 6–0 quarterfinal upset of number-two seed Cretin-Derham Hall. The remarkable performance came in the Lakers' state tournament debut.

WESTON KNOX is an eternal conversationalist. A chatterbox around friends, family, and strangers alike, he could hold court with a traffic cone and there would be nary an awkward silence.

Mark Manney is a talker, too. The Andover coach's refreshingly candid postgame media sessions at the 2022 state tournament were as entertaining as they were insightful.

One of Manney's uproarious salvos concerned Knox, a senior defenseman and co-captain who spent much of the Huskies' semifinal victory over Hill-Murray injecting teammates with positivity from his bottomless well. Just like he did every game.

"Weston . . . is kind of like FEMA on our team," Manney said after the 4–2 triumph over the Pioneers, referring to the Federal Emergency Management Agency. "He cleans up after Hurricane Manney comes through the locker room."

The pair played off each other perfectly.

As an Air Force One pilot, Manney had found that much of his job was devoted to layering contingency plans atop contingency plans. Transporting presidents, after all, involves a bit more preparation and planning than, say, piloting a planeload of tourists to Cabo.

"You assume the worst is going to happen, and that way, you are ready to react if it does," Manney said.

He approaches games in similar fashion.

"[Assistant coach Brett Barta] sees where the other teams are weak," Manney said during the state tournament. "I tend to only see where they're strong. So I go into the game thinking we're going to get smoked no matter who we're playing."

Knox, meanwhile, saw the best in his teammates regardless of the situation. And wasn't shy about reminding them how strongly they were valued.

Andover coach Mark Manney guided the Huskies to their first state championship in 2022 and, in the process, became a media darling with his honesty and array of one-liners. Photo by Tim Kolehmainen/Breakdown Sports Media

"I knew as a senior and a leader I needed to make sure everyone knows that they are a part of this hockey team," said Knox, who also starred in football and was never stingy with encouraging words or pats on the back. "No one is going to play perfect hockey all the time. There are going to be ups and downs."

In their disparate ways, Manney and Knox kept the Huskies focused but loose, hard-driven but fun loving, accountable for their mistakes but willing to take chances.

"They were able to bounce off each other very well," senior forward Logan Gravink said. "It was almost like they were playing good cop, bad cop sometimes."

Regular Season Imperfection

The Huskies were beset with all sorts of adversity, from injuries to horrendous (by their standards) special teams play to inconsistent defense and goaltending to undisciplined penalties to family tragedy in their journey to the program's first state championship.

Victories over highly regarded Cretin–Derham Hall and Hill-Murray in the opening two days of a December holiday tournament had the Huskies brimming with confidence. A loss to unranked Rosemount on the event's final day yanked them back to a harsh reality.

"After beating Cretin and Hill-Murray, we obviously felt like we were the best team in the state," forward Gavyn Thoreson said. "Then we played Rosemount and kind of overlooked them. That made us realize we can't overlook anyone. It helped us."

Andover bottomed out emotionally on January 29. Its 2–1 overtime loss to Rogers was barely an afterthought, as earlier in the day the team learned that the father of senior forward Logan Seward had died of a massive stroke.

"I was up in the shooting room with Sewie getting ready for the game when he got that difficult phone call," Gravink said. "I instantly gave him the biggest hug I could."

Knox gathered the team in the locker room and offered a prayer before the game.

"I think that was pretty much what got me through it . . . those guys," Seward said. "We all grew up together and played hockey together. I think that brought us even closer."

Still, the galvanized Huskies were reeling as they entered the playoffs. They lost two of their final three regular-season games, both to future playoff opponents in Grand Rapids and Maple Grove. Thoreson failed to convert a penalty shot with no time left on the clock against Grand Rapids in a 2–1 loss, but he was more concerned with the Thunderhawks' overwhelming edge in physical play.

"The biggest thing we saw from that game, probably, was that we were pretty soft," Thoreson said. "We toughened up going into the playoffs."

Andover beat Grand Rapids 3–1 in the Section 7AA championship game and in doing so exorcized many of its demons. Thoreson and linemate Cayden Casey, a junior transfer from Elk River, each had a goal and an assist. Senior goaltender Austin Brauns, who could run hot and cold, was brilliant in stopping twenty-nine of thirty shots. And the Huskies successfully killed all four Grand Rapids power-play opportunities (the Huskies allowed eighteen power-play goals in the regular season but none in six playoff games).

Andover was seeded fifth at the state tournament and was hardly a fashionable pick to win it all, especially given the program's history. Andover's inaugural season came in 2002–03. It took the Huskies eight years to post a winning record. They reached a section title game just once in their first fifteen seasons. Andover was described in a 2014 newspaper article as-

sessing the power structure in Section 7 as a "longshot contender in a good year," a line that peeved Manney.

The Huskies reached the state tournament for the first time in 2020 as the number-one seed. The following year they lost just twice in the regular season and made a return trip. They were knocked out in the quarterfinals both times.

Free of lofty expectations, Andover approached the 2022 event in its typical carefree fashion. Most of the players dyed their hair blond. Mustaches were grown out and groomed—some more successfully than others.

"I can't really grow one," Seward said. "I tried to dye mine and ended up with a huge rash on my face. I think [senior defenseman Kyle Law] had the best one."

And the worst?

"If you looked at Thoreson's upper lip," added Seward, "he had maybe three hairs up there."

Master Motivator

Thanks in part to a twenty-two-year military background that included piloting the world's most famous airplane and Presidents Bill Clinton and George W. Bush as passengers, Manney was a master at recognizing and nurturing his players' wide-ranging personalities, priorities, and motivations.

Thoreson, however, was a particularly difficult case.

The ability to agitate opponents with cutting words and stick-blade jabs was a well-used component of Thoreson's toolbox. He was so skilled at throwing players off their games that even Knox, with his forever sunny disposition, would at times reach his boiling point in practice because of Thoreson's antics.

Manney's patience was tested, too.

"He needs to find the line and cross it a little bit less often because he infuriates the other team but he sometimes infuriates me more," Manney said during the state tournament.

Manney said the addition of the quiet, hardworking Casey had something of a calming effect on Thoreson, who took just nine penalties in thirty-one games. Casual friends long before they joined forces for the Huskies, Thoreson and Casey became inseparable. They didn't play on the same line to start the season, but once paired it was obvious their shared ice vision and the strengths in their games—Casey's unflagging commitment to defense and Thoreson's ability to slow the pace and probe for openings in the offensive zone—made them perfectly suited to play together.

The late-season return from injury of junior Cooper Conway, a natural goal scorer nicknamed "the Weapon" and a key member of the Huskies' top forward trio, provided a huge boost entering the playoffs. The three future Division I commits combined for a stunning fifty-three points, including twenty goals, in six playoff games.

"[Casey] brought so much to our team," Thoreson said. "He's probably the best defensive forward I've ever seen. It was perfect for me and Cooper because we are both very offensive, and he helped out the defense.

"And Cooper could score from anywhere on the ice," Thoreson said. "I just think we all complemented each other so well."

Defensively, the Huskies were equally stacked. Knox and Law formed an impeccable top pair, combining their outstanding athletic ability (Law was also a baseball standout) with blue-collar grit and practice habits. Both were co-captains, and, naturally, the gregarious Knox handled most of the speaking duties. The soft-spoken Law occasionally offered words of inspiration, too, deftly picking his spots.

"Law hardly ever spoke to the guys," Manney said. "And when he did, he was really upset, normally. Like, 'Pull your heads out and let's go.'"

Redemption Tour

Andover drew Moorhead in a state tournament quarterfinal. The Spuds had routed the Huskies 6–1 on December 3, Andover's third game of the season. Despite that loss, Manney liked the matchup.

"Maybe it was us playing hard so we didn't have a six-to-one embarrassment in the state tournament," he said. "And so we played with a little extra, and Moorhead didn't."

A little extra proved to be just enough. The score was tied 1–1 in overtime when, with Andover on a power play, a Knox pass at the blue line was intercepted by Spuds goal-scoring phenom Harper Bentz. Despite being at the end of a long shift and finding himself a step behind Bentz, one of Moorhead's fastest players, Knox recovered in time to catch Bentz and limit him to a weak shot. Brauns poked the rebound out of harm's way.

With disaster averted, the Huskies, who had two goals waived off after video review, won 2–1 in double overtime on a Thoreson deflection off a pass Casey feathered through the crease.

The victory over Hill-Murray required different heroics.

All season the Huskies had planted Law in front of opposing goaltenders during power plays because of his willingness to subject his body to all manners of abuse. Law's take-one-for-the-team approach was even more evident in the defensive zone. He blocked a game-high six shots against the Pioneers.

"There are a few things other than a goal that will raise the emotional level of the whole team," said Manney, who starred as a high school player at Moorhead and in college at the Air Force Academy. "When a warrior steps in front of a clapper, and whether he takes it to a sensitive area or not, that gets everybody up."

Roles were well defined for an Andover team that had achieved high-level success at every age group, going all the way back to a championship at a prestigious youth tournament in Fargo, North Dakota: Bill Thoreson, Gavyn's father and a varsity assistant coach, said fifteen of the seventeen players from that Squirt team were on the 2022 state tourney squad.

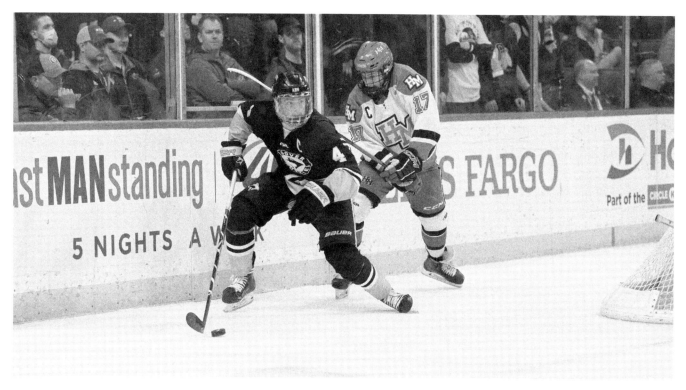

Andover defenseman Weston Knox skates with the puck ahead of Hill-Murray's Dylan Godbout during a state Class 2A semifinal. Knox's leadership and positive attitude were instrumental in the Huskies' push to the state title. Photo by Tim Kolehmainen/Breakdown Sports Media

None were more important than Brauns. He entered the title game having stopped eighty-one of eighty-four shots in the first two rounds.

Brauns might have been at his best in the championship against Maple Grove despite allowing five goals, the most ever surrendered by a winning team in the championship game.

"That game could have been 15–10," Gravink said. "He kept us in it."

As the title game stretched into double overtime, the athletic Brauns stuck with the aggressive style that had served him so well throughout the playoffs. He made a diving blocker save on a Landen Gunderson shot at the left goalpost. The rebound sailed straight up toward the Xcel Energy Center rafters and was swatted away by Law before it could touch down in front of the crease.

Just seconds later, Brauns stopped a deflection attempt by an onrushing Josh Giuliani, who scored three of the Crimson's goals.

"I don't think the pressure really affected him," Gavyn Thoreson said. "He could make any save at any time. Cold-blooded, I guess."

More than nine minutes into the second overtime, Manney trusted his instincts and inserted fresh legs on one of his forward lines. Center Jacob Pierson, who suffered from asthma issues and used an inhaler, was given a breather. Seward, taking just his third shift of the game and first in overtime, replaced Pierson.

Knox started a breakout from behind the Andover goal, juking his way past one Maple Grove player before firing a pass onto the tape of Hunter Zinda streaking down the left boards. Zinda fired a shot off the kneecap of Crimson defender Grant Leneau, and the puck caromed toward a hard-charging Seward in the slot.

Replays are inconclusive as to what happened next, although Seward said he got a piece of the puck as it crossed in front of him.

"It rolled up my stick, then landed on Gravink's stick perfectly," Seward said.

Gravink one-timed the puck past Crimson goaltender Toby Hopp.

Manney, for once speechless, was mobbed by his assistants. Helmets and gloves were flung skyward as Gravink, with Seward close behind, led the celebratory charge to the Andover student section. As the pandemonium subsided, Thoreson made a circle with his hands and gestured them in crown-like fashion toward the top of Gravink's head.

In keeping with his FEMA-inspired nickname, Knox attended to others dealing with hardship. He whispered words of consolation to devastated Crimson players, many of them his friends.

Longtime television commentator Lou Nanne was thoroughly entertained by Andover's 6–5 victory and said as much on the air: "I've enjoyed a lot of tournaments in fifty-eight years, and I really don't know that I have enjoyed a game more than I did tonight."

A Captain's Keepsake

A few weeks after the championship game, Manney bumped into Knox in a hallway at Andover High School. Manney slid the game puck from the Huskies' semifinal victory against Hill-Murray out of his jacket pocket and flipped it to his captain.

Call it a token of appreciation.

"But I think he already knew how much he meant to the team and how important he was to what we accomplished," Manney said. "And how much he meant to me."

~LRN~

THE HEART OF HERMANTOWN
Outdoor hockey culture lifeblood of Hawks' success

Pat Andrews led Hermantown to its fourth state championship, and his first in five seasons as head coach, in 2022. Andrews was a star player for the Hawks, a top youth coach, and a varsity assistant before taking the helm of one of the state's most successful programs. Photo by Tim Kolehmainen/ Breakdown Sports Media

After the 2022 title game, Hermantown head coach Pat Andrews lasted all of two minutes, thirty-six seconds into the postgame media session before breaking down into tears. The Class 1A championship was his first in five seasons as the Hawks' head coach and pierced a blimp-sized balloon of pressure.

Memories flashed through his mind like a series of still photographs.

Hermantown hosting a regionally televised outdoor game against Eden Prairie in 2010 during Hockey Day Minnesota.

Snow falling on grade schoolers as they skate on one of six outdoor rinks adjacent to Hermantown Arena. Another of vibrant sunset—oranges and blues, pine trees and twenty-foot snowbanks serving as the backdrop of a solo outdoor skater.

And then another special memory. One of Andrews's favorite photos is set, of course, on an outdoor rink, dad/ coach Pat Sr. with a hand on young Patrick's shoulder as they struck a pose before Pat played his first game. Pat Sr. was fifty when he passed away in 1995 of lung cancer.

continued next page

A huge Hockey Day Minnesota crowd turned out in Hermantown in 2010 as the host Hawks played Eden Prairie in conditions that included rain and sleet. Photo courtesy of Pat Andrews

continued from previous page

"He never missed a game, even when he was sick," Andrews said.

The collage of Kodak moments became too much.

"I knew I wouldn't get through this without crying," he said after the 3–2 victory over Warroad. "I grew up here in this program since I was four. And I'm speechless, but it means the world to me."

Hermantown's hockey hysteria is something of a new phenomenon, at least compared to more fabled northern Minnesota hotbeds such as Eveleth, International Falls, Roseau, and Warroad. Hermantown, the west Duluth suburb with a population of just more than ten thousand, assembled its first varsity team in the mid-1970s— some thirty years after Eveleth won the state's first championship.

Andrews grew up in a split-level on a gravel road, not far from the high school. Everything in Hermantown is not far from the high school. The arena is just across the street, and those six outdoor rinks, plus a warming house that has undergone two expansions and counting, sit adjacent to it in the shape of a crescent moon.

Arena manager Dave Huttel, another Hawks alum, and his crew polish that outdoor ice to a mirror sheen every day, tantalizing youngsters eager to be the first to carve it up with their steel blades and composite sticks.

"Because what's better than a sheet of fresh ice?" Huttel said.

Andrews played youth hockey on some of those same outdoor rinks. His love for the town and its outdoor hockey culture is as evident as the multitude of championship banners threatening to yank down the arena's metal roof.

"Sometimes, when I look around town, I wonder if we are caught in some sort of time warp," Andrews said.

Dozens of middle schoolers make a mad dash to the arena and its outdoor rinks when school ends at 2:45 PM each day.

"It's almost like a race to see who can get out there first," said Zam Plante, a junior forward on the Hawks' 2022 title team.

A "hockey bus" delivers about forty kids from the elementary school at precisely 4 o'clock each afternoon. More and more players file in as evening approaches. Some head to practice indoors; the rest practice or play shinny games outside. Sometimes there's so much congestion on the rinks the youngest kids play games on the narrow strips of ice between them, making it difficult for the Zamboni to make its appointed rounds [*Beep! Beep!*].

"We would get there after school every day at 3 or whatever it was, and my parents would have to drag us off the ice at 9 o'clock," said Ty Hanson, a junior defenseman on Hermantown's 2022 state championship squad. "It's just a bunch of kids wanting to be better every day and just loving hockey."

The Hawks reached the state tournament for the first time in 1994, finishing sixth. Andrews was a member of the 1998 Hermantown team that finished second at state to Eveleth-Gilbert.

When the Hawks beat Proctor to reach the state tournament that year, Andrews, who scored the winning goal in the waning seconds, was interviewed on the ice. He was jumping out of his skin with excitement.

"I've dreamed of this moment since I was four years old on the driveway, scoring the game-winning goal, and I did it," he said. "It's the greatest feeling of my life."

Andrews studied under Mike Sertich, the ultra-successful former University of Minnesota Duluth coach, when the two led Hermantown's top Bantam team. Andrews then served as a varsity assistant alongside another legend in Bruce Plante, the controversial longtime Hawks coach who stepped down after the 2016–17 season.

Pat Andrews Sr. and son Patrick pose for a photo before Patrick played his first hockey game (dad serving as coach). Pat Sr. was fifty when he passed away in 1995 of lung cancer. Photo courtesy of Pat Andrews

The Hermantown water tower is part of the backdrop as a young hockey player enjoys a sunset skate on a freshly flooded sheet of ice. Photo courtesy of Pat Andrews

Among Plante's 547 victories in twenty-eight seasons were three state Class 1A titles.

For years Plante criticized Class 1A juggernaut St. Thomas Academy for not opting up to Class 2A. The Cadets eventually did move to the larger class. Hermantown, with ten state title game appearances since 2007, became the team critics love to target. Even folks in Hermantown, who have come to expect the Hawks to challenge for a state Class 1A title every year, can get a little testy.

Deep into the 2021–22 season, Andrews was grabbing a couple of steaks for dinner during a trip to Stokke's, the local meat market renowned for its signature smoked beef jerky ("the best you'll find anywhere," Andrews says). The topic of the previous night's loss, the Hawks' second of the season, to high-powered Maple Grove was broached.

What happened coach?

"And I even knew the guy who brought it up," Andrews said.

Andrews plays a starring role in the documentary film *Hockeyland*. The movie followed the ups and downs of Hermantown and Eveleth-Gilbert during the 2019–20 season. Hanson said outsiders sometimes believe Andrews, heart ever-present on his sleeve, put on a show for the cameras.

"There would be guys on my team this year in Sioux City who would say he was so cheesy and that it wasn't real," Hanson said about their reaction to the movie. "I would tell them, 'No, that is actually how he is. That is 100 percent real. He wants the best for us. He really cares about us.'"

Time for one last picture. In this one, the sun is setting, and kids are skating on an outdoor rink. It's different, though, in that the Hermantown water tower is rising in the distance. The same scene washes over Andrews every day as he steps out of the arena, jumps into his truck, and makes the short drive to his home, a split-level much like the one in which he grew up.

"That view brings it all back full circle," Andrews said. "The best part of my day."

~LRN~

TOP OF THE WORLD

MINNETONKA GOALIE KAIZER NELSON, BELOVED BY TEAMMATES FOR PROVOCATIVE POSTGAME SPEECHES, REWARDED HANDSOMELY FOR DARING TO DREAM BIG

DATES	LOCATION	ATTENDANCE	CLASS 2A CHAMPIONSHIP
MARCH 8–11	XCEL ENERGY CENTER, ST. PAUL	121,589	MINNETONKA 2, EDINA 1
			CLASS 1A CHAMPIONSHIP
			MAHTOMEDI 6, WARROAD 5 (2 OT)

 Mahtomedi's Charlie Drage and Warroad's Carson Pilgrim each had hat tricks in the Class 1A championship game, the first time two players from separate teams scored three goals in the same title game.

KAIZER NELSON was a seventh-grader when he first sat atop the high school hockey world.

At approximately 7 PM on March 10, 2018, Nelson, a Minnetonka Pee Wee goaltender of no particular renown, summited the Xcel Energy Center in St. Paul. The time and date coincided with the state Class 2A championship game pitting Duluth East against Minnetonka.

Nelson, perched in Section 227's top row, was fixated on a heavily padded speck on the ice below named Charlie Glockner. A Minnetonka senior, Glockner stopped twenty-seven shots, including thirteen in a frenetic third period, to lead the Skippers to a 5–2 victory and the program's first state title.

"I just remember them winning and being like, 'Oh my god, that is . . . that is crazy,'" Nelson said. "I said to myself, 'I want to make it there.'

"But I never thought I would."

■ ■ ■

Mid-April on-ice training sessions organized by high schoolers typically are giggle fests and nothing more. No hitting. No conditioning. No drills. No coaches. Captains are in charge. On a scale of one to ten, the intensity level generally tops out at about a two.

Minnetonka players were a surly bunch in the spring of 2022. They were coming off a lackluster 16–10–1 season punctuated by an overtime loss to Chaska in a section semifinal. The official start of the 2022–23 season was eight months away, but the Skippers, to a man, decided their push for a state championship started now.

"I think the biggest thing was we set the tone," said junior forward Gavin Garry, a co-captain with senior defenseman Liam Hupka.

Early on it was apparent not everyone was on the same mission. A few of the players prepping for summer junior league tryouts were politely asked not to return.

"There were some older players, seniors, who were kind of in the way of what we were doing," Hupka said.

Put more bluntly: "They removed a couple guys from the locker room," Minnetonka coach Sean Goldsworthy said. "[Hupka and Garry] basically said, 'You're not all in, and you're on our watch now. Not your watch.'"

Indeed, the tone had been set.

Those spring sessions followed the template of in-season practices. Scrimmages sometimes became a bit too intense.

"From day one, we weren't messing around," Nelson said. "We wanted to win it. And it showed in practice. Everyone was all in. There was a fight every other week. I mean, they were for-real fights."

Minnetonka, with at least eight transfers from other youth and high school programs, served as a microcosm of the transient nature of high school athletes in general. But the Skippers didn't suffer from chemistry issues. Hupka saw to that.

"If we had any sort of fight or altercation, five minutes later it would be in the past and we would forget about it," Hupka said.

Hupka also ensured newcomers such as Max Krebsbach, a senior who was Mound Westonka's top scorer the previous season, and Sam Scheetz, a junior who had led Chaska in scoring as a sophomore, were welcomed into the group.

Arrivals and departures were, in effect, a wash for Minnetonka, which had lost several highly regarded youth players to other programs (Drew Stewart to Benilde–St. Margaret's, Beckett Hendrickson to the US National Team Development Program, Kam Hendrickson to Chanhassen by way of Holy Family).

Goldsworthy didn't concern himself with the player movement. Instead, he tweaked the famous line from Herb Brooks, the St. Paul native and legendary 1980 "Miracle" Team USA coach, who said, "I'm not looking for the best players; I'm looking for the right ones."

Goldsworthy puts hours of thought and discussion into whom to choose as captains each spring, obsesses over the team's culture, and distributes a six-point Minnetonka Hockey Expectations document. Top of the list: Have a Vision (Dream Big!).

"I don't think it's a matter of where you're coming from," Goldsworthy said. "I think it's a matter of your character."

The "right" or "character" guys were abundant on the Skippers, going well past Hupka and Garry. Robby House ("best locker room guy ever"), Jack Sand ("probably the nicest kid I've ever met"), Ryan Holzer ("would do anything to help the team")—Garry reeled off name after name when asked about the team's most unsung players.

"I remember looking around the locker room thinking to myself, 'I just love every one of these guys,'" Garry said.

The Skippers' cohesiveness and camaraderie was tested in regular season losses to Chanhassen and Wayzata.

"We got outworked," Goldsworthy said about the 4–1 loss to the Storm on December 10. "The kids admitted it. And they just said, 'That's not going to happen the rest of the year.' It was a really big deal for them."

A 3–1 loss to Wayzata on January 7 gave the Skippers another jolt.

"At that point it was not about, 'Are we good enough or not?' or 'Are we working hard?'" Goldsworthy said. "It was, 'Who's gonna get better in January and February to win in March?'"

The Skippers ratcheted up their intensity. But they were a loose bunch, too. Nelson made sure of that.

As a junior, Nelson was the program's third-string goaltender toiling on the junior varsity. He got his first varsity start midway through the 2021–22 season, against Hill-Murray. The Skippers lost 4–2 as part of a 2–6–1 stretch, but Nelson showed enough promise to earn another start. And another. And another. As he solidified his spot on the varsity, he grew his persona in the locker room.

"Kaizer Speeches" were called for by teammates (*Speeeeeeeeech! Speeeeeeech!*) after every win, and Nelson delivered with high-intensity, high-volume, expletive-filled rants that were completely out of his quiet, studious, Clark Kent–like nature.

"That was the best part about it," Garry said. "You wouldn't see Kaizer do what he would do in those speeches at any other time."

Minnetonka closed the regular season with fourteen straight victories, including a 4–2 triumph over Wayzata on February 2. The Skippers, ranked number one in the state for much of

Minnetonka's Gavin Garry fires a pass past a sliding Landon Cottingham (20) of Hill-Murray during a Class 2A quarterfinal at the Xcel Energy Center in St. Paul. Minnetonka won 4–3 in overtime. Photo by Tim Kolehmainen/Breakdown Sports Media

272

Minnetonka goaltender Kaizer Nelson makes a save on a shot by Edina's Jackson Nevers during the state Class 2A championship game. Nelson stopped twenty-two shots in the Skippers' 2–1 victory. Nelson finished third in the state with a 1.22 goals-against average. Photo by Tim Kolehmainen/Breakdown Sports Media

the season, opened the playoffs with wins over Chaska and Shakopee, setting up a rematch against Chanhassen in the section final.

Adding intrigue to the showdown was the cross-pollination of star players between the teams. Minnetonka forwards Javon Moore, Alex Lunski, and Ashton Schultz all at one point hailed from Chanhassen. Hendrickson played at the Bantam level in Minnetonka and, as a sophomore, at Holy Family before transferring to Chanhassen.

A weird carom off the end boards resulted in a Chanhassen goal and 1–0 lead with 7:31 remaining. But Minnetonka rallied to win in double overtime on a goal by Lunski, a 6-foot-4 junior eventually headed to the University of St. Thomas and one of four Skippers committed to Division I colleges.

After the game Goldsworthy sounded like he had just stepped out of a *Rocky* movie when he declared Minnetonka the number-one team in the state, eager to take on all comers.

"We've played everybody, we've beaten everybody, and every ranking has us at number one," he said. "If we keep playing the way we do, we're going to be a tough out."

Although a bit bold and brash for Minnesota Nice, Goldsworthy wasn't wrong. The Skippers, who had a 6–0 record against the field, entered the tournament with a 26–2–0 record, the number-one seed, and status as the biggest runaway favorite to win the title since Duluth East in 2012 (Lakeville North entered the 2015 tourney undefeated and favored, but 24–1–2 Edina, the defending champion, also loomed as a likely finalist).

Nelson was in the concrete-lined depths of the Xcel Energy Center, sitting on a chair beneath the bleachers and contemplating his just-completed performance against Hill-Murray.

It hadn't been pretty. Nelson allowed three goals on fifteen shots, requiring the Skippers to win 4–3 on an overtime goal (the puck took a fortuitous bounce off a Pioneers player) by defenseman John Stout.

"I talked to [goalie coach Mike Johnson] for maybe twenty minutes after the game," Nelson said. "I was like, 'I don't know what to do. . . . I can't play like that obviously tomorrow against Andover, which was a better team, has got a really good first line, and is coming off a state title.'"

A season that ended with a state championship almost wasn't for Mahtomedi senior forward Charlie Drage

DAMAGE CONTROL

Mahtomedi senior forward Charlie Drage gestures toward his newly chipped teeth while celebrating with the student section after his team's double overtime victory against Warroad in the Class 1A state tournament championship game. Photo by Aaron Lavinsky/*Minneapolis Star Tribune*

In one moment, Mahtomedi senior Charlie Drage was walking home with friends and hockey teammates Jonny Grove, Carson Marshall, Noah Mogren, and David Wolsfeld from the Zephyrs' homecoming football game. In the next, his body was launched onto the hood and windshield of a stranger's car.

Drage remembers the approaching car's headlights bearing down, an odd sight considering he was on foot several yards from the road on that awful late September evening.

The driver stopped and put his car into reverse. He backed up with enough speed to fling the seventeen-year-old Drage to the ground, then fled into the night. Blood poured from a forehead wound opened by a windshield wiper and later closed with seventeen stitches.

Not quite six months later, Drage's mug absorbed another blow. Marshall accidentally planted Drage, sans helmet and gloves, face-first against the Xcel Energy Center Plexiglas during the Zephyrs' Class 1A state tournament championship victory celebration. Drage's two front teeth were chipped almost in half.

Drage mugged his chipped chiclets for television cameras as he skated over to receive his championship medal. He earned a spot on the all-tournament team with game-winning goals in the quarterfinals and semifinals, followed by a hat trick in the championship game.

"You can replace teeth," Drage, a team captain, told the media afterward. "You can't replace this moment."

A glorious finish wasn't on Drage's mind in September as he waited in the M Health Fairview Lakes Medical Center in Wyoming, Minnesota. That's where David Drage, an emergency room doctor at the facility, brought his son for care. The Upper Midwest High School Elite League season, a precur-

sor to the high school varsity season, was not quite three weeks old, and here was Drage, with a damaged face and possible brain injury.

"He asked me to text Chris McAlpine, his Elite League coach, to let him know he'd miss the game the next day," said Jill Drage, Charlie's mother. "He wanted me to apologize for him because he felt bad missing a game. But he ended up missing most of the league."

The good news, however, was a negative brain scan.

"The doctors told me, 'We don't know how there isn't any damage,'" Charlie Drage said.

By the time Mahtomedi began its varsity hockey season in November, Drage was ready. The stitches were out. The bandages weren't needed. All that remained were post-accident nightmares, where Drage would be on foot and illuminated by inescapable car headlights. He would wake with a start, needing several moments to regulate his breathing.

In those moments, he read through the supportive text thread on his smartphone started by his Elite League team, Mpls St. Paul Magazine. The phone also provided motivation. Drage's wallpaper was a Warroad team celebration after defeating Mahtomedi in overtime at the 2022 state tournament semifinals. There was also a photo of a 2022–23 preseason poll that listed Hermantown and Warroad as co-favorites to become state tournament champions with about 40 percent of the vote. Mahtomedi garnered just 7 percent.

Embracing his team's underdog identity, Drage led the mission for relevance. He finished with thirty-five goals after scoring zero as a sophomore and eighteen as a junior. His considerable efforts clinched the Zephyrs' second title in four seasons, captured with upsets of defending state champion Hermantown and previously undefeated Warroad—teams that beat Mahtomedi by three-goal margins in the regular season.

A Cretin-Derham Hall player who arrived at the Xcel Energy Center to prepare for the Class 2A third-place game later shared a detail with Drage to cement just how long the odds of upsetting Warroad were: The Class 1A trophy waiting in the tunnel contained a Warroad team picture. On the ice, Mahtomedi had pulled goalie Charlie Brandt with 1:29 remaining in regulation for what became Drage's tying goal. In the second overtime, Grove clinched the improbable 6–5 victory.

By then, tournament officials had changed the photo. Drage later switched his phone wallpaper to his team posing with the championship trophy.

"It was the perfect way to end the season," Drage said. "We played the best of the best, and everything we had been working for paid off.

"I felt like I would never get there," he said. "To actually win it made it all that much sweeter."

~DL~

Johnson told Nelson that he had a similar conversation with Glockner after the opening round of the 2018 tournament.

"Both Kaizer and Charlie growing up were never on the top teams and were always goalies that had to fight their way through," Johnson said. "I told Kaizer the same thing I told Charlie, 'There is nothing to be afraid of. You have proven yourself over and over. You are a good goalie.'"

Nelson, relieved to hear that Glockner, his childhood idol, also had battled through moments of self-doubt, steadied himself for Andover and its outrageously talented top line of Gavyn Thoreson, Cayden Casey, and Cooper Conway (Division I recruits who combined for a stunning 267 points).

The Skippers won the semifinal 4–1, with a razor-sharp Nelson stopping seventeen shots and, in a key sequence late in the game, drawing a penalty as he stood his ground while a sliding Thoreson barreled into him.

"I think it was a little selfish on his part," Nelson, refreshingly candid, said about the play in the postgame media session. "I think he could have gotten up, but he just wanted to take a cheap shot at me. I'll take that a hundred out of a hundred times."

Minnetonka had defeated championship game foe Edina twice in the regular season, the second game a 1–0 Skippers triumph on February 11 with the lone goal coming late in the third period. As Goldsworthy had predicted, the championship game followed the same script, with both teams playing such stifling defense and so focused on limiting their mistakes that it became chess on skates. One wrong move and . . .

"It looked like a college game," said Goldsworthy, who spent nineteen seasons leading St. Olaf College before returning to coach Minnetonka, his alma mater, in 2017.

A power-play goal by junior forward Hagen Burrows, Minnetonka's leading scorer, gave the Skippers a 1–0 lead after the first period. Edina's Bobby Cowan scored twenty-seven seconds into the third to tie it at 1–1.

Midway through the final period came one of the game's few miscues. Schultz, wheeling into the Edina zone, made a subtle fake that enticed standout Hornets defenseman Eddie Revenig to drop to the ice to block an expected pass. Instead, Schultz, on the short list of the state's top sophomores, drove the net and beat 6-foot-7 Edina goaltender Robbie Clarkowski with a rising shot.

"The problem with a team like Minnetonka is you make one single mistake and they've got enough kids who can finish it and get it done," Edina coach Curt Giles said after Minnetonka's 2–1 triumph. "A lot of teams have one or two; they've got a half dozen."

■ ■ ■

Nelson made twenty-two saves in the title game and got an assist from the hockey gods when a Matt Vander Vort shot in the waning seconds hit the right post, skidded through the crease, then kissed off the left post and out.

"Gave the post a little rub after, saying, 'Thanks,'" Nelson said later.

The wide-eyed seventh-grader who once sat atop the Xcel Energy Center and dared to dream big was now a state champion on center stage, holding court with the media.

"I'd say it's pretty bleeping awesome," he said about replicating that 2018 moment as a player. "I'll let you fill in the blanks there."

~LRN~

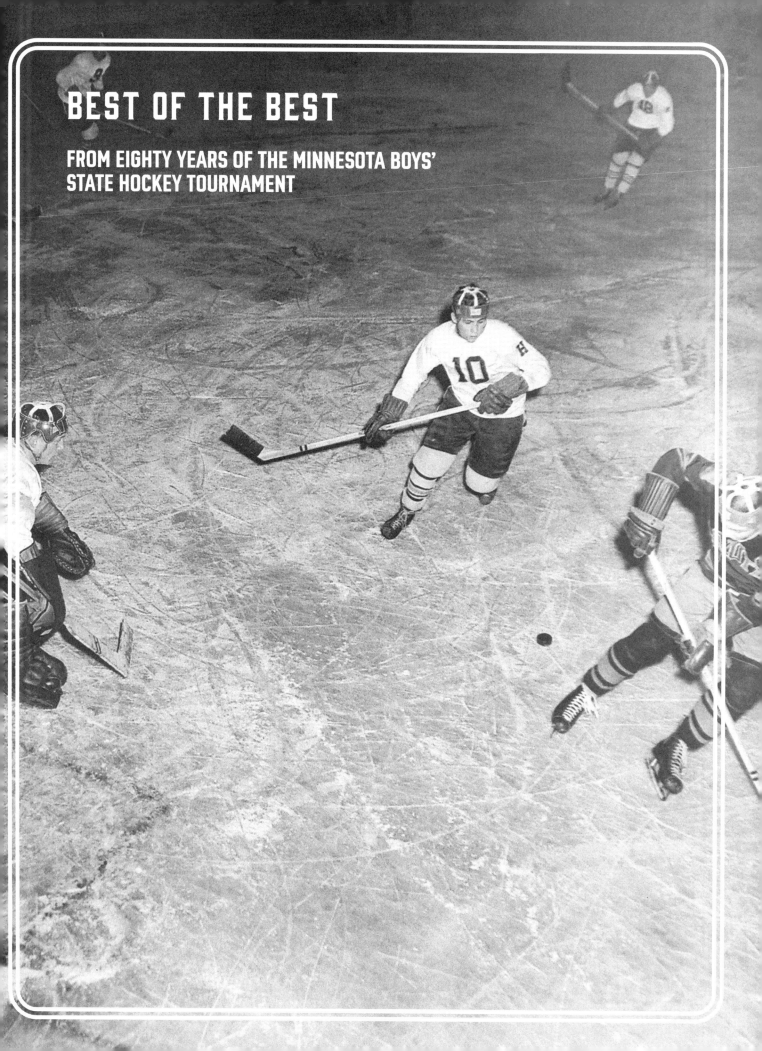

BEST OF THE BEST

FROM EIGHTY YEARS OF THE MINNESOTA BOYS' STATE HOCKEY TOURNAMENT

Greatest Games

1. Apple Valley 5, Duluth East 4, 1996 semi-final. A reckless pace set this five-overtime thriller apart. The teams combined for sixty-eight shots in the overtimes alone. The game lasted a record 93:12 and ended at 1:39 AM.

2. Edina 5, Warroad 4, 1969 championship. The ultimate metro-power-versus-outstate-underdog showdown. The Hornets knocked Warriors star Henry Boucha out of the game and later won in overtime.

3. Minneapolis Southwest 1, Edina 0, 1970 championship. Two undefeated teams went overtime. Southwest prevailed in a first, and so far last, for Minneapolis public schools.

4. Warroad 4, Totino-Grace 3, 2005 1A championship. Three ties, three lead changes, and two overtimes added up to a whale of a game. T. J. Oshie assisted on Aaron Marvin's game-winning goal.

5. Minneapolis South 3, Thief River Falls 2, 1955 quarterfinal. The game extended to a record eleven overtimes. Enough said.

6. Eden Prairie 3, Duluth East 2, 2011 2A championship. Kyle Rau's headfirst slide and goal in the third overtime ended the longest championship game ever played.

7. Edina East 5, Grand Rapids 4, 1978 championship. The two best teams of the 1970s were tied four times before the Hornets escaped in double overtime.

8. St. Thomas Academy 5, Hermantown 4, 2013 1A championship. The Cadets erased a pair of two-goal deficits and won with seven seconds remaining in regulation. This classic marked the teams' third consecutive, and final, title game meeting (St. Thomas Academy opted up to 2A the next season).

9. Hermantown 4, Monticello/Annandale/Maple Lake 3, 2017 1A championship. Down two goals twice, the heavily favored Hawks were in real danger of losing a seventh consecutive title game, this time to an unseeded team making its state tournament debut. But Hermantown rallied to win in double overtime.

10. Bloomington Jefferson 5, Rochester John Marshall 4, 1989 championship. An overtime goal marked the fifth lead change of this fast and physical game. The victory was redemption for returning Jaguars players who felt they had missed a great title chance in 1988.

11. Mahtomedi, 6, Warroad 5, 2023 championship. Having dispatched defending Class 1A state tournament champion Hermantown in the semifinals, Mahtomedi upset previously undefeated (and sentimental favorite) Warroad. For the first time, opponents each tallied a title game hat trick—Warroad's Carson Pilgrim and Mahtomedi's Charlie Drage. There was no quit in these Zephyrs. They trailed by two goals twice and stayed in pursuit. Jonny Grove's goal in double overtime completed the 6–5 victory.

Tournament Coaches

1. Willard Ikola, Edina/Edina East. With the houndstooth hat nicknamed Champ on his head and a stable of talented, opportunistic players at his disposal, Ikola captured a record eight state titles in twenty seasons from 1969 to 1988—one every two and a half years. Championships: 1969, 1971, 1974, 1978, 1979, 1982, 1984, 1988.

2. Larry Ross, International Falls. "Pops" presided over six championship teams, excelling as a motivator and personnel manager. He put players in the right positions and roles to succeed. And on game days, Ross pulled players out of class to get them fired up for the evening. Championships: 1957, 1962, 1964, 1965, 1966, 1972.

3. Cliff Thompson, Eveleth. A commitment to the youth program helped Thompson know his teams years in advance. As a result, the Golden Bears ran to glory while other programs were still learning to walk. Eveleth won the first tournament in 1945, and Thompson later built the first dynasty with four consecutive undefeated seasons. Championships: 1945, 1948, 1949, 1950, 1951.

4. Tom Saterdalen, Bloomington Jefferson. Before each game, Saterdalen gave his guys reports on opposing teams and players. "That's pro level, almost," said forward Chris Tucker, a star of the 1989 championship team. "Sats prepared better than what I saw when I played in Europe." Championships: 1981, 1989, 1992, 1993, 1994.

5. Curt Giles, Edina. The intense former North Stars defenseman restored the program's dominance with four championships in ten seasons. Giles adjusted after falling short in 2008 and 2009. "We had to find character players who would accept their roles," he said. Championships: 2010, 2013, 2014, 2019.

6. Rube Gustafson, St. Paul Johnson. Gustafson never skated. He ran outdoor practices in overshoes. But he knew kids and how to coax their best performances. The Governors were the only metro-area team to win state titles in the tournament's first twenty-four years. Championships: 1947, 1953, 1955, 1963.

7. Oscar Almquist, Roseau. The Eveleth native made tiny Roseau a high school hockey giant. Whether boasting star players, such as Rube Bjorkman in 1946, or the unheralded bunch in 1961 who arrived in St. Paul with little fanfare, Almquist led them to victory. Championships: 1946, 1958, 1959, 1961.

8. Mike Randolph, Duluth East. From 1994 to 1998, Randolph's teams went a combined 12–3 in state tournaments and never placed below third. His teams, occasionally ultraskilled but always tough and disciplined, placed second in 1997, 2000, 2011, 2015, and 2018. Championships: 1995, 1998.

9. Tom Osiecki, Burnsville. Osiecki arrived in the south-of-the-river suburb in 1966 and taught novice players how to put on equipment and tape their sticks. Things got better. The Braves rose to power with four title-game appearances from 1983 to 1987. Championships: 1985, 1986.

10. Bruce Plante, Hermantown. Plante made Hermantown the most unique dynasty in tournament history. The Hawks' six consecutive Class 1A championship game losses (2010–15) were followed by back-to-back championship wins. Championships: 2007, 2016, 2017.

Championship-Game Performances

1. Grant Besse, Benilde–St. Margaret's, 2012. Set a record by scoring all five of his team's goals. Three of them came shorthanded. Two came on electrifying breakaways.

2. Dave Spehar, Duluth East, 1995. His third hat trick in as many games included a penalty-shot goal that held up as the game-winner.

3. John Mayasich, Eveleth, 1951. Capped the greatest career in prep history with a four-goal performance that sent the St. Paul Auditorium crowd into a frenzy.

4. Chris Tucker, Bloomington Jefferson, 1989. Answered critics by completing a hat trick with the game-winning goal in overtime in a 5–4 victory.

5. Gary Aulik, Edina, 1978. Made forty-eight saves, the most ever by a winning goaltender in a title game—a 5–4 victory against Grand Rapids in double overtime.

6. Trevor Stewart, Elk River, 2001. Overcame personal tragedy during the season to tally a goal and four assists for a then championship game record five points.

7. Scott Lecy, Rochester John Marshall, 1977. Lecy was everywhere in the Rockets' 4–2 upset of Edina. He scored twice and assisted on the Rockets' other two goals.

8. Joe Micheletti, Hibbing, 1973. His unassisted shorthanded goal swung the game's momentum. He added two goals and an assist in a 6–3 victory.

9. Joe Bianchi, Bloomington Jefferson, 1992. Blew the game open with three consecutive second-period goals. The Jaguars cruised to a 6–3 victory.

10. Tyler Klatt, Monticello/Annandale/Maple Lake, 2017. His fifty-two saves are tops in a championship game. But the unseeded Moose fell 4–3 in double overtime to number-one Hermantown.

Forward Lines

1. International Falls' Peter Hegg, Dan Mahle, and Tim Sheehy. Hegg could score, fellow wing Mahle could hit, and Sheehy—well, the elite center could do everything. This group propelled the Broncos' 1960s dominance, skating to three consecutive titles (1964–66).

2. Eveleth's Wally Grant, Neil Celley, and Patrick Finnegan. As seniors in 1945, Eveleth's top line overwhelmed foes. They combined to score twenty-three tournament goals. "They were doing things with the puck in the early '40s that the Russians were given credit for innovating fifteen years later," future Golden Bears star John Matchefts said.

3. Eveleth's Ron "Sonny" Castellano, John Mayasich, and Dan Voce. Sure, Mayasich commanded all the attention, but he couldn't do it alone. He and wings Castellano and Voce were united as sophomores and became a staple of three consecutive championships (1949–51). Voce tallied ten career tournament goals.

4. Roseau's Neal Broten, Aaron Broten, and Butsy Erickson. History tells us the deeper Edina East teams simply wore down the Rams in their 1977 and 1978 tournament meetings. But check the video. Roseau's amazing line created myriad scoring chances. If a few more go in . . . who knows?

5. Lakeville North's Jack, Nick, and Ryan Poehling. With Ryan centering his intense older twin brothers, the Panthers fell short in the 2014 Class 2A title game but went undefeated in 2015. Each of the three was talented alone. Together, they were unstoppable.

6. St. Paul Johnson's Mike Crupi, Greg Hughes, and Rob Shattuck. Hughes, the shooter, centered the line. Shattuck, a deft passer, played left wing. The tough and determined Crupi manned the right side. They won the 1963 championship and placed second the following year.

7. Rochester John Marshall's Bruce Aikens, Scott Lecy, and Todd Lecy. Undersized, sure, but hardly overmatched. Sophomore Todd Lecy centered Aikens, a junior, and older brother Scott, a senior. The trio embodied the Rockets' creative playmaking style that produced the 1977 championship.

8 [TIE]. Bloomington Jefferson's Nick Checco, Matt Jones, and Tim McDonald. The signature line on the Jaguars' signature 1992–93 team. McDonald used his big frame to own the corners. Jones's silky mitts made him dangerous around the net. And Checco took off like a bottle rocket and scored big goals.

8 [TIE]. Andover's Gavyn Thoreson, Cooper Conway, and Cayden Casey. Thoreson, a phenomenally talented superpest, teamed with sniper extraordinaire Conway, nicknamed "The Weapon," and criminally underrated two-way phenom Casey to lead the Huskies to the 2022 big-school title and earn a third-place finish in 2023. All Division I commits, they combined for a whopping 267 points during the 2022–23 season.

9. International Falls' Peter Fichuk, Tony Curran, and Keith Bolin. The Broncos' 1964 and 1965 title teams started with Fichuk, the fearless center, flanked by Curran and Bolin. Physically imposing they were not. But this power trio intimidated with puck movement and goals in bunches.

10. Bloomington Kennedy's Joe Decker, Jason Miller, and Chad Pittelkow. Decker, a natural goal scorer, paired well with centerman Miller, the program's career assists leader. Both Mr. Hockey Award finalists benefited from Pittelkow, a hustling, dedicated backchecker. The trio paced the Eagles' 1987 championship team.

Forward-Line Nicknames

1. COTTON ROCKETS,

International Falls. The speedy but supposedly soft-shooting Peter Fichuk, Tony Curran, and Keith Bolin led the Broncos to titles in 1964 and '65. The nickname originated from Broncos goaltender Larry Roche, who joked about the line's "puffball" shots.

2. MAFIA LINE, Hibbing.

Longtime state hockey writer John Gilbert coined this nickname based on the Italian heritage of the deadly Bluejackets' 1967 tournament trio of Bobby Collyard, Bill Baldrica, and Mark Barbato.

3. SOLID GOLD DANCERS, Edina. Wally

Chapman, Mike DeVoe, and Dan Carroll wore gold-colored practice uniforms. The dance-heavy TV series *Solid Gold* was a 1980s teen-targeted staple. Teammates from the Hornets' 1982 championship dreamed up one of all-time goofiest monikers.

4. THE TRIPLETS,

Anoka. Center Sean Fish stood 5 foot 6. His wings were 6-foot-2 identical twins Aaron and Andy LaHoud. The trio had uncanny chemistry starting as Bantams, and twins became triplets. "They adopted me as one of their own," said Fish, co-captain of the Tornadoes' 2003 championship squad.

5. PRODUCTION LINE,

Roseau. Jim Stordahl, brother Larry Stordahl, and Don Ross combined for a never-ending stream of goals, producing against all teams in all situations en route to titles in 1958 and '59.

6. PONY LINE, Thief

River Falls. The unbridled talent of center Jackie Poole and wings Glen Carlson and Cliff "Chipper" Strand was evident when they were sophomores playing behind a bevy of older star forwards. They took the reins as juniors and seniors, playing in two tournaments and winning the championship in 1956.

7. WMD LINE, Duluth

East. This old-school line-naming formula simply strings together the last initials of the Greyhounds' high-scoring 2018 tournament trio of Garrett Worth, Ian Mageau, and Ryder Donovan to form a play on multiple wartime eras' "weapons of mass destruction."

8. WHITEHEADS, Edina.

Just kids from the 1982 champion Hornets team being kids again. White practice jerseys worn by center Dave Maley and wings John DeVoe and Brian Cutshall provided the starting point for a unique moniker.

9. THE SMURFS,

Centennial. Youth hockey phenoms who racked up pinball-wizard point totals, Ben Ollila, Tom Gorowsky, and Tim Ornell formed an undersized trio named after the lovable cartoon characters from the 1980s TV series of the same name. They eventually outgrew their nickname, but the on-ice demolition continued all the way to the 2004 championship.

10. ORANGE CRUSH LINE, Grand Rapids. Gavin

Hain, Blake McLaughlin, and Micah Miller, each of whom was committed to a Division I college program as seniors, combined to score all six goals as the orange-clad Thunderhawks "crushed" Moorhead 6–3 in the 2017 title game.

BEST OF THE BEST

One-Two Forward Combinations

1. Dave Spehar and Chris Locker, Duluth East. To say Spehar the goal scorer was Batman to Locker the set-up man's Robin would be underselling the way these superheroes brought a level of flair and imagination to the game unheard of for a couple of teenagers. Their combined tourney numbers are staggering: twenty-five goals, twenty-four assists, and the 1995 state title.

2. Oscar Mahle and David Frank, International Falls. Legendary coach Larry Ross, winner of six championships, once said he never had a greater duo than Mahle and Frank. Could there be a better stamp of approval? Mahle scored seven goals and Frank six as the Broncos dominated the 1957 tournament, outscoring opponents 17–1.

3. Rube Bjorkman and Bob Harris, Roseau. Bjorkman was bestowed with the grand "Masked Marvel" nickname. Meanwhile, one newspaper described Harris as "chunky" and "little" and called him Bill instead of Bob. Regardless of the reporting, this duo that rarely left the ice was fabulous. They had a hand in nine of the ten goals Roseau scored en route to the 1946 title.

4. Bobby Krieger and Bruce Carlson, Edina. Krieger brought the speed, Carlson the savvy playmaking. Both had a goal scorer's touch. They led Edina to two title games in three tournament appearances, including the championship in 1969.

5. Mike Lauen and Mark Gagnon, Edina. Gagnon had a knack for firing cross-ice breakout passes onto the tape of the jet-propelled Lauen's stick, who routinely blew around opposing defensemen on his way to the net. The combo helped the Hornets reach three straight title games and win two championships, including the 1979 title in overtime against Rochester John Marshall on a trademark Gagnon-to-Lauen stretch pass that resulted in the winning goal.

6. Gino Guyer and Andy Sertich, Greenway. Catalysts of the 2000s revival of the tiny Iron Range program, Guyer (named Mr. Hockey in 2002), Sertich, and the rest of the Raiders were crowd favorites as they stunned metro behemoth Eden Prairie 5–4 in overtime in the 2001 quarterfinals (Guyer scored the winning goal). The duo was involved in all but two of Greenway's eleven goals en route to a third-place finish.

7. Ben Ward and Nick Zwack, Monticello/Annandale/Maple Lake. The lovable Moose, first-time tourney entrants in 2017, played a rope-a-dope, defense-first style that led to low-scoring games and relied heavily on the ability of Zwack and Ward to occasionally break loose for prime scoring chances. The duo delivered a combined six tourney goals, and the Moose pushed Class 1A bully Hermantown to double overtime in an eventual 4–3 loss.

8. Jeff Taffe and Dan Welch, Hastings. In 1999, Taffe was named Mr. Hockey, Welch was the Associated Press Player of the Year, and they shared the *Star Tribune*'s All-Metro Player of the Year honors. Who was better? That's a debate for eternity, although Welch's goal with 0.2 seconds on the clock to beat Blaine in the 1999 quarterfinals is one for the ages.

9. Brock Nelson and Brett Hebel, Warroad. Nelson, a future first-round NHL draft pick, was the do-it-all forward. Hebel was a bull in the corners and, most importantly, knew how to convert Nelson's brilliant passes into goals. They played in three Class 1A tournaments, combining for seventeen goals and eighteen assists and helping Warroad finish second in 2009 and third in 2008 and 2010.

10. Alex Funk and Jason Samuelson, Rochester Lourdes. The Eagles' tandem amassed a combined sixteen goals and twenty-six assists in three tournaments from 2010 to 2013. Lourdes's best finish in that stretch was a consolation title in 2010.

Best Big Men

1. GEORGE PELAWA, BEMIDJI, FORWARD. Bemidji's number 8 was Calgary's top pick in the 1986 NHL draft. No player before or since has blended such extraordinary size (6 foot 3, 245 pounds) and blazing speed in as dominating fashion as the Lumberjacks' "Gentle Giant." Pelawa, who played in the 1985 and 1986 state tournaments, died in a car accident in August 1986.

2. JIM CARTER, SOUTH ST. PAUL, DEFENSEMAN. The rugged Carter (6 foot 4, 210 pounds) played 107 of a possible 108 minutes in the 1966 tournament, leaving the ice briefly only because he lost a contact lens in a semifinal loss to International Falls. He played football and hockey at the University of Minnesota and starred in the NFL for eight seasons as a linebacker with the Green Bay Packers.

3. NICK BJUGSTAD, BLAINE, FORWARD. Cashmere smooth as a skater and the owner of a wickedly powerful and accurate shot, Bjugstad (6 foot 5, 190 pounds) made three straight state tournament appearances starting in 2008. The future first-round draft pick of the Florida Panthers scored four goals in the 2009 tourney, in which the Bengals finished third.

4. DYLAN SAMBERG, HERMANTOWN, DEFENSEMAN. The 6-foot-3, 190-pound workhorse authored one of the classic tournament goal celebrations in the 2017 Class 1A championship game when he raced down the ice, slid on his back, and proceeded to make textbook-perfect snow angels on the ice after scoring in double overtime to lift the Hawks past spirited Monticello/Annandale/Maple Lake.

5. DAN MAHLE, INTERNATIONAL FALLS, FORWARD. Played in four state tournaments. By the time he was a senior, the grinding wing (6 foot 3, 190 pounds) who flanked superstar Tim Sheehy was such an intimidating force, few players bothered to challenge him. A hat trick in the 1965 title game cemented his status as one of the Broncos' all-time greats.

6. JOSH OLSON, ROSEAU, FORWARD. As nasty as he was skilled, the power forward (6 foot 3, 215 pounds) had the singularly focused mindset and colorful vocabulary of a drill sergeant. Olson backed up all his swagger in the 1999 state tournament, scoring game-winning goals against Rochester Mayo (quarterfinals) and Hastings (championship).

7. MATT HENTGES, EDINA, DEFENSEMAN. TV announcers likened Hentges's size (6 foot 6, 210 pounds) to that of an NBA small forward, then continued with the hoops theme by pointing out that Hentges's dad, Dick, had played high school basketball for Sleepy Eye. Matt helped the Hornets hold Hill-Murray to zero shots in the second period of the 1988 championship game as Edina won 5–3.

8. RILEY TUFTE, BLAINE, FORWARD. Seemingly cast from the same mold as previous Bengals big man Nick Bjugstad, Tufte (6 foot 5, 220 pounds) also was a smooth skater with a cannon shot. He even had the blond hair and first-round NHL draft pick status (Dallas Stars) to match his predecessor. Tufte scored twice in the 2015 tournament as a junior, when Blaine finished sixth.

9. MARK ALT, CRETIN-DERHAM HALL, DEFENSEMAN. The son of John Alt, a Pro Bowl offensive lineman for the Kansas City Chiefs, Mark (6 foot 4, 201 pounds) quarterbacked Cretin–Derham Hall to the 2009 state Class 5A championship. The Mr. Hockey finalist registered two assists in the Raiders' surprising quarterfinal win over Duluth East in 2009. Has played in eighteen NHL games.

10. BRETT CHORSKE, EDINA, FORWARD. The son of Tom Chorske, the state's first Mr. Hockey Award recipient as a senior in 1985, Brett (6 foot 6, 185 pounds) blossomed late in his high school career. The center was invaluable in the 2019 state tournament, scoring a goal, adding three assists, and, in the championship game, perfectly screening Eden Prairie goaltender Axel Rosenlund on Peter Colby's overtime goal.

Little Big Men

1. MIKE ANTONOVICH, GREENWAY, FORWARD.

Stood 5 foot 5, weighed 150 pounds, and refused to wear shoulder and elbow pads, making him look more like a Pee Wee than a high school phenom. Assisted on the winning goal and scored the clincher into an empty net in the 1967 championship against St. Paul Johnson. Won another state title in 1968 and racked up twenty-two points (sixth-most all time), including twelve goals, in three-year tourney career.

2. KEITH "HUFFER" CHRISTIANSEN, INTERNATIONAL FALLS, FORWARD.

Prodigiously talented Christiansen (5 foot 5, 145 pounds) scored two goals and added two assists to help International Falls win the 1962 title, leaving fans in awe and opposing coaches in shock. "I hope I never see another player, unless he plays for me, who can do as much as this boy Keith Christiansen of the Falls," Richfield coach Gene Olive told reporters.

3. SCOTT LECY, ROCHESTER JOHN MARSHALL, FORWARD.

Scored his thirteenth hat trick of the season against Minneapolis Southwest to open the 1977 tournament. Something of a player-coach, Scott Lecy (5 foot 8½, 160 pounds) booted his younger brother Todd out of the faceoff circle in the closing seconds of the championship game against Edina East, won the draw, and set up Todd for the clinching empty-net goal in the 4–2 triumph.

4. KARL GOEHRING, APPLE VALLEY, GOALTENDER.

Loomed large in an epic five-overtime 1996 semifinal against Dave Spehar–led Duluth East, throwing his 5-foot-6½, 150-pound body around for a record sixty-five saves. Less than eighteen hours later, the physically and emotionally drained Goehring summoned the energy to make twenty-one more saves in a tightly contested 3–2 championship game win over Edina.

5. KYLE RAU, EDEN PRAIRIE, FORWARD.

Fueled by critics who insisted he was too small to be a success, Rau (5 foot 7, 160 pounds) was an integral part of the Eagles' championship teams in 2009 and 2011. Fearless and relentless, Rau absorbed numerous bone-jarring hits in the 2011 championship game against Duluth East before scoring one of the tournament's most memorable goals in triple overtime.

6. DOUG LONG, ST. PAUL JOHNSON, GOALTENDER.

The kid who stood 5 foot 5, weighed 155 pounds, and enjoyed reading comic books and playing Ping-Pong emerged as a titan of the 1970 tournament, overshadowing the likes of Edina's Bobby Krieger and Bruce Carlson and Minneapolis Southwest's Brad Shelstad. Long's back-to-back sixty-one- and fifty-two-save performances against Greenway (five overtimes) and Edina (three overtimes), respectively, endure as legendary feats.

7. JOE "BIFFY" BIANCHI, BLOOMINGTON JEFFERSON, FORWARD.

Nicknamed Biffy (after a garbage-hauling company in Bloomington) because of his penchant for scoring ugly, short-range, "garbage" goals, the 5-foot-8, 170-pound Bianchi was the last of three brothers to win titles with the Jaguars. As a sophomore, he registered hat tricks in the quarterfinals and championship of the 1992 Tier I tournament.

8. DOUG WOOG, SOUTH ST. PAUL, FORWARD.

A tournament fixture for four years starting in 1959, the precocious Woog (5 foot 7, 155 pounds) had considered playing basketball before wisely turning to a less vertically inclined sport. Had a hand in all but two of the Packers' eight goals as they took third in 1962.

9. SEAN FISH, ANOKA, FORWARD.

The co-captain provided impeccable leadership, diligent defense, and timely scoring as a senior for the 2003 state champion Tornadoes. Fish (5 foot 6, 140 pounds) offered comic relief, too, playing along with the "Triplets" nickname given to his forward line, which included the 6-foot-2, 200-pound LaHoud twins (Andy and Aaron) on his wings. Assisted on both Anoka goals in a 2–1 semifinal victory over defending champion Holy Angels.

10. AARON NESS, ROSEAU, DEFENSEMAN.

A mere toothpick (5 foot 10, 150 pounds), the elusive Ness was a ghost to opposing players bent on driving him into the boards. He took his now-you-see-me-now-you-don't act to St. Paul as a sophomore in 2007 and flourished, earning all-tournament honors for the champion Rams. He won the Mr. Hockey Award as a senior.

Ten Who Played Hurt

1. PETE FICHUK, INTERNATIONAL FALLS.
The gash above Fichuk's left eye was bad enough. But what really hurt was the tooth shoved deep up into his gums. (He thought it had been knocked out until X-rays taken days later showed otherwise.) Fichuk thrived through the pain in the 1964 title game, scoring twice and adding two assists in a 7–3 rout of St. Paul Johnson.

2. DUANE GLASS, THIEF RIVER FALLS.
A freak accident involving his garage door just before the start of the playoffs damaged Glass's right hand severely enough that his glove had to be modified and taped into place before every game. The do-it-all defenseman's performance didn't suffer—he played all but a handful of minutes in the Prowlers' run to the 1956 championship.

3. TOM GOROWSKY, CENTENNIAL.
The state's scoring leader and Mr. Hockey in 2004 limped through the playoffs with a hernia and partially torn medial collateral knee ligament. "It was ruled good enough that I could play," Gorowsky said about his knee. "But I wasn't at full speed."

4. DYLAN MILLS, DULUTH EAST.
The burly defenseman gutted out the 1995 tournament with a pin protruding from his broken thumb. "I couldn't shoot, and there was blood and pus coming out the whole time," said Mills, whose Greyhounds won the title.

5. RYAN POEHLING, LAKEVILLE NORTH.
Complications from a bout of mononucleosis during the 2015 state tournament included an enlarged spleen, and the top-line center was limited to bed rest and intravenous fluids between games as the Panthers won the title.

6. MARTY NANNE, EDINA.
Nanne underwent every available treatment option, including a cortisone shot, to get through the pain of a separated shoulder during the 1984 tournament. Neither the injury nor a bulky shoulder brace proved to be a hindrance, and he scored three goals in three games, almost matching his regular-season output, for the champion Hornets.

7. MARK HORVATH, HILL-MURRAY.
This player couldn't shake a knee injury suffered during fall soccer season. The pain became so great he was transported by wheelchair from the team hotel to the Civic Center. He was wheeled from the locker room to the ice, too, where he summoned the strength to help the Pioneers win the 1983 title.

8. DICK HAUGLAND, INTERNATIONAL FALLS.
The senior defenseman played through the pain of acute appendicitis, even scoring a goal in the Broncos' 1963 title-game loss to St. Paul Johnson. He underwent surgery the next day.

9. NATE WARNER, ST. CLOUD CATHEDRAL.
A painful shoulder injury (torn labrum) limited Warner only in his jump-around exuberance during goal celebrations, of which there were plenty en route to the 2019 Class 1A championship. He underwent surgery nine days after scoring four goals in three games.

10. BOBBY BRINK, MINNETONKA.
The elusive sophomore said a torn meniscus in his right knee limited his speed off the starting line during the 2018 tourney. "Those first explosive strides were tough, especially with the right leg," he said. But once the adrenaline starting flowing, Brink really got going—to the tune of a tournament-best five goals for the champion Skippers.

Former Goalies Who Became State Tournament Coaches

1. Willard Ikola, Eveleth to Edina/Edina East. Won three high school titles as a player and eight as a coach.

2. Larry Ross, Morgan Park (Duluth) to International Falls. All-American 'tender at the University of Minnesota. Coached the Broncos to six championships.

3. Oscar Almquist, Eveleth to Roseau. Solid high school goalie and even better coach. Led Roseau to the pinnacle four times.

4. Ken Pauly, Wayzata to Benilde–St. Margaret's and Minnetonka. Marginal high school goalie (his words) who became a strong coach, winning state titles at Benilde–St. Margaret's in 1999, 2001 (Class 1A), and 2012 (2A).

5. Bruce Plante, Cloquet to Hermantown. Playing career took him from Cloquet to the University of Wisconsin-Superior. Came to Hermantown and built a powerhouse with three titles and six runner-up finishes.

6. Bill Lechner, Cretin to Hill-Murray. Captain of the Cretin varsity team as a senior. Served as assistant coach on Hill-Murray's 1983 championship team and captured his own in 2008 and 2020.

7. Jim Nelson, Roseau to Grand Rapids. Backstopped Roseau to state three times. Kept Grand Rapids churning in the 1970s with the 1976 title.

8. Dave Peterson, St. Paul Harding to Minneapolis Southwest. Won a consolation title with Harding in 1948. Became Southwest's coach and in 1970 captured the one and only state title for a Minneapolis public school.

9. Jeff Poeschl, Hill-Murray to Mahtomedi. Kept the Pioneers undefeated in 1979–80 until the championship game. Mahtomedi won its first state title in 2020 under his watch.

10. Brad Bergstrom, International Falls to Fergus Falls. Played in the 1983 state tournament, the final one of Larry Ross's career. Bergstrom learned well, leading Fergus Falls to its first six state tournaments.

Characters

1. Gene Sack, Rochester John Marshall.
Called "Gunny" or "Bag" as a kid, Sack grew up to be a soft-touch history teacher (he loved to show movies during class) and a flamboyant coach with a nickname for everyone, including "Oleo Margarine" for goaltender Paul Butters. "We've fooled them all so far. Maybe we can do it for one more game," he said on the eve of the 1977 championship, which the Rockets won.

2. Dan Clafton, Grand Rapids.
Chubby as a youngster, Clafton was prone to veering off his diet, thus earning him the nickname Chocolate. He had plenty of go-to catchphrases ("Pitter, patter, let's get at 'er"), but improv skills were also strong for the goalie, who led the Indians to the 1975 title.

3. Bruce Plante, Hermantown.
For better or for worse, this coach's unfiltered postgame Q&A sessions with the media often were more entertaining than the Hawks' many blowout victories in the 2010s. Plante is best known for criticizing St. Thomas Academy's presence on the small-school side of the tournament.

4. John DeVoe, Edina.
Incorrigible to the end, this high-scoring Hornets forward was busted with an illegal stick in the 1982 championship game after scoring a goal and waving his outrageously curved blade in front of the White Bear Mariner bench during the celebration.

5 (TIE). Chuck Grillo, Bemidji.
A notorious wiseacre of a coach, when asked what team he would like to face in the 1974 finals, Grillo responded, "I wouldn't care if it is the Boston Bruins. If it's Edina East, though, I'll take up a vote in the dressing room. If it comes out OK, we'll show up."

5 (TIE). Mark Manney, Andover.
Refreshingly candid, Manney, the former Air Force One pilot, delivered zinger after zinger—all in his signature deadpan style—during uproarious postgame media sessions as the Huskies won the 2022 championship. It makes perfect sense that Manney is believed to be distantly related to Hermantown's Bruce Plante, another all-time tourney character.

6. Lou Cotroneo, St. Paul Johnson.
This fiery Italian succeeded Rube Gustafson as coach in 1964 and reached the state tournament seven times in eight seasons, never placing lower than fourth. One of his more animated motivational speeches ended with his watch flying off his wrist and into a dressing-room toilet.

7. Hank Sorensen, Wayzata.
The defenseman nicknamed the Hammer delighted in agitating opponents with his physical play and verbal jousting. He took command of the postgame interview room after the Trojans won the 2016 title, injecting unsolicited praise for teammates and producing a handful of memorable one-liners.

8. Dick "Beaver" Lick and Don "Whitey" Willer, South St. Paul.
These two beauties switched jerseys before a 1954 state tournament game to "throw off" the competition, resulting in Beaver's name appearing in the official box score when really it was Whitey who scored twice.

9. Mike Antonovich, Greenway.
The T-shirt he wore under his gear remained unwashed when the Raiders were on a win streak. Antonovich preferred to hitchhike home immediately after practice instead of hitting the showers, earning the fun-loving tourney superstar from the late 1960s the nickname Stinky.

10. Clem Cossalter, Eveleth.
This braggadocious senior defenseman on the Golden Bears' 1945 championship squad was nicknamed Iron Guts after claiming he could drink a case of beer. Two bottles later, he was throwing up on the fender of a car.

BEST OF THE BEST

Nicknames

1. Rube **"THE MASKED MARVEL"** Bjorkman, Roseau. Fans and media scribes alike "marveled" at the slick-skating, rocket-shooting forward from the Canadian border who earned the tournament's top billing in 1946 and 1947. Distinctive eyewear—rubber goggles with prescription lenses—led to an array of nicknames, but the Masked Marvel was the one that stuck.

2. Bob **"SLOPJOHN"** O'Leary, International Falls. The feisty and ultratalented junior forward joined buddy Keith "Huffer" Christiansen on a Broncos forward line that terrorized opponents en route to the 1962 title. He missed senior season because of off-ice shenanigans deemed to be career-ending violations of the state high school league's athletic code. Origin of nickname unknown.

3. Wally **"CEDAR LEGS"** Grant, Eveleth. A bow-legged skating style earned him not only the nickname but a place in history as he raced to nine goals in the inaugural tournament. Two of Grant's goals came in the third period of the 1945 championship game as Eveleth rallied to beat Thief River Falls 4–3.

4. Bryan **"BUTSY"** Erickson, Roseau. The least-heralded member of one of the state's all-time great lines, joining neighbors Neal and Aaron Broten, Erickson was a superb talent (he played in the NHL for ten seasons) who doesn't know—or won't say—how the nickname originated. One Twin Cities newspaper initially spelled the moniker "Butzy" upon the Rams' tournament arrival in 1977.

5. Todd **"PUDLY"** Lecy, Rochester John Marshall. This nickname was a hand-me-down for the Rockets forward who starred in three state tourneys, from 1977 to 1979 (teammate Jeff Teal's dad also went by "Pudly"). Lecy was clutch as a sophomore in '77, scoring the lone goal in his team's semifinal win against South St. Paul, then getting the empty-net clincher in the championship against Edina East. Family and friends still call him Pudly.

6. Mike **"LEFTY"** Curran, International Falls. Many of the great Bronco goaltenders have been left-handed, longtime Minnesota Wild goaltending coach Bob Mason among them. But only Curran, who starred for International Falls en route to the 1962 championship, was tagged with the "Lefty" nickname. He went on to star at North Dakota and was named MVP of the 1972 silver medal–winning US Olympic team.

7. Mac **"QUADZILLA"** Jansen, White Bear Lake. Jansen acquired his nickname through legendary offseason squat workouts and resulting tree trunks for legs. He entered the 2011 Class 2A tournament with thirty-five goals but was held pointless in the Bears' double-overtime quarterfinal loss to Duluth East.

8. Chris **"SWISS"** Schwartzbauer, Edina. That's Swiss, as in cheese. Teammate Chris Bonvino is believed to have authored the nickname for the Hornets' goaltender as part of good-natured locker-room ribbing. There were no holes in Schwartzbauer's game during the 1984 tournament, when he allowed just three goals on seventy-one shots.

9. David **"IZZY"** Marvin, Warroad. The eleventh of Beth and Cal Marvin's twelve children, Izzy was a senior defenseman on the Warrior team that reached the state tournament in 1987, ending a seventeen-year absence. Marvin has parlayed the childhood nickname into a brand—he owns Izzy's Lounge and Grill in Warroad. He also guided the Warroad girls' team to nine state Class 1A tournaments, winning titles in 2010 and 2011.

10. Jim **"BUZZ BOMB"** Renstrom, St. Paul Johnson. Impact player? How about a guy named after a World War II version of the cruise missile? Renstrom left his mark on the 1947 state tournament, scoring a goal and adding a couple of assists as a key forward for the champion Governors.

Notable Tournament Streaks

1 White Bear Lake's quarterfinal futility. Starting with the first tournament in 1945 and most recently in 2019, the Bears have played in nineteen quarterfinal games, losing them all.

2 Centennial's back-to-back-to-back shutouts. No team before or since the 2004 Cougars, led by goaltender Gregg Stutz, has shut out all three of its tournament opponents.

3 Hermantown's title game hex. From 2010 to 2015, the Hawks lost six consecutive Class 1A championship games, three of them to St. Thomas Academy.

4 Eveleth's yearly residency in St. Paul. The Golden Bears played in a record twelve straight tournaments from 1945 to 1956, winning five titles and finishing second twice.

5 Moorhead's role as all-time runner-up. The Spuds have lost all eight state championship games they've played in, a streak that started in 1992 and most recently continued in 2017.

6 Eveleth's guaranteed goal scorer. The great John Mayasich went a record twelve consecutive tournament games from 1948 to 1951 scoring at least one goal.

7 Hermantown's reserved title game seat. The Hawks have dominated the small-school portion of the tournament like no other team, appearing in a record eight straight championship games from 2010 to 2017 and winning titles in 2016 and '17.

8 Eveleth's four of a kind. The Golden Bears ruled the tournament's early years, winning a record four straight championships from 1948 to 1951.

9 Edina's extra-time insistence. The Hornets played in a record five straight overtime games from 1969 to 1971.

10 Eveleth's hat trick hero. In yet another record that is unlikely to be matched, the Golden Bears' John Mayasich had a streak of five consecutive games with hat tricks in 1950–51.

BEST OF THE BEST

Biggest Upsets

1. ROCHESTER JOHN MARSHALL 4, EDINA EAST 2, 1977. Nobody—not fans, not opposing teams, not even the media—thought the southerners from John Marshall belonged at the state tournament. Doubters' faces were as red as the Rockets' helmets following a 4–2 championship game upset of Edina East.

2. BLOOMINGTON 3, ST. PAUL JOHNSON 2, 1965. The undefeated Governors found their path to a third consecutive championship game repeatedly blocked by Bears goaltender Terry Smith, who overcame lingering knee pain and a 38–10 Johnson advantage in shots on goal.

3. COLUMBIA HEIGHTS 2, EDINA 0, 1983. What more can you want from a first-time state tournament entrant blanking the defending champions in the quarterfinals? How about this? The Hylanders' goalie was Reggie Miracle. The headlines practically wrote themselves.

4. LAKEVILLE SOUTH 3, DULUTH EAST 2, 2012. In 2012, Thursday's Class 2A quarterfinals weren't kind to the favorites. All four seeded teams lost, including number-one Duluth East. The Greyhounds (27–1) were tamed by Mr. Hockey Award–winner Justin Kloos and the Cougars.

5. MOORHEAD 5, EDINA 2, 2009. A relentless, physical Spuds team outplayed number-one seed Edina in the quarterfinals—this despite a 3–0 Hornets victory against Moorhead earlier in the season. The Spuds closed the game strong with two goals in the final six minutes.

6. ALEXANDRIA 6, HERMANTOWN 1, 2018. The two-time defending champs rode a forty-eight-game unbeaten streak against Class 1A opponents and hoped to reach its ninth consecutive title game. Number-four seed Alexandria killed those plans in the semifinals.

7. DULUTH EAST 3, EDINA 1, 2015. The matchup everyone wanted, number-one Lakeville North against number-two Edina, went to the dogs. The Greyhounds, that is. A Duluth East team with ten losses dethroned the two-time defending champs in the semifinals.

8. GRAND RAPIDS 3, EDINA 1, 1972. A quarterfinal matchup between Grand Rapids, a tournament newcomer with seven losses, and Edina, top ranked and the defending champion, did not go as scripted. Goaltender Dan Benzie made thirty-seven saves for the up-and-coming Iron Range power.

9. BURNSVILLE 3, ROSEAU 2, 1991. Number-twelve Burnsville, featuring a new head coach and eight losses, stunned the defending champion and top-ranked Rams in overtime. The Braves overcame a 2–1 deficit and rallied for the quarterfinal victory.

10. ROCHESTER 2, EVELETH 1, 1946. In just its second running, the state tournament offered a glimpse of the unpredictability that would provide its charm for decades. In this case, the Rockets were the field's lone automatic entry yet upset defending champion Eveleth in the semifinals.

Best Tournament Teams That Didn't Win the Title

1. Edina, 1970. The defending champs featured senior stars Bobby Krieger and Bill Nyrop. But the Hornets (22–0–1) fell to fellow undefeated Minneapolis Southwest 1–0 in overtime in the championship game.

2. Hill-Murray, 1980. A roster loaded with ten future Division I players entered the tournament 25–0 but got clipped 2–1 by Grand Rapids in the title game.

3. Duluth East, 2012. Runners-up in 2011, the Greyhounds rolled through the season on a mission. They were 27–1 but fell 3–2 to Lakeville South in the quarterfinals.

4. Minnetonka, 2010. Led by a trio of Division I–committed defensemen, the Skippers (25–1–2) seemed unsinkable. However, a fired-up Edina team outplayed them for a 4–2 title game victory.

5 [TIE]. Warroad, 1988. Top-ranked Warroad (24–0) boasted two Mr. Hockey Award finalists in defenseman Larry Olimb and goaltender Chad Erickson. Tournament nemesis Edina struck again, edging the Warriors 2–1 in double overtime of the semifinals.

5 [TIE]. Warroad, 2023. Undefeated and considered by many to be the best team in the state regardless of class, the Warriors, featuring winners of the Mr. Hockey (forward Jayson Shaugabay) and Frank Brimsek (goalie Hampton Slukynsky) awards, suffered their lone loss in their thirty-first and final outing—and 6–5 double-overtime setback against Mahtomedi in the Class 1A title game.

6. Edina West, 1981. The Cougars (22–1) took a seventeen-game winning streak and the number-one ranking into the state tournament, then got dumped 2–1 in the quarterfinals by South St. Paul.

7. Duluth East, 1997. Undefeated (26–0–1) and facing Edina, a team they had beaten during the regular season, the Greyhounds were blanked 1–0 in the championship game.

8. Edina, 2018. The Hornets were 27–2 and had routed eleven opponents by six goals or more before running into a physical Duluth East team in the semifinals and losing 4–2.

9. Roseau, 2008. The defending champion Rams (28–0) earned the number-one seed in the Class 2A state tournament but got manhandled throughout a 6–2 semifinal loss to eventual champion Hill-Murray.

10. St. Paul Johnson, 1967. The consensus favorite to win their first state title in four years, the Governors (23–0) reached the final game but fell 4–2 to Greenway.

BEST OF THE BEST

Best Teams That Didn't Make the Tournament

1. 2000 ELK RIVER. The Elks, featuring one of the state's all-time great athletes in defenseman Paul Martin, a Mr. Hockey Award winner, were ranked number one for most of the season and boasted a 22–1 record when they were slayed by unranked, nine-loss Osseo 5–4 in double overtime in a section semifinal. Elk River, third-place state finisher in 1999 and champion in 2001, had routed eventual 2000 champion Blaine 7–1 late in the regular season.

2. 1960 ROSEAU. The Rams, champions in 1958 and '59, returned so much talent they seemed all but assured of a three-peat. Forwards Don Ross and Larry Stordahl, goaltender Richard Roth, and defenseman Keith Brandt (each of whom were all-tournament picks at least once) were among the bevy of stars who were shocked by Warroad and its goaltender Jerry Lindsay (thirty-one saves) 1–0 in the Region 8 semifinals. Roseau had defeated Warroad twice by five goals in the regular season.

3. 1958 ST. PAUL JOHNSON. Nine-loss St. Paul Harding's 4–3 victory over undefeated St. Paul Johnson in the Region 4 playoffs sparked a firestorm of criticism over such a "flawed" postseason system that could leave a team as talented as the Governors, who went 17–0–2 and allowed just thirteen goals in the regular season, out of the state tournament. Goaltender Tom Martinson and all-tournament selections Mark Skoog and Harold Vinnes were among a group of twelve Johnson seniors who had finished fourth in 1957 and were expecting more in 1958.

4. 1986 EDINA. Spectacular in making thirty-six saves, Richfield junior goaltender Damian Rhodes was the architect of one of the most shocking playoff losses suffered by Edina coach Willard Ikola in his thirty-three-year career. The Hornets were 19–2 and ranked number one in the state when they lost 4–3 to Rhodes and the upstart Spartans, who were 9–11–1 and ranked number eighteen.

5. 1961 INTERNATIONAL FALLS. With Mike "Lefty" Curran in goal, Keith "Huffer" Christiansen and Bob "Slopjohn" O'Leary at forward, and Larry "Pops" Ross behind the bench, these Broncos weren't just an all-time collection of nicknames. This über-talented group—superstar forward Jim Amidon included—was 22–1 entering its brawl-marred 3–2 region final loss to defending state champion Duluth East.

6. 1986 WARROAD. Featuring a defense corps led by future NHLer Danny Lambert (a transfer from Manitoba) and 1988 Mr. Hockey Award winner Larry Olimb, the Warriors were 19–0–1 entering the playoffs. The state's only unbeaten team, with another future NHLer in Chad Erickson in goal, was upended 5–4 by a 9–10–3 Moorhead squad in one of the biggest section playoff upsets ever.

7. 1979 EDINA WEST. Led by superb center Greg Moore, Edina West pounded archrival Edina East, the eventual state champion, 6–2 and 6–1 in the regular season. When sixth-ranked West, the Lake South Conference champion, was defeated by Cooper 2–1 in the section semifinals, East players rejoiced. "We were jumping up and down because our chances of getting to state were very slim if we would have had to play them," Hornets star Mike Lauen said.

8. 2010 WAYZATA. The Trojans beat eventual state champion Edina three times, tied state runner-up Minnetonka twice, and beat semifinalist Apple Valley and quarterfinalists Lakeville North and Duluth East in a 20–2–3 regular season. Wayzata, fueled by top scorers Scott Holm, Tony Cameranesi, and Mario Lucia, lost 4–1 to defending state champion Eden Prairie in a section semifinal.

9. 2016 BENILDE-ST. MARGARET'S. Few people—OK, nobody—would have predicted an undefeated season for this overachieving Red Knights group led by scoring ace Cade Gleekel (fifty-eight points) and goaltender Ryan Bischel (2.09 goals-against average). The team's 24–0–1 regular season record included a 3–0 mark against eventual state finalists Wayzata and Eden Prairie. Downed by Cretin–Derham Hall 4–3 in a section semifinal.

10. 1976 EVELETH. With future 1980 Olympian Mark Pavelich as the playmaking centerpiece and Ronn Tomassoni as his high-scoring sidekick, Eveleth reeled off eighteen consecutive victories to finish the regular season 18–2. The Iron Range Conference champion Golden Bears avenged season-opening losses by trouncing Grand Rapids 7–3 and International Falls 6–0. Lost 3–0 to eventual state champ Grand Rapids in the section final to finish 21–3.

BEST OF THE BEST

Players Who Never Played in the Tournament

1. Corey Millen, Cloquet. The state's best forward in 1981–82, Millen suffered a broken ankle in the playoffs. Cloquet made the state tournament, but Millen watched from the bench with a cast on his right foot and crutches at his side.

2. Tom Chorske, Minneapolis West/Southwest. The inaugural Mr. Hockey Award winner as a senior forward in 1985, Chorske was taken number sixteen overall in the NHL draft. He played three seasons for the Minnesota Gophers. In 1995, he hoisted the Stanley Cup with New Jersey.

3. Jack McCartan, St. Paul Marshall. An overlooked goaltender from an overmatched high school program, McCartan kept climbing. A walk-on at Minnesota, he became an all-American in 1957 and 1958. In 1960, he led the US Olympic team to gold.

4. Alex Goligoski, Grand Rapids. His Thunderhawks fell in the Section 7 finals his junior and senior seasons, but Goligoski, a 2004 graduate, was a superb defenseman and a Mr. Hockey finalist. He earned all-American honors with the Gophers in 2007 and two years later helped the Pittsburgh Penguins win the Stanley Cup.

5. Eric Strobel, Rochester Mayo. An elite forward, Strobel went on to win the NCAA championship with Minnesota in 1979 and the Olympic gold medal in 1980. "He's the best there is, no question about it," Jefferson coach Tom Saterdalen told John Gilbert of the *Minneapolis Tribune* in 1976.

6. Dave Merhar, Ely. Who? From where? Merhar was a gem from the state's northeast corner. Recruited as a senior forward in 1965 by Minnesota coach John Mariucci, Merhar opted for West Point. In 1968–69, he became the first collegiate player to surpass one hundred points in a season.

7. Mark Pavelich, Eveleth. The best of several strong players unable to push some good mid-1970s Eveleth teams through a loaded Section 7. Pavelich became an all-American forward at Minnesota Duluth, won Olympic gold in 1980, and posted five strong seasons with the New York Rangers.

8. David Backes, Spring Lake Park. A 2002 Mr. Hockey finalist and power forward, Backes enjoyed three solid seasons at Minnesota State. He earned second-team all-American honors in 2006. From there, he made two appearances in the Winter Olympics and was a 2011 NHL All-Star.

9. Wally Olds, Baudette. The Baudette native graduated high school in 1967 and played at Minnesota. A swift-skating and cerebral defenseman, Olds earned all-American status in 1970 and was an Olympic silver medalist in 1972. He played professionally in the World Hockey Association.

10. Erik Rasmussen, St. Louis Park. The 1995 Mr. Hockey Award winner, Rasmussen tallied twenty goals and twenty-four assists playing both forward and defense while averaging thirty-five minutes per game. He played two college seasons at Minnesota and was selected number seven overall by Buffalo in the NHL draft.

Celebrity Sightings

1 Tom Hanks. Not yet a mega-actor, a young Hanks drank in the sights and sounds of the state tournament in 1982 as he promoted his soon-to-be-canceled TV series, *Bosom Buddies.* "This is my first visit to the Twin Cities, and the electricity in this building is absolutely infectious," he said after watching Edina beat Bloomington Jefferson in overtime in the semifinals.

★ ★ ★ ★ ★ ★ ★ ★ ★ ★ ★ ★ ★ ★ ★ ★ ★ ★

2 Howard Cosell. Another star brought in to promote KSTP's affiliation with ABC, Cosell of *Monday Night Football* fame was at the apex of his sports broadcasting career in 1979 when he took the St. Paul Civic Center by storm, smoking stogies, hobnobbing with *Star Tribune* columnist Sid Hartman, and waxing poetic about the hockey below. "This is sport the way it should be," he said.

★ ★ ★ ★ ★ ★ ★ ★ ★ ★ ★ ★ ★ ★ ★ ★ ★ ★

3 Cheryl Tiegs. A Minnesota native, Tiegs was well on her way to becoming the first American supermodel when she appeared at the state tournament in 1979 with photographer and future husband Peter Beard to promote an episode of ABC's *The American Sportsman.*

★ ★ ★ ★ ★ ★ ★ ★ ★ ★ ★ ★ ★ ★ ★ ★ ★ ★

4 André the Giant. The 7-foot-2 professional wrestler billed as the "Eighth Wonder of the World" was one of several stars from Verne Gagne's American Wrestling Association brought in by TV analyst Lou Nanne to spice up 1960s and '70s tourney broadcasts. "He would grab your hand, and you couldn't believe how big he was," Nanne said.

★ ★ ★ ★ ★ ★ ★ ★ ★ ★ ★ ★ ★ ★ ★ ★ ★ ★

5 Barry Melrose. Playfully billed as ESPN's "Senior Hair Correspondent," the mullet-topped Melrose made his inaugural appearance at the state tournament in 2016 and chronicled the lasting infatuation with players' locks in a piece titled "Minneflowta."

6 Richard Dawson. The former *Hogan's Heroes* actor was in the midst of his first run as host of the game show *Family Feud* when he joined Cosell and other ABC stars at the 1979 tourney. The British-born Dawson admitted to knowing little about hockey but said, "The young people here are an absolute joy, they really are."

★ ★ ★ ★ ★ ★ ★ ★ ★ ★ ★ ★ ★ ★ ★ ★ ★ ★

7 Reginald "the Crusher" Lisowski. Another pro wrestler brought in to promote the WTCN-televised American Wrestling Association, the Crusher was a three-time world heavyweight champion known for his "hundred-megaton biceps" and eagerness to pummel "da bum."

★ ★ ★ ★ ★ ★ ★ ★ ★ ★ ★ ★ ★ ★ ★ ★ ★ ★

8 Ted McGinley. The actor who appeared on popular TV shows ranging from *Love Boat* to *Dynasty* to *Married . . . with Children* was in his second season as a *Happy Days* regular in 1982 when he got his first taste of state tournament hoopla—and hockey. "I'm having a great time," he said. "I'm being introduced to hockey at [what] I think is the best level possible."

★ ★ ★ ★ ★ ★ ★ ★ ★ ★ ★ ★ ★ ★ ★ ★ ★ ★

9 Maren Jensen. Jensen, a B-lister who portrayed Athena on the short-lived original *Battlestar Galactica* TV series, was among the group of ABC stars who converged on the 1979 tournament. The California beauty, when asked if she knew how to skate, replied, "I do skate. I roller skate, though."

★ ★ ★ ★ ★ ★ ★ ★ ★ ★ ★ ★ ★ ★ ★ ★ ★ ★

10 Don Chevrier. Canada's version of Howard Cosell, the iconic Toronto-born Chevrier called games in 1983 as WCCO stepped up the coverage of the tournament in its first year broadcasting the event.

BEST OF THE BEST

Tournament Career Scoring Leaders

	GOALS	ASSISTS	POINTS
JOHN MAYASICH, Eveleth (1948–51)	36	10	46
JOHN MATCHEFTS, Eveleth (1946–49)	19	12	31
DAVE SPEHAR, Duluth East (1994–96)	21	8	29
BEN HANOWSKI, Little Falls (2006–09)	19	9	28
JOHNNY POHL, Red Wing (1995–98)	11	17	28
MIKE ANTONOVICH, Greenway (1967–69)	12	10	22
ALEX FUNK, Rochester Lourdes (2010–13)	11	10	21
JASON SAMUELSON, Rochester Lourdes (2010–13)	5	16	21
AARON BROTEN, Roseau (1977–79)	10	10	20
CHRIS LOCKER, Duluth East (1995–96)	4	16	20
BROCK NELSON, Warroad (2008–10)	11	9	20
RYAN SANDELIN, Hermantown (2015–17)	10	10	20
JAYSON SHAUGABAY, Warroad (2020–23)	8	12	20
RYAN MILLER, Fergus Falls (1999–2002)	11	8	19
TOM MOORE, Red Wing (1996–98)	12	7	19
DOUG WOOG, South St. Paul (1959–62)	12	7	19
RYAN KRAFT, Moorhead (1992–94)	13	5	18
JOHN BADER, Irondale (1979–80)	6	11	17
DIXON BOWEN, East Grand Forks (2013–15)	5	12	17
MIKE CASTELLANO, Eveleth (1950–53)	7	10	17
CASEY MITTELSTADT, Eden Prairie (2015–17)	8	9	17
T. J. OSHIE, Warroad (2003–05)	7	10	17
SHEA WALTERS, Hibbing (2003–04)	7	10	17

Tournament Goaltending Records

MOST SAVES IN A SINGLE GAME

65 — Karl Goehring, Apple Valley, 1996 semifinals

63 — Henry Welsch, Lakeville South, 2019 quarterfinals

61 — Doug Long, St. Paul Johnson, 1970 quarterfinals

MOST SAVES IN A SINGLE TOURNAMENT

131 — Henry Welsch, Lakeville South, 2019

124 — Doug Long, St. Paul Johnson, 1970

119 — Jim Nelson, Roseau, 1966

MOST CAREER TOURNAMENT SAVES

252 — Jim Nelson, Roseau, 1965–67

241 — Peter Waselovich, International Falls, 1971–73

241 — Paul Butters, Rochester John Marshall, 1977–79

MOST CAREER TOURNAMENT VICTORIES

10 — Willard Ikola, Eveleth, 1947–50

9 — David Zevnik, St. Thomas Academy, 2011–13

7 — Jim Jetland, Grand Rapids, 1976–78
Peter Waselovich, International Falls, 1971–73
Tom Wahman, St. Paul Johnson, 1954–56

HIGHEST TOURNAMENT AND CAREER SAVE PERCENTAGE

1.000 — Gregg Stutz, Centennial, 2004
(53 saves on 53 shots on goal)

ACKNOWLEDGMENTS

This book as you see it today wouldn't exist without the relentless work of Kyle Oen. Kyle spent hundreds of hours at the Minnesota History Center's Gale Family Library carefully sifting through boxes of negatives, some dating back to the 1940s, from the Minneapolis and St. Paul newspapers. Dozens of the fantastic photos used in *Tourney Time* were curated by Kyle, who not only captured images of more than thirty-five thousand state tournament negatives but allowed us to thumb through his massive personal collection of tourney photos. His love for all things related to the history of the state tournament knows no limits. In that way, Kyle, the founder and owner of Vintage Minnesota Hockey, is a kindred spirit. We're lucky to count him as a friend.

Kyle, thank you so much for all your contributions.

—David and Loren

To my amazing wife, Sarah, and my wonderful daughter, Michaela: thank you for your love, patience, and support. This book is for you two. Thanks, Loren Nelson, for being a true believer. And thanks to the former players, coaches, referees, fans, and others for trusting us with their stories. To modify a Herb Brooks quote, the names inside this book are a hell of a lot more important than the ones on the cover.

—David

To my wonderful wife, Helen; daughter, Katherine; and son, Luke, I offer my deepest gratitude for your love, support, patience, and creative encouragement as we counted down the chapters remaining to be written. To my co-author, David La Vaque, thank you not only for the inspiration for this book but also for asking me to partner with you in writing it. I am honored to have been given this opportunity. Finally, I am forever indebted to all the former players, coaches, referees, fans, and others who have been so gracious and accommodating while sharing their memories of an event that, only because of their involvement, truly is like no other.

—Loren

The authors would further like to acknowledge the
following people for their contributions:

BRIAN ARVIN	BEN HANKINSON	SKIP PELTIER
HENRY BOUCHA	JIM HOEY	BARB REGAL
AARON BROTEN	WILLARD IKOLA	CRAIG ROBERTS
NEAL BROTEN	TIM KOLEHMAINEN	ERIN ROTH
PAUL BROTEN	KEVIN KURTT	MICHAEL RUSSO
BRUCE CARLSON	MARK LODGE	KARL SCHUETTLER
TOM CHORSKE	DON LUCIA	HERB SELLARS
JOE CHRISTENSEN	MYRON MEDCALF	MIKE THILL
TONY CURRAN	BRIAN MURPHY	JOHN WAREHAM
JOHN DECENZO	CHRIS MURPHY	ERIC WHISLER
DICK FISHER	KYLE OEN	BRYAN ZOLLMAN
JACE FREDERICK	JASON OLSON	
RICH GLENNIE	TRACY OSTBY	

Introduction
John Gilbert, "Olympic, 'U' Coaches Fire Up Prep Hockey Players," *Minneapolis Tribune,* March 9, 1972.

1945
Interviews: John Aldrich, John Resler, Gorman Velde.
Jack Horner, "Horner's Corner," *Skyway News,* March 3, 1976.
Patrick Reusse, "Heritage on Ice," *Minneapolis Star Tribune,* February 28, 1999.
Jim Ryan, "State Ice Champs Had Great Time," *Eveleth News-Clarion,* February 22, 1945.
Bob Sansevere, "The First Ice Kings," *St. Paul Pioneer Press,* March 7, 2001.
Howard Sinker, "Glory Is Just a Memory, but Eveleth Remembers," *Minneapolis Tribune,* March 8, 1981.
"1,500 Attend Annual Ice Show at George Myrum Field House," *St. Peter Herald,* February 21, 1940.
"City Sportswriters Laud Fighting Spirit of Granite Hockey Players," *Granite Falls Tribune,* February 22, 1945.
"Eight Hockey Teams Honored at Luncheon," *St. Paul Pioneer Press,* February 15, 1945.
"George Kieffer Scores Opener," *St. Paul Pioneer Press,* February 16, 1945.
"High School Hockey Meet," *Roseau Times-Region,* February 26, 1942.
"Seven High Schools in G.A. Hockey Meet," *St. Peter Herald,* February 16, 1940.
"T.R. Falls is Hock'y Champ," *Roseau Times-Region,* March 5, 1942.

1946
Interviews: Orv Anderson, Rube Bjorkman, Bob Harris, Clark Wilder.
"Roseau Tips White Bear," *St. Paul Pioneer Press,* February 15, 1946.

1947
Interviews: Orv Anderson, Rod Anderson, Lou Cotroneo, Howie Eckstrom, George "Skip" Peltier, Jim Sedin.
"Roseau's Pucksters Boast Big Cheering Section," *Minneapolis Tribune,* February 16, 1947.

1948
Interviews: Ron Castellano, Dave Hendrickson, Willard Ikola, Bob Kochevar, John Mayasich, Tony Tassoni, Dan Voce.
Dick Cullum, "Cullum's Column," *Minneapolis Tribune,* February 25, 1952.

1949
Interviews: Ron Castellano, Dave Hendrickson, Willard Ikola, Bob Kochevar, Jim Matchefts, John Mayasich, Tony Tassoni, Dan Voce.

Loren Nelson, "Iron Range Jackrabbit," *Minneapolis Star Tribune* MN Boys' Hockey Hub, 2011.

1950
Interviews: Ron Castellano, Dave Hendrickson, Willard Ikola, Bob Kochevar, John Mayasich, Tony Tassoni, Dan Voce.

1951
Interviews: Roger Bertelsen, Vincent Bugliosi, Ron Castellano, Dave Hendrickson, Willard Ikola, Bob Kochevar, John Mayasich, Tony Tassoni, Dan Voce.
Tom Briere, "Mayasich Betters Hat Trick," *Minneapolis Tribune,* February 27, 1950.
Jim Byrne, "Southwest Six Tackles Eveleth," *Minneapolis Star,* February 23, 1951.
1951 "Founding Families" Sidebar
Interviews: Gary Alm, Rick Alm, Steve Jecha, Bob Lundeen, Dick Meredith, Chris Middlebrook, Jim Westby.
Patrick Reusse, "Alms, Westbys Remember Golden Era," *Minneapolis Star Tribune,* June 20, 2004.

1952
Interviews: Jerry Calengor, George Jetty, George Perpich Jr., Jim Perpich, Herb Sellars, Joanne Tomaino, Don Vaia, Loren Webb.
Halsey Hall, "State Prep Puck Meet Best Yet," *Minneapolis Tribune,* February 25, 1952.
"Hibbing's Ace Shoes in Shreds," *St. Paul Pioneer Press,* February 24, 1952.

1953
Interviews: Rod Anderson, Stu Anderson, Roger Bertelsen, Jack Holstrom, Larry Paul, Gene Picha, Gary Shea, Bob Wahman.
Hank Kebhorn, "Bedlam on Ice," *St. Paul Pioneer Press,* February 22, 1953.
Ted Randolph, "Heartbreak by a Heartbeat," *St. Paul Dispatch,* February 20, 1953.

1954
Interviews: Glen Carlson, Bob Kochevar, Mike McMahon, Joe Poole.
Lewis Patterson, "Thief River Falls Boys Versatile // It's Wonder Hockey Star Has Time to Tie Skates," *St. Paul Dispatch,* February 26, 1954.
Ted Randolph, "Poole Wins Fans' Raves," *St. Paul Dispatch,* February 26, 1954.
"Thompson: Thief River No 'Shinny Team,'" *Minneapolis Tribune,* February 27, 1954.
"Wrong Place! Prep Star's Injury Fools Announcer," *St. Paul Pioneer Press,* February 28, 1954.
1954 "Whitey and Beaver" Sidebar
Interview: Richard Lick.

1955
Interviews: Rod Anderson, Stu Anderson, Lou Cotroneo, Ken Fanger, Jack Holstrom, Roger Wigen.
Jim Byrne, "Johnson Ice Coach Can 'Good Turn' Old Scoutmaster," *Minneapolis Star,* February 26, 1955.
Ted Randolph, "Twin Cities Teams Face Challenge," *St. Paul Dispatch,* February 25, 1955.
"'No Alibis' Says Tiger Coach Kogl," *Minneapolis Tribune,* February 26, 1955.
1955 "Endurance Test" Sidebar
Interviews: Glen Carlson, Duane Glass, Jim Westby.

1956
Interviews: Glen Carlson, Duane Glass, Jim Hall, Jack Poole.

1957
Interviews: Glen Carlson, Les Etienne, Tom Neveau, John Prettyman, Jim Wherley.
Sid Hartman, "Falls' Stars Raised Together on Skates," *Minneapolis Tribune,* February 21, 1957.
"Miggins Surprised at Record," *St. Paul Pioneer Press,* February 26, 1957.

1958
Interviews: Ed Bulauca, Dick Roth, Joe Schwartzbauer, Jim Stordahl, Larry Stordahl.
"Not Robbed! Johnson Icers Pledge Support," *St. Paul Pioneer Press,* February 18, 1958.

1959
Interviews: Jackie McDonald, Don Ross, Dick Roth, Jim Stordahl, Larry Stordahl.
Ralph Reeve, "Rams Ace 'Disappears' // Is Only Sleeping," *St. Paul Dispatch,* February 21, 1958.

1960
Interviews: John Bonte, Dick Fisher, Larry Hendrickson, Bill McGiffert, Jim Ross.
Jim Byrne, "Rolle Says Sivertson Goal Fired East Drive," *Minneapolis Tribune,* February 28, 1960.
"Third Period Best All Season—Rolle," *St. Paul Pioneer Press,* February 26, 1960.

1961
Interviews: David Backlund, Paul Dorwart, Gordie Hipsher, Charles Oseid, Rick Ulvin.
Dwayne Netland, "Prep Puck Brawl Results in Injuries, Criticism // Falls, East Crowds Fight," *Minneapolis Tribune,* February 20, 1961.
"Packers Hope to Break Jinx," *Minneapolis Tribune,* February 24, 1961.
1961 "Tournament Darling" Sidebar
Interview: Doug Woog.

1962 ....
Interviews: Jim Amidon, Evie Christiansen, Ken
    Christiansen, Mike Curran, Don Milette, Mike Sertich.
Jim Byrne, "Falls 'Thanks' Bjorkman for 'Firing Us Up,'"
    Minneapolis Tribune, February 25, 1962.
Jim Byrne, "Lillo vs. Christiansen in Puck Finals; Two of
    State's Top Centers Lead Roseau, Falls," *Minneapolis
    Star,* February 24, 1962.
Sid Hartman, "Canadians Star for Roseau Six,"
    Minneapolis Tribune, February 21, 1958.
Jim Klobuchar, "Coleraine Coach Accuses O'Leary of Foul
    Play," *Minneapolis Tribune,* February 24, 1962.
"Falls, Coleraine Players Injured," *St. Paul Pioneer Press,*
    February 25, 1962.
1962 "Slopjohn's Revenge" Sidebar
Interviews: Jim Amidon, Mike Curran.

1963 ....
Interviews: Kathy Brullo, Lou Cotroneo, Stephen
    Gustafson, Greg Hughes, Bill Metzger, George "Skip"
    Peltier, Hank Remackel, Rob Shattuck.
Sid Hartman, "Amidon, Boysen Musts for Maroosh at 'U,'"
    Minneapolis Tribune, February 23, 1963.
Glenn Redmann, "I'm Proud of Them—Rube," *St. Paul
    Pioneer Press,* February 24, 1963.
Ralph Reeve, "Johnson Wins State Title in Overtime," *St.
    Paul Pioneer Press,* February 24, 1963.
"Govies Eye New Coach, More Titles in Future," *St. Paul
    Dispatch,* February 25, 1963.

1964 ....
Interviews: Ron Beck, Lou Cotroneo, Tony Curran, Pete
    Fichuk, Larry Roche.
Dick Dillman, "Coach Calls Falls 'Resilient,'" *St. Paul
    Pioneer Press,* February 22, 1964.
Jim Klobuchar, "Varying Memories of 1963," *Minneapolis
    Tribune,* February 20, 1964.

1965 ....
Interviews: Ron Beck, Jim Carter, Rod Christensen, Tony
    Curran, Peter Fichuk, Dan Mahle, Tim Sheehy.
Sid Hartman, "Ross Will Seek Wisconsin Puck Job,"
    Minneapolis Tribune, February 28, 1965.
Dwayne Netland, "Ross: Falls Six Sound, Very Deep,"
    Minneapolis Tribune, February 22, 1965.

1966 ....
Interviews: Jim Amidon, Ron Beck, Jim Carter, Rod
    Christensen, Dan Mahle, Tim Sheehy.
Sid Hartman, "Gopher Letdown Worries Kundla,"
    Minneapolis Tribune, February 19, 1966.

1967 ....
Interviews: Mike Antonovich, Bob Gernander, Jim Hoey,
    Mike Holland, Paul Rygh.
1967 "Danger Zone" Sidebar
Interviews: Ron Beck, Jim Carter, Bob Gernander, Willard
    Ikola, Bill Joy, Grant Standbrook.
Mike Lamey, "Playing Like Pro Trips Up Goalie,"
    Minneapolis Star, February 25, 1957.

1968 ....
Interviews: Mike Antonovich, Bob Gernander, Jim Hoey,
    Mike Holland, Paul Rygh.

1969 ....
Interviews: Henry Boucha, Bruce Carlson, Willard Ikola,
    Jim Knutson, Frank Krahn, Bob Krieger, Mike Marvin,
    Dick Roberts, Bob Storey, Dale Telle.
John Gilbert, "Boucha Knew He Was 'Done,'" *Minneapolis
    Tribune,* February 24, 1969.
1969 "Bag of Rags" Sidebar
Interviews: Henry Boucha, John Lindberg.

1970 ....
Interviews: Bruce Carlson, Willard Ikola, Bob Krieger,
    Larry Larson, Bob Lundeen, Bill Shaw, Dixon Shelstad,
    John Taft.
Dick Gordon, "'Backyard Barnburner,' SW Players Want—
    and Get—Edina," *Minneapolis Star,* March 7, 1970.
Dick Gordon, "'Non-Playing' SW Line Outplays All,"
    Minneapolis Star, March 9, 1970.
Jim Kaplan, "50th & France—State Title Crossroad,"
    Minneapolis Star, March 7, 1970.
1970 "Long on Talent" Sidebar
Interviews: Lou Cotroneo, Jim Hoey, Doug Long.

1971 ....
Interviews: Bill Broback, Rick Cabalka, Bruce Carlson, Tim
    Carlson, Willard Ikola, Scott Nieland, Todd Nieland.

1972 ....
Interviews: Terry Burns, Craig Dahl, Jim Jorgenson, Jim
    Knapp, Robert LaFond, Pete Waselovich.
Sid Hartman, "Waselovich Report," *Minneapolis Tribune,*
    March 13, 1972.
1972 "'Pops' Knows Best" Sidebar
Interviews: Ron Beck, Dean Blais, Terry Burns, Craig Dahl,
    Dan Mahle, John Prettyman, Steve Waselovich.
"DECC Athletic Hall of Fame: Ross Led Falls to Hockey
    Greatness," *Duluth News Tribune,* September 7, 2010.
"Young Ross 'Weaned' on Hockey," *Minneapolis Tribune,*
    March 1, 1965.

1973 ....
Interviews: Dave Herbst, Don Micheletti, Joe Micheletti,
    George Perpich Jr., Jim Perpich, Tim Pogorels.
Roman Augustovitz, "'Magic Stick' Paces Hibbing," United
    Press International, March 10, 1973.
Bruce Brothers, "Back at the Border, Bronko Beams,"
    Minneapolis Tribune, March 9, 1973.
Dick Gordon, "Burma Soccer Started Goalie," *Minneapolis
    Star,* March 10, 1973.

1974 ....
Interviews: Willard Ikola, Craig Norwich, Tim Pavek, Steve
    Polsfuss, Bill Thayer.
John Gilbert, "Edina-East Wins State Title 6-0,"
    Minneapolis Tribune, March 10, 1974.
Bob Schrank, "Edina East Called Best in 16 Years,"
    Minneapolis Star, March 8, 1974.
1974 "Gone in Six Minutes" Sidebar
Interviews: Willard Ikola, Craig Norwich, Tim Pavek, Bill
    Thayer.
Jim Wells, "Edina Scores as Sibley Quits Hitting," *St. Paul
    Pioneer Press,* March 9, 1974.

1975 ....
Interviews: Bill Baker, Buzz Christensen, Dan Clafton,
    Peter DeCenzo, Gus Hendrickson, Don Lucia, Jim
    Nelson, Erin Roth, John Rothstein, Mike Sertich.

Bruce Brothers, "Lincoln Coach Likes Position,"
    Minneapolis Tribune, March 6, 1975.
John Gilbert, "Injured Fleming Is 20-20 as Inspiration,"
    Minneapolis Tribune, March 9, 1975.
Ken Hickman, "Shooting the Rapids," *Grand Rapids
    Herald,* March 10, 1975.

1976 ....
Interviews: Buzz Christensen, Peter DeCenzo, Jim Jetland,
    Don Lucia, Jim Nelson, Erin Roth.
Dick Gordon, "3-Goal Cleveland Not Here Just for Ride,"
    Minneapolis Star, March 6, 1976.

1977 ....
Interviews: Bruce Aikens, Paul Brandrup, Paul Butters,
    Steve Carroll, Willard Ikola, Scott Lecy, Todd Lecy.
Bruce Brothers, "John Marshall's Scott Lecy Takes 13th
    Hat Trick in Stride," *Minneapolis Tribune,* March 18,
    1977.
Bruce Brothers, "Rochester's Sophomore Goalie Cool
    Facing S. St. Paul Barrage," *Minneapolis Tribune,*
    March 19, 1977.
John Gilbert, "John Marshall Coach Still on Cloud Nine
    After Section 1 Victory," *Minneapolis Tribune,* March
    14, 1977.
John Gilbert, "John Marshall 4, Southwest 1," *Minneapolis
    Tribune,* March 18, 1977.
John Gilbert, "Rochester Mystery," *Minneapolis Tribune,*
    March 19, 1977.
Charley Hallman, "Rockets' Button Tells the Story: 'Let's
    Win It,'" *St. Paul Pioneer Press,* March 19, 1977.
Sid Hartman, untitled column, *Minneapolis Tribune,*
    March 20, 1977.

1978 ....
Interviews: Gary Aulik, Steve Brown, Tom Carroll, John
    Donnelly, Mark Gagnon, Willard Ikola, Mike Lauen,
    Mike Vacanti.
John Gilbert, "Edina-East Wins Title in Overtime,"
    Minneapolis Tribune, March 12, 1978.
1978 "Fabled Family" Sidebar
Interviews: Aaron Broten, Neal Broten, Newell Broten,
    Paul Broten, David Drown, Bob Harris, Gary Hokanson.

1979 ....
Interviews: Steve Brown, Paul Butters, Tom Carroll, John
    Donnelly, Mark Gagnon, Willard Ikola, Mike Lauen,
    Todd Lecy, Mike Vacanti.
1979 "Gift of Gab" Sidebar
Interviews: Willard Ikola, Mike Vacanti.
Joe Soucheray, *Minneapolis Tribune,* March 18, 1979.

1980 ....
Interviews: Scott Billeadeau, Jon Casey, Buzz
    Christensen, John DeCenzo, Jeff Hovanec, Robb Leer,
    Tom Rothstein.
1980 "Sight to Behold" Sidebar
Interviews: Phil Housley, Doug Woog.
Dan Stoneking, "In NHL or at the 'U,' Phil Housley's Family
    Ties Will Remain Strong," *Minneapolis Star and
    Tribune,* June 10, 1982.

1981 ....
Interviews: Jim Becker, John Bianchi, Steve Bianchi, Tom
    Saterdalen.
Mike Augustin, "Jefferson Wins Hockey Crown 3-2," *St.
    Paul Pioneer Press,* March 15, 1981.

Gregg Wong, "Hockey Once Impossible for Robideau," *St. Paul Pioneer Press,* March 15, 1981.

1982 ....
Interviews: Bill Brauer, Dan Carroll, Wally Chapman, John DeVoe, Willard Ikola, Bart Larson.

1983 ....
Interviews: Tom Follmer, Pat Heffernan, Mark Horvath, Bill Lechner, Mark Krois, Terry Skrypek.
1983 "Name Recognition" Sidebar
Interviews: Elly Froiland, Reggie Miracle, Tom Palkowski, Brad Schlagel.

1984 ....
Interviews: Greg Dornbach, Peter Hankinson, Willard Ikola, Jeff Johnson, Lou Nanne, Marty Nanne, Paul Ranheim.
1984 "Sweet Lou" Sidebar
Interviews: Willard Ikola, Lou Nanne, Marty Nanne.

1985 ....
Interviews: Scott Bloom, Kevin Gorg, Matt Larson, Mike Luckraft, Mark Osiecki, Tom Osiecki.
Dennis Brackin, "Chorske Closing Out Prep Career Still on Outside," *Minneapolis Star Tribune,* March 5, 1985.

1986 ....
Interviews: Scott Bloom, Matt Larson, Mark Osiecki, Tom Osiecki.
Jay Weiner, "Backup Denfeld Goalie Gets Most Out of Off-Ice Role," *Minneapolis Star Tribune,* March 7, 1986.

1987 ....
Interviews: Joe Decker, Mark Hultgren, Chris Lind, Jason Miller, Jerry Peterson.

1988 ....
Interviews: Matt Bertram, Rob Copeland, Willard Ikola, Tom King, Larry Olimb, Noel Rahn, Mike Terwilliger.

1989 ....
Interviews: John Bianchi, Tony Bianchi, Kelly Hultgren, Sean Rice, Tom Saterdalen, Chris Tucker.
Roman Augustoviz, "Jefferson Works Overtime for Title," *Minneapolis Star Tribune,* March 5, 1989.
John Gilbert, "Broken Foot Can't Stop Edina Star," *Minneapolis Star Tribune,* March 5, 1989.

1990 ....
Interviews: Dean Blais, Chris Gotziaman, Terry Gotziaman, Dane Gunderson, Bill Lund.
1990 "Lovable Rodents" Sidebar
Interviews: Derrick Brown, Mike Curti, Paul Deutsch, Mark Hultgren.

1991 ....
Interviews: Jeremy Hackman, Mark Strobel, Mike Strobel, Jeff Whisler, Jim Young.
1991 "Tradition in Transition" Sidebar
Interviews: John Bartz, Willard Ikola, Bob Kochevar, George Larson, Herb Sellars, Jeff Whisler, Jim Young.
Roman Augustoviz, "Faceoff // Sides Drawn for Two-Class Tournament," *Minneapolis Star Tribune,* April 30, 1989.
Roman Augustoviz, "Groups Don't Share Goals for Hockey Tournament," *Minneapolis Star Tribune,* January 14, 1990.

Dan Barreiro, "The Only Place to Watch Games," *Minneapolis Star Tribune,* March 8, 1991.
Curt Brown, "It's Official: Hockey Tourney Is Split in Two // Classes Based on Team Strength," *Minneapolis Star Tribune,* April 25, 1991.
Charley McKenna, "Centaur Coach Seeks 2-Class Hockey Tourney," *Minneapolis Star and Tribune,* February 24, 1983.
Bob Sansevere, "Blame These Guys for Two-Tier Hockey," *St. Paul Pioneer Press,* March 9, 1991.
Robert Whereatt and Roman Augustoviz, "It's the Law: Hockey Will Have Two State Tournaments," *Minneapolis Star Tribune,* May 27, 1989.

1992 ....
Interviews: Joe Bianchi, John Bianchi, Nick Checco, Mike Crowley, Cort Lundeen, Tom Saterdalen, Dan Trebil.
Roman Augustoviz, "Tier Titles to Jefferson, Greenway // Bianchi Lifts Jaguars 6–3," *Minneapolis Star Tribune,* March 15, 1992.

1993 ....
Interviews: Joe Bianchi, John Bianchi, Derek Camuel, Nick Checco, Mike Crowley, Cort Lundeen, Mark Parrish, Tom Saterdalen.
Roman Augustoviz, "Unbeatable to the Very End // Jefferson Charges Past Hill-Murray for Title," *Minneapolis Star Tribune,* March 14, 1993.
John Gilbert, "Jefferson Too Much for Moorhead // Unbeaten Jaguars Romp to Hockey Tourney Title," *Minneapolis Star Tribune,* December 30, 1992.

1994 ....
Interviews: Joe Bianchi, John Bianchi, Derek Camuel, Mike Crowley, Mark Parrish, Toby Petersen, Tom Saterdalen.

1995 ....
Interviews: Chris Locker, Matt Mathias, Dylan Mills, Mike Randolph, Dave Spehar.
Roman Augustoviz, "Hail to Threes for Class AA Champs," *Minneapolis Star Tribune,* March 12, 1995.
Mike Fermoyle, "Spehar's Third Hat Does the Trick," *St. Paul Pioneer Press,* March 12, 1995.
John Gilbert, "East Turns Trick in AA; Falls Wins in A," *Minneapolis Star Tribune,* March 12, 1995.
John Gilbert, "Jefferson After No. 4; Jaguars Open against No. 4 Minnetonka Tonight," *Minneapolis Star Tribune,* November 29, 1994.
David La Vaque, "Three Hat Tricks Turned Him into Legend," *Minneapolis Star Tribune,* March 4, 2015.
1995 "Ladies First" Sidebar
Interviews: Amber Hegland, Amy Murphy.

1996 ....
Interviews : Aaron Dwyer, Karl Goehring, Rick Larsen, Chris Locker, Paul Otsby, Mike Randolph, Dave Spehar, Erik Westrum, Pat Westrum.
David La Vaque, "Game Finally Ended, but Legend Lives On," *Minneapolis Star Tribune,* March 2, 2016.
Patrick Reusse, "Westrum Takes Page from Dad's Book," *Minneapolis Star Tribune,* March 10, 2001.

1997 ....
Interviews: Dan Carlson, Peter Fitzgerald, Jeff Hall, Bart Larson, Ben Stafford.

Roman Augustoviz, "Young Hornets Show Mettle When It Counts," *Minneapolis Star Tribune,* March 10, 1997.
1997 "Southern Charm" Sidebar
Interviews: George Nemanich, Johnny Pohl.

1998 ....
Interviews: Nick Angell, Adam Coole, Patrick Finnegan, Mike Randolph.
Kevin Pates, "Carlsons, East Get to State," *Duluth News Tribune,* March 4, 1998.

1999 ....
Interviews: Jake Brandt, Mike Klema, Phil Larson, Jim Lundbohm.

2000 ....
Interviews: Brandon Bochenski, Matt Hendricks, Steve Larson, Steve Witkowski.
2000 "The Venues" Sidebar
Interviews: Ben Gustafson, Matt Hendricks, Jared Hummel, Willard Ikola, Bob Krieger, Phil Larson, Noel Rahn.
Frank Rajkowski, "Duluth East Captured the Final State Hockey Title at Civic Center 20 Years Ago," KSTP-TV, March 8, 2018.

2001 ....
Interviews: Nate Droogsma, Ben Gustafson, Tony Sarsland, Trevor Stewart.
Michael Rand, "Elks Seize Their Moment," *Minneapolis Star Tribune,* March 11, 2001.
Michael Rand, "A Season of Pain, Pleasure," *Minneapolis Star Tribune,* March 8, 2001.

2002 ....
Interviews: Jack Hillen, Jared Hummel, Jimmy Kilpatrick, Guy Olson, Mike Taylor.
John Millea, "Ice Investigation," *Minneapolis Star Tribune,* December 17, 2002.
2002 "Miracle Man" Sidebar
Interviews: Jack Hillen, Jared Hummel, Guy Olson, Mike Taylor.

2003 ....
Interviews: Sean Fish, Jack Hillen, Tim Manthey, Todd Manthey.

2004 ....
Interviews: R. J. Anderson, Erik Aus, Tom Gorowsky, Jack Hillen, Guy Olson, Tim Ornell, Gregg Stutz.
2004 "March Sickness" Sidebar
Interviews: Wally Chapman, Blake Wheeler.

2005 ....
Interviews: Joe Bennek, Kyle Hardwick, Albert Hasbargen, Rob Hoody, Mark Loahr, Aaron Marvin, Dave Norling, T. J. Oshie.
2005 "Blonds Have More Fun" Sidebar
Interviews: Kyle Hardwick, T. J. Oshie.
2005 "Forgotten Misfit" Sidebar
Interviews : Keith Hendrickson, Willard Ikola, Matt Niskanen.
Patrick Reusse, "Long Wait Is Over," *Minneapolis Star Tribune,* March 1, 2005.

SOURCES

2006
Interviews: Chris Hickey, Corvin Kieger, Ben Kinne, Ryan McDonagh, Jim O'Neill.

2007
Interviews: Tyler Landman, Mike Lee, Aaron Ness, Nick Oliver, Scott Oliver.

2008
Interviews: Bo Dolan, Ryan Furne, Bill Lechner, Joe Phillippi, Pat Schafhauser, Dan Sova.
Ray Richardson, "Phillippi Hungry," *St. Paul Pioneer Press,* March 7, 2008.
Pam Schmid, "While Others Got Away, They Stayed to Play," *Minneapolis Star Tribune,* January 30, 2007.
Dean Spiros, "Hill-Murray Completed a Run through the Top Two Seeds and Won the Title," *Minneapolis Star Tribune,* March 9, 2008.

2009
Interviews: Andrew Ford, Nick Leddy, Curt Rau, Kyle Rau, Des Shavlik, Lee Smith, Taylor Wolfe.

2010
Interviews: Blake Chapman, Steve Fogarty, Curt Giles, Brett Stolpestad.

2011
Interviews: Andrew Ford, Andrew Kerr, Curt Rau, Kyle Rau, Nate Repensky, Des Shavlik, Lee Smith.
2011 "The Smokers' Doors" Sidebar
Interviews: Dan Beaudette, Andrew Kerr, Dan Kovarik, Jim O'Neill, Kyle Rau, Lee Smith.

2012
Interviews: Grant Besse, Jack Jablonski, Leslie Jablonski, Mike Jabolonski, Justin Kloos, Ken Pauly, Craig Perry.
David La Vaque, "Poised and Proud, Kloos Is Mr. Hockey," *Minneapolis Star Tribune,* March 12, 2012.
Pam Louwagie, "'This Is Like a Calling Almost,'" *Minneapolis Star Tribune,* January 20, 2012.
Jeremy Olson and David La Vaque, "Family Says Hockey Player Won't Be Able to Walk Again," *Minneapolis Star Tribune,* January 5, 2012.

2013
Interviews: Curt Giles, Matt Nelson, Anthony Walsh.
2013 "The Height of Lunacy" Sidebar
Interviews: Bruce Plante, Greg Vannelli.

2014
Interviews: Curt Giles, Miguel Fidler, Dylan Malmquist, Lee Smith.

2015
Interviews: Ryan Edquist, Trent Eigner, Jack McNeely, Jack Poehling, Ryan Poehling.
2015 "Best in Flow" Sidebar
Interview: Luke Seper.
Ben McGrath, "The Glories of Minnesota Hockey Hair, from the Mullet to the 'Portobella,'" *New Yorker,* March 14, 2019.

2016
Interviews: Billy Duma, Pat O'Leary, Alex Schilling, Mark Senden, Lee Smith, Hank Sorensen.

2017
Interviews: Jack Bowman, Gavin Hain, Trent Klatt, Blake McLaughlin, Micah Miller.

2018
Interviews: Bobby Brink, Sean Goldsworthy, Luke Loheit, Joe Molenaar.
2018 "Paintings Speak Volumes" Sidebar
Interviews: Terrence Fogarty, Tim Poehling.

2019
Interviews: Peter Colby, Kevin Delaney, Curt Giles.

2020
Interviews: Ben Dardis, Grant Dardis, Nathan Gruhlke, Colin Hagstrom, Adam Johnson, Jeff Poeschl.
David LaVaque, "Green Wave Wears Down Zephyrs // The Defending Champs Returned to the Title Game," *Minneapolis Star Tribune,* March 7, 2015.
David LaVaque, "The Zephyrs Held Up under Pressure to Win Their First State Title," *Minneapolis Star Tribune,* March 8, 2020.
David LaVaque and Loren Nelson, "Mahtomedi Sets Record for Fewest Shots by Title Winner," *Minneapolis Star Tribune,* March 8, 2020.
Loren Nelson, "Crusader Trips—In Introductions," *Minneapolis Star Tribune,* March 9, 2019.
Loren Nelson, "Early-Season Broken Leg Doesn't Deter Mahtomedi Goal-Scoring Hero," *Minneapolis Star Tribune,* March 7, 2020.
2020 "Surprise Appearance" Sidebar
Interviews: Bill Lechner, Joey Palodichuk.

2021
Interviews: Carter Batchelder, Jackson Blake, Mason Langenbrunner, Bill Lechner, Bob Madison, Luke Mittelstadt, Lee Smith.
Paul Klauda, "Last Year's Champs Out of 2A Tourney," *Minneapolis Star Tribune,* March 31, 2021.

Paul Klauda and David LaVaque, "Minnesota Legislators, Parents Decry Mask Order As Youth Sports Restart," *Minneapolis Star Tribune,* January 8, 2021.
David LaVaque, "Jackson Blake, in the Right Spot, Winds Up a Two-OT Hero at State," *Minneapolis Star Tribune,* July 13, 2021.
David LaVaque and Loren Nelson, "Wayzata Is Enjoying 2A Quarterfinals on TV," *Minneapolis Star Tribune,* April 1, 2021.
Loren Nelson, "COVID-19 Disrupting Boys' Hockey State Tournament," *Minneapolis Star Tribune,* March 30, 2021.
Loren Nelson, "Eden Prairie Hands Benilde–St. Margaret's Its First Loss of the Season," MN Boys' Hockey Hub, February 16, 2021.
Rick Weegman, "Hermantown JV Unable to Silence Lamb, Dodge County," therinklive.com, March 30, 2021.

2022
Interviews: Austin Brauns, Logan Gravink, Weston Knox, Kyle Law, Mark Manney, Logan Seward, Bill Thoreson, Gavyn Thoreson.
Loren Nelson, "Manney Emerges As Media Sensation," Legacy.Hockey, March 17, 2022.
Bruce Strand, "Commentary: Cash Trumps Fairness in Elks Hockey Section," *Elk River Star News,* April 5, 2014.
2022 "The Heart of Hermantown" Sidebar
Interviews: Pat Andrews, Ty Hanson, Dave Huttel, Zam Plante.
Loren Nelson, "True to Their Schools," Legacy.Hockey, March 31, 2022.
Rick Weegman, "An Unbelievable Story," *Duluth News Tribune,* March 2, 1998.

2023
Interviews: Gavin Garry, Sean Goldsworthy, Liam Hupka, Mike Johnson, Kaizer Nelson.
Drew Herron, "Lunski Lifts Minnetonka Past Chanhassen," Legacy.Hockey, March 2, 2023.
Loren Nelson, "Class 2A Title 'Pretty Bleeping Awesome' for Minnetonka," Legacy.Hockey, March 11, 2023.
Loren Nelson, "Minnetonka Goalie Stands His Ground Against Andover Star," Legacy.Hockey, March 10, 2023.
2023 "Damage Control" Sidebar
Interview: Charlie Drage.

SOURCES—General Bibliography

Arend, Robert G. *Edina High School Varsity Hockey 1950–1984.* N.p., 1984.

Bernstein, Ross. *America's Coach: Life Lessons and Wisdom for Gold Medal Success: A Biographical Journey of the Late Hockey Icon Herb Brooks.* Eagan, MN: Bernstein Books, 2006.
——. *Legends and Legacies: Celebrating a Century of Minnesota's Greatest Coaches.* Minneapolis: Nodin Press, 2003.
——. *More . . . Frozen Memories, Celebrating a Century of Minnesota Hockey.* Minneapolis: Nodin Press, 2007.
Big Team, Little Me. Free-Style Productions, Inc. Produced by Dale Kivimaki, 2002.
Borzi, Patrick C. *Minnesota Made Me.* Mendota Heights, MN: Press Box Books, 2018.
Boucha, Henry. *Henry Boucha, Ojibwa: Native American Olympian.* N.p., 2013.

Engel, Bruce. *Iron Range Conference Hockey: The Finest High School Hockey in the U.S.A. 1972–83.* N.p., [1983/84?].

Gilbert, John. *Herb Brooks: The Inside Story of a Hockey Mastermind.* Minneapolis: Voyageur Press, 2008.
Glennie, Rich. *The Streak: And the Guys Who Made It All Happen.* N.p., 2018.

Haag, Ken. *Johnson High Hockey: A 40-Year Retrospect and Other Puckish Delights.* St. Paul: Country Images, 1987.
Hoey, Jim. *Puck Heaven: Minnesota State Boys Hockey Tournament Trivia.* Minneapolis: Nodin Press, 2011, rev. 2015.

Ice Dreams: The Minnesota State High School Hockey Tournament. Fox Sports Net North. Produced by Paul Hipp, Matt Hoover, Doug McLeod, and Dan Truebenbach, 2003.
Ikola, Willard, and Jim Hoey. *"Ike": Minnesota Hockey Icon.* St. Louis Park, MN: Nodin Press, 2015.

Just, Jim, and Ryan Shanley. Hill-Murray Pioneer Hockey. hmpioneers.net.

Kirchoff, Maggie, ed. *A Complete History of the Minnesota Boys and Girls High School Hockey Tournament 1945–2000.* Minneapolis: D&M Publishing, Inc., 2000.

Nordquist, Stuart. *64 Years of Bronco Hockey, 1948–2012.* N.p., 2012

Oen, Kyle. Vintage Minnesota Hockey. www.vintagemnhockey.com.

Phillips, Gary L. *Skate for Goal! Highlights from Minnesota's State Hockey Tournament.* Afton, MN: Afton Press, 1982.

Rippel, Joel A. *75 Memorable Moments in Minnesota Sports.* St. Paul: Minnesota Historical Society Press, 2003.
Rosengren, John. *Blades of Glory: The True Story of a Young Team Bred to Win.* Naperville, IL: Sourcebooks, 2004.

Schofield, Mary Halverson. *Henry Boucha: Star of the North.* Edina, MN: Snowshoe Press, 1999.
——. *River of Champions.* Edina, MN: Snowshoe Press, 1995.
Solz, Arthur. *Minnesota State High School Hockey Tournament 1945–1968.*

Vosejpka, John. Minnesota State High School Boys' and Girls' Hockey Tournaments: Results, Records and Rarities. rrr.hockey.

INDEX

ABOUT THE AUTHORS

DAVID LA VAQUE is a reporter for the *Star Tribune* and has been the newspaper's point person for high school hockey since 2010. He has covered the state tournament in its entirety each year, writing enterprise pieces on the sport and selecting the paper's All-Metro teams and Metro Player of the Year. A graduate of the University of Minnesota, he covered sports for the *Minnesota Daily* and his work has also appeared in such media as *Athlon Sports Magazine, Atlanta Journal-Constitution*, CSN-Chicago, *Duluth News Tribune, Miami Herald, Cleveland Plain Dealer, USA Junior Hockey Magazine*, and US College Hockey Online Magazine, among others. He grew up playing hockey on St. Paul's East Side. La Vaque now lives in Woodbury, Minnesota, with his wife, Sarah, and daughter, Michaela.

L. R. NELSON is an author, freelance journalist, and photographer and the founder and president of Legacy.Hockey, Minnesota's number-one resource for high school hockey's past, present, and future. A recipient of numerous state, regional, and national writing awards, he researched, wrote, and published a series on Minnesota's top 100 high school players as managing editor of the Minnesota Hockey Hub. He covered Stanley Cup runs as a beat writer for the Tampa Bay Lightning and Anaheim Ducks, and he has covered multiple Super Bowls, college football national championship games, golf major championships, and the World Series. Nelson grew up playing hockey in and around International Falls, Minnesota, and now lives in Excelsior with his wife, Helen. They have two children, Katherine and Luke.

Authors David La Vaque (david_lavaque@yahoo.com) and Loren Nelson (loren.nelson@legacy.hockey) welcome your corrections or story ideas.